TOTAL QUALITY MANAGEMENT

TOTAL QUALITY MANAGEMENT

P.N. MUKHERJEE

Professor and Chairperson
Total Quality Management and Supply Chain Management
Narsee Monjee Institute of Management & Higher Studies
(Deemed University)
Mumbai

Formerly, Professor and Head
Department of Operation and Logistics & Supply Chain Management
K.J. Somaiya Institute of Management Studies and Research
Mumbai

Prentice-Hall of India Private Limited

New Delhi - 110001
2006

Rs. 325.00

TOTAL QUALITY MANAGEMENT
P.N. Mukherjee

ISBN-81-203-3056-0

The export rights of this book are vested solely with the publisher.

Published by Asoke K. Ghosh, Prentice-Hall of India Private Limited, M-97, Connaught Circus, New Delhi-110001 and Printed by Mudrak, 30-A, Patparganj, Delhi-110091.

To
My Mother, Wife & Children

Contents

Section II

Preface

There is an ancient story about some visually impaired men who were once asked by a rajah to tell him what sort of a thing an elephant was. The man who touched the tail, interpreted the elephant as a rope; the man who touched its leg, thought it to be a pillar; the one who touched the elephant's ear, interpreted the elephant to be a fan; and the one who touched its body, thought it to be a wall. Each formed his own opinion and did not fully understand the object touched by him. This story is often told to make people realize that though each person was partly right, all were wrong. The same analogy can be extended to the methodology of Total Quality Management (TQM). It stands explored in parts and its implementation remains sporadic, so to say.

It is a well-known fact that it was the adoption of the concept of TQM in its totality that accelerated the rise of Japanese industries to world-class performance. Soon the entire world followed their lead to capture the benefits of TQM.

In 1991, six US multinational organizations with global presence, Ford, IBM, Motorola, American Express, Procter & Gamble and Xerox, sponsored the Total Quality Management Forum. The objective of this forum was to discuss the role of TQM in the United States industries and the US campuses, particularly in the business management schools and engineering institutes. Similar things happened in Europe where 14 leading European corporations founded the European Foundation of Quality Management in 1989. With the participation of European universities and industries the membership of this Foundation grew to more than 300 by 1995. The Americans looked at TQM as a tool to enhance the global presence of US industries. On the other hand, the objective of European Foundation of Quality Management was to make TQM of an integrated value to the European society and management to achieve the global competitive advantage. Though several organizations have substantially benefited from the use of TQM tools and techniques, not all have exploited and understood its full potential. This especially applies to the Indian industries.

During my interaction with leading Indian Industries, TQM appeared to be treated more as a fad, with top management acting as the cheer leader. The understanding and implementation of TQM in Indian industries has to improve substantially in order to achieve the desired result of world-class performance and global leadership.

The Japanese industries stand out from the rest of the world in the sense that they not only achieved global leadership by the mid-1970s but have since sustained the same for more than three decades. The reason is simple. The Japanese industries first worked

1950s how to be the global leader by the 1970s. This was nothing but the process of 'Strategic Quality Planning', supported by the Japanese lifestyle of 'Kaizen' or 'Continuous Improvement' embedded in it. The top management wholly participated in understanding and implementing TQM. The principle of **Total Organizational Involvement** and the integrated business strategy, made Japanese organizations build strong infrastructure that provided the platform for achieving world-class performance and excellence in every sphere of their operation.

The success of TQM therefore depends a lot on the Foundation and Infrastructure of an organization. This is the crux of my theory of 'Holistic Management System for World-class Performance and Leadership' expounded in this book. This is also where this book endeavours to bridge the gap and introduce TQM to management and engineering students so that they acquire a sound knowledge of all facets of TQM.

There are a number of books on various tools of TQM focusing on the improvement aspects of each technique. Indian industry too has focused on TQM just as an improvement process, whether it is Quality Circle, Kaizen, Taguchi's Experimental Design, TPM, or JQI. For example, with relevance to Juran's Triology every industry does churn out a number of quality improvement projects (JQI), forgetting altogether the other two important processes of 'Quality Planning' and 'Quality Control'. In fact, the most important process of Juran's Triology is quality planning, the other two activities being part of it. According to my understanding, Juran's Triology is probably the most comprehensive of all the TQM techniques. The other prevalent TQM tools are by and large the improvement tools. The six sigma is again only the statistical process control tool. The effectiveness and efficiency of TQM tools will multiply exponentially if practised with a sound foundation and infrastructure. The 'holistic approach to the understanding and practice of TQM' integrates all of the efforts in the field of TQM in a structured manner with a view to converting them into a management system as explained in the book.

The book systematically covers in the first three chapters most of the work done by TQM Gurus and various activities thereof related to the understanding and implementation of TQM in an organization. Chapters 4–8 explain in detail the subject of TQM as per my theory of 'holistic management system for world-class performance and leadership'. Chapters 9–10 are devoted to the 'Statistical Process Control' and 'Six Sigma' respectively. Chapter 11 elaborates on the subject of 'FEMA', 'POKA YOKE' and Taguchi's experimental design. The concluding part of the book explains and analyses certain cases related to TQM. The book also brings in a lot of new concepts like the little known Japanese practice of 'Muri', 'Muda' and 'Mura', the logistics and supply chain management, the value analysis, the various management techniques like brainstorming, NGT, ISO 9000:2000, benchmarking, business process reengineering, etc. The book thus provides wide coverage of areas related to TQM and integrates all of the processes, tools and techniques under one management system. This is the *unique* feature of this book.

The book has been the outcome of my years of research in the field of 'TQM-based World-class Management System'. Besides, the book covers the entire curriculum of TQM prescribed for management and engineering students. It is your journey to a storehouse of knowledge of theory, tools, techniques, and practices of TQM, integrated into a well-structured management system.

Bon voyage!

P.N. MUKHERJEE

Chapter 1

Introduction to Total Quality Management, Management of Process/Operation and Customer Satisfaction

CHAPTER OBJECTIVES

In this chapter, we will discuss the following:

- Definition and concept of management and its features
- Concepts of production and operation management
- Difference between manufacturing and service industries
- Managerial functions—conventional and current concept
- Deming's P-D-C-A cycle
- Mission, Vision and SWOT analysis
- Concepts of process approach and productivity
- Managerial roles and skills under TQM paradigm
- Concept of customer satisfaction
- Importance of return on investment
- Functions of a world-class TQM organization and its departments
- Managerial roles and skills
- The working of a contemporary organization and current functional orientation
- Horizontal quality thinking

Outdated management theories and business principles are still taught in most of the management institutes. The curriculum needs to be updated with the same speed of change in business environment that has taken place in the 1990s as well as in the new millennium with the occurrence of liberalization and globalization. The Indian business scenario is not an exception either. We find most of the conventional business houses still following the outdated definition of management and managerial practices. Ninety percent of the advertisements for job opportunities clearly insist on previous experience in the same function or department in the same type of industry or industries of the similar nature. Students in the management institute also aspire to specialize only in certain areas like marketing/finance/HR and tend to put a blind eye towards acquiring the basic knowledge of other areas.

The key factor for survival and performance excellence of any industry is 'Customer Satisfaction' and 'Return on Investment (ROI)'. This applies to both the manufacturing and service sectors. Even if everybody talks about it as a fad, hardly anybody understands the meaning in the correct prospective. The result is that industries after industries both in the manufacturing and service sectors are closing down. The scenario is common in a visit in any industrial area in any corner of the country whether it is Peenya Industrial Area in Bangalore, Wagle Industrial Estate in Thane near Mumbai, Bhosari Industrial Area in Pune, Faridabad Industrial Area near Delhi in Haryana or Padi in Chennai. Seventy percent of the industries have closed down their shutter unable to face the international competition and the forces of globalization. Hence the pertinent question emerges—How to reverse the trend and survive in the current turbulent challenging business environment?

The survival strategy is not adequate. The industries should aim for excellence in their performance to survive and prosper. In today's business environment, either you have to move ahead or you have to move out. The options are clear. The onslaught of foreign multinationals has been fast and drastic in every field of manufacturing—be it FMCG, automobile, textile or chemical industries. The liberalization and globalization took place in the 1990s, much faster than the Indian industries could imagine and cope up with. The management thoughts and practices also needed to be upgraded to current international theories and practices on the latest management techniques. The essence of current cases of business success of globally-renowned enterprises has to be looked into in redefining the successful business strategies in a systematic and scientific manner.

With the same speed of change in business environment and fast emerging international competition, the industries need to change their way of functioning, redefine management and managerial roles as well as have clear cut objectives and goals integrated with the same intensity and functional unification of individual functions with the organizational goal. The industry should think today only of a managerial style and functioning equivalent to the world-class performance oriented towards the business excellence. After an intensive research in this direction, a simple holistic approach has to be adopted and the conventional approach has to be replaced by a world-class performance orientation as described hereafter.

1.1   DEFINITION AND CONCEPT OF MANAGEMENT

In industrial and business circle, there is so much importance given to the concept of 'management'. However if one asks practising managers from all levels to explain its meaning, there would be many explanations widely varying from each other. You come across various management activities like General Management, Purchase Management, Materials Management, Production Management, Operation Management, Marketing Management, Personal Management, Human Resource Management, Maintenance Management, Logistics Management, Supply Chain Management and so on. With the new challenges emerging with the globalization and liberalization, the management has undergone a sea change in its concept and interpretation. For each function, each individual differs widely in understanding and interpretation of the concept of management. But they all agree on one common point, i.e. 'management is vital to running a business or for that matter any activity whatsoever successfully'. Let us get the fundamental concept of 'management' clear before we proceed any further.

The universal conventional definition of 'management' is: "The art and science of getting things done from others."

If at all we agree to this definition which is a century old, a basic question arises—What is the manager supposed to do? He is supposed to get work done from others, but do nothing himself. It defies the fundamental principle of leadership wherein 'leaders' have to lead by example. It has been found that excellent organizations have a leader at the top who is the role model for the rest of his team. This signifies that a successful manager also practises what he preaches to his team. Successful management practitioners like Bill Gates of Microsoft, Azim Premji of Wipro, Narayan Murthi of Infosys, Jamshedji Tata of Tata Group and Dhirubhai Ambani of Reliance have been a role model for the rest of the team. Many of them might have not been highly educated and management postgraduates but they had one thing in common—extremely successful business management skills. Each one of them was a role model who practised himself every bit of what he preached about the business management to the rest of his team.

Hence let us define 'management' in its correct prospective as: *'Management is a continuous process of creating and maintaining an environment conducive for performance for a group of people working together towards attainment of a common objective or goal in time.'*

The definition can be explained as follows:

- Management is a process-oriented approach.
- Management is not a one time activity.
- Management creates and maintains an environment conducive for performance.
- Management is teamwork for a group of people bound by a common objective.
- The last two words 'in time' are extremely important. Every activity and, every objective has a time element beyond which it is null and void.

For example, you have consumed least amount of resources for producing some goods and the quality is of the highest order. But it was to be ready by 10th of the month as per the 'letter of credit' delivery norms. Instead it got completed by 20th of the month. Everything is fine but 'in time' element is not maintained. The result is zero as the delivery date has expired. Nobody will pick up the consignment unless of course the customers agree to reopen the letter of credit extending the date which may be a remote possibility.

1.2   THE CONCEPT OF PRODUCTION AND/OR OPERATION

The difference between the concepts of production management and operation management is often not clearly understood. These two areas are distinctly different streams of management. Production management mainly deals with the manufacturing of any products, i.e. the conversion of the raw material into the finished goods. Production management is a relatively old concept of management. It is applicable only to the manufacturing activity. Operation management is altogether a new management concept universally applicable to all functions including the production, materials, human resources, marketing, logistics and supply chain management. Operation management imparts knowledge as to how to handle any process in any functions efficiently and effectively. A process or an operation has an input and an output (value-added input) and the process itself consists of the value addition through conversion. Operation management involves the efficient and effective handling of the same wherein the value addition to the input is maximum, and the utilization of the resources are minimum aimed towards the maximization of the customer satisfaction and return on the investment. The concept of production management and operation management can be further elaborated in a simplistic manner by the explanation given hereafter.

If one were to distribute free of cost a stainless steel sheet (1 m × 1 m), nobody would be interested in taking it. But if the same stainless steel sheet is processed and converted to a utensil with the deployment of men and machines and then offered at an attractive discount of 25–30%, many people would be interested now to take it as this product has value to them.

The example cited above is relevant to a manufacturing industry. Production is a typical key activity of a manufacturing industry.

Hence 'production' can be defined as 'value addition by conversion and/or transformation of input raw material into the finished product with the deployment of men and machines and/or tools'.

If we elaborate this basic concept we will come to the following conclusion:

- In a manufacturing industry the input is the 'raw material' and output is 'value-added raw material' or the 'finished product'.
- The finished product obviously has more value to the end user than that of the raw material.
- Production is value addition by conversion to input raw material.
- The 'hard factors' of production are men, machines and materials.
- The 'soft factors' of production are management, money and technology.
- This 'value addition' process needs certain input resources like raw material, men, machines and/or tools.
- Each of these input resources cost money. Hence 'money' is another factor of production. However 'money' is considered as a 'soft factor' of production.
- Management teaches the process of adding maximum value by consumption of least amount of resources for attainment of the end objective.
- The cost of all these input resources added together constitutes the 'cost of value addition' to the input raw material.
- For an organization to survive, it must have the ability to create 'surplus' which can be explained as the value added minus the cost of value addition.

In this example say Rs. 40 is the input cost of raw material and another Rs. 30 is the cost of value addition. Rs. 70 becomes the total cost of input resources. The product has to be sold at a price higher than Rs. 70 to create surplus. If the customer is ready to pay Rs. 100 for the finished product, the value added is Rs. 100 – Rs. 40 = Rs. 60. The cost of value addition is Rs. 30. Hence the 'surplus' generated in this case is Rs. 60 – Rs. 30 = Rs. 30.

- The efficiency of an organization is its ability to create surplus.

1.3   THE CONCEPT OF SERVICE INDUSTRY

In the service industry the input is the 'customers' and the output is the 'value-added customers'. The process of value addition is also by conversion. The value addition to the customer should be more than the cost of value addition. This process should also be both efficient as well as effective, i.e. the entire process should follow a time schedule and as per the target. The efficiency of a service sector is also its ability to create surplus.

There were times till the 1980s when the contribution of the service sector to a Nation's GDP (Gross Domestic Product) was in single-digit numbers. Today the service sector comprises more than one third of GDP for most of the nations in the world. The contribution of the service sector to the national wealth is substantial.

The input to a management institute is the fresh graduate students. The management institute adds value to them by imparting management knowledge and converts them into management postgraduates whose market value with the industries is substantially higher than the students' status as fresh graduates before joining the institute. The input to a pleader is a litigated customer having a fear of either paying money or fine for economic offence or a client facing criminal proceeding of fear of being jailed. To retrieve himself from this litigation, he pays fees to the lawyer and the expected output is a litigation-free client. Input to a doctor is a sick human being and the output is a healthy human being.

While the word 'production' is normally confined to the area of manufacturing, the concept of operation can be applied to any industrial sector—manufacturing or service sector as also on any function apart from production to any business process of marketing, materials, human resource or any other function whatsoever.

1.4   OPERATION MANAGEMENT

Operation management is the management of a process or sub-process consisting of a distinctive input and a well-defined process for value addition by conversion leading to a value-added output. Operation management principles are uniformly applied to both the manufacturing and the service sectors. For the manufacturing industry, the input is the raw material and the output is the finished goods or the products and the associated services (refer to Figure 1.1). For the service sector the input is the customer and the output is the value-added customer. Here again operation is the process of adding value by conversion (refer to Figure 1.2). In both the cases the input resources are men, machines, finance, management and technology. The operation management ensures that the process should be both efficient and effective and generates a surplus.

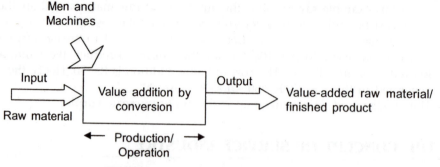

FIGURE 1.1 Manufacturing industry.

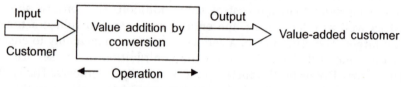

FIGURE 1.2 Service sector.

Hence operation management can be defined as "the effectively and efficiently carrying out a business process or an activity which leads to accomplishment of goal and/or objective normally related to an organization with creation of maximum possible surplus in time."

This definition can be expanded for understanding as follows:

- Operation management is the management of a business process.
- The management of business process should be both 'effective' and 'efficient'.
- The 'effectiveness' can be defined as the ability to achieve the target or rather the extent of nearness to the target.
- The concept of operation management has been introduced to the industry with the advent of 'CWQA' or company-wide quality assurance activity.
- The 'efficiency' can be defined as the ratio of value of the output to the value of the input resources consumed for achievement of the end objective with least amount of resources. The efficiency of the process under focus should always be more than one for the organization to survive and make a profit for the organizational growth and sustenance.
- 'Value added' is the value of the output minus the value of the input. The 'cost of value addition' is the value of resources consumed like men and machines for the purpose of the value addition.
- The 'surplus' is the difference between the value added and the cost of value addition. For an organization to survive, the surplus should always be positive and more than one.
- The performance of a manager is measured by his/her ability to generate the surplus as well as the achievement of the organizational objective.
- For management of any operation there is always a goal or objective to be accomplished in a certain time frame.

- The concept of operation management can be equally and effectively applied to all functions including Production, Marketing, Finance, General Management, Human Resource Management, etc. It can also be applied equally to both manufacturing and service sectors.

The final universal model of operation management can be depicted as in Figure 1.3, where the various input resources are also portrayed. The inputs are clearly defined as men, machines, material, money, management, technology and environment. Men, machines and materials are hard factors or well-defined resources mandatory for the value addition by conversion. The conversion process follows a well-defined technology for conversion. The technology enables the product and/or services to meet the specifications of performance and manufacturing/processing and defines a clear flow process chart for conversion which is the best alternative among the various options. Here the best alternative is the technology of conversion which satisfies the product feature requirements as well as the process requirements for conversion with the least consumption of input resources. The management ensures the optimum utilization of all resources for attainment of the business objective of the maximization of the customer satisfaction and the return on the investment in time. The finance to an organization is like blood in the human body which ensures effective circulation of various resources towards attainment of the defined organizational objective. The environment plays a lead role in today's global business environment and international competition, shorter product life cycle, frequently changing political relationship between nations, constantly emerging threats from substitute products and technological innovations, etc. A systematic understanding of the political, social, economic and technological environment is mandatory for the survival and world-class performance of an organization. The most important aspect of operation management is that it leads to the position of market leadership, all round performance excellence and multiplying return on investment with the same resources without any additional investment whatsoever.

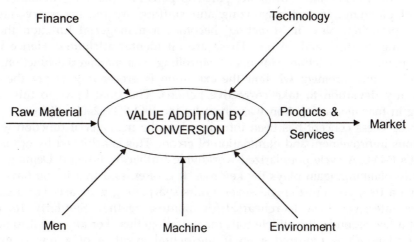

FIGURE 1.3 Model of operation management.

The seventies were the era of new products and services innovations and belonged to engineers. The eighties belonged to marketing professionals whose job was to sensitize customers of these innovations of seventies and eighties and capitalize on the same to gain market leadership. The focus was basically on the product. The era between the end of the eighties to the first two years of the nineties were dominated by financial managers who displaced traditional chartered accountants who only kept details on inflow and outflow of money and auditing. From the early nineties to the beginning of the next millennium belonged to information technology management. Currently information technology has been recognized as an enabler to all other functions without exception. Service industry was traditionally a single-digit contributor to the GDP of most of the nations in the world. In the last two decades, it has steadily jumped to a major contributor to the GDP of most of the nations in the world. In some of the world's leading economies, it is contributing nearly as much as the manufacturing sector. In this kind of emerging dynamic environment, operation management is the latest field of management which enables an organization to have an all-round performance excellence both in the manufacturing as well as the service sector. It is, therefore, strongly felt that the dominance of the principle of operation management, which is the current management trend for the last couple of years, is going to be the deciding factor in the emerging business environment for the next decade.

1.5 MANAGERIAL FUNCTIONS

Managerial functions are redefined under the total quality management concepts. Conventionally the functions are *planning, organizing, staffing, directing and controlling*. This concept was discarded by the Japanese industry more than 50 years ago. By the mid 70s and early 80s European, American industry and rest of the world's industry also realised the flaws in these managerial functions. The reasoning was simple. Can you ever draw a 'plan' without an organization before you and without staffing, i.e. without knowing the profile of the people going to execute the plan? It is just not possible. Therefore, organizing and staffing are part and parcel of 'planning' or rather they are the subset of planning. In fact organizing and staffing are the necessary data input for effective planning. Next if 'directing' becomes a managerial function then why not coordinating, leading and so on? These are all mental attributes. Hence it cannot be called a managerial function. However 'controlling' is a managerial function. Controlling is periodical measurement whether the execution is proceeding as per the plan and in case of any deviation to take corrective actions. The final blow to this conventional thinking in managerial function was given by the ISO 9000:2000 edition.

The process concept has been introduced as the managerial function with focus on continuous improvement and elimination of errors. This is achieved by opting for Walter Shewart's P-D-C-A cycle popularized worldwide further by Edward Deming (Figure 1.4).

Here planning again plays the key role. It is often said that if you have one hour to cut down a tree, you must spend seven hours sharpening your axe. For a stage show of a few minutes, you have to rehearsal for months together. Similarly, for an Olympic event of a few seconds, the athlete toils for years together. For any event to be successful, a lot of planning is required even if the actual event is of a few minutes. Let us

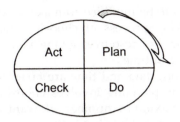

FIGURE 1.4 P-D-C-A cycle.

understand planning in the right perspective. Most of the industry does plan. But do they work out a complete 100% plan? Conventionally the definition of planning is 'deciding the course of action in advance'. It is as simple as that. For some organizations they are a bit advance and they modify the definition by adding another phrase like 'Planning is defining the course of action in advance and arranges resources for the same'. You tend to agree that this is a good definition and settle down to carry out the actual work of planning.

Let us take an example. Your work is located at a suburb. You have to go to the centre of the city to attend the crucial meeting at 6:00 p.m. in the evening—a simple activity. Now let us evaluate the number of alternatives for this simple work. Remember each alternative consumes resources in terms of money and takes some time for its execution. The alternatives could be as follows:

- Take an air-conditioned company car to the meeting.
- Since time of meeting is in the evening, it may overshoot the driver's working hours needing overtime. You may hire an A/C car for attending the meeting.
- You may walk down to the nearest railway station and catch a train nearest to the point of the meeting and walk down to the place.
- You may take a local transport to a railway station where you get a faster train and get down at a nearest station and take a cab to the meeting point.
- You can take a cheap local transport to the outskirt of the city limit and then change over to a cab to the meeting point.
- You can take a local transport to the bus station and catch a direct bus to the meeting point.

Still, there are more alternatives for this simple work. But you will notice that for each alternative, there is a different level of resources needed, cost involved, different time element and different level of efforts and associated comfort.

But what you actually do is: Take a hired A/C tourist car from your work and leave at 4:30 p.m. knowing that the drive time is one hour and you plan half an hour as a cushion. However what actually happens is that you get stuck in the routine traffic jam of the evening at outskirts of the city as all offices get over around 5:00 p.m. to 5:30 p.m. You reach the meeting point one hour late by 7:00 p.m. and by that time the person, whom you were to meet, might have left his office. Hence next time you have a meeting in the town at the same time, you will probably catch a train to the nearest station and take a cab to the meeting place so that the failure of last time is not repeated again. It could also lead to consumption of least amount of resources for attainment of the desired objective in time.

Planning definition needs to be modified to make it perfect. Hence, planning can be defined as the 'decision-making process of choosing the best alternative leading to consumption of the least amount of resources giving you the maximum output towards attainment of the end objective in time'.

Maximum amount of effort, data and time are taken for working out the plan. The decision making process of the planning involves choosing the best alternative which satisfies all the musts and maximum number of wants with least consumption of resources on a time-phased manner. Planning is the most important managerial function which ensures systematic efforts and approach to achieve the end result in time rather than achieving the same by default.

Once the plan is perfected, there is no discussion. Just go ahead and 'do' it, i.e. execute the plan. Before execution of the plan starts, the organization must ensure that all the resources are available as per the plan. The resources must be of right quality and available in right quantity at right time, right place and at right cost. The sequential flow process chart of the process of value addition at each stage should be charted out with well-defined resource and technology need at each and every stage with the control points. The accomplishment of the plan as envisaged is the main objective of the action of 'do' or the execution.

However, as explained earlier execution may not be 100% identical to the plan. The next step is to 'check' for the concurrence of the execution with the plan by periodic measurement at the defined control points as stated above. If the execution of plan is proceeding exactly as per the schedule, then hold on to the same charted out flow process chart or the route schedule. However in case there are 'deviations' from the plan to your execution, then the organization should have incorporated a mechanism of back-up actions to rectify the deviation by taking a suitable corrective action. This will put execution of the plan back on the right track.

Once you identify the deviations, check out the root cause for the deviations and 'act', i.e. take corrective and preventive actions so that next time you plan, you take precautions and you do not repeat the same mistake. In future if you have to attend any such meetings in the city, you will obviously not opt for the same plan but opt for a plan which will enable you to avoid the traffic jam in the evening office hours. This you can probably do by combining other work in city leaving early to avoid the traffic jam or take an alternate route consuming more time but not congested to a common traffic jam or else you can take an alternative route of travel, i.e. by rail route or so. This example is an indicator of choosing the alternative action plans or the routes for attainment of the end objective in time. Here the routes means the different actions consuming different resources and time for attaining the defined business plan.

Another feature is that the P-D-C-A cycle is a cycle. Normally, the situation in an organization repeats cyclically and periodically every month, every week, etc. since the men, materials and machines are more or less the same every month and month after month in the same organization. Hence, the P-D-C-A cycle can be made more effective as illustrated in Figure 1.5.

An effective and improved P-D-C-A cycle can be modified in a manner that once a deviation or mistake has occurred, it does not repeat again. This will lead to a continuous process of refinement and mistake elimination in an ongoing process. The Japanese call it 'Poka-Yoke' or mistake proofing. However, it follows an elaborate complicated path, but

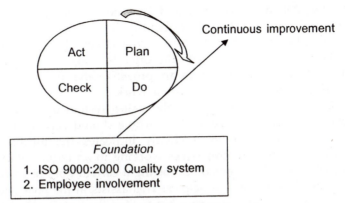

FIGURE 1.5 Effective and improved P-D-C-A cycle.

the objective is the same. The methodology is different. Here the objective is to simplify and synthesize all healthy management practices under one continuous process so that it is simple to implement without complicated management jargons which normally the management gurus are so fond of.

Since the basic three hard factors of production men, materials and machines are the same month after month and you keep on eliminating your mistakes and deviations every month and do not allow them to repeat, you are automatically on a path of continuous improvement. Today if you are measuring your errors in a percentage, tomorrow the organization will measure the errors in parts per million (p.p.m.)

However, to 'hold the gain', i.e. to ensure that the improvement does not fall back to original situation after some time, the organization's function should be sound enough to permanently absorb the improvement in its system. The best system is to have a quality management system as per ISO 9001:2000. Every improvement should lead to a change in the manual by making relevant change in procedure, work instructions and/or quality record so that change/improvement is permanently absorbed in day to day working of the organization or its quality system. The ISO 9000:2000 quality management system not only ensures organizational stability by way of holding the gains and maintaining the organizational performance, but also it creates an environment and approach for the continuous improvement of organizational performance.

Another important input to the organizational health is the 'total employee involvement'. Whatever you want to accomplish, unless the employees are involved in their job, nothing great can be achieved. All your best management practices can be grounded unless the employees are with the organization's goals and objectives. It is the employees in an organization who differentiates between a world-class organization and an ordinary organization with both operating in the same market with the same resources.

Hence fundamental to any good management practice is 'total employee involvement' and it starts right with the top management. It is mandatory for the top management to declare the 'vision' for the organization. A 'vision' can be defined as the long-term goal (minimum 10–15 years) of the organization as to where the organization wants to reach after a specified period of time. The 'vision' should be Specific,

Measurable, Attainable, Realistic and Time bound (SMART). The vision makes the people working in the organization clear about their goals and objective and synchronism of the same with the individual goals and objectives. This ensures the unification of the objectives of the employees with the organizational goals and objectives. This creates a situation where all the employees are proactive and involved in their work leading to all-round performance excellence in their work.

'Mission' can be defined as the value system of the organization as to how the employees and the organization as a whole should conduct itself to enable it to achieve the vision. Mission statement clearly indicates the means (ethical, legal, moral or otherwise) by which the employees working in an organization should accomplish their end objectives. This will ensure attracting a certain kind of employees who believe in the organizational values and principles. This assists in the goal integration of the employees and the employer enabling each other to give the best for the organizational performance excellence.

The vision is normally broken up into 'annual milestones'. The annual milestones are the goals and/or objectives of the organization. To attain these goals and objectives, the organization must have a proper business plan. The business plan is an outcome of the development of a business strategy which is determined after a 'SWOT' (Strengths, Weaknesses, Opportunities, Threats) analysis.

In the SWOT analysis, an elaborate analysis is done on two fronts:

1. *Assessment of the strengths and weaknesses of an organization vis-a-vis its competition.* Here the competition implies the organizations manufacturing the similar products and marketing the similar services including the substitute products and services. Here the organization should employ Michael Porter's theory of 'Competitive Advantage' by product or service differentiation to give customers that bit extra to differentiate the organization's products and services from the rest of the crowd. The strategy for the organization is to sensitize its customer about its strengths in the product and its services to enable it convince the customer to purchase the products and services of the organization. On the other hand the organization should overcome its weakness related to its products and services through proper research and development, product development, product innovation, customer training regarding the usage of the company's products and services, etc. The ultimate goal of the organization is to eliminate its weakness and if possible to convert the same into strength.

2. *Assessment of the opportunities and threats vis-a-vis the environment.* The environment analysis consists of the 'PEST' analysis, i.e. the Political, Economical, Social and Technological environment existing as well as emerging in every potential market. The organizational objective is to develop a strategic action plan capitalizing on its strength and opportunities and finding out the ways and means to convert the threats into opportunities through mergers, acquisitions or realignment of its facilities.

The outcome is an 'action plan' for a world-class performance aiming to reach the top of the corporate ladder assuming a leadership position. The action plans are for achievement of the annual targets, their periodic review for performance and taking corrective actions if needed to attain the end objective as stated above. The action plan and its execution involves the arrangement of the resources, laying out the technical processes and flow process chart, their periodic measurement and taking corrective actions in case of any deviation to ultimately achieve the quality objectives in the short run and the vision in the long run.

1.6 LATEST TREND IN TOTAL QUALITY MANAGEMENT

1.6.1 The Process Approach

The adoption of the P-D-C-A cycle as managerial function leads to the concept of 'process approach'. In fact the main improvization in ISO 9000:2000 over the 1994 standard is a total shift from product approach to process approach. It is concluded that 'if the process is correct and within total control, the product cannot be defective'.

In fact this process approach divides the entire business operations as an inter-linkage of processes. The ISO 9000:2000 clearly states that it promotes the adoption of a process approach.

A process can be defined as 'an activity needing resources and managed in order to transform an input in to a value added output'. In the interlinking of process the output of one process becomes the input for the next process.

According to ISO 9000:2000, the application of a system of processes within an organization, together with the identification and interaction of these processes and their management can be referred to as 'process approach'.

Under the concept of the process approach, ISO 9000:2000 has defined in P-D-C-A (Plan-Do-Check-Act) approach all the four activities as follows:

- *Plan:* Establish the objectives and processes necessary to deliver result in accordance with the customer requirements and organization's policies.
- *Do:* Implement the processes.
- *Check:* It has been defined as 'monitor and measure the processes and product against policies, objectives and requirements of the product and report the results'.
- *Act:* Take action to continually improve process performance.

The P-D-C-A approach of managerial function has already been explained in detail earlier.

ISO 9000:2000 propagates a process-based approach of a quality management system as shown in Figure 1.6, illustrating the process linkage in conjunctions with the interpretation and manifestation of the four major clauses.

However the standard clearly specifies the importance of customer satisfaction as the major objective of an organization in accordance with the policies of the organization. The organization policy of an organization is the outcome of its business plan. The business plan is the output and interpretation of the organization mission, vision, goals and objectives as explained earlier.

The process approach redefines the functions of the departments and organization structure in different prospective. It defines the purpose of the business as customer satisfaction and maximization of return on investment. With these two objectives being translated into measurable parameters, the rest of the business is broken up into inter-linkage of process culminating into the attainment of the above two fixed end objectives.

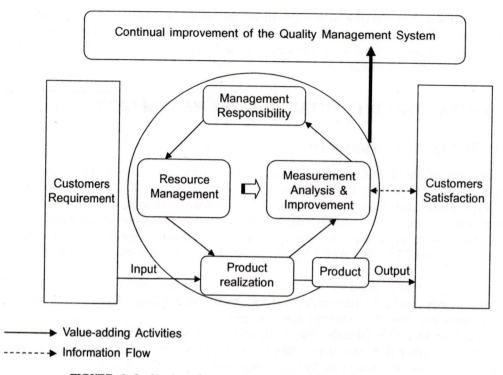

FIGURE 1.6 Model of process-based quality management system.

At every stage of such process as mentioned above there should be 'value addition'. At every process continuous value addition and inter-linkage through a flow process chart ensures that the output of one process becomes the input to the next process. Hence it leads to minimization of confusion, emergence of clear guidelines and objectives enabling the employees to be clear in their perception and leading to the participation and involvement of the employees totally in their respective jobs.

The six sigma (6σ) approach for zero-defect is also a process-oriented approach. It is a part of the concept of the 'statistical process control'. Here the control limits are fixed on the plus and minus three sigma from the zero or the mean line. As per normal distribution curve principle (Figure 1.7), the probability of percentage of population falling within $+ 3\sigma$ (sigma) is 99.73%. This implies that if the control limits are fixed at $+ 3\sigma$, there is a probability of only 27 parts per ten thousands to go out of the control limit. This obviously is a fairly low level of products going outside the control limits. We put the working signals like hooter or light or some such mechanism, the moment the parts tend to cross the control limits. The tolerance limits are always fixed beyond the control limits. Therefore, the process ensures that there is no rejection at any point of time. The parts that cross control limit (i.e. $\pm 3\sigma$) is still under the tolerance limit. This ensures zero rejection and zero-defect in the product.

Hence it can be concluded that if the process is under control the product can never get rejected.

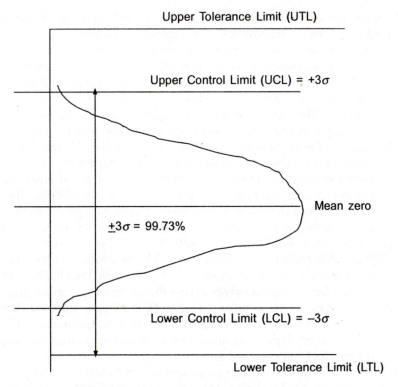

FIGURE 1.7 Normal distribution curve.

The terminology used in statistical process control is as follows:

$$\text{Mean} = \overline{X} = \frac{x_1 + x_2 + x_3 + \dots + x_n}{n}$$

Range, $R = X_{max} - X_{min}$

$\sigma = $ standard deviation $= \sqrt{\dfrac{\Sigma(x - \overline{x})^2}{n}}$

$z = $ variance $= \sigma^2$

Process capability, $C_p = \dfrac{\text{total tolerance}}{6\sigma} \geq 1$

Process capability factor, $C_{pk} = $ Minimum of $\dfrac{(\text{UTL} - \text{zero/mean})}{3\sigma}$ or

$$\frac{\text{zero/mean} - \text{LTL}}{3\sigma} \geq 1.0$$

Ideally both the C_p and C_{pk} should be around 1.27 to 1.33 for the process capability of a process to be good. The statistical process control ensures that the process is under control through periodic measure of the result and in case of deviation taking suitable remedial actions to ensure that the process is put back on the right track. This will ensure a self-renovating system producing products and services of zero defects and assured quality. The statistical process control ensures reliable performance of the product and services as per the customers' needs. It also ensures that both the machines as well as the process are capable to produce the product and services leading to total customer satisfaction. The statistical process control leads to the process and product standardization leading to uniform performance across the product and the customer. It ensures fulfillment of the customers' expectations repeatedly and reliably.

The statistical process control is dealt in detail in Chapter 9.

The six sigma concept maintains the control limits at $\pm 6\sigma$ ensuring to keep the product performance practically perfect as per norms with 99.99966%. This implies that the probability of the product failure is 3.4 parts per million. The six sigma concept is an extension of the statistical process control. It was originally started at Motorola in 1979. Mikel Harry left Motorola in 1993 to join 'ABB' in 1993. The six sigma effectiveness was proved in ABB by 68% reduction in defects and 30% in product costs. Mikel Harry and Richard Schroeder started six sigma academy in 1994. Jack Welch, the CEO of General Electric, popularized the six sigma drives across the globe by implementing it strongly in all its divisions as well as its vendors. Today TCS, Wipro, Infosys, Patni Computer systems, etc. all practices six sigma due to their tie up with General Electric.

The six sigma can be defined as 'a statistical measuring system to gauge and attain perfection of the product, process and services'.

There are many instances where you cannot afford to fail even 3.4 parts in a million or at six sigma performance level also, for example landing system of aircraft, your own heartbeat, loss of important documents, failure in a surgery, testing of a nuclear plant and management of dangerous affluent.

However, under the circumstance the organization has to attempt to do the best that is possible to achieve at least a performance level of six sigma. The six sigma philosophy always attempts for an error-free performance.

The six sigma concept is dealt in detail in Chapter 10.

1.7   CONCEPT OF PRODUCTIVITY

World-class companies create 'surplus' through productive operations, i.e. the output is always more than the input of resources.

Productivity is defined as 'the ratio of output to input within a defined time period with due consideration for quality'.

$$\text{Productivity} = \frac{\text{output}}{\text{input}} \text{ (within a defined time and quality)}$$

This formula can be elaborated as follows:

- Both the output and input should be quantified in tangible monetary terms for correct assessment.

- Productivity can be improved by the following:
  (a) Increasing output with the same input
  (b) Increasing output more than the increase in input
  (c) Decreasing input for the same output
  (d) Increasing output with decreasing the input
- Productivity implies effectiveness and efficiency in individual and organizational performance. Here the 'effectiveness' means the achievement of the set individual and the organizational target or the objective whereas 'efficiency' is the output input ratio or the value addition to input resources minus the cost of value addition, i.e. surplus generated by a process or an organization as a whole.
- Managers should clearly know their goals and those of the organization to ascertain whether they are productive or not. It is therefore important for the organization to declare its mission, vision and annual objectives to chart out a clear unambiguous path without any confusion in the organization.

1.8 MANAGERIAL ROLES AND SKILLS UNDER TQM PARADIGM

All managers have one objective, i.e. to create surplus. All managers need four types of skills to adapt themselves to their role.

1.8.1 Technical Skills/Technological Skills

Managers should have technical skill in terms of the following:

- Knowledge about the product
- Technical knowledge about the process
- Technical knowledge about the usage of the product
- Technical knowledge about the competency of the people to do this task in the team

The technical skill is more required for the first line managers and supervisors. This enables them to understand the product and process to effectively guide and lead his team to carry out the assigned responsibility. This also enables a first line manager to lead his team by example or as such help the team in maximization of the value addition at this junction. The technical knowledge about the product, process and its usages increases product quality, its better applicability, longer life and after all enhanced customer satisfaction. It also brings down the cost of production and better utilization of men, machines and materials.

However as the manager goes up the ladder, the technical knowledge does not play a key role and its significance reduces substantially. The technical knowledge as per the modern management concept is required maximum at operator's and supervisor's level. The need becomes lesser and lesser as the manager's level or hierarchy goes up.

1.8.2 Human Relation Skill

The human relation skill is divided into two parts, namely the communication skill of recipient and disseminator of information as well as presentation of departmental information and output to rest of the organization. The manager has to represent the departmental interest at the various forums on behalf of the department and get the best deal for the department. At the same time the manager has to convey and convince his people regarding the implementation of the organizational policies and directives and ensure that the department gels well with the rest of the organization. The other aspect of human relation skill is liasoning or interpersonal skill which is a key attribute for the enhancement of employees' moral and motivation.

Informational role/Communication skills

The manager represents the department or a group of people reporting to him/her. Hence on behalf of the group, he receives information and interaction about operations, processes, organizational policies, principles, etc. He has to pass the information effectively to the subordinates. The subordinates need help from the manager to understand and interpret their input information. He has to get their doubts and queries cleared.

He also has to represent the department as its spokesperson at various meetings, and forums.

It is said that most of the labour problems and unrests are due to lack of communication between the management and workmen. It is here that the manager's ability to perform effectively the recipient, disseminator and spokesperson role is the key to proper and healthy communication. All managers at all levels require good communication skill.

Inter-personal role/liasoning skills

All managers at all levels have to play the role of the head of a group of people they represent. A manager has not only to play the role of a leader but also has to act as a ceremonial head of the group. The manager also does the liasoning role. He has to play an intermediately liasoning role in terms of getting the best deal for the people whom he represents as also he has to get the best productive output from the group of people reporting to him.

All managers at all levels require this inter-personal and/or liasoning skill which is of equal importance. The inter-personal and/or liasoning skill is one of the essential skill elements required to be a successful manager.

1.8.3 Decision-making Role/Entrepreneurship Skills

A manager has to have entrepreneurship skills wherein his ability to take timely effective decisions becomes the key to business success. This attribute of decision making assumes more importance as the level of manager becomes higher and higher. In fact at the 'CEO' or General Manager level, his main role is that of decision making on vital issues. The importance of the conceptual skills at the top is of vital importance. Refer to Figure 1.8.

A manager has to act as an entrepreneur for his own department. He has an objective or goal to accomplish. He has some resources, i.e. men, money, equipment and material at his disposal. These resources may not be adequate to accomplish the goal. Hence, he has to play a negotiator role to optimize the resources to achieve the end result. He has to allocate the resources to the best and optimal use. In case of any

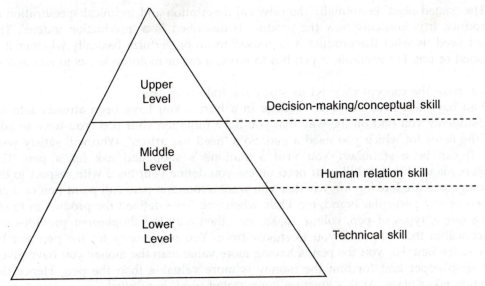

FIGURE 1.8 Level of manager.

disturbance in execution of the plan or deviation, the manager has to handle the same efficiently to attain the end result.

On the whole the manager has to act as an entrepreneur as if it is his own business where the key issue is to create a surplus by value addition on a consistent basis. He has to maximize the 'return on investment' by enhanced speed of business, minimum consumption of resources and maintain value addition by transformation.

1.9   THE CONCEPT OF CUSTOMER SATISFACTION

An organization survives because of its customers. An excellently managed technically sound organization with international certification may also go out of business due to lack of customer support. A business enterprise irrespective of whether in a manufacturing or service sector has to have regular order to keep its wheels running. In fact it is the customers who pay for the employees' salary as well as meets all the expenditure and creates surplus for an organization.

Hence another improvement the ISO 9000:2000 standards incorporated as its key focus is the customer focus. Edward Deming, Philip Kotler and Joseph Juran have all insisted on one thing for success of a business enterprise—customer orientation or customer satisfaction.

'A customer is stated to be satisfied if his/her stated and implied needs are fulfilled'.

An evidence of customer satisfaction is 'repurchase' or repeat business as well as becoming goodwill ambassador for the organization. The other evidences are the increase in the market share with the same customer or increase in the sales. The organization may also have a written assessment of its performance giving a rating from its customers.

Now let us understand the concept of customer satisfaction, i.e. the fulfillment of the customer's stated and implied needs.

The 'stated need' is normally the physical description and technical specification of the product. It is normally how the product is described in a 'production indent'. The 'implied need' is what the product is supposed to do or perform basically whether it is mentioned or not. For example, a pen has to write, a car or motorcycle has to run and so on.

To make the concept clear let us study the following case:

You have left your house for college in a hurry. You have been already late for class. Suddenly you find on the way that you have forgotten your pen. You have to take down the notes for which you need a pen. So a 'need has arisen'. Who will satisfy your need? It can be a stationer. You visit a stationer's shop and ask for a pen. The shopkeeper is unable to fulfill your need unless you define your need with respect to the price range you are looking for, whether you want a fountain pen, ball point pen or a gel type pen or any particular brand, etc. Only when you have defined the product in terms of price range, types of pen, colour, make, etc., then only the shopkeeper provides the product within that range for you to choose from. You pay money for the pen and he gives you the pen. For you the pen is having more value than the money you have given to the shopkeeper and for him the money is more valuable than the pen. Hence the transaction takes place. At this juncture your 'stated need' is fulfilled.

As is stated earlier, you are already late for the class. Hence you do not have time to keep on scratching the pen to make it write and so on. When you enter your class, what is implied that the pen should write clearly, and without any obstruction to the flow of ink. If the pen starts performing these functions without any problem and gives a reasonably good life till the ink is exhausted, your 'implied need' is also fulfilled.

Now you are a satisfied customer. You look for the brand of the product as to the make and type so that next time you have a need, you will buy the same product.

We can now formulate a formula of customer satisfaction and state it as follows: A customer is satisfied if his stated and implied needs are fulfilled. Once if he is satisfied, he will continue to buy the same product of the same brand unless influenced by an external force.

Here, the external force could be better price, service, better technology, etc. Whatever may be the influence, a satisfied customer will always resist to change over to a new product. Hence, customer satisfaction becomes a key factor in an organizational vision statement or quality policy. The modern concept is to orient the entire organizational activity towards fulfillment of the customer's stated and implied needs. The entire supply chain is managed to fulfill the customer's needs.

A customer is fundamentally satisfied by use of a product and the service associated with it while fulfilling the stated and implied needs. With reference to the product, the quality and quantity are the two predominant features the customer looks for. With reference to the service, time utility, place utility and price play a pivotal role in customer satisfaction wherein he looks for 'value for money'.

1.9.1 The Concept of Right Quality

Joseph Juran defined: "Quality as fitness for use by the customer."
Philip B. Crossby defined: "Quality as conformance to requirement consistently."
W. Edward Deming stated: "Quality is a key to competitive advantage".

Quality is the ability of the product to meet the functional usage associated with the product. It is interesting to know that the customer's perception about quality varies along with the functional requirement. A product is supposed to be of good quality at one place can be considered as a product of bad quality for some other usage.

For example, a normal home floor and table cleaning liquid with nominal disinfectant power but of good fragrance could be a sought-after product of good quality for day-to-day domestic use. The same product can be called of poor quality while used in hospitals and operation theaters. Hence, the concept of quality is product-specific, usage-specific and customer-specific. However, it has some features in common under all circumstances, i.e. trouble-free performance, ease of handling and usage.

1.9.2 The Concept of Right Quantity

The concept of quantity is partly associated with the product usage and partly with the service factor. For example, the same quantity of food served in a restaurant could be enough for a middle-aged man or woman on diet and it could be inadequate for a young sportsman. The amount of soap and toiletries required by a domestic household, a medium-sized hotel and a large group of hotels, their buying habits as well as the concept of quantity are all different.

It is well known that a sales promotional campaign, quantity discount, packaging, transportation mode and the 'Distribution Requirement Planning (DRP)' depend largely on the concept of quantity.

Hence the customer satisfaction depends on the concept of providing goods and services of right quantity as well as right quality. For example, if a beauty soap manufacturer offer a sales promotional scheme of one soap free on purchase of every six soaps, it is bound to be a failure as the consumer usually need soaps in lots of 3/4 per month for a normal household of husband, wife and two children. On the other hand, if a soap manufacturer offers a scheme of one extra soap on purchase of two or three soaps, the scheme is more likely to become a hit. Hence the concept of right quantity is very important in customer satisfaction.

1.9.3 The Concept of Right Time

The concept of right time is very important for the product usage and buying habit of the consumer. For example, when you are hungry you may eat any bare minimum right quality of food in right quantity. If required, you may make some compromises also in quality and quantity. But if you are offered a sound tasty good quality meal when your stomach is full, you will not even look at the food. Similarly, one may not like to have ice-cream when the outside temperature is around 0°C. He may rather prefer a hot cup of tea. Hence the concept of right time of selling a product to a customer/consumer is when he needs it as well as he has the resource to buy the product and use it. The concept of right time is very important towards providing customer satisfaction. The seasonal factor in terms of time always plays a role in the market place. For example, the sales of fans, refrigerators and air-conditioners are maximum during the summer season. The sales of colour television peak before a world cup event in football or cricket. The sales of clothes and white goods rise during Diwali and Dassera in India and during

Christmas in Europe and America. Hence, the concept of right time is an extremely important aspect in marketing and customer satisfaction.

1.9.4 The Concept of Right Place

The product should be available at the right place where the demand exists. Most of the people who stay in cities are aware that the main/whole sale market is hardly a few kilometres away where goods are available at least 10–20% cheaper than a next-door grocer or vegetable vendor. People still buy from the next-door grocer or vegetable vendor at a higher price of 10–20%. This is the premium people pay for the place utility for saving time and transportation cost. We can explain it in another way. Suppose you are a brand loyal to Coke and you are thirsty. If you do not get a Coke in the nearby outlet, you would not travel a kilometre to get a Coke. Rather you may settle down to buy a competitive product like Pepsi.

To create the place utility, a manufacturer develops a distribution network which is a powerful tool to make the product available where the demand exists. This PDM or Physical Distribution Management is a key factor for the company's market share and customer response.

For example, in an important metro city in India like Mumbai, Pepsi struggled to get its market share in spite of heavy advertisement because it could not create a powerful distribution network and thereby the place utility. Dukes was a dominant brand in Mumbai with its powerful physical distribution management for many years. When Pepsi tied up with Dukes, Pepsi gained its market share and strengthened it substantially. On the other hand Coca-Cola had foreseen this factor and all along had this advantage due to taking over of Parle Soft Drinks Limited, a manufacturer of a dominant soft drink brand named Thums Up.

Procter & Gamble (P&G) had an instant access to the Indian market through its smart move of tying up with Godrej Soaps Ltd., having a wide distribution network to make the P&G product available at every possible retail outlet in the country thereby creating a place utility.

1.9.5 The Concept of Right Price

The concept of right price is so obvious to understand that it needs little explanation. It can be redefined as value for money. Today customers are technically knowledgeable and smart. They have a choice of global products and global pricing. All other factors being the same like right quality, right quantity, right time and right place, the right price plays a decisive role in affecting and influencing the decision of purchasing. Today a product priced lower is no more considered a inferior product. Both products are compared by the customer and other things being equal, the product which is priced lower is still considered to be a better product and the organization producing the product is considered to be more cost efficient or competent in its operation management.

In 'industrial marketing', the customer is competent to technically access and compare two products in terms of quality. Hence there is no scope for paying higher for a particular brand. The product which is priced lower gets the order.

In 'consumer marketing', the concept of esteem value and brand may add value to the product. However, with the presence of so many brands and global competition and better product knowledge, the concept of esteem value giving a price advantage is gradually diminishing and a few years down the line, it may be an outdated concept.

Hence the right price or the value for money plays a lead role in customer satisfaction. Now we can conclude that customer satisfaction is attained by satisfying the stated and implied needs of the customer. This is in intangible terms. When we translate this concept in tangible, definable and measurable terms, we can define customer satisfaction is achieved by providing products and services of right quality, right quantity, at right time, right place and at right price leading to the fulfillment of the customer's stated and implied needs.

1.10 THE IMPORTANCE OF RETURN ON INVESTMENT

Customer satisfaction is the key to survival of an organization. But if we look from the point of view of management and investors/shareholders in an organization, their main objective is the Return On Investment (ROI).

If one keeps money in a fixed deposit, which is one of the safest forms of investment and securities, he can earn around 7–8%. If he takes slightly more risk and keeps the money in a private or co-operative bank, he may earn a percent more. The next safest investment is gold which has both liquidity and lesser risk. The average annual increase in the price of gold is around 10%. The next opportunity for the investment is in real estates. But the liquidity of the investment is gone and return is not assured. The next option offers the highest earning as well loosing opportunity. It is the share market. The risk is high and the possibility of the gain is also equally high. The option which is most challenging, multifunctional, lucrative and serves individual as well social objective is the entrepreneurship of starting an organization. The thumb rule is that it takes one to two years to reach its break-even point and three to five years to recover the investment in an organization. This is why an individual invests in business fundamentally.

Hence the main objective of a businessman or the management of an organization is to maximize the return on investment. If this is not attractive, one will not invest in business. The return on investment depends on two factors:

- The profit per transaction
- The number of times the working capital is turned round per annum

Therefore,

$$\text{ROI} = \text{Profit} \times \text{No. of working capital cycle per annum}$$

For understanding the concept of profit, let us first understand the importance of break-even point (BEP). Refer to Figure 1.9. For a businessman or an investor, the BEP is the crucial point beyond which the firm starts making profit. The organization incurs two types of cost: fixed cost and variable cost.

The variable cost is directly proportionate to a single unit being produced and is the cost of direct input resources like cost of material, man, running cost of machines like electricity, fuel, etc. The variable cost is incurred when the factory is in running condition.

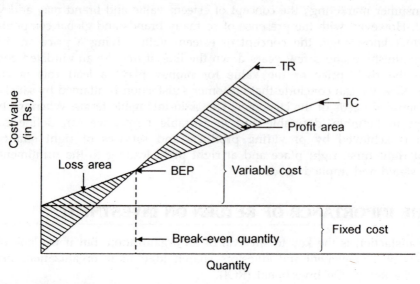

TR : Total revenue/Total sales value
TC : Total cost
FC : Fixed cost
VC : Variable cost
BEP : Break-even point

FIGURE 1.9 Break-even point.

The fixed cost is incurred even if the factory is closed. It consists of interest on loan, salary, plant maintenance cost, etc.

Contribution is the difference between the selling price (SP) and the variable cost (VC), i.e.

$$\text{Contribution} = \text{SP} - \text{VC}$$

Below the break-even point, the business is in loss since the total contribution is not enough to cover the fixed cost. At the break-even point the contribution becomes equal to fixed cost and it is a 'null balance point' where the business neither makes loss nor makes profit.

Beyond the break-even point, the contribution becomes equal to profit and the more the firm sells, the more is the profit. In other words, profit is equal to surplus generated by the business.

Now let us probe into the second concept of turning round of a working capital cycle. The working capital is the capital invested in meeting the variable cost of the business. In accounting terms, the working capital means the capital invested in stock, i.e. raw material, WIP (work in progress) and finished goods, goods in transit, debtors and expenses during this period, i.e. wages, electricity, power and fuel cost, etc. The working capital cycle has important 'time element'. It starts with the receipt of orders from customers and goes through the process of procuring material from the supplier, processing it and converting it into finished goods, dispatching to customers and ultimately recovering money from the customers. The entire process duration is the working capital cycle time.

On completion of one working capital cycle, one earns one profit. Hence if the firm completes two working capital cycles, it earns two profits. What it means is that if a firm's investment in the raw material is for one month, WIP for one month, expenses for one month, and debtors for three months for recovery, the total working capital cycle time is six months. Therefore the turning round of working capital per annum is two. The firm earns one profit per completion of working capital cycle. Hence in this case the firm will earn two profits as its return on investment. In case the firm can compress its working capital cycle to four months from six months, it will turn round the working capital three times a year. Hence the return on investment will be three times the profit. Therefore,

$$\text{ROI} = \text{Profit} \times \text{No. of times turning round of working capital}$$

Here the investment means total investment, i.e. capital + short-term and long-term loans and advances.

To illustrate the concept further, let us analyze the following case.

A manufacturing industry has certain goods in stock. It has two customers A and B. The customer A agrees to allow the organization a profit margin of 20% with the payment terms as three months after the supply and acceptance of the goods. The customer A is a large organization. It takes up the processing of invoice for payment after three months and by the time the organization gets its cheque and realizes the payment, four months is over. The customer B allows the organization a profit margin of only 5% (one-fourth of profit compared to the first situation), but agrees to pay against delivery. The entire transaction of delivery of goods till realization of the payment is over in a maximum of five days including the week-ends. Which of these two situations is more beneficial to the organization as far as the return on investment is considered?

Obviously the dealing with the customer B is more beneficial. Let us analyze the case. Money is a scarce resource and every organization has limitation of this resource. It therefore has the alternative uses and opportunity cost. In both the situations, let us assume that the customer places an order of Rs 1.00 lakh. In the case of the customer A, the organization keeps on supplying Rs. 1.00 lakh worth of goods every month. At the end of the fourth month he realizes Rs. 1.00 lakh invoiced in the first month. Then onwards every month the organization gets Rs. 1.00 lakh and earns a profit of Rs. 20000. The outstanding with the customer A will be always Rs. 4.0 lakh. Hence the return on investment with the customer per month will be $(20000/400000) \times 100 = 5\%$ only.

In the case of the customer B, every five days the organization invoices to the customer B (or any other similar customer) Rs. 1.00 lakh and realizes Rs. 5000. This way in thirty days or per month the organization can complete $30/5 = 6$ transactions. Every transaction he earns Rs. 5000. Hence the organization earns Rs. $5000 \times 6 = $ Rs. 30000 per month on an investment of Rs. 1.00 lakh, i.e. 30% per month. Hence the return on investment is six times more beneficial in the case of the customer B (30%) than in the case of the customer A (only 5%). Hence the current concept in business is the maximization of the return on investment and not only the profit. This concept is also known as increasing the 'throughput' of the business. This also adds to the liquidity and better cash flow management in any contemporary business organization.

1.11   FUNCTIONS OF A WORLD-CLASS TQM ORGANIZATION AND ITS DEPARTMENTS

It is now conclusively proved that for an organization to survive and prosper, it has clearly two major objectives:

- To maximize customer satisfaction
- To maximize the creation of surplus or rather maximize the return on investment.

In most of the organizations, people follow strict department orientation and each department is a power centre by itself. An additional factor of departmental loyalty and departmental objective come to play over and above the organizational objective and loyalty. More often than not, these two objectives clash with each other nullifying each other's effort and producing zero result.

In a typical monthly review meeting, the reason for not meeting the target will be discussed and each department representative normally the department head will give his explanation for non-performance. The marketing department would tell that they are the best marketing team in the world but they could not achieve the target as the product quality was much inferior as compared to the competitors's and/or the cost of production is too high to market the product competitively in the market. They will back up these statements with a number of field failures and customer complaints.

The production department people are equally smart. They will claim that they are the most competent and technically sound production department in the world. They are producing the product of world-class quality and their cost of production is lowest. They will back up this statement with in-house trial results against the world's best product. The report will show that the company's product is superior to even the world's best product. Their explanation will be that the marketing team is incompetent and not as capable as the competition. Hence the reason for lower sales performance is pushed to the other side.

This meeting will last for hours together. But it may not yield any result. It is like two sides of the same river looking at each other all their life but never meeting each other at a common point or coming to a common understanding. This could be called anything but team work. If one says 'yes' the other says 'no'. It leads to a situation where +1 and −1 makes the result as zero. If the top CEO is very powerful, he may overrule by close supervision making the result at the most one plus one two.

The strong non-permeable departmental walls, individual departmental objective and goals leads to non-sharing of ideas, stone walling each other creating a situation of converting departments into vertical chimneys where all these non-productive waste of energy and gases go up in the air like that of chimneys and of no use to the organization (Figure 1.10). The vertical chimney organizations are symbolic of strong power centres, autocratic working culture without goal integration of individual with the organizational goal and cannot survive in today's highly competitive global environment. They are invariably the non-productive and non-performing outdated organizations struggling for survival.

The organizational goals and objectives thus get lost in this way and these organizations waste their productive energy in in-fighting whereas the competition has a field day outside. The outlook of this type of the organization tends to become negative and that of a loser or laggard rather than positive or that of a winner.

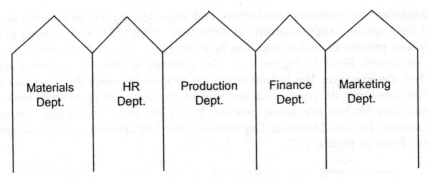

FIGURE 1.10 Vertical chimney organizational structure.

The functions of the departments and the organizational structure have to be reoriented to face the global competition as well as to survive and succeed in today's turbulent environment. The departmental walls should be thin and transparent mingling into each other into a continuous process wherein the output of one department becomes input for another department. The department's objective and goals are to be integrated with the organizational goals and objectives. Refer to Figure 1.11.

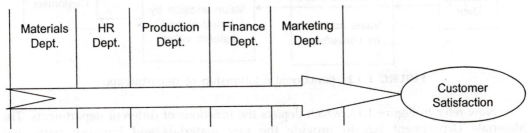

FIGURE 1.11 Horizontal quality thinking.

Each department supplements and complements each other producing the result by their individual as well as cumulative contribution by each one standing next to the other producing a result as one and one eleven (1 + 1 = 11). The concept of 'internal customer' is introduced wherein one function becomes the internal customer for the other department. The Marketing Department becomes the internal customer for the Production Department and the production department becomes the internal customer for the Materials Department. This argument can be mathematically depicted as follows:

$$
\begin{array}{ccc}
+1 & +1 & 1 \ \& \ 1 = \\
-1 & +1 & 11 \\
\hline
0 & 2 & \text{eleven}
\end{array}
$$

As is explained earlier the organization as well as each department has only two major objectives:

- To maximize the customer satisfaction externally and internally
- To maximize the return on investment

To maximize the customer satisfaction, and organization has to provide goods and services of right quality, right quantity, at right time, right place and at right price.

The entire process of 'value addition by conversion' has to be broken up into sub-functions/processes. Refer to Figure 1.12. The concept of internal customer has to be introduced at this juncture. The output from one process becomes the input for the next process. The consumer of goods and services of the succeeding process becomes the internal customer for the preceding process. It implies that 'Production' becomes the internal customer for the Materials Department, HR Department and the Maintenance Department. Refer to Figure 1.12.

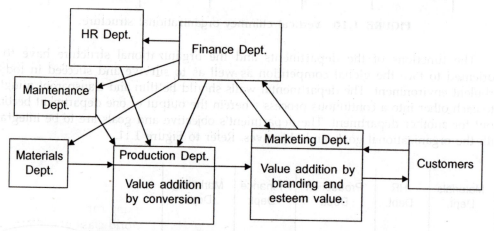

FIGURE 1.12 Functional relationship of departments.

Now refer to Figure 1.13, which depicts the functions of different departments. The Materials Department has to provide the raw materials and buy out parts and components of right quality, right quantity, at right time, right place and at right price to the Production Department aiming towards satisfying the Production Department's stated and implied needs.

Concept of Internal Customer

Maintenance Dept. Machines of right quality, and quantity, cost and at right time and place	**Finance Dept.** Finance of right quality, quantity, cost at right time and place	**HR Dept.** Human Resource of right quality, quantity at right cost time and place

| **Materials Dept.** Raw materials of right quality, quantity, price at right time and place | **Production Dept.** Value addition by conversion | **Marketing Dept.** Creation of esteem value | **Customer** |

FIGURE 1.13 Departmental functions.

Similarly, the HR Department has to provide human resources, i.e. workers, staff, and managers of right quality, right quantity, at right time, right place and at right price to the Production Department who is an internal customer.

The Maintenance Department has to provide machines and tools of right quality, right quantity, at right time, right place and at right price to the Production Department.

The Marketing Department is the internal customer for the Production Department, and the Production Department has to provide products and services of right quality, right quantity, at right time, right place and at right price to the Marketing Department.

The Marketing Department represents the organization and it has to provide products and services of right quality, right quantity, at right time, right place and at right price to external customers/consumers for their satisfaction.

The Finance Department has to arrange for money of right quality, right quantity, at right time, right place and at right price. The Finance Department gets the payment for goods and services supplied through the Marketing Department and in turn provides these resources to respective departments.

The maximization of return on investment is principally concerned with reduction in cost of production. The profit can either be increased by an increase in selling price or reduction in cost of production. Due to the global competition and highly competitive marketing environment the increase in selling price may lead a firm to go out of business. Therefore, the second part of 'reduction in the cost of production' is the only way to increase profitability. The other areas where the firms are concentrating to enhance their return on investment are by proper logistics and supply chain management as well as debtor control and the faster turning round of working capital. The minimum norm of the turning round of working capital for a normal world-class organization has to be minimum four or above per annum. Certain good organizations have achieved the turning round of working capital period to once in a month, i.e. 12 per annum.

Additionally you should create a concept of 'listening post' in the organization. Under this concept, you should put personnel from the Production Department, HR Department, Materials Department or Finance Department at the customer's end like a dealer shop or a customer premise. These personnel should listen quietly to the customer/consumer without even letting them know of their identity. This listening post concept is very effective in understanding the true feedback from the customer/consumer without any bias or influence. This helps the entire organization understanding the customer's stated and implied needs.

Organizing a dealer meet in the factory as well as organizing a customer visit to the factory and having interaction with factory personnel is also an effective way of understanding customer's stated and implied needs.

The organization should understand and believe in the importance of satisfying the customer. All the employees including the top management should trust and respect the customer and build that into the value system of the organization. Additionally give the employees the responsibility, authority and skills to deliver high levels of customer satisfaction.

Undertaking the above approach of management style needs a lot of effort and total rethinking and reorientation of managerial practices and working for a conventional organization. First of all the management of kind of orthodox and outdated organizations rarely have the honesty to accept and acknowledge that they need to change and improve to survive in the current highly competitive global environment. As it is rightly said an organization and its employees' survival depends a lot on their ability to learn, unlearn and relearn to adapt to the new turbulent business environment and global competition where clearly only the best and fittest will survive and excel.

EXERCISES

1. Define the latest concept of 'Management'. Explain the statement: "Operation Management is a key activity for achieving success in any Business functions".

2. How will you apply the concept of management for attaining both the 'effectiveness' and 'efficiency' in manufacturing as well as service sectors.

3. Explain Deming's P-D-C-A cycle and how it helps in continuous improvement.

4. What are the main business objectives to be fulfilled by an organization for its survival and performance excellence?

5. This chapter describes in detail 'the changing phase of management for survival in current business environment'. Please discuss.

6. Explain the horizontal quality thinking and the functional orientation of various departments.

7. Elaborate on the process approach. How is it different from the product approach?

8. Design a contemporary modern organization for world-class performance in the current global business environment.

Chapter 2

Total Quality Management System—Its Various Concepts and Tools

Conventionally 'quality' has been associated with the 'product'. Marks like 'ISI' for technical products and 'Agmark' for food products are considered to be symbols of good quality. However with the globalization, emergence of intense international competition and market transformation from sellers' to buyers' market has lead to a situation where the same product features may not be acceptable to the entire user segment. Hence quality has also become user segment specific. A product which is good quality for a certain user segment may be bad quality for another user segment under similar or different conditions of use. This chapter will deal with the concepts and importance of quality.

2.1   QUALITY AND ITS DEFINITION, CONCEPTS AND FEATURES

Dr. Juran, the most acclaimed management and quality guru of the 20th century has defined 'quality as fitness for use'. Philip Crosby, another leading exponent of total quality management has defined 'quality as conformance to requirement'. ISO 9000:2000, the international standard on Quality Management System has defined 'quality as the degree to which a set of inherent characteristics fulfills requirements'.

To sum up all the contemporary definitions:

'Quality can be defined as the totality of the features or state of the products and/or services that satisfies the stated and implied need of the customer.

This definition brings out a universally applicable definition of quality for both the manufacturing and the service sectors. This definition also makes it amply clear that quality is the outcome of well-planned and researched combination of the features of the product and services associated with the product or the service itself derived in combinations with the factors of the use of the product and/or service along with the conditions of usage. Quality has become a complex and key aspect of current business management and success of an organization. With the evolution of the contemporary management theories and creative work done by world-class companies in this dynamic and challenging global business environment, the vital paradigm of organizational success has shifted from other functions to quality. Hence quality is the key parameter for business success as defined by Edward Deming who states: 'Leadership in quality decides the market leadership'.

Quality has many facets as described hereafter:

2.1.1   Quality Satisfies Three Fs—Fit, Form and Function

Quality satisfies three Fs—fit, form and function. This is a conventional and orthodox definition of 'quality' which is basically confined to a product satisfying the need for the required dimensions, fitment, required form and aesthetics. The product should also be able to fulfill the functions desired to be performed by the product. This definition is more product-focussed and does not include the services under its paradigm.

2.1.2   Fitness for Use

Dr. Juran defined quality as fitness for use. A product or service is considered to be of good quality if it is fit enough for the intended use, i.e. it can be used satisfactorily. A product or service need not to be perfect. In spite of other drawbacks, if the product or service satisfies the end use conditions, it is said to be having good quality.

2.1.3 Fitness for Purpose

The product or service should serve the purpose for which it is used. If the product is used efficiently, but it does not serve the purpose for which it is intended to be used, it is not supposed to be having good quality. It is like the old story that if you give a woodcutter an axe made of gold instead of steel, it is bad quality since it does not serve his purpose. He needs an axe made of steel only to cut wood. Therefore, a product or service should serve the purpose if it is to be of good quality.

2.1.4 Totality of Features and Characteristics

An organization striving to excel in business as well as in the field of quality must offer the product and services together as a complete package so that the customer is not required to look beyond the organization. This also needs a detail research to find out the customer's requirement so as to translate the same into design and development of the product and services to give shape to the totality of features and characteristics.

2.1.5 Conformance to Requirement

Conformance to requirement is a definition of quality according to Philip Crosby. Here the requirement may go beyond the customer's stated needs. The customer may not be fully aware of his needs or the customer may not be aware that such kind of product or service exists which is better suited to fulfill his requirement. The true quality is achieved when the customer's requirements are exactly investigated and understood by the organization, and the products and services are offered accordingly.

2.1.6 Stated and Implied Needs

The stated needs are the needs which the customer specifies for procurement of the goods or services. They are the purchase indent for an organization and the physical parameters or the tangible description of the product or the service. Implied needs are the associated functions the product is supposed to perform irrespective of whether they are stated or not. For example, the stated need for you while purchasing a pen may be a certain specification and price range, whereas implied need is that the pen should be able to write clearly, legibly and smoothly till the time the ink gets exhausted. The quality goal is achieved by an organization if it makes efforts to understand the consumer's stated needs as well as implied or latent needs correctly, and it offers products and services in accordance with the same. In case this can be achieved, the customer who is going to use the product or the service is bound to be satisfied or delighted.

2.2 CUSTOMER SATISFACTION

The buzzword in today's marketing management or total quality management is the customer's satisfaction. A customer is satisfied when his stated and implied needs are fulfilled. Here the need could go much beyond the product and service to enter into the areas like aesthetics, time of delivery, place of delivery, life, the way the sales transaction is handled, etc. The true definition of quality emerges only and mainly from customer satisfaction.

Customer satisfaction can be achieved through the fulfillment of the stated and implied needs of the customer by the use of the products and/or services offered by the organization.

The effect of customer satisfaction is the continued brand loyalty, repurchase of the products and service as well as the customer acting as an opinion leader in the market for the organization. To satisfy a customer, the extremely important task for an organization is to understand what the customer actually needs. The need could be partially understood by the customer who is in a position to state and define the same whereas a part of the need may be dormant or latent which the customer may not be in a position to state or define. Both the needs should be understood and defined, and suitable steps like addition of product features, have to be undertaken to satisfy both the stated and the implied needs. Then only the customer satisfaction is possible. It is this customer orientation that has made the Japanese industries secure world leadership in their respective fields of operation. The evidence of customer satisfaction or its measure should be obtained periodically by market surveys, market share, percentage of customers coming back for repurchase of the product or the service, periodic customer satisfaction and need assessment surveys and measure of percentage return of goods or the rejection.

The required quality values for customer satisfaction have to be embedded in an organizational culture. A concept of internal customer can be imbibed into an organization. By this system, the Marketing Department becomes the customer for the Manufacturing Department who in turn becomes the customer for the Materials or Human Resources Department. Periodic training programmes can be conducted in this regard to 'understand, trust, believe the customers and respect them', and this culture can be built in an organization. An organization can develop a formal and informal listening post to stay in touch with the customer and can ensure all level employees participation.

Having accepted and implemented the required quality in an organization, the next step would be to institutionalize it, i.e. develop a 'Quality Management System' which will ensure that the organization is in a position not only to retain the quality at the desired level, but also to continuously improve it and bring it at the level that is considered to be the best in the trade. The best way to remain firm in the path of quality is to make the organization's intensions clear to its employees, customers and society at large. In this direction getting a third party audit of the quality management system as per a well- known international standard and an international quality body like 'ANSI-USA' or 'UKAS-United Kingdom' does help the organization to achieve its quality goal. Hence a certification as ISO 9000:2000 for the organization's quality management system definitely helps the organization to reconfirm its business leadership through the well-accepted and time-tested path of quality and customer satisfaction.

2.3 INTRODUCTION TO TOTAL QUALITY MANAGEMENT

All through the 1950s, 1960s, 1970s and 1980s, Indian industries had a comfortable period due to 'License Raj', which in other words meant that the supply of product in the market was always lower than the demand. This enabled even a junk product to have a customer. The industries followed a 'push' strategy, i.e. produce product to optimize the plant capacity and then look for the customer. The customer orientation was totally missing leading to ever widening a gap between the customer's needs and products provided. The industry environment was stagnant with no innovation and no improvement in product, service, technology, modernization, etc. Following of the socialist economic and labour policy led to non-productive lethargic work force. The result was that India developed a conglomerate of private and public enterprises with outdated technology, lower productivity, poor product quality, and stagnant industry.

In the mean time Japanese industries followed the path and guidance of Joseph Juran and Edward Deming and followed the total quality management principles, and by the mid 1970s became a world leader in most of the industries and consumer product segments, for example, Sony in consumer electronics, Toyota and Honda in four-wheeler automobile industry, Honda and Yahama in two-wheeler industry, Seiko, Citizen and Ricoh in watch industry and Mitsubishi in heavy vehicles, etc. Pioneering work in total quality management was also done by Taichi Ohno who implemented the famous Just-in-Time manufacturing or the Kanban and Toyota Production System (TPS). There were other Japanese management gurus like Matsushita, Sheigo Shingo, Ishikawa and recently Masaaki Imai who contributed substantially in the field of total quality management.

Gradually the concept of TQM spread to most of the world's industries in Korea, Europe and USA and it was accepted as a universal mantra for world-class performance and excelling in individual fields of operations. The concept of big Q overlooked small q and TQM became a way of life for most of the progressive industries in the world. The importance of product quality as well as associated services was universally accepted. The result was that while Japan had a revolutionary rate of growth in the 1960s and 1970s Europe, USA and some of Asian countries like China, Taiwan, and Korea had similar fast pace of progressive production and growth in the late 1970s and 1980s.

When the floodgate of liberalization and globalization was opened in India in the early 1990s, a wide gap had been developed between the products produced by Indian industry and products produced by above-stated countries. The Indian industry was caught as a sitting duck and on the top of it, the inertia of lethargic working settled down so much over the years that Indian industry just could not successfully face the global competition. The conventional Indian industry was unable to face this international competition which entered the country along with globalization and liberalization.

The TQM principles started getting appreciated in the Indian industry as well. But its understanding was very little, particularly at the top management level. Industries tried to implement TQM principles in a loosely coordinated sporadic manner without involvement of the top management. A new branch of management consultants emerged who hardly understood the subject of TQM. Somebody spoke about Statistical Quality Control (SQC), somebody about Job Quality Index (JQI), and somebody on Kaizen and some on Quality Circle. This piecemeal practice of TQM without the involvement of top management gave minuscule benefit as 'holistic approach of TQM' was grossly missing. What was needed by the industry was acceptance and implementation of the TQM principles in totality. Juran's theory of TQM and Juran's Triology was hardly understood by the industry and it was reduced to the sporadic mindless adoption of Joint Quality Improvement Process (JQIP) in the areas selected at random. The result was obvious, most of the existing Indian industries could not face the stress and strain of globalization, liberalization and international competition, and closed their shutter. But a new group of Indian industries like TVS Group, Wipro, Infosys, Reliance Industries, PCS, etc. who practised TQM principles like customer focus, continuous improvement, employees empowerment, statistical process control like six sigma, ISO 9000 quality management system adoption, adoption of knowingly and unknowingly quality planning, quality control and quality improvement emerged as winners compared to others. Existing Indian industries such as Mahindra Group, Tata Group, L&T Group, Kumarmangalam Birla Group, etc. who adopted and practised TQM, survived and gained success even in this challenging industrial environment.

2.3.1   Equivalence of TQM with World-class Management System

With the current scenario of globalization and liberalization, organizations have no options but to face the international competition. They have to 'think globally but act locally'. Every day the market is becoming competitive as new steps in liberalization like reduction of import duty, full convertibility of rupee on trade account, abolition of license raj, signing of WTO, etc. are introduced. Earlier the Indian industry enjoyed monopoly for a long time. Then the market was the sellers' market. For simple items like a scooter or car, the customer had to wait for years. The product quality was much below the international standard. Even for items of regular day-to-day use like soaps, detergents, kitchenware, electronic items, the options were limited and that too of poor quality. Every substandard product also had a customer since the government ensured that the demand is always more than the supply. Today the consumers have the entire world at his disposal. The latest designs and models of almost all the products are freely available giving consumers a wide choice. Under the circumstances, only the 'best' can survive.

Today the Indian industry has learned to live in the 'buyers' market' where customer satisfaction has become the key word.

Customer satisfaction is the state in which customers' needs, wants and expectations are met and exceeded resulting in repurchase and continued loyalty. The customer is said to be satisfied when his stated and implied needs get fulfilled by the use of the product and associated services.

The two simple words 'customer satisfaction' have changed the whole complexion of not only the Indian industry but also of the world industrial scenario. The key to the success of Japanese industry has been their orientation towards customer satisfaction. All these factors combined together have made it imperative for the Indian Industry to adopt successful management practices like Total Quality Management to survive and compete globally. The best part of it is that the TQM practices multiply profitability, productivity and efficiency leading to excellence in every field of business without any investment.

The key to customer satisfaction has to go beyond the concept of product quality or small q. For customer satisfaction is the adoption of the big Q or total quality management. ISO 9000 is only a part of total quality management. ISO 9000 is an international standard on 'quality management system' aimed towards customer satisfaction. TQM, a part of which is ISO 9000, goes much beyond Quality Control Department or product quality and embraces in its fold all functions including marketing, production, materials, personnel and even finance.

In fact under the 'TQM' theory, the Marketing Department assumes a critical function where the TQM activity begins and ends. As far as the organization is concerned, marketing becomes the internal customer for the organization and a channel of communication with the external customer or the actual customer. The Operation/ Production Department's function is value addition by conversion and all other departments' function is to support the operation.

TQM redefined the management as 'the process of designing and maintaining an environment conducive for performance for a group of people working together for attainment of the common objective in time'. The term 'total quality' encompasses the totality of the entire business operation.

The basic objective of an organization or a manager is to create a surplus. The business operation ought to be productive both in terms of 'efficiency'—output should be more than the input and 'effectiveness'—nearness to goal or objective.

Here planning is not merely budgeting but an elaborate 'quality plan' which selects the best alternative for attainment of the end objective in time with least consumption of resources. The next step is to execute the plan, i.e. 'Do it'. However in actual situation, what you plan and what you do, there is a deviation. Hence the next logical step is to check the deviation and then analyze its root cause, and then take corrective action so that any mistake once done should never be repeated again. As every month it is the same organization, same product, and the same machine setup, managerial function is an ongoing process—a cycle. Every time you analyze the root cause of deviation and take corrective action in the next plan so that mistake once committed is never repeated again. Therefore, in an organization if the deviations today are in % (percentage), after some time the deviations will reduce to parts per million (ppm). The entire organization will be on a path of continuous improvement. The entire system should be backed up by a sound quality management system which allows the improvements to be sustained on a long-term basis. This quality system is nothing but the ISO 9000:2000 quality system. It defines the entire management system, resource allocation, marketing, design and development, purchasing, production, housekeeping, quality assurance, inventory management, training and after sales service verse by verse and word by word. There is this process orientation with the P-D-C-A cycle approach leading to externally the maximization of customer satisfaction and internally for the organization highest possible Return on Investment (ROI). These two factors combined together lead not only to Market Leadership but also ultimately the attainment of the Global Business Leadershup.

The departmental orientation of vertical chimney type of organization is replaced by 'horizontal quality thinking' where the entire organization is oriented towards the attainment of the common objective or goal. The departmental boundaries are thin in the current organizational structure. The ultimate objective of a world-class organization is customer satisfaction leading to its business success and market leadership position. Its objective is to maximize customer satisfaction by providing the right quality of product in right quantity, at right place, right time and at right price. The same concept is brought towards the function of the internal department supplementing and complementing the production or rather the operation function. Hence the function of Materials Department is to provide right quality of material, in right quantity, at right place, right time and right price. The Human Resource Department provides right quality of manpower, in right quantity, at right time, right place and at least cost. The same is applicable to finance function of providing right quantity of finance, of right quality, at right time, right place and at right price. This attainment of 'customer satisfaction' with optimization of input resources will not only ensure cost competitiveness and 'market leadership' but also enable the organization to maximize its return on investment.

Here the concept of the 'internal customer' can be effectively introduced to increase accountability, better efficiency, effectiveness and measurement of 'value addition' at each stage or function or department towards the fulfillment of the overall objective of the organization, i.e. measured in terms of market leadership, customer satisfaction, profitability and return on investment. Thus Marketing Department becomes an internal customer for the Manufacturing Department or the factory, the Manufacturing Department becomes an internal customer for the Materials or the Human Resources Department.

2.3.2 Definitions of Various Quality-related Terms

The various quality-related terms are defined as per the universally accepted ISO 9000:2000 standard.

Quality

Ability of a complete set of realized inherent characteristics of a product, system or process to fulfill requirements.

Quality policy

The overall intensions and directions of an organization related to quality as formally expressed by the top management.

Quality management

Coordinated activities to direct and control an organization.

Quality system

A set of interrelated or interacting elements.

Quality planning

Part of QMS focused on setting quality objectives and specifying necessary operational processes and related resources to fulfill the quality objectives.

Quality management system

A management system is to direct and control an organization with regard to quality.

Quality objective

Something sought, or aimed for, related to quality.
Objectives should be specific, measurable and quantifiable.

Quality control

Part of QMS focussed on fulfilling quality requirements.

Quality assurance

Part of QMS focussed on providing confidence that quality requirements will be fulfilled.

Customer satisfaction

Customer's opinion of the degree to which a transaction has met the customer's needs and expectations.

Top management

A person or group of people who direct and control an organization at the highest level.

Quality improvement

Part of quality management focussed on increasing the ability to fulfill quality requirements, i.e. effectiveness and efficiency of QMS.

Effectiveness

Measure of the extent to which planned activities are realized and planned results achieved.

Efficiency

Relationship between the result achieved and the resources used.

Document

Information and its support medium. Examples include: record, specification, drawing, report, standard (Medium can be paper, magnetic, electronic or optical computer disc, photograph or master sample, or a combination thereof.)

Quality record

Document stating results achieved or providing evidence of the activities performed.

2.4   DEFINITION, CONCEPT AND FEATURES OF TQM

Total quality management can be defined as 'an organized scientific approach towards continuous improvement of quality involving everyone in the organization covering every function aimed towards total customer satisfaction'.

2.4.1   Goals of TQM

The goals of TQM are as follows:

Customer delightment/Satisfaction in totality

The total quality management concept according to the Japanese industry is customer-related or user-related concept than a product-related concept. It is the customer who runs the wheel of an organization. This implies the very existence of an organization depends on its customers. The organization can only survive and excel when it produces products and services fulfilling the customers' stated and implied needs leading to their satisfaction. The vital factor to an organization's performance excellence is its ability to be user friendly and develop as close a relationship with customers as possible.

Continuous improvement

The best organizations in the world are not keeping quiet, but growing at a good pace. Juran clearly states that the organization with a revolutionary growth rate can only reach and sustain the global leadership. Deming's basic principle of the P-D-C-A cycle is heavily growth or continuous improvement oriented. Change for better at a revolutionary pace is the ideal business mantra for business excellence in the current highly competitive environment.

Total employee involvement and empowerment

The difference between the winners and also runs is not the machine or raw materials but the difference between motivational levels of their employees. The employee involvement and their proactiveness can only create an environment for performance excellence of each and every individual leading to an all-round business leadership.

Optimization of resources

In today's competitive world the market force decides the price. Unless an organization's cost of production of the product and/or services are the least, the organization cannot survive. This is where the Japanese concept of controlling 'Muda' and methodology of reduction of 'cost of poor quality' by Juran's methodology play a vital role in world-class performance of the organization.

Do it right the first time

To fulfill the requirement of customer satisfaction of providing products and services of the right quality, in right quantity, at the right time, place and least price depends only on the concept of do it right the first time because in the current competitive world nobody is going to give you the chance second time. An organization has to capitalize on the opportunity first time itself if it has to survive and excel.

The importance of TQM and quality is not only to the goods, products and services produced by industries, but also to the industries themselves and ultimately to the society in general. Edward Deming and Joseph Juran are seen as the principal force in converting non-significant, low profile Japanese companies of the 1950s and 1960s to world class, world leader in their respective field of operation by the end 1970s and 1980s. These are the two management gurus who made the world realize the key to the business leadership is the management of quality on all aspects of business operation and not merely to the product quality. Joseph Juran was the first to publish a 'Quality Control Hand book' way back in 1949. The total copies sold of this book are over 3,50,000. Juran along with Edward Deming has started a silent revolution all over the world, 'The Quality Revolution'. This has led to a remarkable growth in the importance of quality to society generally. Today's industrial society provides its citizenry with the marvelous benefit of technology. The continuity of this very life style depends on the quality of goods and services available. Today the survival of an organization depends on its ability to satisfy its customers. The customer satisfaction is derived from the fulfillment of the customer's needs by use of the product and its services. Quality as defined by Juran is 'Fitness for use'. Hence quality plays the lead role in customer satisfaction. TQM embraced the paradigm of quality for not only the products but also to the services. Hence quality became prime organization-wide activity.

Total quality management shifts the paradigm of the organizational focus from the product to the process. Refer to Figure 2.1. The concept believes that if the process is correct and under control, the product cannot be defective. Total quality management is a long enduring journey of infinite length. It has a bottom-up approach at the operational level. To implement total quality management, an organization has to move the ideas to each employee at their speed. The organization should not try to force strategies but try

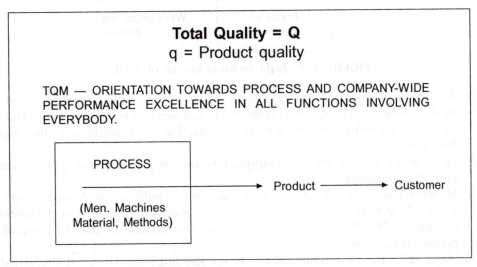

FIGURE 2.1 Process-oriented TQM.

to change people's mind set. Total quality management is a people's process. Hence never underestimate the people's power. Every body in the organization should be oriented towards the common goal of maximization of the customer satisfaction as well as attainment of the organizational vision. The organization should always challenge the 'business as usual' attitude and develop a self-renovating business organization with focus on continuous improvement.

The attainment of desired quality requires commitment and participation of all members in an organization whereas responsibility of quality management belongs to the top management.

2.4.2 Eight Building Blocks of TQM

The internationally recognized building blocks of total quality management can now be summed up into eight building blocks (Figure 2.2) and are detailed as follows.

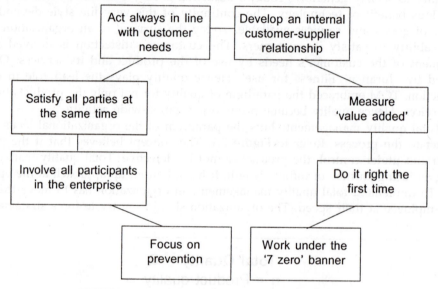

FIGURE 2.2 Eight building blocks of TQM.

1. Act always in line with the customers' needs by understanding their stated and implied needs and supplying the products and services as per the same. This will lead to achieving the customers' satisfaction and ultimately the market leadership.
2. Develop an internal customer-supplier relationship as explained in the earlier part of this chapter in detail.
3. Measure the value added to the process or the subprocess. Measure both the value added to the input and the cost of value addition, i.e. cost of the resources consumed. The difference will give the surplus created or the efficiency of the process management.
4. Do it right the first time. This calls for the implementation of the statistical process control or the six sigma to ensure the reliability in terms of the zero

defect in the products, elimination of wastages and timely delivery of the products and services.

5. Work under the 'seven zero' banner. The seven zeros are as follows:
   - Zero disdain for others
   - Zero stock or inventory
   - Zero delay
   - Zero paper
   - Zero downtime
   - Zero defect
   - Zero accident
6. Focus on the prevention to prevent the repetition of mistakes. Any failure or the mistake has to be analyzed to find out the root cause and take the suitable corrective and preventive actions so that the mistake or the failure never repeats.
7. Involve all the participants in the organization. Total quality management advocates involvement of not only its employees, but also the organization's suppliers, vendors as well its customers.
8. Satisfy all parties at the same time. The organization should make endeavour to satisfy not only its employees, suppliers and customers, but also the environment, its share holders, society and the country at large.

These eight building blocks are practised together in a cycle for the implementation of Total quality management. The objective is to attain the performance level of the highest order for each and every employee as well as the suppliers so that the organization attains the market leadership. The twelve TQM steps to be the world's best organization in its class along with these eight building blocks can take an organization to an invincible position as compared to not only its competitors but also by the industry standards. This will enable an organization to attain the market leadership position globally as well as implement the world-class management system.

2.4.3 Pre-requisites for Success for TQM

Committment at the top

For TQM to be successful, only the involvement of employees is not enough. The commitment should come from the top management who has to implement total quality management in the organization by declaring the organizational vision, mission and quality policy. The top management has also to arrange for the resources for fulfillment of the objective. The top management has also to walk the talk to make TQM implementation successful.

Organization for quality

An organization for implementation and success of TQM should create a 'quality council' at the highest level to decide and implement all the vital decisions. The quality council members are the head of the various functions and the chairman of the quality council is the chief executive officer of the organization. The organization should have different quality improvement teams at different levels for the implementation of TQM activities and problem solving.

Strategic direction

The strategic direction consists of formulating a long-range plan known as the 'vision' and a value system for the organization known as the 'mission' along with the annual business plans formulated after 'SWOT' analysis and formulation of function-wise strategic action plan. This is extremely important and explained in detail in twelve steps to implement world-class management system.

Customer orientation

As is explained in detail in the first chapter, the main objective of an organization for its survival and performance excellence is maximization of customer satisfaction and the return on investment. The first objective of customer satisfaction can only be achieved by customer orientation, understanding the customer's stated and implied needs and developing user friendly customer-oriented products and services. It is the customers who run the wheels of an organization.

Need-based education and training

Total quality management is the concept which changes the working of an organization totally. To adapt to this concept and the techniques involved, extensive as well intensive education and training are must to make the total quality management system work. Even the total quality management system warrants continual improvement at all levels thereby needing a system constant upgradation of the skill level of its all the employees which can only happen by continuous education and training.

Total involvement of employees

Depending on the work environment and work culture, people contribute differently for the attainment of organizational objectives. A person with a negative attitude will not do any value addition even if he is capable of doing so. Similarly, a neutral person does his bare minimum bit. The active employees with a positive attitude will contribute positively for the attainment of the organizational goal. A proactive person will not only perform per excellence himself but also help others to achieve the organizational goal.

Supportive culture

Total quality management system will expect support from the various functions as well from the suppliers of the organization. The concept of internal customer develops into a supportive culture for performance excellence, supplementing and complementing each other.

Teamwork

Total quality management focuses on the teamwork for performance excellence. The horizontal quality thinking with common objective of maximization of customer satisfaction and return on investment is based totally on a cohesive teamwork, pulling the entire resources for achievement of the organizational goal. The importance and significance of teamwork is also explained in the first chapter.

Prevention-based systems

Total quality management makes the prevention-based system compulsory so that mistake once committed is never repeated again. Whether the working is as per the Deming's P-D-C-A cycle or ISO 9000:2000 quality management system or various problem solving techniques like quality circle or Kaizen Gemba, the fundamental principle of all these systems is formulation of a prevention-based system. For any failure or mistake, the prevention-based system finds out the root cause for the same and takes a corrective and preventive system so that the mistake or failure is not repeated again.

Recognition and reward system

The total quality management system is based on the principle of rewarding the performers after their identification and training and educating the non-performers to upgrade their skill level. A non-performer after improvement can stake his claim for recognition and reward. Total quality management tools like Kaizen Gemba, quality circle, etc. believe in rewarding a contributing person.

2.5 COST OF QUALITY

The total quality management system must include methods and procedures to determine and evaluate the impact of the cost of quality or the cost of poor quality (COPQ) on the profitability of the organization. Here the cost of quality is a measure of the level of quality the organization wants to maintain and the associated cost of the same whereas the cost of the poor quality or COPQ is a measure of all the nine wastages as listed later under the subject of 'Muda' or the wastages.

The purpose of the cost of quality reporting system is to provide management with a tool to identify the improvement areas. Refer to Figure 2.3. In the initial stage, the external failure and rejection is high. As the inspection system gets effectively

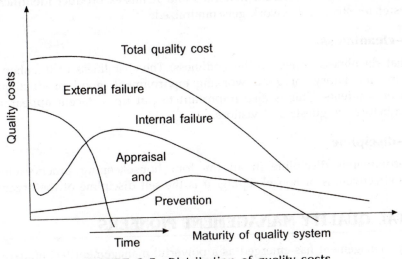

FIGURE 2.3 Distribution of quality costs.

implemented, the external failure gets eliminated at the cost of increase in the internal failure. As the quality management system matures further, the appraisal and prevention steps are taken. The moment the root causes of the failure are identified and who is responsible for the same, the failure rate comes down considerably. This is the point where the total cost of poor quality and overall failure rate takes a fast dip within a short time. The external and internal failure gradually becomes zero as the appraisal cost starts coming down. The root causes of the failure are identified and the corrective and preventive actions are taken. Hence as the system matures, the preventive cost goes up and it should ideally be the only cost.

2.6   5S OF HOUSEKEEPING

Housekeeping is given a lot of importance in the total quality management system. It reduces wastage of time and improves the efficiency and effectiveness of work. Improper housekeeping may lead to accidents, dull working environment and other work-related problems. The five 'S' of housekeeping are as follows:

Seiri—orderliness

The orderliness of manufacturing aids, proper arrangement of raw materials near the machines and keeping the files and drawings in order make the working fast, effective and efficient without wastage of the effort or time and material.

Seiso—clarity

The clarity of work process, flow process charts, arrangement of raw material, finished goods and intermediary services make the work place more efficient and effective.

Seiton—tidiness

Tidiness ensures adequate space for the machines and movement of men is made easy. Tidiness avoids mixing of different materials and it makes product identification easy. The chances of rejection and rework gets minimized.

Seiketsu—cleanliness

It is said that cleanliness is next to the godliness. The cleanliness of the shop floor and the office are mandatory for good working environment, good product quality and elimination of accidents. This is also important to put up a decent appearance of the organization before the guests and visitors.

Shitsuke—discipline

Shitsuke recommends discipline in all the four housekeeping practices together to enhance the effectiveness of housekeeping. It is the self discipline of the organization.

2.7   TOTAL QUALITY MANAGEMENT PIONEERS

Total quality management has emerged as a powerful management technique worldwide over the last five decades. This is also known as the world-class management system.

The people who made substantial contributions towards the field of TQM are highlighted as follows:

1. Walter Shewart
   - Founder of P-D-C-A cycle
   - Originator of statistical procss control at A&T bells lab in 1930
2. W. Edward Deming
   - Led quality revolution in Japan during the post-world War II period.
   - Quality is a key competitive advantage
   - Deming quality award by Japan is the most prestigious quality award
   - Deming's fourteen points for excellence
   - Deming's seven diseases
3. Joseph M. Juran
   - Led quality revolution in Japan during the post-world War II period
   - He defined quality as fitness for use by customer
   - Juran's triology of quality planning, quality control and quality improvement
   - Started Juran's institute in USA
   - Introduced cost of poor quality
4. Philip B. Crosby
   - Started Crosby quality college
   - Created the concept of 'zero defect'
   - Defined quality as conformance to requirment
   - Crosby's 14 steps of quality improvement
5. A.V. Feigenbaum
   - Originator of TQM concept
   - His theory of three steps to quality:
     Quality leadership, modern quality technology and organizational commitment
6. Taiichi Ohno
   - Formulated the flexible manufacturing system (FMS)
   - Father of the just-in-time and kanban system of manufacturing
   - Father of (TPS) or Toyota Production System
7. Sheigo Shingo
   - Originator of 'single minute exchange of dies'
   - Introducing the concept of modular manufacturing
8. Kaoru Ishikawa
   - Originator of fish bone or the cause and effect diagram
   - Originator of concept of Company Wide Quality Control (CWQC).
   - Responsible for initial deployment of quality circles
   - Remove the root cause and not the syptoms
9. Masaaki Imai
   - Popularized the Kaizan concept of continuous improvement
10. E. Goldrat
    - Theory of constraints.

All of them advocated 'involvement of top management' for successful TQM implementation.

2.8 ELEVEN TQM STEPS TO BE A WORLD-CLASS ORGANIZATION

Having understood the various aspects of total quality management, now let us sum up the overall concept and convert into the practical application to make an organization a 'world-class organization'. There are eleven well-defined steps (Figure 2.4) to make a world-class organization. The steps are discussed as follows.

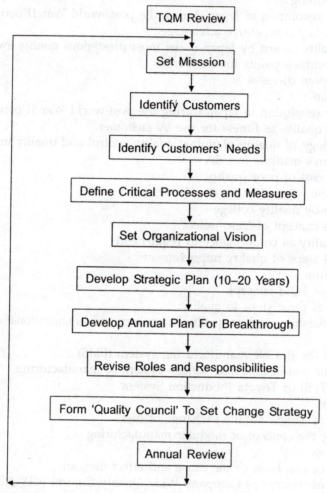

FIGURE 2.4 Eleven steps to be a world-class organization.

TQM overview

Total quality management is people's process and involvement of the top management is a must for its success. Hence the entire organization must have a review of total quality management and accept to implement it in earnest. This assurance for the total commitment is mandatory for the total quality management implementation to start.

Set mission

The organization should define its value system for every employee to follow. Total adherence and commitment to its value system known as 'mission' is the vital first step towards the attainment of the world-class management system.

Identify customers

The third step is to identify customers who respect the similar value system and who have the potential to make the organization reach the status of a world-class organization by way of quantity and quality.

Identify customer's needs

Break up the product into attributes and classify the attributes into 'musts' and 'wants' or 'vital few' and 'trivial many' as per the customer's perception collected during the market survey. The 'vital few' or the 'must' attributes decide the customers' preference for buying a particular product. The product which performs the best on these attributes in the market invariably becomes the market leader. For example, the outcome of various workshops conducted by the undersigned in this respect and market survey, the 'must' or the 'vital few' attributes of a colour television are picture quality and sound. For a pen, it is the ability of the pen to write clearly without any obstruction to the flow of ink.

Define critical process and measures

The 'must' or 'vital few' key attributes are the outcome of a certain process and its control to ensure consistent production of these attributes. These processes are defined as the critical processes, and control point for these processes are called measures. The input raw material for these processes, the machinery required for its conversion and the process itself should be nothing less than the world's best. For example, the picture quality of a colour television depends on the quality and flatness of the picture tube and the electronics parts used for reception of video and audio signals. Further, for sound system the quality of the magnets used in the speakers, the shape of the speaker for resonance and permutation and combination of the sound waves for the required reproduction of the required quality of sound are the examples of controlling the quality of the critical processes to have the best performance on the must or the key attributes.

Set organizational vision

Now the product performance is defined as the best as per customers' requirement. This is now based on customers' feedback on the product performance and validation by the chosen group of customers. Now the long-term goal or the objective as to where the organization wants to position itself after 15–20 years is defined as the 'vision' statement which should be 'SMART', i.e. Specific, Measurable, Attainable, Realistic and Time bound.

Develop strategic plan (10–20 years)

After all these steps are over, then perform a SWOT analysis. This means the strength and weakness assessment vis-à-vis the competitors and assessment of the opportunities and threats vis-à-vis the environment under different environmental conditions of PEST analysis, i.e. Political, Economic, Social and Technology. Develop the strategic plan sensitizing your customers about the positive points, and inside the factory develop product attributes to convert weaknesses into strengths. The strategic plan should also try to capitalize on the opportunities and try to convert the threats into the strengths. This is a long-term strategic plan to achieve the organizational vision.

Develop annual plan for breakthrough

The next step in the total quality management is to break up the long-term strategic plan into the annual business plan for breakthrough. This business plan should further generate the marketing plan and financial plan followed by the production plan. This is further followed by the other function's individual plans. But all these plans are integrated to the business plan.

Revise roles and responsibilities

Here we are looking for a world-class performance excellence from all the employees without exception. Hence the employee's individual assessment and core competencies are to be decided, and suitable training and education need to be provided to overcome the deficiencies. Once this is done the organization has to be reoriented, and roles and responsibilities have to be redefined and revised to attain this world-class management system and related performance.

Form 'quality council' to set change strategy

An individual can make mistakes when he takes the decision in isolation. The task of world-class performance excellence is a tough job to be accomplished. Hence it needs a more composite organizational structure. Normally total quality management organization forms a 'quality council' consisting of all the functional heads and chaired by the Chief Executive Officer or the Managing Director. This apex body takes initiative to implement the change strategy.

Annual review

Now the periodic or annual measurement of performance is carried out to find the performance is going as per the business plan for the year or not. In case there is a deviation or shortfall, corrective actions are taken to put the business plan back on the track. This feedback is given for correction in the performance as also to keep the organization abreast of the emerging opportunities.

2.9 DEMING'S THEORY ON TOTAL QUALITY MANAGEMENT

The first pioneering effort in the field of 'TQM' was done by Walter Shewhart of Bells Laboratory who not only initially gave the concept of the P-D-C-A cycle but also introduced the statistical quality control to the industry. His disciple W. Edward Deming popularized the process approach and the P-D-C-A concept, i.e. if the process is under control it is impossible to produce a defective product. This concept has already been described in great detail in the first chapter. Deming made quality management as an organization-wide activity rather than the task of a specialized inspection or the quality assurance department. He introduced the concept that 'quality' cannot be inspected but it has to be produced. Quality has to be integrated right from the design stage through the production process to arrive at the desired product and service features leading to the fulfillment of the customer's stated and implied needs. This obviously leads to the customer satisfaction.

Deming's theory states that increase in quality leads to decrease in rejection rework material and time wastages, etc. thereby improving the productivity of the entire system. Increase in the productivity makes the company's product and services of better quality and cheaper in cost leading to a greater market share and market leadership. This makes a sound and healthy organization growing steadily thereby generating more employment and better facilities to its employees.

Deming made it very clear that a problem is a problem and needs to be eliminated from the process and the organization. There is nothing like a major or minor problem. Deming firmly believed in the three basic philosophies of the company-wide quality control activity. These are all people-oriented approach, which constitues employees and top management. First is the commitment to the continuous improvement and innovation in all the organizational processes, products and services. The second important criterion is the Total Employee Involvement (TEI) and the third is the scientific knowledge about the product, process technology as well as the knowledge of the various quality improvement tools and techniques.

Deming propagated a systematic approach to business success and separated business forces and practices into two categories. The first category takes an organization down the line of disasters and factors detrimental to the progress of an organization. Deming named this as 'Seven Deadly Disasters'. The second category comprises the points that lead to progress of an organization and make the organization world class. These points are popularly known as 'Deming's Fourteen points'. These points are necessary for the survival of business and to be competitive today.

2.9.1 Deming's Seven Deadly Disasters

The following are Deming's seven deadly disasters:
1. Lack of consistency of purpose to plan product and services that have a sufficient market to keep the company in business and provide jobs.
2. Emphasis on short-term profits; short-term thinking that is driven by a fear of unfriendly takeover attempts and pressure from bankers and shareholders to produce dividends.
3. Personal review system for managers and management by objectives without providing methods or resources to accomplish objectives. Performance appraisals, merit rating, and annual appraisals are all parts of these disasters.
4. Job hoping by managers.
5. Using only visible data and information in decision making with little or no consideration given to what is not known or cannot be known.
6. Excessive medical costs.
7. Excessive cost of liability driven up by lawyers that work on contingency fees.

2.9.2 Deming's 14 Points to Reach World Class Performance Standard

Edward Deming gave a holistic approach of 14 points to his Japanese industrial clients to reach to the top of the world in business excellence. The fourteen points are as follows:

1. *Achieve constancy of purpose.* Deming suggested that the top management of an organization should define the organization's vision, mission and objectives to be followed by the entire organization so that an unified objective with the constancy of purpose can be established by the organization. The goal integration between the organization and individuals working there is extremely important for individuals to give their best for achievement of the organizational objectives.
2. *Learn a new philosophy.* All growth comes from change by learning and implementing a new philosophy or something new. Always challenge the business as usual approach. Today's management is learning, unlearning and relearning the subject matter relevant to the organization. It is the speed and frequency with which the organization and its employees learn a new philosophy and decide the growth rate and the market leadership of the organization.
3. *Do not depend on mass inspection (Use statistical sampling technique).* Deming emphasized heavily deployment of statistical techniques in the area of inspection. He was of the opinion like his guru Walter Shewart of the Bell's Laboratory that the behaviour of the whole group is going to be more or less the same as that of the sample lot taken up for inspection. Then why unnecessarily waste precious resources of manpower and time for 100% inspection.
4. *Reduce the number of vendors for better control and consistency.* Deming considered the vendors or the suppliers as part of the organization. He advocated a direct involvement of the organization in the Statistical Process Control of the vendors so that there is no need to do 100% inspection as well as to improve their process capability. For achieving the above objective you need lot of effort as well time and money. Hence if you change vendors frequently for cheaper price, the quality of supplies will never stabilize. Hence number vendor per component should be either one or two to have better control and consistency in the supplies.
5. *Recognize two sources of faults: (a) management and production systems (b) produc-tion workers.* There are two types of errors or faults. One is due to random causes and the other due to assignable causes. The random causes are due to faulty production systems. The factors responsible could be a faulty process design or inadequate machine capability. The management only can solve such problems. The assignable errors are due to the workers and occur due to faulty workmanship. This can be eliminated by providing training to the workers and motivating them properly.
6. *Improve on the job training.* Deming always insisted on-the-job training. He described on-the-job training as the best method of training where the absorption of knowledge imparted during the training is the maximum. Identify the training needs and the skill level required for each operator and employees. Now identify suitable job on which the training to be imparted and conduct the training for best results.

7. *Improve supervision.* Improve the supervision at the process level so that not only the errors or the mistakes are minimized, but also the on-the-job training to the operators are strengthened. This will lead to continuous improvement, better productivity and enhanced quality of the products, process and services.

8. *Drive out fear.* The entire organization should be self sustaining, proactive and employees should be involved. Fear should not be the driving force to achieve the end results. It may give temporary benefits, but it will fail in the long run.

9. *Improve communication.* The majority of labour problems are due to lack of communication between the workers and the management of an organization. Communication has to be immaculate in terms of training, learning of new philosophy and techniques, unification of objective, constancy of purpose, etc.

10. *Eliminate fear.* This point is repeated and overstressed by Deming to highlight that fear can never achieve the end result. An organization driven by the fear psychosis is bound to collapse like a pack of cards sooner or later. Hence take extra care to eliminate fear in the organization.

11. *Consider work standards carefully.* This is the Japanese concept of 'Muri' or 'unreasonableness'. Deming has advised to critically examine each work standard from the functional point of view whether it is over designed or the tolerance is tighter or the finishing standards are unnecessarily rigid. If it is not required from the customer's point of view and not adding any value, why unnecessary incur additional expenditure when customers are not ready to pay for it.

12. *Teach statistical methods.* Deming emphasized the implementation of statistical process control system in manufacturing leading to establishment of process capability, machine capability and zero defect in products and services, enhancement of productivity as well as reduction in effort for attainment of the end result.

13. *Encourage new skills.* New skills, innovations and development bring in a fresh leash of air into the health of an organization invariably. A product innovation and product development increase the market share. The same innovation in the process enhances productivity and quality as well reduces the cost of production. An organization should have a system like suggestion scheme, quality improvement teams, etc. to encourage new skills and their implementation.

14. *Use statistical knowledge.* The statistical knowledge reduces efforts by sampling technique, gives a fair amount of accuracy in the result and enhances labour and material productivity. At the same time it enables the organization to test various theories, sensitivity analysis, etc. in minimum amount of time and cost to arrive at the least cost.

Deming's contribution to the Japanese industry was so much that the Japanese Government named the highest quality award for the industry after his name as the 'Deming Award'. Deming firmly believed like Joseph Juran that it is the quality leadership that will decide the market leadership and ultimately the global business leadership.

2.10 RELEVANCE OF JURAN'S TRIOLOGY TO TODAY'S BUSINESS SCENARIO

Juran gave a similar holistic approach for all-round business excellence known as the 'Juran's triology' involving the three-step approach for business excellence:

- Quality Planning
- Quality Control
- Quality Improvement.

He described quality planning similar to Deming's 'P' of the P-D-C-A cycle. However, Juran made it more organized by way of deciding the mission, vision and quality objectives in advance and working out the plan to achieve the same in least cost. He introduced the concept of cost of poor quality (COPQ) to focus on wastages and taking suitable steps to eliminate the same.

Juran defined quality control in a few simple words as 'control over the process'. It involves periodic measurement of events proceeding as per the plan or not and taking corrective steps in case there is a deviation. Quality control will retain the chronic deficiencies at the same level and not allow them to increase.

It is the quality improvement that eliminates the hatchery of the chronic deficiencies in a systematic manner involving Juran's Quality Improvement Projects (JQIP) leading to reduction in COPQ, thereby increasing profit as well as quality and customer satisfaction.

While JQIP focuses on the major cross functional areas of performance improvement leading to a quantum jump in organization improvement, there are other TQM techniques of problem solving involving workers in their same work area for regular small improvements known as Kaizen Gemba or Quality Circle or TPM Techniques. These techniques fundamentally focus on the problem solving techniques in a sporadic manner and are tools of TQM.

TQM is a vast subject and a very powerful management technique. When it is implemented in a holistic manner in any organization or business irrespective of its status or position, it is bound to increase the performance of the organization continuously and substantially to enable it to reach to the position of business leadership and world-class performance. The best part of TQM technique is that it does not warrant any investment.

Juran has been carrying out his research work in the field of quality and its importance not only to the goods, products and services produced by industries, but also to the industries themselves and ultimately to the society in general. He is still alive at an age of over ninety-two years, active and practising quality principles in industries all over the world and turning industries into world-class performers. Along with Edward Deming, he is seen as the principal force in converting non-significant, low profile Japanese companies of the 1950s and 1960s to world class, world leader in their respective field of operation. He was the first to publish a 'Quality Control Handbook' way back in 1949. Total copies sold of this book are over 3,50,000. He has started a silent revolution all over the world called 'The Quality Revolution'. This has led to a remarkable growth in the importance of quality to society generally. Today's industrial society provides its citizenry with the marvelous benefit of technology. The continuity of this very life style depends on the quality of goods and services available. Today the survival of an organization depends on its ability to satisfy its customers. Customer satisfaction is derived from the fulfillment of his need by use of the product and its services. Quality as defined by Juran as 'fitness for use'. Hence quality plays the lead role in customer satisfaction. Juran embraced the paradigm of quality for not only the products but to the services also. Hence quality becomes prime organization-wide activity.

Juran has compared two companies A and B (Figure 2.5). Company B is initially much below company A. Over a period of time company B overtakes company A to become the market leader as it has followed the revolutionary rate of quality improvement and growth and company A has followed the normal evolutionary rate of quality improvement and growth. Juran has clearly proved by his detail research work that an organization, which has the quality leadership is also the market leader. Hence there is an intense international competition in quality. Quality is now a critical element in international trade, buyer-seller dyad, in defense capability, in safety and health and in maintaining the environment.

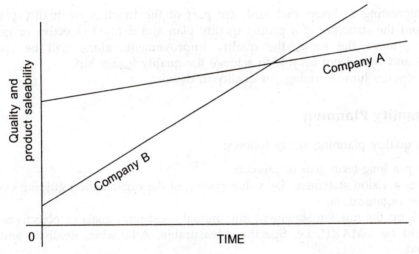

FIGURE 2.5   Quality improvement rate vs. time.

While ISO 9000 is the first step towards the attainment of the TQM, Juran's theory of quality concept shows the ways of attainment of total quality management in a systematic holistic manner. The Indian industry has realised this need and is attempting to adapt quickly to Juran's triology to attain the international standard of quality and service. Leading industrial houses like Ajay Piramal Group consisting of Morarjee Goculdas Spinning and Weaving Mills Ltd., Nicholas Piramal Ltd., Roche Products Ltd., Gujarat Glass Ltd. etc., Mahindra & Mahindra Group consisting of their Auto Division Tractors Division, etc., OTIS Elevators, Mukand Industries Ltd., Tata group including Voltas, TISCO, Telco, etc., Bombay Dyeing Ltd., Marico Ltd, Punjab Tractors Ltd., Gujarat Heavy Chemicals and numerous others to name a few of leading industrial enterprises in India have already adopted the Juran methodology of quality improve-ment, i.e. improvement project by project aimed towards better customer satisfaction, reducing COPQ (cost of poor quality), better profitability, better product salability and ultimately to attain total quality management. However, the other two aspects of Juran's trilogy of Quality Plan and Quality Control have not been implemented to that extent. This lack of holistic approach has not led to a world-class performance level on the whole. Even if by taking up JQI projects, the organizations had marginal gain in the relevant areas.

Industrial companies have been responding to the growth in the importance of the 'quality function'. The Scope of 'quality' has been broadened to include the following:

- Product quality
- Quality of services

The Juran methodology of quality improvement is aimed at the attainment of quality leadership. Juran Institute Incorporation, USA under leadership of Juran has summed up the lesson learnt from failures of various organizations into two:

- Lesson 1:   The poor choice of strategy for managing quality.
- Lesson 2:   Upper management lacked the knowledge of 'how to manage for quality?'

It is interesting to know that both are part of the function of quality planning. Hence without the structure of a proper quality plan and defined objective or goal and strategy to achieve the same, the quality improvements alone will be sporadic, directionless and would not be able to achieve the quality leadership.

Let us discuss Juran's triology of quality in detail.

2.10.1   Quality Planning

The steps in quality planning are as follows:

1. Set up a long-term goal or mission.
2. Define a vision statement, i.e. value system of the organization guiding everyone in the organization.
3. Break up the mission statement into annual short-term goals or objectives which should be 'SMART', i.e. Specific, Measurable, Attainable, Realistic and Time bound.
4. Identify customers who will help the organization to achieve the goals.
5. Discover their needs.
6. Develop product features responding to customer needs.
7. Establish product goals.
8. Develop systems and processes to produce these product features.
9. Prove process capability and hand over to production, i.e. develop the plan at operating level.

Quality planning is the starting point of the journey to be a world-class organization. It is a systematic step by step approach adopted by the organization to become a business leader in its field irrespective of the status or current position of the organization. Juran has stated through his research work the following findings:

1. 20% deficiencies are normally inherent, due to bad quality planning.
2. The best quality control can do is to maintain 20% deficiencies and not allow the deterioration.

3. Quality planning integrates the attainment of organization's mission and achievement of milestones of organizational progress with its routine activities and makes it a habit.
4. Quality planning replaces the conventional system of budgeting and is the starting point for an organization to be world class.

2.10.2 Quality Control

Quality control as defined by Juran is control over process.

Quality control consists of two major processes:

1. Statistical process control
2. Training on statistical tools

For quality control, it is to be from within or the concept of self-control has to be developed. For attainment of self-control, three conditions are to be satisfied. Everybody in an organization, workers as well as management, should be provided with:

1. Means for knowing quality goals
2. Means for knowing his performance on the quality goals
3. Means for regulating/correcting his performance

The 'quality control' activity in short means the continuous appraisal and measurement of the performance of an individual, department/function and organization vis-a-vis the 'quality plan' and find out the deviations from the plan, and take corrective action to eliminate the deviation and put the process back on the track. The quality control activity also warrants taking preventive actions so that the deviation does not occur in the future.

Juran's triology does not believe in becoming a 'cheer leader'. Slogans, exhortations, etc. do not work. It involves vagueness, which cannot compete with the structured and systematic process.

Juran has clearly stated that every successful quality revolution has included the participation of upper management without exception. The quality control activity helps to retain the present performance at the current level and ensures consistency in the performance of the product, process and service.

2.10.3 Quality Improvement

The quality improvement activity under the Juran methodology is extremely popular across the globe and popularly known as Juran's Quality Improvement Project, (JQIP). Juran clearly states that it is the number of JQI projects undertaken by an organization that decides the rate of growth of an organization, i.e. revolutionary or the evolutionary rate of growth. According to him this decides the market leadership.

Juran's ten-step quality improvement plan is detailed as follows:

1. The organization should build awareness for both needs and opportunities for improvement which should be an ongoing activity. Juran says that the rate of quality improvement projects taken by an organization decides its rate of growth and prosperity and thereby its market leadership.

2. The quality council identifies specific projects/goals for improvement based on the 'Pareto analysis' by choosing those vital few projects which if successful will give the organization a substantial jump in its performance. The projects chosen for the JQI are chronic in nature, if solved it will give a quantum jump in organizations performance either in process, products or services.

3. The quality council should choose a heterogeneous cross-functional team to work on the JQI project. This gives a holistic approach to the problem solving. The leader is the most affected person. For example a JQI project on increasing market share will chose the marketing functional head as the leader of the JQI team.

4. The organization should provide training to the entire JQI team in the advanced problem-solving tools and techniques.

5. The team now carries out a brainstorming session followed by a cause and effect diagram analysis to discover the root causes. This is known as the 'diagnostic journey'. The heterogeneous multifunctional team facilitates this session due to their approach to solve the problem from different angles and then integrating the same into the likely solution.

6. Once the root cause of the problem is identified and problems are clearly defined, the next step is to evolve the remedies to overcome the causes. This is known as the 'remedial journey'.

7. The project team should prove adequacy of the remedies by testing them one by one and ultimately deciding on the best remedy which satisfies all the 'musts' and the maximum number of 'wants'. Now implement the remedies first under controlled condition and get it validated. Once the remedies are validated, now implement the same across the organization.

8. The JQI project team should address the change to the relevant persons and train and convince them to implement the solution. This way the project team must overcome the resistance to the change and institutionalize the solution for implementation.

9. The quality council and the top management should give recognition to the good JQI projects and its team members. The quality council should communicate results in the open house meetings and sessions as well as in the house journals, etc. Suitable rewards and benefits can also be given depending on the quality and benefit of the project work.

10. Involvement of the quality council, the project team as well as the concerned officials in the day-to-day activity concerned with the project work should ensure that there is a suitable control mechanism to hold the gain.

For a project to qualify for JQI, it must satisfy the following parameters:

1. All quality improvements take place project by project and in no other way.

2. The organization should develop a habit of undertaking quality improvement projects in its area of weaknesses on a regular basis.

3. To ensure effectiveness of quality improvement projects, a new organization structure and new managerial processes are required for quality improvement.

   (a) Establish infrastructure like the quality council consisting of the members as functional heads and the chairman is the chief executive officer. The quality council spearheads the quality improvement activities supplemented by a coordinator and individual project teams.

(b) Nomination and screening of projects should be done on the basis of 'Pareto analysis'. The vital few projects that contribute to the 80% of the organization's problems and which are chronic in nature are chosen first to be resolved. This is due to the fact that these vital few problems may happen to be a critical success factor for the organization.

(c) Cross-functional project teams should be set. The heterogeneous team members bring in a holistic view to the problem solving or the growth opportunities, and chronic problems apparently seem unsolvable by individuals get easily solved by this holistic view. The team leader is normally the most affected person.

(d) The JQI project team provides a structured quality improvement process with management tools and techniques like Pareto analysis, brainstorming, cause and effect diagram and systematic problem analysis in finding the root cause and giving the remedies.

(e) The project team and the top management then organize resources like time, facilities, diagnostic and analytical tools to make the project effective, efficient and successful. Normally costly resources are not required for JQI.

(f) The project team reviews the process which is the root cause for the success or failure of the products, services and the entire organization's systems. The root cause for performance failures are identified and suggested remedies are worked out for the implementation.

(g) The project team now implements the suggested remedies and validates the solutions after their implementation. After successful implementation and institutionalizing there is 'dissemination of results' in the other relevant areas where similar situation exists.

(h) The organization's top management should recognize the good performance of the project team and reward them suitably. The rewarding system has to be evaluated depending on the organization's policy and modalities of working.

(i) The organization's top management should revise of the 'merit rating system' following the Management by Objective (MBO) system and giving suitable weight to the quality improvement activities in the Key Result Areas (KRAs).

(j) The quality council should revise the strategic business plans to incorporate annual improvements as part of the organizational goals and objectives.

4. The quality improvement is to fine-tune the existing process only by studying process variables impacting product results.

5. It is interesting to note that the quality improvement is not capital intensive.

6. Quality improvement can increase your return on investment many times; enhance productivity and customer satisfaction without having to go for investment in new plant and machinery which is otherwise costly.

7. The role of upper management is vital. Personal participation is a must while performing the tasks, viz.

(a) Serve on quality council

(b) Approve strategic quality goals

(c) Allocate needed resources

(d) Review progress

(e) Give recognition

(f) Serve on project teams—leadership by example.

8. The syndrome 'here comes another one' psychology has to be broken by creating awareness programmes and benefits of quality improvement projects. If upper management performs the above six tasks personally, such syndrome is overcome.

9. It is important that leadership by upper management is not delegate able. Upper Management MUST personally carry out the responsibilities.

Different phases of quality improvement

The following are the different phases of quality improvement:

1. Start up—create organization and infrastructure
2. Test (Pilot phase)
3. Scale up
4. Institutionalize
   (a) It takes several years to establish through the above phases and to lock in the habit of annual quality improvement.
   (b) The number of quality improvement projects undertaken by an organization decides its quality leadership.
   (c) It is time for Indian industries to take up the quality planning and quality improvement to shut down hatchery of chronic deficiencies.
   (d) Two changes are required:
       (i) Structured and disciplined approach;
       (ii) Training to planners
5. Provide lessons learned from feedback for quality improvement projects—create database and implement in other relevant areas.

It was mainly Japanese industries who benefited from practising Juran's triology and became a world leader in their respective business fields by the mid 1970s from nowhere in 1950. They not only became the leader but defended their leadership position for decades thereafter by following Juran's triology. Gradually the rest of the world's leading business houses including those of USA and Europe adopted the same methodology to attain and defend their market, quality and business leadership. Many Indian industries have also started following JQIP. However the effectiveness of Juran's triology is in its holistic approach of practising simultaneously all the three activities of quality planning, quality control and quality improvement for all-round performance excellence in the business. This approach is apparently missing with most of the Indian industries who are mainly practising 'JQI', ignoring the more important activity of quality planning and also the quality control.

In today's environment when Indian manufacturing as well as the service sectors are facing the intense international competition due to globalization, adopting the time-tested contemporary latest management technique of Juran's triology is probably the only alternative for them not only to survive but also to attain a position of global leadership.

The quality planning, quality control and quality improvement will be dealt with in detail in separate chapters considering their importance to the subject of total quality management.

2.11 CROSBY'S THEORY ON QUALITY MANAGEMENT

Philip B. Crosby is an eminent management guru who wrote a number of books on the subject of quality like 'Quality is free', 'Quality without Tears' and 'The Eternally Successful Organization'. His extensive work in the field of quality in USA earned him wide acclaim from allover the world. His client included famous organizations like IBM.

Like Joseph Juran and Edward Deming, Crossby also worked extensively on creating awareness in the organizations the importance of quality. While Juran propagated that 'higher quality costs less, Philip Crosby tried to popularize the concept that 'the quality is free'.

Crosby is famous for his **6 Cs**:

- **Comprehensions** or ability to understand and absorb the quality related activities, its sustenance and improvements.
- **Commitments** by all, i.e. top management, employee's, suppliers and the customers to the quality management system performance.
- **Competence** for improvement and then sustaining the improvement on a long-term basis. Here the competence means the effectiveness and efficiency of the entire quality management system.
- **Corrections** that is fool proofing the quality management system by rectifying the mistakes and deviations and putting the quality management system back on the track for world-class performance.
- **Communications** in the organization should be clear without ambiguity and honest. This will ensure support to the quality management system from the employees, suppliers and the customers alike,
- **Continuance** of the organization's good performance and its continuous improvement is the essence of a world-class organization and its successful operation.

Crosby propagated that quality or lack of it depends on the management rather than employees. He formulated his theory on how to get results by spending a small percentage of the organization's operating cost on education and the error prevention. He educated the organizations how to get things right the first time and achieve the goal of 'zero defect'.

Crosby again focused more on the quality improvement activity. He made it clear that the key to quality improvement was to understand the concepts and implementing it and not implanting a complex system difficult to execute. He emphasized that causing quality was an ordinary part of the management. The organization does not need a separate group or a separate department to implement quality.

Crosby's main theory is explained that what originally began as 'quality' for him had expanded with experience into an understanding that 'quality improvement' is nothing but 'hassle elimination'. He has taken the basic three elements of improvement—determination, education and implementation, and broken them down in their essence. When the organization hassles its employees knowingly or unknowingly, it has a negative impact on the result of the organization.

Crosby has defined the four absolute requirements to be fulfilled for the attainment of quality. They are as follows:

1. *The definition of quality is conformance to requirement.* The objective of the quality improvement is to get everyone to do it right the first time. To achieve this, an organization must get its employees to understand the requirements clearly. The management has to perform three tasks to accomplish this. First of all the organization should establish the requirements that employees are to meet. Next job of the organization is to supply the resources needed by the employees to meet these requirements. The final step for the organization is to encourage and help the employees to meet these requirements.

2. *The system of quality is prevention.* Appraisal is inspection and testing, checking the products after the job is over. If there is no conformance, you cannot do much about it except rework, re-grade or salvage. All these create a lot of ongoing hassles and there is no improvement. Hence according to Crosby, appraisal is an expensive and unreliable way of getting quality. What has to happen is 'prevention'. Once the concerned person understands the process, the prevention activity becomes easy. The concept of prevention is based on understanding the process that needs preventive action. The preventive activities are to look at the processes and identify opportunities for the error. These errors can be controlled by eliminating the cause of the problem.

3. *The performance of the standard is zero defects.* Organizations with millions of individual actions cannot afford to have a percent or two of it to go astray. Less than complete compliance with the required level of performance could cause big trouble in the organization. Companies try all sorts of ways to help their people not to meet the requirements by declaring things like AQL (Accepted Quality Level). SPQL (Shipped Product Quality Level), etc. The concept has to be 'zero defect' that is absolute conformance to the requirement. There cannot be a grade or percentage of performance. The employees should be aware of what they are supposed to do and do exactly that. This should be the focus. The employees have to do it right the first time to make the organization hassle free.

4. *The measurement of quality is the price of non-conformance.* The 'cost of quality' consists of two factors:

   (a) *Price of conformance:* The price of conformance consists of costs like all prevention efforts, training and education on quality. It is not more than 2% of the sales.

   (b) *Price of non-conformance:* The price of non-conformance consists of faulty handling of a customer's enquiry to loss of orders, rejection, delayed delivery, rework, salvaging, etc. It can be as high as 20% and it can eat up the organization's profit. The price of non-conformance is everything that the organization would not have done if it was done right the first time.

2.11.1   Process of Creating a Hassle-free Organization with Zero Defects

In order to create a hassle-free organization where all operations are executed with zero defect and every thing is right the first time, we have to take a systematic approach for development of such an organization. Let us describe the procedure of developing such organization.

Identification of a problem organization

The products and services produced by a problem organization will have deviations from the agreed-upon and defined requirements. The organization will have an extensive and efficient service network for rectification and corrective actions for meeting warranty commitments of the organization and to keep the customer satisfied. The management does not provide a clear performance standard or definition of quality. So the employees develop their own individual standards. In this organization, the management does not pay attention to the price of non-conformance and does not take responsibility for the problems.

Prevention of non-conformance

Crosby calls it the 'vaccination against non-conformance'. To prepare preventive measures, he has suggested three-key ingredients—determination, education and implementation. The management has to have a strategy that is to be continually administered with the above three distinctive managerial actions.

Determination: The management should first of all be determined to implement the principle of 'zero defect' and 'do it right the first time'. The management should recognize that their action is the only tool that will change the organizational performance. Once this is made known to the employees, they will automatically pull their efforts in this direction and the result is bound to come in a slow but steady manner.

   The efforts for the quality improvement should be a well-organized programme rather than a process. All the efforts should be aimed at the lower level of the organization. The process should have a strong determination of both the management and the employees for the implementation.

Education: Education and training is the process of educating all the employees of the common language of quality and do it right the first time, and understand their individual roles in the quality improvement process. The management should provide special knowledge to handle non-conformance and take preventive measures for attainment of the zero defect and the skill to do it right the first time. Education and knowledge will also help the organization to motivate the employees and have the confidence in their work. This is very important for the effective implementation of Crosby's theory on quality and zero defect.

   According to Crosby, producing a hassle-free organization requires a continual transfer of information from person to person. Education has to be routine and focused. Every one has to have the common language, the skills to do the job and the understanding of each one's personal role in running the organization. Every body has to understand the common language of quality. The fourteen-step quality improvement process has to be understood by the management team since they are responsible for the implementation of the same. The individual role in quality must be understood by each and every person in the company. Those who are involved in the specific functions has to be given special education in order to carry out their role efficiently and effectively. The education must be imparted at all the three levels of Management, executives and employees.

Implementation: The implementation of the quality management or the quality improvement is a fourteen-step implementation procedure as detailed here after.

1. *Management commitment:* The management should show their commitment by declaring a clear cut corporate policy on quality needs. The commitment in 'quality policy' should be simple, real and easily understandable. Secondly the quality should be periodically and regularly discussed in the 'Management Review Meeting' in specific quantifiable terms. The CEO in all his talks should reflect his commitment to the quality and motivate the employees accordingly.

2. *Quality improvement team:* The quality improvement team is cross-functional and the members should be capable of helping the individual teams and employees in quality improvement activities. The quality improvement team needs a clear direction and leadership. This team is one of the key parts of the process and helps in coordination and support. The quality improvement team should schedule the education programs and create company-wide events. The chair person of the team should be one of the members of the top team and should have a clear understanding of the overall strategy and the power to influence the same. The quality improvement team focuses on improving the things on a continuous basis.

3. *Measurement:* The quality improvement team must devise ways and means of measuring the evidence of improvement from the existing way of doing the things. Every function and sub-function is a process which has an input and an output. The objective of the process is value addition at the expense of some resources needed for the value addition. The cost of input resources should be less than the value added for the process be efficient. The effectiveness of the process is determined by its extent of achievement of the organizational objective. All the assessment of input, output, value addition, cost of resources, business objective, etc. needs quantified measurement and units against which the same can be evaluated.

4. *Cost of quality:* The quality improvement team plans and implements a strategy to measure the cost of non-conformance and undertake quality improvement projects to minimize the same progressively until it reaches the target of 'zero defect' by installing a full proof system 'do it right the first time'. The quality improvement team should be able to bring the cost of non-conformance to nil. The cost of conformance should be maintained at a reasonable level to retain the improvements and hold the gains.

5. *Quality awareness:* The quality improvement team should create a number of education and training programmes to create the awareness about quality and its various aspects as propagated by Crosby. The team should create the significance

of quality for the organizational success and hassle-free working. The team should also define the losses due the cost of non-conformance and how to reduce it. The creation of quality awareness in the organization will create self-motivated employees for an excellent performance.

6. *Corrective action:* The quality improvement team should identify all the cost of non-conformance and plan corrective actions and get it implemented to reduce the cost of non-conformance to zero. All the employees as well as the management should develop a habit of taking immediate corrective actions as and when the deviations take place.

7. *Zero defect planning:* When the performance of the organization and its employees has reached a reasonably good level, the quality improvement team moves ahead and plans for a foolproof system of the zero defect or the Do-it-right-the-first time culture. The suitable quality improvement tools are implemented for elimination of the organizational problems.

8. *Employee education:* Now the quality improvement team with the help of the consultants imparts training and education on the 'quality improvement tools' for systematically and scientifically undertaking the quality improvement projects and reducing the cost of non-conformance.

9. *Zero defect days:* The quality improvement team plans for occasional zero defect days as the practical implementation of the zero defect planning. The team closely monitors the processes and activities on a zero defect day and ensures that the employees actually believe that the zero defect is possible by seeing the actual zero defect day happening.

10. *Goal setting:* The quality improvement team should help individual functions and activities set up their own individual objectives and goals and suitable quality improvement project for the same. The team should set up for itself the attainment of the organizational objective or the goal and a strategic action plan for the same.

11. *Error cause removal:* The quality improvement team should not settle down for the corrective action alone after finding out the root cause of the problem as it will give only temporary relief from the cost of non-conformance. There is a good likelihood that the problem may repeat again. Hence the quality improvement team should find out the root cause of each problem and try to take preventive action for the removal of the root cause of the error so that the same is not repeated ever.

12. *Recognition:* The quality improvement team should recognize good efforts done by the individual or the quality improvement team by giving awards, promotions, acknowledgement, etc. The recognition is extremely important for the growth and prosperity of the organization and the motivation of employee.

13. *Quality council:* The quality improvement team should submit a periodic report of the activity of the quality improvement projects to the quality council. The quality council discusses all the quality improvement activities and takes a decision on their implementation along with the resource allocation, and reviews their implementation periodically.

14. *Do it over again:* The quality improvement team takes stock of the successful quality improvement projects and measures the gain from such projects. The

quality council and the quality improvement team now examine critically all the functions and try to identify the area where the similar spin-off projects can be taken up straightway for implementation.

Philip B. Crosby's theory on 'zero defect' and 'do it right the first time' has been accepted worldwide over even if he practised management mainly in USA. He has advocated that one can create an organization of eternal success by following the above theory.

2.12 MURI, MURA AND MUDA—THREE MAGIC WANDS OF JAPANESE MANAGEMENT SYSTEM

During the Second World War, the Japanese lost the most and the American industry gained the most. Post-war Japan was a ruined country where everything was to be rebuilt and replaced. The requirement was monstrous and resources were scarce. The country whose focus was manufacturing war arsenals was suddenly required to reorganize in manufacturing civilian products of day-to-day consumption. The factory manufacturing war planes was to realign itself with manufacturing of automobiles. The 'Made in Japan' was not a symbol of good quality in the world market compared to its western counterparts. On top of it Japan had limited natural resources to cope up with this tremendous challenge. On the other hand, the West enjoyed period of steady growth for 30 years from the post-war period till the oil crisis of 1973. The market was the 'sellers' market' all over the world. The focus was on production rather than sales. The result was the steady growth of western industries.

However way back in 1950, the Japanese industries under the stewardship of Joseph M. Juran, Deming, Taiichi Ohno, Shigeo Shingo and other management experts decided to catch up with the West and obtain world leadership in various Industrial segments by the 1970s. One by one the Japanese industrial entities overtook the western industry leaders by the mid seventies and retained their leadership even after three decades till date in most of the segments. Japanese industries did learn from the West, but did emulate them ditto. They blended the best from the West with their original ways adapted to their constraints to make the end output the world's best. The tough local condition of scarce resources led to the birth of methods based on waste (Muda) elimination, maximizing production and productivity to produce products and services at the least cost. This coupled with the customer orientation pushed the Japanese industries up the ladder for the leadership position. 'Ford's production model' adopted by western industries believed in 'push sales' where large production quantity in small product variety led to supply exceeding the demand. This led to global competition and market transforming into the buyer's market. The customers were not fully satisfied due to the offer of limited choice of product varieties. On the contrary the Toyota Production System focused on cost management and a 'customer pull strategy'. This implied a customization and manufacturing small batch quantity as per specific customer's requirement, leading to the customer satisfaction. Manufacturers could no more push their design, their product at their cost to the customer. They had to adapt to a new era of the buyer's market where the organization has to respond to spot demand as per the client's desire in a time bound, quick and economically effective manner.

The development of the post 1990s has magnified worldwide the consumer's total dominance over the market. Breakingdown of protective dykes of duties in socialist and communist countries across the globe, signing of WTO, unipolar world, globalization, etc have led to intense global competition where good quality at least cost has been the order of the day for survival and growth of the industry. The selling price of any product or service is decided by the market forces. There is the effect of the routine inflation, rising cost of labour, material, etc. threatening the profit margin continuously. The opportunity of price increase is not there, leaving the only option for survival and growth is to reduce the cost of production. The three Japanese mantras of 'muri', 'mura' and 'muda' popularly known as 'the big 3' or '3M practice' is an integral part of Japanese manufacturing system. The 3M practice brought down the cost of the production to bare minimum without effecting the quality or rather the user friendliness. The effect of elimination of muda or wastage can be immediately visible and its effect appreciated. The impact of the other two concepts of mura and muri are subtle and not that visible but equally significant in attaining the end objective of customer satisfaction and cost reduction. Let us understand the concept and implication of the effect of these three magic wands of muri, mura and muda step by step and systematically.

2.12.1 MURI

The word 'muri' fundamentally means 'unreasonable' or 'irrational' approach to any field of operation whatsoever. This might have been adopted in various ways in various fields like 'unreasonable or excessive strain' in 3M checklist of Kaizen activities. The Kaizan checklist tries to look into improvement by identifying and eliminating the unreasonableness or excessive strain in all the eleven areas such as manpower, technique, method, time, facilities, tools, materials, inventory, place, production quantity, quality and way of thinking.

Muri looks for irrationality with four major approaches:

1. Things or activities that are extremely difficult to do and at the moment beyond the reach—should be identified and eliminated from our activities as there is no meaning behind perusing these activities and currently beyond the individual's or the organization's capability.
2. There is futility in perusing the things or the activities that do not make any sense or it is difficult for the individual or the organization to find reasons for.
3. You should also eliminate the things or activities you do just because you are told to do so without understanding the reason for doing the same or its underlying benefit from performing such activities.
4. You should eliminate irrational actions or operations that cause undue or excessive fatigue due to a lot of physical effort, frequent stress to body movement, mental fatigue due to unwarranted work place stress, to remember a lot of unnecessary things, constantly worrying about defects or breakdowns, struggling to read illegible words and symbols, etc.

In this context a vital area of 'muri' application which made Japanese automobile and machine tool industry go miles ahead of western industry is illustrated here. The American and European car and machine tool industry designed a car or two-wheeler or a machine tool to last for next twenty to thirty years and to give consistent performance. Therefore, they multiplied the calculated dimension by the factor of safety of two. This led to increasing dimensions of the components. Therefore, the cost of the raw material was double. The weight of the automobile or the machine tool was heavier and, it was less flexible and difficult to handle. As per the thumb rule half the cost of an automobile or a machine tool is the raw material, and if it doubles, the price of the final product also nearly doubles as all other costs are also directly or indirectly related to the processing of the raw material.

The Japanese thought differently and of course rationally. The difference was their 'customer orientation'. Their view point was the following:

- Is the customer going to use the same 'car' or the 'two-wheeler' for the next twenty or thirty years?
- Is the customer going to use the same 'machine tool' or the 'manufacturing technology' for the next twenty or thirty years?
- Is the product development and upgradation of technology in this most dynamic and vibrant field going to be negligible in next two to three decades?

If the answers to all these questions are no, then the Japanese argue that why design and manufacture a car or two-wheeler for twenty to thirty years when you know that you are going to use the same maximum for a period of four to five years? Why manufacture a machine tool to last for thirty to forty years when you know that the technology for manufacturing is going to change every five years. This is precisely 'muri' or 'irrationality' or 'unreasonableness'. Therefore, the Japanese did what was rational. They designed a car or two-wheeler for five years because that is normally the life span for which the product is effectively used. Therefore the Japanese used a 'Factor of safety' of 1.25 instead of two. Their raw material cost was about 62.5% of the western design. The other direct and indirect cost was also reduced around the same figure. The end product was identical in terms of product features and user friendliness. The cost of raw material and manufacturing was also lower. Hence the end price of the product to the consumer was also proportionately lower by almost 30% to 35%. The automobiles were also lighter in weight due to lower percentage of the raw material used. This led to the reduction of dead weight to be carried by the vehicle thereby increasing the pick-up of the vehicle as well as reduction in fuel consumption. The end result of practising 'muri' was a better performing product which is more user friendly priced much lower than conventional western products. The outcome was obvious. The Japanese industry became a world leader in their respective field by the mid seventies and continued to defend their leadership position till date in most of the fields.

2.12.2 MURA

The Japanese word 'Mura' means irregular, uneven or inconsistent. Technically, this word is the opposite of 'heijo' which means ordinary, regular or even. Either due to lack of interest or over enthusiasm we tend to deviate from the laid out standard leading to inconsistent actions. Such inconsistency can easily give rise to the irrationality and waste. Both the 'Bottleneck Theory' and 'Theory of Constraints' originate from the principle of mura.

The bottleneck theory states that the neck of a bottle or the least diameter of a bottle decides the rate of flow out of the bottle. This theory when applied to an industry states that the department in the manufacturing chain with the least capacity decides the plant capacity. The corrective action is strengthening this weak department by increasing its capacity by minimum investment. The result will be a quantum jump in overall performance of the organization as the extra capacity is already lying unutilized in other areas.

Eliyahu M. Goldratt's 'theory of constraints' also tends to be developed around the same principle of 'mura'. The theory infers: 'The weakest link in a chain decides the weight that can be lifted by the chain.' The objective is to identify this weakest link and keep on strengthening it to make the organization stronger and stronger and make it grow steadily. Of course both the theories have been developed extensively much beyond what is stated above to make them comprehensive and effective in offering a complete solution to organizational problems.

Kaizen also uses 'mura' as a powerful improvement tool. However, instead of terming it inconsistency, Kaizen prefers to term it 'discrepancy'. It calls for identifying the discrepancy in the eleven defined areas such as men, technique, method, time, facilities, tools and manufacturing aids, materials, production volume, inventory, place and way of thinking. Once the discrepancy is identified, it is analyzed and a solution is found out to eliminate or remove the discrepancy leading to a culture of continuous improvement.

In Joseph Juran's triology of quality planning, quality control and quality improvement, the quality control is defined as control over the process. The aim of this activity is to have the consistency in the performance of the product, process and people. This consistency in performance on the above parameters is extremely important for customer satisfaction and the maximization of return on investment from the business, which are the two vital parameters for the survival and growth of an organization. This need for consistency in performance in all areas of an organization is reflected in developing the ISO 9000:2000 series of standard for the 'Quality Management System' by the international standard organization.

Mura calls for a minimum deviation between the best and the worst product or service. It calls for minimizing the range of deviation and minimizing the standard deviation in the statistical process control. It develops the confidence of the customer as well as the management who knows precisely what to expect from the organization, its product and processes.

2.12.3 MUDA

'Muda' means waste. Waste is any activity that does not add value. Joseph Juran has called all the activities that do not add value the Cost of Poor Quality (COPQ). Juran has summed up this as the total cost of external product/service failure plus the cost of internal failure plus the cost of various preventive measures. Taichi Ohno of Toyota Motor Company has done an elaborate work on the 'mudas' or wastes. He has identified seven mudas or seven wastes which have further been modified to nine mudas. The objective in either case is the same. First identify and analyze the Mudas and then take suitable corrective and preventive actions to eliminate the same. This obviously reduces the cost of production, enhances productivity, reduces the cycle time and leads to better customer satisfaction.

Taichi Ohno has focused on the seven mudas or seven wastes as elaborated below:

Waste from overproduction

The waste from over is normally not detectable. The tendency of an organization is always to overproduce to ensure no shortage of material in the market under any circumstance or to fill up the idle plant capacity during the lean period. In today's dynamic highly competitive world, the products and services have a shorter life cycle. If a product is in inventory for a long time, it may become obsolete in the market. It may occupy plant capacity for products that are already in stock whereas some of the products for which customers are waiting cannot be produced due to this blockage of useful plant capacity. It also leads to piling up of excess inventory, occupying more storage space, excessive material handling cost, interest cost on unsold stock, etc.

Waste due to waiting time

Any time wasted in waiting for the parts to arrive due to improper line balancing or waiting for job instructions due to improper planning or non-aligned objectives is a drain in the organizational resources. All such waiting time has to be identified and eliminated from the system.

Waste due to unwarranted transportation

Waste due to unwarranted transportation happens due to unplanned and improper plant layout leading to things or parts being moved multiple times. If parts are not properly placed, they are difficult to find leading to further wastages. It can also aggravate the alignment of processes.

Waste from excess inventories

Excess buffer inventory takes care of a lot of inefficiencies like faulty sales forecasting, late deliveries from suppliers, delayed production, etc. In the Just-In-Time production system the inventory is progressively reduced to increase the operational efficiency. Excess inventory leads to increase in Inventory Carrying Cost consisting of interest Cost (ICC) on capital invested in extra inventory, storage space, extra material and product handling, insurance cost, product pilferage, product obsolescence, etc.

Processing waste or useless operation in processing waste

Processing waste occurs due to inefficient process design and improper technology. This can be improved by proper method study, incorporating proper technology, proper training to the operators, work study, SMED (Single Minute Exhange of Die), etc.

Waste of motion due to unnecessary human movements

Unnecessary human can be eliminated by study of Human motions, ergonomics and applying the principles of Motion Study. This includes the incorporation of simple human motion, proper arrangement of work place, proper location of operating switches, simultaneous and opposite movement of both hands, reduction of fatigue as well as pre-arrangement of tools and accessories lead to reduction of 'Motion Muda'.

Waste from product defects or defective parts

The waste from product defects or defective part is a major muda which not only affects the cost of production but also leads to loss of sales due to customer dissatisfaction. This involves the major cost of rejection, rework and replacement. The cost of an external failure is ten times the cost of detecting the same failure internally which is again ten times the cost of detecting the failure at the point of origin. Hence the emphasis should be in the process control or implementation of the six-sigma practice which makes it almost impossible to produce a defective part.

The further research in this area of muda leads to the **'eighth muda'** as 'the development of product or services or for that matter even the product features which does not add value to the product or service from the customer's point of view or his needs and expectations'. In the lean manufacturing approach, any activity or effort which does not meet a customer's need or expectation is qualified as a waste.

The **'ninth muda'** as per the latest concept has been defined as **'the waste of opportunities'**. An organization may be contented with its growth, purchasing price or quality of the goods produced unaware of the fact of a new entrant performing better in these areas, a cheaper and better substitute raw material, a new technology, etc. being availed by the competitor or available in the market. Any loss due to not utilizing this potential area of gain could be classified as an area of muda.

The opportunities of identification and elimination of muri, mura and muda are generally assessed and revealed by a comparison to other standard either a competitor or someone who is the best in the class. The common practices could be by 'benchmarking', 'strategic planning' or 'business process reengineering', etc. The endeavour should be to attempt for a revolutionary rate of growth. This can be done through step by step through Kaizen Gemba, quality circle, continuous improvement or with a breakthrough improvement through 'JQI', **Kaikaku or Reengineering** or a combination of both of the approaches. The organization should strive for perfection, to aim beyond the limited objective of being the best in the class by benchmarking. The organization should get close to perfection, understand customer's needs and expectation, undertake value analysis and reach to a position of outstanding competitive advantage.

2.13 QUALITY CIRCLE

2.13.1 Definition

A quality circle is a group of employees from the same work area and doing similar type of work voluntarily meet for an hour periodically either every week or fortnightly to identity, analyze and resolve work related problems in their own work area.

The common number of employees for a quality circle group is about 10–12 individuals.

2.13.2 Philosophy of Quality Circle

The philosophy of quality circle respects human dignity and motivates employees at grass root levels to use their brain power along with their physical effort.

2.13.3 Benefits of Quality Circle

In 1962 in Japan, a small group was formed of operators or task performers known as 'Quality Control Circle' for problem solving in work area by team effort. This was the first time that workers at the shop floor level were involved in decision making process and quality improvement effort. It started a quite but powerful revolution in work culture and productivity improvement world wide. The peer knowledge was utilized for the benefit of the organization as well as the fellow worker bringing in a strong team spirit and creating an environment of continuous improvement. The key reason to the success of Japanese industry and their fast growth in the 1960s and 1970s is believed to be attributed to the quality circle movement. In India Bharat Heavy Electrical Limited popularly known as BHEL is one of the 'Navaratnas' of Indian government undertakings, and it has done exceedingly well under all circumstance at all times and can be called a world-class organization with round performance excellence in all its units at Haridwar, Jhanshi, Hyderabad and Tiruchirapalli. One of the main contributors in making BHEL what it is today is definitely the quality circle movement in all its plants as stated above.

The benefits of quality circle can be detailed as follows:

1. The periodic meeting of the shop floor workers to solve their work-related problem in the quality circle will develop mutual trust and cooperation between management and workers as well as involve the workers in the decision making process in their work area.
2. Quality circle will lead to the improvement in productivity which in turn will lead to increase in employment.
3. The benefit of improved productivity should be evenly distributed between management, labour and customers.
4. Quality circle changes the total attitude to a constant, self renovation force of business enterprise.
5. It develops the 'knowledge management' culture in the organization at the workers level. The peer knowledge is shared and nurtured to solve the worker's own work-related problem.
6. The quality circle effort improves the quality of the products and services provided by the organization to its customers.
7. Productivity improvement effort in quality circle leads to increase in sales and reduction in the cost of production.
8. Quality circle efforts focus on higher safety and reduction in accident.
9. Quality circle ensures better housekeeping.
10. Quality circle movement increases profitability by reduction in waste.
11. Quality circle creates better motivation and involvement of the employees leading to reduced Absenteeism & Grievances.

12. Quality circle activities lead to enriched quality of work life.
13. It creates an atmosphere of positive and proactive work force with harmony and mutual trust.
14. Quality circle activities create better communication and effective team-work.
15. It creates better human relation and participative culture.
16. The quality circle movement promotes job knowledge.
17. The quality circle creates a greater sense of belonging.

2.13.4 Structure of Quality Circle

The structure of quality circle is detailed in Figure 2.6. The structure of the quality circle is headed by the top management who forms a steering committee known as the quality council. The quality council has all the heads of the functions as its member and chaired by the chief executive officer. All important activities in the organization are monitored by the quality council. All the important decisions are taken in the quality council. The quality circle is basically formed by workers from the work area known as the members. Their supervisor is normally the leader. The facilitator is the head of the coordinating agency which implements the quality circle. The non-members are the specialists in a particular area. The non-members are invited as a consultant to solve the work-related problems of a quality circle group.

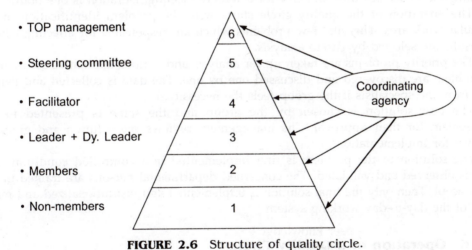

* TOP management
* Steering committee
* Facilitator
* Leader + Dy. Leader
* Members
* Non-members

Coordinating agency

FIGURE 2.6 Structure of quality circle.

2.13.5 Implementation of Quality Circle

The step by step implementation of the quality circle starts with the formation of the 'structure of the quality circle', which primarily consists of workers numbering about ten to twelve from the same work area. The leader of the group is their departmental supervisor or the foreman to whom they are reporting normally. The quality circle group is helped by a facilitator in their activities. The non-members are the specialists in their respective areas. The service of a non-member is sought to solve the technical problem which is beyond the group's capability. A coordinating agency is formed to coordinate the quality circle activities in the entire organization. (The quality circle activities of each group are periodically reported by the coordinating agency to the steering committee which is normally the quality council formed by the head of the functions as its members and the chief executive officer or the managing director as its chairman.) The top management here implies the board of directors who are rarely involved in the quality circle activities directly.

Once the structure of the quality circle is formed, now present the concept of quality circle and its salient features to senior management including the managing director. Explain philosophy of quality circles to middle level executives. The steering committee takes the decision to implement the quality circle activity in the organization. The steering committee conducts a 'Pareto analysis' and identifies the areas of initiating quality circle is identified. The most important department or the most problematic department is chosen as the preferred choice of starting the quality circle activity.

A quality circle is formed by members from the relevant area. The leader and deputy leader is normally the members' hierarchical superior, i.e. their foreman or supervisor. The coordinating agency or the steering committee organizes a training programme on quality circle for the leader, deputy leader and workers.

Once the members are trained on the quality circle activities as well as on the seven tools of quality circle for problem solving, they start holding the meetings. The members of quality circle decides time and day for a weekly meeting. Duration is one hour.

The operation of the quality circle starts with the problem identification in the particular work area. The vital few problems which are responsible for effecting 80% of the results are selected by Pareto analysis.

The priority problems are taken up for analysis and various alternative solutions to the problem are discovered and discussed one by one. The data is collected and help is taken from the specialists if the group feels the necessity.

The best solution is chosen by the group and the same is presented to the management for their approval. The management reviews the solution and gives its approval for implementation.

The solution to the problem is first implemented in a controlled condition. The result is observed and validated. The concerned departmental persons are trained in the new concept. Then only the final solution is implemented and institutionalized and made a part of the day-to-day working system.

2.13.6 Operation of a Quality Circle

The operation of a quality circle is depicted in Figure 2.7. The quality council formulates the quality circle operation coordinating agency that identifies problems to be taken up on priority for solving. It identifies the problems in consultation with the functional heads. The problem is selected by the team member of a particular quality circle. The problem is analyzed in the quality circle meeting and attempt is made to find out a solution to the problem. If the quality circle team needs the assistance from an external expert or specialist, the expert is invited in the quality circle team meeting. Alternative solutions are discussed and the most suitable alternative solution which satisfies all the musts and the maximum number of the wants is selected as the best solution.

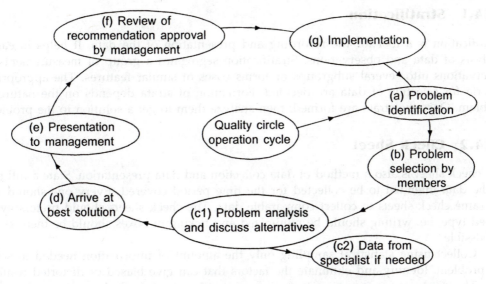

FIGURE 2.7 Operation of a quality circle.

The quality circle team recommends the best solution to the quality council that reviews the problem and solution. If it deems fit and finds it acceptable, the quality council gives its approval for the implementation of the solution. The suggestion of the quality circle team is now implemented by the concerned department.

2.14 SEVEN TOOLS OF TQC/QUALITY CIRCLE

The seven universal problem-solving tools of 'total quality control' or the quality circle are as follows:

- Stratification
- Check sheet
- Scatter diagram
- Histogram
- Ishikawa diagram/Cause and effect diagram
- Pareto diagram
- Control charts (X and R charts)

We shall be discussing the seven problem-solving tools one by one in detail with their applicability. While the stratification, check sheets and scatter diagrams are the methodology of displaying the data in a systematic manner in groups or classes indicating where the problem lies, the typical problem-solving tool is a combination of histogram for problem presentation in groups, Pareto analysis for prioritizing the problem to be taken up first to the drawing of the Ishikawa or fish bone diagram to identify the root cause. Once the root cause of the problem is found out, then solution is found out, tested, validated and implemented to derive the required result.

2.14.1 Stratification

Stratification is a tool for the recording and presentation of the data. It helps in easier analysis of data and observations. Stratification segregates a group of measurements or observations into several subgroups or forms bases of similar features. The appropriate criteria for selection of data are decided. Formation of strata depends on the nature of problem. Once the strata are formed, then analyze them to get a solution to the problem.

2.14.2 Check Sheet

The check sheet is also a method of data collection and data presentation. State a full title of the data intended to be collected for the time period covered. Every one should use the same check sheets to collect comparable data. The check sheets should preferably be closed type, i.e. writing should be minimized and ticking in boxes should be there as far as possible.

Collect using statistical sampling only the amount of information needed to solve the problem. Identify and eliminate the factors that can give biased or distorted results.

The dimension measurement of a component is put in a tabular form as shown in Figure 2.8.

Faults	1st shift	2nd shift	3rd shift	Total
Size oversize	I	III	IIII	8
Size undersize	I	II	III	6
Ovality	I	II	II	5
Material crack/hard	–	I	I	2
	3	8	10	21

FIGURE 2.8 Dimension measurement of a component.

2.14.3 Scatter Diagram

The scatter diagram is drawn to a scale for collection of data and plotted on a graph. The analysis consists of finding out the relationship between the hypothesis and the result. Two correlated data are plotted on a graphical scale. One is drawn on the horizontal x-axis and the other is drawn on the vertical y-axis. The respective points are drawn which indicate the relationship between the dependant variable and the independent variable. This helps in decision making.

The scatter diagram is illustrated in Figure 2.9.

2.14.4 Histogram

A histogram (Figure 2.10) is a visual presentation of the spread on distribution of data to monitor a process to see if it consistently meets the customer's requirements.

This is drawn over a fixed period of time and a fixed range of data.

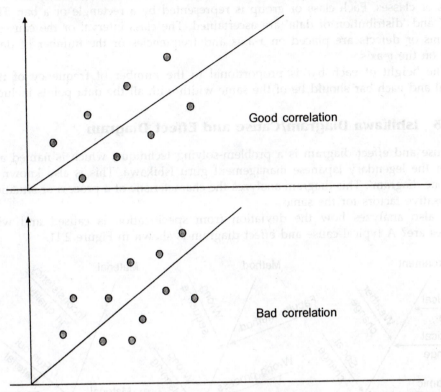

Good correlation

Bad correlation

FIGURE 2.9 Scatter diagram.

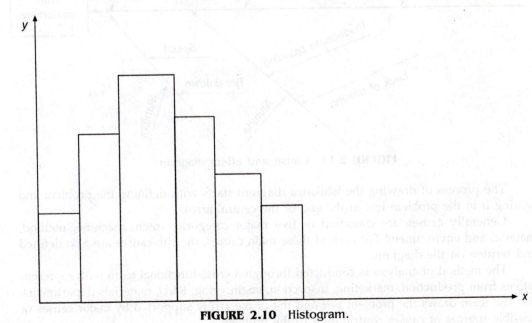

FIGURE 2.10 Histogram.

The population in the data is classified on the basis of their similarity into different groups or classes. Each class or group is represented by a rectangle or a bar. Then the 'range' and 'distribution of data' are ascertained. The class interval or the causes of the problems or defects are placed on x-axis and frequencies or the number of defects is placed on the y-axis.

The height of each bar is proportional to the number of frequency of its class interval and each bar should be of the same width with all the data points included.

2.14.5 Ishikawa Diagram/Cause and Effect Diagram

The cause and effect diagram is a problem-solving technique, which is named after its founder the legendary Japanese management guru Ishikawa. This is also known as the 'fish bone diagram'. This diagram analyzes the characteristic of a process or situation and the causative factors for the same.

It also analyzes how the deviation from specification is caused and what its remedies are? A typical cause and effect diagram is shown in Figure 2.11.

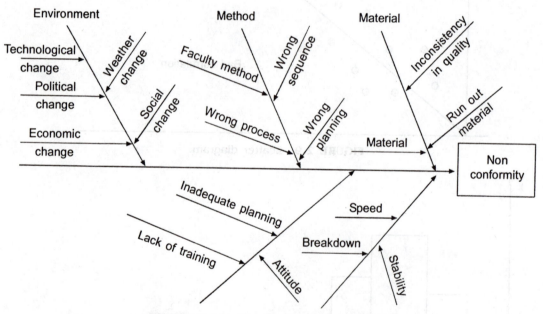

FIGURE 2.11 Cause and effect diagram.

The process of drawing the Ishikawa diagram starts with defining the problem and writing it in the problem box at the end of the central arrow.

Generally causes are classified in five major categories: men, machine, method, material and environment. For each of these main causes, the sub-causes are also defined and written on the diagram.

The method of analysis is conducted through a cross-functional team with representatives from production, marketing, inspection, engineering, R&D, materials departments, etc. The team draws the problem box and the prime arrow supported by major causes or possible sources of causes contributing to the problem.

Now brain storming is employed by the team to identify possible causes of the problem and take the corrective action. The causes are discussed one by one among the team members and eliminated leaving behind the most likely causes and find their solutions.

Once the root cause is identified, the group tries to find the solution which should take care of both the corrective actions and preventive actions so that not only the problems are corrected but also they are eliminated from the system. This will ensure a permanent solution to the problem and prevent its recurrence again.

2.14.6 Pareto Diagram

Pareto has been a great statistician who proved that 20% of world's population held 80% of its wealth. The 20% of land area irrigated provided for 80% of the food grains and so on. He put forth the 80–20 theory and applied it to the industrial situation also and proved it. Similarly, 20% of the employees of an organization are responsible for 80% of the sales of the organization. The 20% of problems in an organization are related to 80% of its result. The Pareto principle is employed to prioritize the problems to be taken up first. These problems if solved will give the quantum jump in the performance of an organization.

Method

The problems are plotted according to priority using a bar-graph format with 100% indicating the total amount of value cost.

Then the types of non-conformities are identified. The non-conformities are classified into various groups or categories based on identical or similar features. Now the data is collected about the non-conformities over the same period of time. The frequencies of number of non-conformities for various categories are measured and noted. The non-conformities are listed in the descending order of frequencies.

The frequency percentages are calculated and cumulative frequency for each category is measured starting from the largest frequency or the left-hand side of the graph.

The scale of the Pareto diagram on the left-hand side is the actual frequency of occurrences which is plotted and on the right-hand side, the cumulative frequency is drawn (Figure 2.12). This is followed by plotting the frequency bar and cumulative frequency percentage.

Now it will be observed as per the Pareto principle that 20% of the non-conformities will have 80% of the frequency or occurrences. Identify these 20% causes as the 'vital few' non-conformities and separate them from 'trivial/useful' many (Figure 2.13).

2.14.7 Control Chart

For details refer chapter on "Statistical Process Control".

X-chart

X is the average of each sub-group. R is the average of the ranges. The central line of

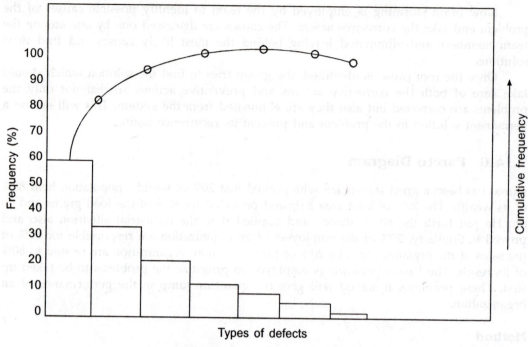

FIGURE 2.12   Pareto diagram.

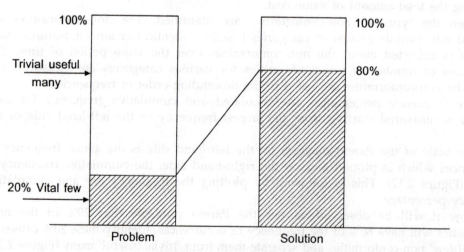

FIGURE 2.13   Pareto analysis.

X-chart (Figure 2.14) is found by adding the averages and dividing the result by the number of sub-groups (*p*), i.e.

$$X = \frac{\sum x}{p}$$

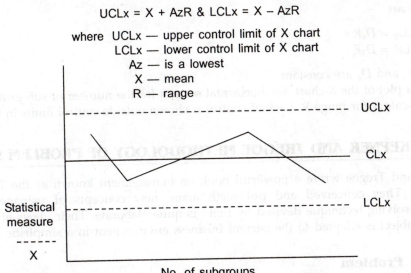

$$UCLx = X + AzR \ \& \ LCLx = X - AzR$$

where UCLx — upper control limit of X chart
LCLx — lower control limit of X chart
Az — is a lowest
X — mean
R — range

Horizontal scale is used for sub-group number and the vertical scale is used for statistical measure of X.

FIGURE 2.14 X-chart.

R-chart

The range of each sub-group is obtained by

$$X_{max} - X_{min} = R_1, R_2, ..., R_n$$

The central line of R-chart (Figure 2.15) is found by adding the sub-group ranges ($R_1, R_2, ..., R_n$) and dividing them by the number of sub-groups p, i.e.

$$R = \frac{R_1 + R_2 + ... + R_n}{p} = \frac{\Sigma R}{p}$$

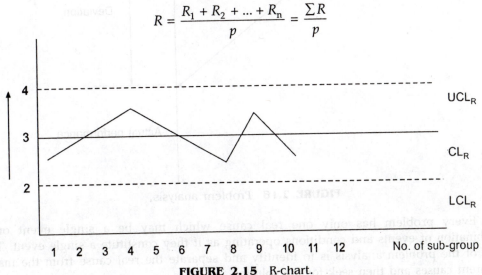

FIGURE 2.15 R-chart.

For R-Chart

$$UCL_R = D_4R$$
$$LCLR = D_3R$$

where D_3 and D_4 are constant.

In a plot of the R-chart, the horizontal scale is for the number of sub-groups and the vertical scale is for range R. Lack of control is shown outside control limits in the R-chart.

2.15   KEPNER AND TREGOE METHODOLOGY OF PROBLEM SOLVING

Kepner and Tregoe wrote a powerful book on management known as the *The Rational Manager*. They conceived and put forth many new concepts of management. The problem-solving technique devised by them is quite elaborate. Their views and thinking on the subject is adapted to the current business environment in a simplistic manner.

2.15.1   Problem

A *problem* is an unwanted effect due to a deviation from the plan. It is something which is to be corrected or eliminated. Refer to Figure 2.16.

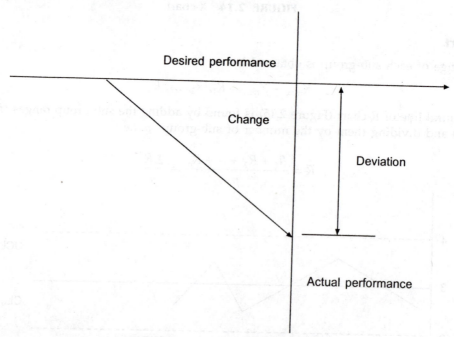

FIGURE 2.16   Problem analysis.

Every problem has only one real cause which may be a single event or a combination of events and conditions operating as if they constitute a single event. The crux of the problem analysis is to identify and separate the real cause from the many apparent causes and then seek for the solution.

A problem is a deviation or an imbalance between what should be and what actually is happening. The imbalance is caused by a 'change' of one kind or the other. This change needs to be precisely found and that will enable to decide the 'root cause of the problem'.

2.15.2 Seven Basic Concepts of Problem Analysis

The methodology of problem analysis basically has seven basic concepts:

1. The problem analyzer has an expected standard of performance—a benchmark against which he has to compare the actual performance. This standard of performance is derived from the objective or the goal of the plan which is followed for implementation.
2. A problem is a deviation from the standard of performance. The control mechanism or the periodic measurement of the performance against the expected standard of performance identifies that there is a deviation from the standard of performance. Once this is detected, the problem is now recognized and identified.
3. In the next step, the problem needs to be precisely defined. The deviation from the standard must be accurately identified, located and described with respect to the four dimensions, i.e. identity, location, time and extent. The questions need to be answered in terms of: What is the problem? Where is the problem? When has the problem happened? What is the extent of impact of the problem on attainment of the end objective?
4. There is always something distinguishing from that which has been affected by the cause from that which is not. Analyze and conclude without any ambiguity what is the actual impact of the deviation and differentiate from the diffused impacts.
5. The cause of a problem is always a change that has taken place through some distinctive feature, mechanism or condition to produce a new unwanted effect. This root cause of the problem needs to be identified and its step-by-step impact on the performance is to be evaluated.
6. The possible changes are ascertained from the relevant changes found in analyzing the problem. Once the precise factors responsible for the changes are ascertained, the root cause of the problem can be identified.
7. The most likely cause of a deviation is the one that precisely explains all the facts in the specification of the problem. The description of the cause of the deviation and the description of the problem are almost identical.

2.15.3 Problem-solving Methodology

Kepner and Tregoe propagated a problem-solving methodology of seven steps. The steps are required to be followed systematically in order to effectively find out a solution to the problem.

1. *Specify a problem:* The problem has to be specified clearly and distinctly so that it has clear-cut boundaries, demarcating sharply in each four dimensions as to what the problem is than what it is not.

2. *Draw a problem analysis work sheet search:*   The objective is to separate important and relevant one from irrelevant ones. This is the most important step of the problem-solving process. The accuracy of problem specification will decide the accuracy of the problem solution.

A problem analysis sheet is drawn with reference to the four dimensions of the problem. Refer to Figure 2.17. On the left-hand side of the problem sheet, it clearly specifies what the deviation object is, where it is observed, when it has occurred and the extent of occurrence, i.e. in terms of the quantity and depth of the deviation or the damage.

	IS	IS not	Distinctive of the IS	Any change
What: Deviation object				
Where: On object observed				
When: On object observed				
Extent: How much, how many				

FIGURE 2.17   Problem analysis worksheet.

3. *Search for the cause:*   The search for the cause proceeds in two ways:
   (a) The process further searches and demarcates distinctively those characteristics distinctive of IS and not of the IS NOT (Figure 2.17).
   (b) A search is carried out for the 'changes' occurred within and have effect upon and in conjunction with a given distinctive area.
4. *Differentiation of IS and IS NOT:*   The dividing line between the IS and IS NOT of the problem should be as distinct as possible. A sharp dividing line between the IS and IS NOT will help to distinguish between the two sets of facts that will provide clues to the cause.
5. *Analysis for distinctions and changes:*   Facts are analyzed to search for the change that precisely produced the effects observed through some area of distinction found in the specification. There is always one change—simple or complex. The simple change is normally the single elements change. The complex change consists of multiple elements and conditions. Either the simple or the complex change which is the likely cause of the deviation produces the exact effect observed in the problem. We can only find the change through the analysis of the facts in specifying the problem. The principal skill in the problem solving exercise is the accuracy and acumen for the 'analysis of the facts'.
6. *Find the cause:*   The cause is one specific constellation of events producing the problem. The possible causes are defined in the form of testable, positive statements of cause and effect. Each hypothesis is tested against the facts of specifications. The one which produces the same observed outcome as the problem is the cause.

7. *Test the cause determined:*   The cause explains both the effects that were observed (the IS) and the absence of effects where none were observed (the IS NOT) simply, logically and completely. Once the root cause of the problem is determined, the necessary interim, corrective and preventive actions are taken so that the root cause is permanently eliminated from the system and it never ever repeats again.

The Kepner and Tregoe methodology of two stages of 'problem analysis' and 'problem solving' is a fool-proof method of problem elimination from the system. Both the techniques are of seven steps each as explained earlier.

2.15.4   Decision Analysis

Decision making is a process of choosing between the alternatives and finding out the 'best alternative' in getting a job done.

After finding out the root cause of the problem, the solution to the problem or the elimination of the problem may have many alternatives. The decision-making process is to choose the best alternative among the options which consumes the least amount of resources, i.e. least costly but at the same time gives the best solution to the problem.

Five alternative actions

The problem solving or the problem elimination exercise may warrant one or more actions to be taken in this regard. A manager can take five different alternative actions in dealing with a problem. The five types of the actions taken are as follows:

Interim action: The interim action is an immediate stop-gap action which gives temporary solution to the problem. It gives temporary relief from the problem. The interim action gives the management time to complete the identification and analysis of the problem to find out the root cause and take corrective action.

Adaptive action: The action is taken after locating the cause of the problem but unable to correct the deviation or eliminate the problem completely. This decision is basically taken from the past experience of handling similar problem and applying the same analogy to the current problem.

Corrective action: Corrective action is the action that eliminates the deviation by removing the cause that produces problem. Corrective action eliminates the problem from that particular area and instance only. It does not eliminate the possibility of recurrence of such problem in other areas.

Preventive action: The action that foresees a problem and eliminates the cause even before it starts taking shape. This is the ultimate objective of problem identification, analysis and problem solving. The preventive action ensures that the problem will never ever repeat again in any area in the same organization.

Contingency action: For the critical projects and operations, a set of back-up actions is planned to take care of likely problem based on past data and happenings. This ensures that the production or the project always proceeds as per the plan even if there are certain unforeseen circumstances.

Seven concepts of decision making

1. *Setting objectives against which to choose:* This is derived from the expected result as outcome of the decision taken. This is the objective of the decision and arrangement of the resources to carry out the decision.

2. *Classify objectives according to importance:* Depending on the importance all objectives are classified into two categories. In the order of importance 'musts' are more critical for the decision making objective and 'wants' are the desirable objectives. Musts are compulsory to have whereas wants are not mandatory but desirable if possible.

3. *Develop alternatives from which to choose:* Now the alternatives are developed in the light of the musts and wants objectives which are translated in terms of certain defined specifications to be fulfilled for attainment of these objectives. The alternatives should perform well-defined specific performances and functions which may or may not fulfill all the must and want objectives.

4. *Evaluate alternatives against the objectives to make a choice:* Each alternative is tested and evaluated against the objectives. The alternatives are first evaluated against the 'must' objectives. If an alternative fails to function as per the must objective, it is discarded. This process eliminates most of the alternatives. The balance few alternatives are then evaluated against the want objectives.

5. *Choose the best alternative as the one which satisfies all the must objectives and maximum number of want objectives:* This is the best course of action and called a 'tentative decision'. This decision may or may not be the perfect one.

6. *Assess the adverse consequence of the tentative decision:* This tentative decision may introduce a change in the system to solve the problem or correct the situation. This change should not worsen the problem, but eliminate the problem. This tentative decision should not create any new problem. This pre-emptive step to eliminate side effects of any change has to be worked out before introducing the alternative.

7. *Control effect of final decision by preventing adverse consequences and by follow up:* Once a decision is decided to be implemented as the best solution, every adverse consequence should be assessed. The adverse consequences should not be allowed to become a potential problem. The possible causes should be identified, analyzed and the preventive action should be taken. However, if a possible cause cannot be totally removed, a contingency action plan has to be worked out to handle such potential problem when it actually occurs.

2.15.5   Potential Problem Analysis

Potential problem analysis solves problems by anticipating the same in advance either by eliminating the cause or minimizing their effect if any deviation takes place. This forms the base of the preventive and contingency actions.

The crux of this potential problem analysis is answering the following seven basic questions.

1. What could go wrong?
2. What specifically is each problem?
   All potential problems need to be defined as to where, what, when and to what extent?
3. How risky is each problem?
   Prioritise the potential problems.
4. What are the possible causes of each problem?
5. How probable is each possible cause?
6. How can a possible cause be prevented or its effect be minimized?
7. How can the most serious potential problem be handled?
   Prepare a contingency plan for each such eventuality.

2.16 KAIZEN GEMBA

'Gemba' means workplace and 'kaizen' means improvement.

Kaizen Gemba can be defined as 'the systematic organized effort to continuously improve the performance at the work area by individual efforts in a group who assemble periodically to discuss their work-related problems'. The Kaizen Gemba is nothing but an improvised form of the quality circle with certain minor deviations. Kaizen is a way of living in Japan wherein an individual believes that with his/her age he/she gains experience and that should be reflected in his/her work area by his/her better performance and a better way of doing the things. The same principle applies to a department or an organization. As the organization becomes older, it should do things differently and in a better manner with continuous small improvements in its product, process and overall performance.

The customer satisfaction is derived from the use of the products and services by the customer. This customer orientation by the Japanese industry has led to small continuous improvements and additions to the product features and innovations which help the Japanese industry to gain market leadership by 'Product Differentiation' which according to Michael Porter's theory is a key to gain competitive advantage in the market place. The Kaizen focus enables organizations to gain global market leadership.

The Kaizen focus on the continuous process improvements leads to better productivity and the elimination of wastages leading to the reduction in the cost of production. This thereby makes the product cost to go down and be more competitive with better quality leading to the situation of 'cost leadership'. According to Michael Porter's theory on competitive advantage, this is the other factor for gaining competitive advantage in the market place. Following the Kaizen principles, both the factors combined together will invariably make an organization global market leader.

The basic thinking of Kaizen Gemba is that there is always a room for improvement in all work and facilities, and methods for such improvement always exists. Several small improvements will ultimately lead to overall major improvements. Kaizen Gemba focuses on the 'ego needs' to bring out the best in a worker as a motivational factor. All wants to reach higher level of achievement by his/her own thinking and effort. At the same time he/she expects others to be impressed by the same and recognize his/her effort.

2.16.1 Comparison between Quality Circle and Kaizen Gemba

The following are the comparison between quality circles and Kaizen Gemba:

1. Both the Kaizen Gemba and quality circle are a quality improvement activity in the own work area of the workers aimed towards continuous small improvements.
2. In both of the cases, the number of participants are around 8–10 and are homogeneous in nature. The leader of the group is normally the hierarchical superior of the worker, i.e. their supervisor or the foreman from the same area.
3. Both the Kaizen Gemba and quality circle are organized to solve the work-related problem by periodic meetings of the workers.
4. Both use the same seven tools of total quality control for problem solving.
5. The benefits out of quality improvement efforts in quality circle is shared equally between the worker, management and customers whereas in Kaizen Gemba the entire benefit goes to the management.
6. Participation in quality circle activity is voluntary whereas in the Kaizen Gemba it is compulsory.
7. The benefits in Kaizen Gemba are quantified and published all over the organization to satisfy the worker's ego needs. No such activity may take place in the quality circle.
8. In Kaizen Gemba, the improvements are to be made by all in their own work by own ideas, own efforts and continuously in small steps. In the quality circle the improvements are brought in by a few who dominate all the proceedings due to a group dynamics. The others are silent participants. In Kaizen Gemba, everybody has to speak for a few minutes and even if no improvement is done, he/she has to get up and say 'no improvement done during the month'.
9. In Kaizen Gemba the participants can talk about their own work area and improvements done by them only whereas in the quality circle, you can suggest improvements in other's work areas.

2.16.2 Common Subjects of Kaizen Gemba

The common subjects of the Kaizen Gemba are either process improvement, reduction or elimination of wastages as well as saving in energy, manpower, etc. One of the major focuses of the Kaizen Gemba is the 5 S of housekeeping. The specific focus areas for the Kaizen Gemba are as follows:

- Improvement in methods
- Improvement in work content
- Improvement in workmanship
- Improvement in quality
- Reduction in wastage
- Reduction in defectives
- Reduction in rework
- Reduction in errors/mistakes

- Saving in power/energy
- Saving in fuel
- Saving in space
- Saving in time
- Use of improved tools
- Economy of efforts
- Machine maintenance
- Inventory control
- Housekeeping

2.16.3 Implementation of Kaizen Gemba in a Company

The quality council decides to implement the Kaizen Gemba in the organization. It selects the departments where the Kaizen Gemba has to be implemented to start with. This is done by the Pareto analysis. The departments that are invariably the most problematic departments or the critical departments whose performance decides the organizational performance, the supervisors in charge of these departments are chosen as the 'Kaizenees'.

The Kaizenees are trained on the basic principles and methods of the Kaizen Gemba. Each Kaizenee forms a group of ten workers from his/her department. The Kaizenee then in turn trains the team members on the principles and guidelines of the Kaizen Gemba.

The 'Kaizen Meeting' is started once in a month on a particular day at a particular time, e.g. first Monday of every month between 11 a.m. to 12 noon. The duration of the meeting is an hour. The attendance to the meeting is compulsory. Each of the team members has to speak on Kaizen or the improvement carried out during the month. The maximum time allotted per member is six minutes. Questions or clarifications if any can be asked only at the end of the meeting in the last ten minutes. All members will tell all improvements done by them in the preceding month and the results of such improvements. They may supplement their presentation by sketches, diagrams, samples etc. The members are also allowed to say that they have not done any improvement during the month. The Kaizen Gemba meeting should be conducted with a lot of seriousness and without interruptions. Every member has to listen carefully and cross questions or interruptions are not allowed. At the end of the meeting, necessary clarifications or guidance can be given. This gives the opportunity and freedom for everybody to improve.

The responsibility of the Kaizenee is to recognize the efforts made by the team members. The Kaizenee should be a mentor and not a boss and should be able to tap the imagination of all the team members. A Kaizenee or the team members should not impose their ideas on the individual team members. It is to be ensured that there is honest give and take of ideas, thoughts and experience.

The strength of Kaizen Gemba is that every idea is implemented to get results. The implemented ideas generate more ideas which can be applied in other areas. This shifts the decision-making activity to the lowest level going in line with the bottom-up approach of total quality management. The Kaizen Gemba is a self supporting activity and does not require an elaborate organization. It transforms the organization into a self renovating organization continuously, improving its performance with the involvement of all its employees.

All Kaizenees submit the monthly scores of their members to the Kaizen Gemba coordinator who in turn submits the summary of the scorers to the quality council. The quality council keeps track of progress of the company-wide Kaizen Gemba activities. The Kaizenee maintains the files of individual Kaizen reports and the Kaizen Gemba coordinator maintains a record of all the outstanding Kaizens.

2.16.4   Criteria for Good Kaizen

The Criteria for good Kaizen is assessed on the basis of the following factors:

- Independent initiative by contributors
- Improvement in routine job
- Improvement actualy done
- Long time efforts for improvement
- Improvement in methods
- Implementation of suggestions of co-workers
- Improvement in unexplored area
- Systematic diagnosis of problem.

2.16.5   Evaluation of Kaizen Gemba

The evaluation of Kaizen Gemba is done after the meetings. The total 20 marks are divided as follows:

- Gravity of problem: Marks 0–2
- Suitability of solution: Marks 0–4
- Implementation of solution: Marks 0–6
- Results obtained: Marks 0–8

The 'Recognition for Performance in Kaizen' Gemba is given mainly to the workers and the Kaizen groups getting maximum marks. The Kaizen scores are displayed on the noticeboards, in-house journals and are publicized widely. The selected Kaizens are presented to the quality council.

Masaaki Imai has brought together the Japanese management philosophies, theories and tools under a single and readily understandable concept—The Kaizen. He has written a number of books on the subject and described Kaizen as the key to Japan's competitive success. The basic philosophy propagated by Kaizen is a mind set to continuously improve the organization as well as that of an individual in terms of product, process and housekeeping, leading to an all-round performance excellence. The Kaizen Gemba inculcates self-renovating culture in an organization where everybody is thriving for excellence in their individual as well as group efforts for a performance level which is the best in the industry. The Kaizen Gemba is a powerful total quality management tool at the workers' level.

2.17 GROUP TECHNOLOGY

Group technology is also popularly known as the *Cellular manufacturing*. The group technology layout is a hybrid between both the product layout and the process layout. It meets the needs of both automated factories and flexible manufacturing system. A product is the final assembly of the individual parts and components in subsequent stages of the value addition by conversion either by the means of machining and fabrication as explained at the beginning of this chapter or by assembly. The final product can be used by the end user for its intended use. This is the level zero. We break the product into the major sub-assemblies, sub-assemblies to individual parts and components till the parts or raw material is sourced from outside. This process is known as the *explosion* of the product into individual components and raw materials at various levels of zero, one, two, etc. These levels show the entry point of the part or the components and after entry how many times it will undergo conversion to be part of the final assembly. After this process, the parts are grouped together depending upon the similarity in the process of the manufacturing. This is known as formation of *Groups by segregation*. The final process is adding up all the identical parts in the same group together known as *aggregation*. This process of grouping the parts and components into groups of a similar process of manufacturing is known as the process of *Explosion, segregation and aggregation*. The production of each individual group having a similar manufacturing process is accomplished by a group of machines arranged sequentially as per the process requirement. The production batch is small, but the layout of the machines of each group is similar to the line layout or the product layout. This is like a group of small plants separated on the basis of process differentiation, but combined together to form the main plant. This is part of the 'Flexible Manufacturing System (FMS)'. The items handled under the group technology are the 'Dependent Demand Items'. Dependent demand items are the items which are part of the final assembly or the final product.

The individual groups of items in a particular group are produced in a 'cell' where a number of machines are laid as per the manufacturing technology to convert the raw materials into the finished components or the sub-assembly. This is the reason why group technology is also known as *cellular manufacturing* where parts are grouped in sub-families of similar manufacturing functions. Each sub-family needs similar machines and processing. Group technology is suitable for large firms producing a wide variety of parts to moderate on high volumes. The processing required by each family can be performed within the cell where the machines are arranged to accommodate a common flow pattern for the parts of the family. Refer to Figure 2.18.

Group technology is thus a concept of organizing manufacturing resources to increase process productivity focused on small lot situations involving parts and products that are similar. The result is a group of small plants within a plant. For a similar type of components, similar machines are grouped together in a process-focused system, but the flow of the family of parts or products would be arranged in a line fashion. This grouping of equipment can be arranged in a sequence that fits the various sizes and types very well.

Group technology concepts can include a computerized classification and codification system.

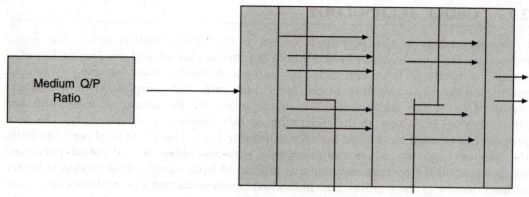

FIGURE 2.18 Group technology layout.

The coding system exploits the commonalities in the family of parts and products and can be coupled to computer-aided design, computer-aided manufacturing and integrating them together into Computer Integrated Manufacturing (CIM). CIM reduces the set-up time to bare minimum, practically a few minutes, reducing the pressure of lot sizes on the production and making it adapt to small lot size production and frequent deliveries as per just-in-time as well as flexible manufacturing system.

2.17.1   Advantages of Group Technology

Group technology is the best form of a plant layout. It has the combined benefit of both the product layout and process layout. It thus makes the only and best type of the plant layout for the world-class manufacturing system. Group technology has the following advantages:

1. Group technology combines the benefit of both the product layout and process layout.
2. It reduces work-in-process by production smoothing and line balancing. Small lot sizes also reduce work-in-process and the inventory in the system.
3. It reduces set-up time by the use of computer-integrated technology and similar individual jobs in the same group.
4. It reduces material handling cost by automation of the material handling system.
5. It leads to better scheduling.
6. It makes the optimum use of the input resources like men, machines and material.
7. In a modernized plant, group technology is the only type of plant layout resorted due to its adaptability to flexible manufacturing system, just-in-time manufacturing and Kanban system, etc.

2.17.2   Disadvantages of Group Technology

Group technology has hardly any disadvantages. However, a few can be looked into:

1. There is difficulty in grouping into the sub-families.

2. In group technology, the flow analysis may be difficult.
3. Sometimes group technology may need duplication of machine tools in separate cells which can be overcome by creating a technology centre within the group technology cell.

2.17.3 Types of Group Technology Layout

There are three types of group technology layout giving it further adaptability to the world-class manufacturing system and giving the best results. The features of all three different types of group technology layout are detailed as follows:

Group technology flow line

When the product families are closely related and the quantity per product ratio is high, the group technology flow line (Figure 2.19) is applicable for the best result. Process routes have close relationship with each product being processed. The group technology flow line is a line flow within a family. It gives advantages of both line layout, i.e. low process inventories and cycle time along with that of functional layout, i.e. excellent equipment utilization and broader job design.

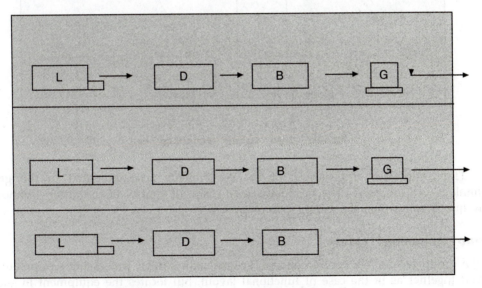

FIGURE 2.19 Group technology flow line.

The group technology flow line gives the best benefit of the manufacturing system where close relationship with each product category exists in line with the processing route being followed for each individual product. The group technology flow line gives the highest productivity and production efficiency with the least cost of processing.

Group technology cell

The group technology cell concept (Figure 2.20) is applied when processing flow for the families of parts are different. Here neither the group technology flow line nor the group technology centre concepts can be applied. For this kind of parts and components, all the operations for one or more of the families of parts are accomplished by a group technology cell that contains the alignment and presence of the necessary equipment needed to accomplish the necessary tasks. The group technology cell concept is then replicated to accommodate different families of parts. The concept represents a compromise between the group technology flow fine and group technology centre.

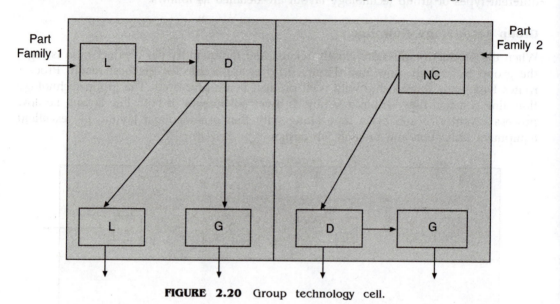

FIGURE 2.20 Group technology cell.

The complexity and variety of the components accommodated in the group technology cell are more. The productivity and ease of control of the group technology flow line is better than the group technology cell.

Group technology centre

In the group technology centre concept, groups with similar processing equipment are placed together as in the case of functional layout, but locates the equipment in such a manner that a part family can be processed by the same equipment as far as possible. This is exactly similar to the group technology flow line plant layout but skips the line or the cell to avail a costly and special machine which is not available in the cell or the line. The part may or may not come back to its original group or the line depending upon the stage of processing. This group technology layout mainly avoids duplication of costly machines having spare capacity to accommodate parts of the other group.

In the example shown in Figure 2.21, the component from sub-assembly family 1 is quitting the line after processing in the third work station and joining the third machining centre in family 2 to finish the operation on that particular part.

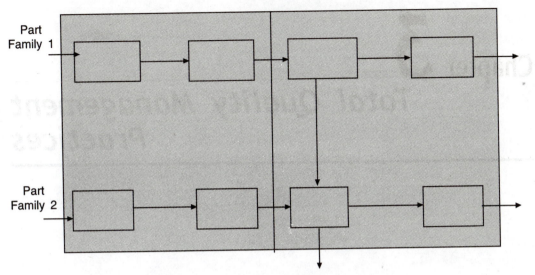

FIGURE 2.21 Group technology centre.

EXERCISES

1. Define and explain 'quality' and the various terms related to quality.

2. Define 'total quality management'. Elaborate on the concepts and features of total quality management.

3. Explain the eight building blocks of total quality management.

4. What are the prerequisites for the success of total quality management.

5. What steps will you follow to make a world-class organization in the following sectors:
   a. A food processing industry
   b. An automobile component manufacturer
   c. A pharmaceutical industry
   d. A software development company

6. Explain Deming's theory on Total Quality Management.

7. Explain Jurans Triology and its applicability to the existing business environment.

8. Elaborate on Philip Crosby's theory on quality management.

9. What are the effective quality improvement processes on the shop floor? What are the similarities and difference between quality circle and Kaizen Gemba.

10. Explain how the Japanese system of 3 M practice of Muri, Muda and Mura helped the Japanese industries to attain global leadership.

11. Explain in detail the Kepner and Tregoe methodology of problem solving. Take a practical example.

12. Explain the significance of the group technology in world-class manufacturing system.

Chapter 3

Total Quality Management Practices

In this chapter, we will discuss the following:

- Value analysis and value Engineering
- Brainstorming, Delphi and Nominal Group Technique. Whole brain thinking
- Quality Function Deployment (QFD)
- Ergonomics
- Single Digit Minute Exchange of Dies (SMED)
- Total Productive Maintenance (TPM)
- Benchmarking
- Business Process Re-engineering (BPR)

In Chapter 2, we have introduced the topic of total quality management in depth. We have discussed the pioneering work done by the famous total quality management gurus and their concepts and practices. We have also discussed the various quality improvement tools. In this chapter, we will deal with the related subjects, principles and concepts with total quality management. Activities like value analysis, value for money, benchmarking, business process re-engineering, quality function deployment, brainstorming, ergonomics, etc. are all the integral part of the total quality management system and practices.

3.1 VALUE ANALYSIS AND VALUE ENGINEERING

3.1.1 Definition

Value Analysis (VA) and Value Engineering can be defined as an organized and systematic approach to provide the required function at the lowest cost consistent with specific performance, quality and reliability.

3.1.2 Features of Value Analysis

Value analysis is a functionally oriented scientific method to improve the product value from the customer's point of view with reference to the elements of the product cost in order to accomplish the desired functions at the least cost of the resources deployed to produce the product. Value analysis pertains to the existing product and services whereas value engineering is concerned to the design of new products.

The main objective of value analysis is to increase profit by critical examination of the areas of high cost in the manufacturing of a product or a service and finding out the ways and means of reducing or elimination of unnecessary costs. The focus of value analysis is the reduction of the material cost while the method study and the time study are mainly concerned with the reduction in the labour cost.

The value can be increased in three ways:

1. Retain the value but reduce the cost.
2. Retain the cost but increase the value.
3. Increase the cost if necessary, but increase the value much more than the cost.

The value analysis is a group activity. The value analysis team is a cross-functional team. If the objective of value analysis is enhancement of the market value, then the value analysis team leader will be the head of the marketing department. If the objective of value analysis is to reduce the cost or the product innovation, then the value analysis team leader will be the head of the manufacturing.

3.1.3 Concept of Value

The value is of two types, namely the *use value* and the *esteem value*. They can be elaborated as follows:

Use value

The product quality is fundamentally defined as fitness for use. Having a product and not having a product makes a tremendous difference to the user. Value analysis is primarily concerned with the 'use value'. This is also known as the primary or the basic value of the product.

Esteem value

The esteem value is the enhanced value associated with a brand or a product created by smart marketers. This is a notional or snob value for which the customer is ready to pay higher. This is also known as the secondary value associated with the product.

3.1.4 Steps in Value Analysis

The following steps are to be followed for the value analysis.

1. Collect data about cost function, customer needs, history and likely future developments related to the product and its use. Determine the function of the product.
2. Develop alternative designs. The selected alternatives should be able to fulfill the functional requirement of the product as detailed above.
3. Ascertain the cost of the alternatives.
4. Evaluate the alternatives in all respect. The alternative which fulfills all the basic or primary value considerations and maximum number of secondary value considerations is the ideal alternative subject to the cost consideration which should be minimum.
5. Recommend and implement the best solution. Identify the control point and devise a plan for periodic measurement of the performance and correct the deviations if any.

3.1.5 Factors Influencing Product Design or Redesign

The factors influencing product design or redesign are either from the customers' perspectives or from the organizational perspectives. Let us discuss it first from the customer's perspective.

Customer's perspectives

The product redesign should be as per the customers' requirements. The product alteration should be customer oriented. The aim of the product redesign or the alteration or modification is to fulfill the customers' stated, implied and the latent needs. The customers' perspectives are normally in four different sectors as detailed hereafter.

Functions: The product or the service should be fit for the use by the customer. The functions of the product or the service can be divided into two types of needs—the 'musts' and 'wants'. The musts are the basic requirements for the product or service has to fulfill, and the wants are the desirable features of the product or service. The product or service which fulfills all the musts and the maximum number of wants is functionally the best product or the service.

Aesthetics: The aesthetics or the external look of the product or service constitutes the basic requirement of any product or service to decide its market acceptability and the value or the price it can command in the market. The aesthetic is a marketing requirement across the products or services to be marketed.

User friendliness: The user friendliness of the product or service decides its market share or the market leadership. Sometimes many of the good products or services fail to take off in the market place if they are introduced before time, i.e. before the customer is ready to accept the products. The user friendliness or the ease of use, service and maintenance adds substantial value to the end products or services.

Esteem associated with possession: As we have discussed earlier, all the products or services in the market have two types of value—the use value and the esteem value. The products or services must fulfill the basic needs of customers to survive in the market. The products or services in the upper end of the market has esteem value over and above the use value for gaining its market share. In this market segment, the customers want the products or services with special or additional distinguishing features for which they are ready to pay. The customers feel that the value-added products or services would increase their social esteem or prestige because others in the society cannot afford such costly products. Therefore, these value-added products or services and the associated brand name become a status symbol in the society. The example could be possession of cars like 'Rolls-Royce'.

Organizational perspective: The products or services manufactured and marketed by the organization has certain internal factors to be taken into consideration while undertaking the value analysis of the products or services. This is pertaining to the optimum utilization of the internal resources used for the production of the products or services by the organization. This will enable the organization to keep low its cost of production so that it can defend its profitability and offer the products or services at competitive rates than the competition thereby gaining higher market share.

Intrinsic cost of material: The main objective of value analysis is to reduce the material cost by the way of elimination of wastages, reduction in the material consumption and elimination or substitution of the non-value adding components in the products or services. The reduction in the cost of material can also come from the cheaper and better substitute parts and components in the products or services. As the material cost is normally 50% of the selling price of the products or services, a small reduction in the material cost is going to reduce the cost of production substantially.

Intrinsic cost of labour: More important aspect than the cost of labour is the quality and the competency of labour. The intrinsic cost of labour is an important aspect of the value analysis of the products or services. This aspect of labour cost and productivity is handled effectively by management techniques such as work measurement, time study, motion study and method study. These techniques bring down the intrinsic cost of labour with better quality of the products or services and better labour productivity.

Replacement, exchange and disposal: The cost of replacement, exchange, disposal or removal of personnel, machines or material due to the product design or redesign is an important aspect of the value analysis, which has to be looked into not only from the point of view of direct impact, but also from the point of view of the spinning of effects on the product, market, employees and the management. This is a major area which has to looked into critically, otherwise it may spell a disaster to the organization or it may also bring a boon to the organization.

3.1.6 Methods of Value Analysis

The method of the value analysis pertaining to the products or services is by asking certain fundamental questions in relation to the elimination, simplification, substitution, relaxation or the standardization of the operations, materials, tolerances or the components. Let us examine critically all these possibilities.

Eliminate parts in operation

Critically examine all the parts and components which constitute the final assembled product, and find out if each one of them is adding any value to the product. If the answer is no, then eliminate the part or component from the product. An example can be given that of a car audio system. In the past due to poor reception of medium and short wave radio signals in a moving car, the radio and consequently the aerial were eliminated from the audio system as it was not providing any value to the customer. Now with the clear reception of FM radio channels in moving cars, the car stereo systems are once again being provided with Radio channels, thus adding value to the customer.

Simplify parts in operation: After critical examination of the parts and components, if it is found that a part or component cannot be eliminated, then look into the possibility whether it can be simplified or combined with other parts and components performing the same function effectively. The best example could be the multi-functional switches in a four-wheeler or two-wheeler.

Substitute alternative materials: After critical examination of the parts and components, if it is found that a part or component can neither be eliminated nor simplified or combined with other parts or components, then look into the possibility whether it can be substituted by cheaper and better alternative materials. An excellent example of the value analysis in this regard is the substitution of heavy rigid steel car bumpers with lightweight collapsible fibre glass reinforced ABS plastic bumpers. In case of an accident, the steel bumper will have a marginal dent, the car will be relatively safe and the entire impact of the accident will be transmitted undiminished through the chassis of the car to the steering rod. The driver will surge forward due to sudden impact on the vehicle and will be hit by the steering rod on the chest with such a magnitude of the impact that he may die on the spot. However, the lightweight collapsible fibre glass reinforced ABS plastic bumpers, in case of an accident, absorb 75% of the impact and only 25% of the impact gets transmitted further. There is a weak point deliberately incorporated in the steering wheel which collapses when the safe impact goes beyond the limit. In this value analysis exercise the driver of the car is safe as well the car.

Use standard parts in materials: Today in the manufacturing and service sector emphasis is given on the modular manufacturing where the sub-assemblies and parts are standardized so that the flexibility in the product range with the reduction in the cost of manufacturing is attained at the shortest possible lead time between receipt of the order and its execution. The concept of modular manufacturing has already become popular in the construction and furniture industry. The concept of modular manufacturing is already being tried out in the automobile industry by various leading car manufacturers in the world.

Relax manufacturing tolerances: The more are the manufacturing tolerances specified, the more is the cost of production in controlling the same. Also, the tighter is the tolerance specified than required, the more is the cost of production in maintaining the same. Hence in the value analysis, the parts and components are critically examined to reduce the number of specified tolerances as well as the relaxation of the closeness of the tolerances. For example, now-a-days nobody specifies the radius of sharp corners. Only one sentence is written at the bottom of the drawing that all sharp corners to be rounded off.

Use standard manufactured parts: The use of standard manufactured parts makes the cost of such parts to be cheaper and quality consistent. There will be no need to keep excess inventory since such types of items are readily available in stock.

Eliminate unnecessary design features: The unnecessary design features that do not add value to the final product or the services should be eliminated to bring down the cost of production. Specify only that many dimensions that are required bare minimum.

Change design to suit manufacturing: Every organization has a well-defined manufacturing facility. The design of the parts and components should be changed or modified so that it can be processed in house at the least possible cost. This also helps in closer monitoring of the parts and components.

Buy if cheap than make: The emphasis of most of the organizations currently is to outsource parts or components if feasible. In case the parts or components are outside the technical competence of the firm or the cost of manufacturing the components is higher in house, the decision is to outsource the parts and components.

Use pre-finished materials: To speed up the manufacturing and assembly operation as well as execution of the projects, the pre-finished materials are used. The pre-finished parts and components also reduce the inventory and reduce the cycle time of production process.

Use pre-fabricated parts: To speed up the manufacturing and assembly operation as well as execution of the projects, the pre-fabricated parts are used. The pre-fabricated parts and components also reduce the inventory and reduce the cycle time of production process.

Rationalize product range: The profitability of the individual products, the positioning of the product at the product life cycle graph and the contribution to the organization are to be considered together to arrive at the product range that gives the best results in terms of the customer satisfaction, return on investment and future expansion. The rationalization of the product range is an important decision in the redesigning of a product.

Substitute labour cost manufacturing process: The product redesign should have a focus on eliminating or substituting labour cost manufacturing processes. This will eliminate human error from the manufacturing process, lower cost of production and provide better quality of the end product.

Rationalize and standardize low cost purchased parts: The redesign of the parts and components should be able to rationalize and standardize the low cost purchased parts so that there is no shortage for these items during the production. The cost of holding inventory will also be minimum in view of their low cost.

Eliminate material waste: The redesign of the product should ensure the optimum utilization of the material and avoid excessive use of the material. All causes of material wastages should be eliminated.

3.1.7 Value Analysis—Areas of Improvement

In value analysis, the areas of improvements are basically identified in four areas. They are: (a) the functional aspect of the product and services, (b) the intrinsic cost of the materials, (c) manufacturing and (d) specification. While the functional aspect is related to the adding of value to the products and services, the other three factors aimed at reducing the cost of production. Certain questions are asked from the checklist of all the four areas. The answer to these questions gives the scope and means of improvements in these areas.

Functions

- Details of the basic functions.
- Details of secondary functions.
- Are all the functions necessary?
- Substitute the factors.
- Combination of the factors.

Materials

- What materials are used?
- Look for alternative materials.
- Reduction in waste materials.
- Standardization of materials.
- Use of cheaper and better substitute materials.
- Price of materials.
- Make or buy decision.

Manufacturing

- Define operations.
- Can it be eliminated?
- Can it be substituted?
- Can it be simplified?
- Can it be standardized?
- Can standard tools be used?
- Can pre-fabricated parts be used?
- Make or buy the parts.

Specifications

- Define specifications.
- Can dimensions be reduced?
- Are the parts oversized?
- Are tolerances very close?
- Are tolerances very critical?
- Can tolerances be increased?
- What type of finish is required?
- Are finish standards essential?

3.1.8 Phases of Value Engineering

Value analysis or value engineering is normally carried out in eight successive phases which are enumerated as follows:

- Orientation
- Information
- Functional
- Speculation/Creation
- Evaluation/Analysis
- Recommendation
- Implementation
- Audit/Follow-up

Now let us take the phases one by one and understand the activities and objectives at each stage of the activity.

Orientation phase

The orientation phase of value engineering consists of imparting 'training' to the members of a department or the organization proposing to undertake the value engineering activity. The next value engineering activity will involve in selecting the 'subject of study'. Once the subject of the study is selected, the 'selection of the project' is normally done by priority depending on the urgency and criticality of the situation. The project prioritization can be done by either ABC analysis, Pareto analysis, contribution analysis, New product development or new system/process development.

The value engineering team consists of members from the different functional areas and should be as heterogeneous and creative as possible. In case the objective of value engineering is value addition to the products and service, the team leader is the head of the marketing department. If the main objective of the value engineering team is cost reduction, the team leader will be the head of the manufacturing department.

Information phase

The information phase of value engineering starts only after deciding the objective or the mission of the value engineering activity. The information to be collected should hover around the 'key questions of cost' and collect data about 'spercial waste' and 'work procedures', and install the facts about the correctness and validity of the data collected as well as the source of the information. The 'sources of information' can be the government publications, government reports, information from the suppliers, commercial information provided by the competitors about their products and services, projects data, historical data, experimental data, etc.

Functional phase

The next phase of value engineering is the functional aspects of the products and services. The value engineering activity starts with determination of the objective and the key question of function. The functional phase of value engineering has to answer the following important questions:

1. What does it do?
2. What must it do?
3. How much does it cost?
4. What is its function/work?

Once these questions are answered the value engineering team analyzes the answers and determines the functional requirement of the products and services.

Speculation/Creation phase

The next phase of the value engineering activity looks for the 'alternatives'. This phase of the value engineering activity consists of a brainstorming session by the value engineering team where a number of alternatives are blasted and created. Then all these alternatives are analyzed from the point of view of which alternative will satisfy the needed function. Most of the alternatives are eliminated leaving behind a few most likely and feasible alternative substitutes.

Evaluation/Analysis phase

The evaluation of the ideas created during the brainstorming session is the next phase. What is the cost of implementation of each idea? Will the idea perform the basic function or the 'musts'? Will it perform the secondary functions or 'wants' and to what extent? Will it work satisfactorily? What will be the savings? The idea which satisfies all the musts and the maximum number of wants is the best solution. However, this idea should be better than the existing way of doing the things and should either add value to the products and services or reduce the cost of production.

Recommendation phase

Now develop a prototype of idea into the controlled condition and conduct the trials. Get the market's or the customers' feedback and assess the customers' satisfaction. Assess the management's needs in terms of profitability and return on investment. Pre-empt any objections for the acceptability of the idea and make presentation to the customers, organizational people and the dealers for the acceptance of the idea. If everything goes favourably and the chances of the idea becoming successful are high, recommend the same for implementation as a validated idea.

Implementation phase

After finding out the best solution, the value engineering team will work out an action plan for systematic implementation of the idea with required resources and in a time-bound manner. The value engineering team will now translate the idea into actions and remove the bottlenecks as and when they arise. The progress of the implementation of the idea will have to be monitored by the value engineering team and the team has to ensure its smooth implementation for obtaining the desired result.

Audit follow-up

The value engineering team keeps a constant watch on the actual process even after the same has been successfully implemented. The team prepares periodic reports after evaluating that the desired results are obtained also under the normal working condition by the regular people handling the matter as usual. After being certain about the success of the idea and its implementation, the value engineering team looks for the spin-off projects in other similar areas and initiates new projects and the process repeats again as stated above.

3.1.9 Darsiri Method

'Darsh' in Sanskrit means to reconsider. The darsiri method of value engineering is the systematic approach to improve the value of product and its components by reconsideration of the cost & quality. Focus in the process of reconsideration is on the quality of the product based on its functions, esteem and cost.

Steps of Darsiri method

Data collection: The data is collected based on the functional aspects of the products and services. The cost associated with each function is also ascertained during the data collection process.

Data analysis: The data analysis is focused on saving in cost with improvements in the product features without compromising on the performance and reliability of the product and the related services.

Recording of ideas: After the data collection, the team goes through the process of the generation and recording of ideas through brainstorming exercise.

Speculation and selection: The ideas are selected based on whether they are previously tried and failed, technological viability, availability of material, etc. and a few best ideas are approved.

Investigation: After detailed analysis and investigation, suitable prototypes are developed on the approved ideas. These prototypes are tested to ascertain performance against the required level of performance. A comparative study is done to select the best alternative which satisfies all the basic functions and maximum number of secondary functions.

Recommendation: The value engineering team now recommends for the implementation of the best alternative as discussed above and arranges for the required resources.

Implementation: The value engineering team now shifts the responsibility of implementing the best alternative by the most affected department. If the exercise is for better market share, the department will be the marketing department. On the other hand if the objective of the value engineering is cost reduction, the implementing department will be the manufacturing department.

A periodic review is always required after implementation to find out the scope for further improvement as well as for implementing in the other relevant areas.

3.2 BRAINSTORMING, DELPHI AND NOMINAL GROUP TECHNIQUE

All the three total quality management techniques of the idea generation follows the basic brainstorming technique of generating a maximum number of ideas in minimum possible time. The Delphi method calls for the presence of an expert in the brainstorming team. The specialized information from an expert is made available to the brainstorming team. In the nominal group technique, each group generates individual solution to the problem or the decision to be taken. Then one or two representatives from each group meet for the final brainstorming and takes the decision or zeros on to the solution to the problem.

Here we shall be discussing the brainstorming process in detail followed by the nominal group technique since the Delphi method as explained above is exactly similar to the brainstorming exercise except that it has an expert or an expert opinion on the subject.

3.2.1 Brainstorming

Brainstorming is a management technique of problem solving where a group of people (6–20) of heterogeneous nature of age, sex, background and functions generate a large number of ideas in a small time.

Guidelines of brainstorming

The guidelines of the brainstorming are detailed as follows:

Create an atmosphere for brainstorming: The brainstorming exercise is a creative activity where a lot of ideas have to be generated for the solution to a problem or to take a decision in any particular matter by creating many alternatives. Here the right brain has to be activated for the idea generation. The right brain gets activated by music, laughter and freewheeling of ideas and sharing of views. Hence the session has to start with a tension-free environment.

Free generation of ideas: The ideas should be generated without inhibition. All the participants should be given equal opportunity for the presentation of their ideas in as much numbers as the individual participant deems fit. There should be absolute free generation of ideas from the participants and the leader should make a record of all the ideas generated during the brainstorming session.

No interruption: During the brainstorming session, there should be no interruptions, cross-questioning, evaluation or judgment on ideas generated. Any interruption even praise or criticism makes the right brain to coil back into its shell leading to a situation wherein it will not be able to generate any further ideas which is the main objective of the brainstorming.

Quantum of ideas: The brainstorming session puts emphasis on the quantity of ideas rather than the quality, i.e. the large number of ideas irrespective of quality has to be generated in the shortest possible time aimed towards the solution to a problem or a decision to be taken.

Pick up other people's ideas: In the brainstorming session, the objective is to pick up other people's ideas and develop them into the useful ones as the likely solution to the problem or the best decision from the alternatives. You know your ideas or perception of a problem and its solution. The brainstorming session tries to extract a maximum number of ideas from a diverse heterogeneous group in the shortest possible time.

Stages of brainstorming

Brainstorming has the following distinctive stages:

1. The problem is explained to the participants by the leader and a short discussion is held on the same.
2. The problem is restated in as many ways as possible by all the participants and a short discussion is held on all such statements.
3. A basic statement or two is selected by the group as a lead.
4. Then there is a warm-up session to get the participants freewheeling. This is carried out with a lot of fun to activate the right brain so that a maximum number of ideas are generated within short time by the heterogeneous group.
5. The leader writes the statement on a piece of paper and recalls for ideas. All ideas are displayed and discussed. The process is continued till all ideas dry out.
6. Now the leader gives a self hypnotic suggestion as 'the well is dry', i.e. all the ideas are recorded and there are no more ideas. This is also a signal to the participants to switch over from the right brain to the left brain. This process is facilitated further by maintaining a couple of minute silence to enable to switch over to the left brain which is analytical and helps in the decision making process of choosing the best alternative.
7. The ideas are taken up one by one and tried to convert them into useful ones to get the likely solution to the problem. This exercise eliminates most of the useless ideas leaving behind the most useful ones which are the likely solution to the problem.
8. The brainstorming session is ended on a high note.
9. The useful ideas are implemented in a systematic manner with periodic measurement of the performance.

3.2.2 Nominal Group Technique

The nominal group technique (NGT) is already explained in the beginning of this chapter. This is a brainstorming exercise with group discussion on the subject or problem. The important features and the process of the nominal group technique (Figure 3.1) are discussed as follows:

1. NGT goes beyond brainstorming.
2. It brings together a small group of individuals who present and systematically discuss their ideas and then select the most favoured one.
3. NGT is a group decision.
4. Each member is given the problem in written form.
5. Each one of the group works independently without consulting each other and develops a solution and puts it in writing.
6. Discussion is held on each recorded idea for clarification and evaluation.
7. A hierarchic superior or designate selects the ideas to be implemented or alternatively members vote for the priority ideas with the group discussion derived through rank ordering or rating.
8. NGT gives equal importance of both *idea generation* and *idea separation* for specific individuals.
9. The session allows two hours or so to complete.
10. The technique allows evaluation of many ideas without pressure to conform to those of high status persons.
11. The technique requires the use of a trained group facilitator and deals with one problem at a time.

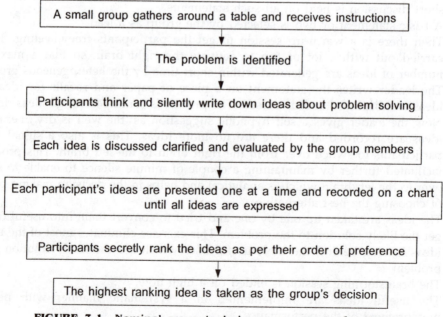

FIGURE 3.1 Nominal group technique—sequence of activities.

3.2.3 Whole Brain Thinking

The human brain is divided into two hemispheres—left brain and right brain. The right brain is more creative while the left brain is more analytical. The whole brain thinking is a scientific and systematic approach of problem solving by making the best use of the properties of the left brain and right brain.

The people with the right brain more developed are more innovative and intelligent than the people whose left brain is more developed. The people whose left brain is more developed are more practical and analytical and are more focused on their work. However, the objective of the whole brain thinking is to develop both the right brain as well as the left brain so that maximum potential of the brain can be utilized.

Both the left brain and the right brain are utilized systematically and alternately to solve any problem or in the decision making process.

The process is normally deployed with the brainstorming and Ishikawa methodology of the total quality management tools. Most of the human beings do not use even 10% of the brain power. Hence imagine a situation if someone develops the usage of the left and the right brain to even 50% what extra ordinary human being he or she will be. The people, whose right brain or creativity is more developed, are with extrovert personality and they talk or laugh loudly. The people whose left brain gets more developed are introvert and they talk less and rarely laugh loudly. The process of the whole brain thinking process is detailed in Table 3.1.

TABLE 3.1 Whole brain thinking process

Steps	Process	Feelings
1. Writing out the problem or need	Listening, defining, verbalizing	Efficient, focused, controlled
2. Brainstorming (Right brain)	New ideas, sounds, pictures and concepts which may be irrelevant and defocused	Sense of expectation and curiosity
3. Evaluation (Left brain)	Ask 5 'W's and 1'H' questions: Who? What? When? Where? Why? and How?	Surprised at volume of ideas, analyze the ideas, value initiatives, idea separation and synthesis.
4. Selection (Right brain)	Eliminate irrelevant ideas, focus on attractive ideas.	It would work
5. Integration (Left and right brain	See the whole solution or concept and fill in detail or they just fall into place.	Stimulated, excited, positive and self-confident.

3.3 QUALITY FUNCTION DEPLOYMENT

The 'Quality Function Deployment (QFD)' can be defined as the process of incorporation of the 'Voice of the Customer' into the design and development of a certain product and service and subsequently standardization of the process of manufacturing.

The QFD brings the concept of the customer orientation to the shop floor of the organization. It makes the new product development process and product alteration and modifications. It is a scientific and systematic process aimed towards customer satisfaction and the reduction of manufacturing cost.

3.3.1 Benefits of QFD

The following are the benefits of QFD:

1. QFD increases the assurance of meeting 'voice of the customer' with a new product.
2. It provides a mechanism to target selected areas where competitive advantage would help increase market share.
3. QFD reduces a number of engineering changes due to lack of engineering knowledge, mistakes or errors.
4. It reduces engineering costs by using fewer engineers and a greater portion of entry level engineers.
5. It provides a method for training managers to improve their engineering knowledge and discipline interaction between departments.
6. It identifies conflicting design requirements where optimization is needed.
7. It achieves individual target values.
8. It focuses various company activities on customer oriented objectives.
9. It reduces product development cycle.
10. It reduces costs of engineering, manufacturing and service.
11. It improves the quality of product and services.

3.3.2 Assessment of the 'Voice of Customer'

QFD is a systematic procedure for translating the 'Voice of the Customer' (VOC) into technical requirements and operational terms, displaying and documenting the translated information in matrix form. Here the customer could be the internal or the external customer.

The process to identify the customer 'CTQs' is described below. Here 'CTQ' means 'critical to quality'. The first step is to identify the potential customers. The organization should find out all its potential customers and then filter the list to create the targeted customers' list. The organization should review the existing VOC data; decide what data to collect and then select the VOC collection tools to be deployed and collect the data. The tools to gather the VOC are customer complaints, customer satisfaction index (CSI), listening posts at the market place or at the customer's end and the competitive comparison. The proactive tools are the one-to-one interviews, visits to customers, customer surveys, data from the focus critical group and playing the role of a customer in market. After the entire customer data has been collected, the data should be compared, integrated and synthesized into the real customer needs. Now the organization should define the 'CTQs' or the factors critical to the quality for the fulfillment of the customer needs and prioritize them.

Figure 3.2 show the different houses which integrate the different processes. The customer needs are converted into the internal measures through various 'Houses of Quality'.

3.3.3 Conversion of Customer's Needs into Product and Process Development

QFD focuses on the most important items that need to be improved and provides the mechanism to target selected areas where improvement would enhance competitive advantages and would therefore help increase market share. The critical information of the VOC is defining the customer's needs. What is the customer's perception on the organization's process performance? What can be done to improve the organization's performance? How is the process performance measured by the customer? What are the performance levels expected by the customer? The QFD process converts the high level voice of customer needs into the real customer needs, which are again converted in tangible terms of the Project Y output characteristics or the CTQs.

QFD aids in converting the customer's needs into the internal process measures that can be controlled and monitored. This results in the development of the quality product and the services that meet the customer's requirements. QFD is a tool to convert the customer's requirements into technical specifications through a series of matrix or tables.

QFD integrates quality assurance into the design process, provides the basis for selecting items for manufacturing control and identifies conflicting design requirement where optimization is needed to achieve individual target values. It reduces the product and/or the service development cycle time. It also develops innovative products for value additions as per customer need and reduces the error and deviations after the product's introduction.

Depending upon the specific product, the technique of quality function deployment may be used as an alternative for the quality planning process. In particular, QFD Phase I—Product Planning translates customer requirements, i.e., VOC, into counterpart control characteristics. It provides a means of converting general customer requirements drawn from market evaluations, comparisons with competition, and marketing plans into specified final product control characteristics.

3.3.4 'House of Quality'

QFD is a mechanism to deploy VOC horizontally through all departments, i.e., product planning, product engineering, manufacturing (controls). Refer to Figures 3.2 and 3.3.

Figure 3.2 show the different houses which integrate the different processes. The customer needs are converted into the internal measures through various 'houses of quality'. 'How' at one level becomes the 'what' at the next level.

QFD is formed by the horizontal bar which represents the customer's portion and the vertical column which represents the technical portion. The QFD matrix is formed by the intersection of the customer table and the technical table, as shown in Figure 3.3.

.The voice of the customer is the input required to begin. This defines the customer's needs and wants. The output is the customer's competitive evaluations. The organization defines the operational goals or targets, i.e., CTQs. A competitive technical assessment is

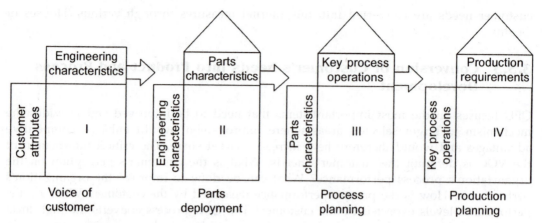

FIGURE 3.2   A continuous process for QFD—House of quality.

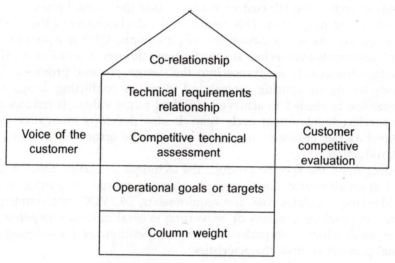

FIGURE 3.3   House of quality.

carried out. A relationship is ascertained between the VOC, the customer's competitive evaluations and the organization's technical capabilities to meet the CTQs. This is translated in the technical requirement and a co-relationship is established among the above factors.

The two dimensions of QFD are the deployment of quality characteristics in product development and production needed to achieve objectives and the assignment of specific roles to individual job functions in order to achieve objectives.

QFD is much more than summations and multiplications. A multifunctional group works on defining the customers' requirements and fill the matrix after good amount of technical and marketing discussion. QFD integrates the marketing and the manufacturing together with the unified objective of customer satisfaction and the reduction of the cost of poor quality. It can handle mutually independent requirements and needs.

3.4 ERGONOMICS

'Ergos' means work and 'nomos' means study.

Hence 'Ergonomics' is basically a study of the workplace to bring changes that make the place of work conductive to higher productivity by reducing the stress and strain of the workforce. The objective of ergonomics is to achieve higher efficiency and effectiveness in terms of work by providing a work environment that is conducive for performance as well as better means of doing the work by incorporating the knowledge of science, technology and other relevant areas.

It deals with studying the following entities that are responsible for the achievement of the end work with least amount of effort.

Study of human body

The human body and its requirements must be appropriately studied so that the workplace can be designed to suit the body and its physical and psychological requirements. All human capabilities have to be designed and directed scientifically for the attainment of the end objective of doing the work in the least amount of time with the least possible effort within the threshold of human capabilities.

Design of the workplace

The workplace should be so designed as to result in maximum productivity among the workers with least amount of fatigue to them. The workplace should have cross ventilation, adequate light and must be scientifically designed for the flow of fresh air and exit of warm and stale air. The workplace should also provide adequate space for the movement of the men, machine and materials.

Design of machines and jobs

The machines and tools must be arranged such that they are conducive to the operation by human beings without any stress or strain to the human beings. The key here is to achieve synergy between the workplace and the employee so that the productivity increases.

The factors affecting it are:

Anthropometric data

The anthropometric data pertains to the study of human being in its various forms with relation to the work being done. The fundamental study pertains to the study of the structural dimensions, which is the study of the work being done when the human body is in standing or sitting position and the study of the functional dimensions, which is the study of the human body when in motion.

Human activity analysis

The factors considered for the human activity analysis basically pertain to the study of the following three areas:

(i) The speed and accuracy desired of the human activity,

(ii) Movements desired in relation to the human activity, and

(iii) The strength and endurance of the human body.

Principles of motion economy

The principles of motion economy relate to the motion of the human body for doing work or performing the task and it is to be studied in relation to the following factor.

(a) Design of the workplace. The workplace should be designed such that it provides adequate space for movement of men, material and maintenance of the machines, proper ventilation, temperature, working environment and other factors necessary for the effective operation of the organization.

(b) Design of tools and equipment. The cutting tools, equipments, jigs, fixtures and manufacturing aids should be designed and made available in a manner such that the work can be done easily, effectively and efficiently with the least amount of effort and least cost in the least possible time.

(c) Use of human body in the operation. The various rules pertaining to the use of human body in the operation in an effective manner, like simultaneous use of both the hands in synchronous and opposite direction, use of ballistic movements, operating the control points without changing the direction of the body, etc., are the important rules for the effective and efficient use of human body in work.

3.5 SINGLE DIGIT MINUTE EXCHANGE OF DIES

Increased variety or small lot sizes lead to increase in the number of changeovers. Each changeover leads to new set-up and loss of valuable production time due to increase in idle time. Mr. Sheigo Shingo worked for many years to solve this problem and came out with a methodology to ensure that all the dies' changeover time is restricted to a single digit minute thereby saving a lot of useful production time otherwise lost in machine set-up. Normally dies are needed in manufacturing a lot of components. All the plastic and rubber components need dies for their manufacturing. The castings of steel and non-ferrous metal need dies. The forging process also needs dies for manufacturing.

'Single Digit Minute Exchange of Dies' (SMED) is a structured procedure of reducing the set-up time to a single digit minute, i.e., between 1 to 9 minutes.

As set-up cost reduces, the total cost of production reduces substantially and the pressure on lot size enhancement also reduces, as shown in Figure 3.4.

3.5.1 Steps of SMED

In 1950, Sheigo Shingo first introduced this study in Toyo Kogyo's Mazda plant. He introduced following four-step procedure for SMED:

Step I: Observe and analyze how the set-up is being currently performed. Carefully observe set-ups and draw activity charts, worker machine charts and if possible video tape the process and look for improvements. Break up the process into sub-

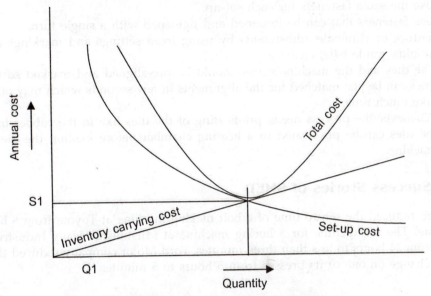

FIGURE 3.4 Optimum cost curve.

processes and look for the time wasters. Eliminate the time wasters and combine the operations for reducing the set-up time as well to carry it out effectively and efficiently.

Step II: Separate internal operation and external operation of set-up activity. Internal operations are those operations for which the production has to be stopped, e.g., actual changing of the die. External operations are those operations which can be carried out concurrently with the production without stopping the productive activity, e.g., arranging for the tools, bolts and materials beforehand.

The objective is to reduce both the operations as far as possible and if the operations cannot be eliminated, it should be at least converted to external operation so that the machine stoppage time is bare minimum.

Step III: Convert internal operation set-up activities to external operation set-up activities. The activities like pre-arrangement of tools for changeover, cleaning of machine and area of old material, etc., bringing and arranging new material for production, preheating of dies and moulds, providing duplicate alignment facility, etc. should be completed before the machine is actually shut down for the changeover. The internal operation set-up time should be as low as possible.

Step IV: Simplify and streamline the activities. After assigning as many activities as possible to external set-up, internal set-up time can be further reduced by simplifying and streamlining the work, thereby reducing the internal set-up activities and ultimately reducing the production system idleness. For instance,

(a) Each work station should have its own tools and the tools should be easily retrievable. As far as possible they should be put on a board on the wall next to the machine and arranged in a systematic manner.

(b) Standardize the external sizes and shapes of the dies, moulds, jigs and fixtures and its holding arrangements so that they can be of quick change type.

(c) Use the same fasteners for each set-up.

(d) Use fasteners that can be loosened and tightened with a single turn.

(e) Reduce or eliminate adjustments by using fixed settings and markings on dies, moulds, guide bars, etc.

(f) The dies and the machine's axis should be pre-aligned and marked so that the lines can be just matched for the alignments in few seconds which may otherwise take much time.

(g) Whenever the process needs pre-heating of the dies like in the rubber industry, the dies can be pre-heated in a heating chamber before loading the die on the machine.

3.5.2 Success Stories of SMED

Mr. Shingo reduced the set-up time of a bolt making machine at Toyota from 8 hours to one minute. The set-up time for a boring machine at Mitsubishi Heavy Industries was reduced from 24 hours to less than three minutes. Ford Motor company reduced the time for a die change on one of its presses from 5 hours to 5 minutes.

3.5.3 Examples of SMED

- Cap of jam bottle opens in half turn.
- Metal clip on wrist watches takes less time than leather strap and buckle.
- Twin razor is quicker than shaving stick.
- Press buttons on zippers are faster than loop buttons.
- Changing of dies on presses is like changing cassettes in tape-recorders due to standardization of sizes and shapes.

3.5.4 Four Principles by Shingo for Achieving SMED

1. No matter what the current set-up time may be (hours, days, weeks), it is possible to reduce the set-up time to a single digit value in minutes, i.e., less than ten minutes.

2. The reduction in set-up time should be done in stages and not in one go.

3. Only a small amount of money should be permitted at each stage.

4. Only through participation of all, SMED can be attained.

SMED along with the computer integrated manufacturing (CIM) has made the loss of production and idle manpower due to set-up time to practically single digit minute or almost negligible. This has reduced the pressure on the manufacturing for taking up economic batch quantity to compensate for the setting time. Hence the modern manufacturing concepts like just-in-time could be implemented. Smaller lot size with frequent deliveries to the market or the customer has become the norm of the world class manufacturing system. All these modern manufacturing techniques have been made possible to a great extent by the SMED. The underlying principle of the SMED has been applied to the concept of the 'modular manufacturing' which is quite popular in the construction and furniture industry and under the process of implementation in the automobile industry.

3.6   TOTAL PRODUCTIVE MAINTENANCE

Sudden breakdown of the machine tools results in substantial loss of production due to stoppage of the production line as well as rejection of the products. Before the machine actually breaks down, it produces lots of products which are substandard in terms of quality due to deteriorating condition of the machine tools. The cost of the breakdown maintenance is higher than the preventive maintenance cost of the machine. Hence the significance of 'Total Productive Maintenance' (TPM).

3.6.1   Effect of Poor Maintenance

The effects of poor maintenance are as follows:

1. It is expensive and harmful.
2. Fixing major machine failures are costlier than preventive maintenance.
3. When machines are being repaired, the workers remain idle.
4. Production reliability is lost due to machine breakdowns leading to product shortages and late deliveries.
5. Breakdowns lead to waste of capacity.
6. Production is lost because of unplanned shut-downs due to machine failures.
7. Inadequately maintained machines may produce defective parts.

3.6.2   Causes of Machine Failures

The causes of the machine failures are enumerated below:

1. Inadequate and irregular preventive maintenance leads to the deterioration of the machine and ultimately its failure.
2. Overusing machines and operating them at excessive speeds over and above its specified limit results in reducing the working life of the machine as well its accuracy and consistency of performance.
3. Improper cleaning of the machines leads to the accumulation of dirt, oil, etc. on the machine parts, resulting in the chemical change causing the erosion and corrosion of the machine parts. This makes the machine to work in a defective manner producing non-conforming products.
4. Inadequate maintenance of the machines results in loosening of the parts including nuts and bolts. The parts may fall off leading to the collisions and accidents.
5. Incorrect machine set-up for operation by loading with parts beyond the machines' capacity and taking cuts or performing an operation beyond the machines' capability will result in machine breakdown or cutting tool breakage or slippage of the job under operation.
6. Materials fed into the machine may be processed inadequately due to inconsistency in the quality of materials or their specifications leading to the rejection of the parts produced on the machine for reason of quality.

3.6.3 Focus of TPM

1. TPM aims to eliminate the six causes of machine failures.
2. It aims at maximizing the effectiveness of its equipment throughout its entire life.
3. It involves everyone in all the departments and at all levels.
4. It motivates people for plant maintenance through small group and voluntary activities.
5. It develops a maintenance system.
6. It provides training in basic house-keeping, problem solving skills and activities to achieve zero breakdowns and prevents six big loses, viz:
   (a) Breakdown due to equipment failure,
   (b) Set-up and adjustment time lost,
   (c) Idling and minor stoppages,
   (d) Reduced speed,
   (e) Defects in process and reworks, and
   (f) Start-up loss of yield.

3.6.4 Features of TPM

Total productive maintenance can be achieved by installing a sense of ownership in the mind of the operator for the machine being run by him for years together. The TPM work can be both routine maintenance work as well as preventive maintenance work to be done regularly by the machine operator himself/herself. The preventive maintenance work should be delegated from the specialized maintenance staff to the routine machine operators and must be done as a normal part of the operator's job so that it is more reliable and regular. It is also costless since it can be done while the machine is running or when it is idle for other reasons.

To make the TPM work effective and productive elaborate training on fault finding, noticing early warning signals of machine malfunctioning and preventive maintenance should be imparted to the regular machine operators. The possibility of machine failure is maximum when it is run for long periods regularly without break and also if it is run more than 80% of its rated capacity, as shown in Figure 3.5.

Cleanliness and good housekeeping not only prevent machine failures, but also reduce accidents, rejections, rework, etc. A major cause of machine failure or poor product quality is the build-up of dirt, chemicals or oil on the machine or the material. The dirt, chemicals and oils corrode the machine parts leading to faulty working, which results in poor quality of the components produced and weakening of the machine parts.

Structured set-ups driven by SMED technique ensure quick changeovers, better quality of product and no rejections. Incorrect set-up leads to material jamming in the machine or other processing problems leading to damage of machine and accidents. The proper set-up on the machine can only be ensured by the machine operators and no maintenance man whatsoever.

Proper job design and work aids ensure that no time is wasted in looking for materials or other work aids. They also ensure optimum utilization of the input resources of man, machine and material. This also can be ensured by the machine operator only.

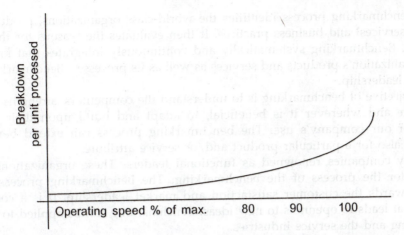

FIGURE 3.5 Relation between operating speed and product failure.

Machines should be as simple as possible and standardized while still accomplishing the required functions effectively. The machine operator should be properly trained to handle the machine and work on the same efficiently. The worker's training not only in terms of using the machine but also in terms of its maintenance as well as various problem solving techniques should be ensured for the effective implementation of TPM.

Machine history cards should be properly filled in and maintained to prepare adequate data for preventive maintenance work. This will enable the operator to plan the routine spare parts requirements like V-belts, bearings, etc. for the machine in advance and as per schedule. Procurement should be carefully planned such that all the parts are available when needed but there is no excess inventory.

When one part of the machine wears out, it affects other parts also. It is better to change all such related parts in one go rather than opening the machine frequently. Hence under the TPM philosophy the machine operator not only takes responsibility for the quality and quantity of production, but also the routine preventive maintenance of the machine.

3.7 BENCHMARKING

A benchmark is a point of reference against which other things are compared or measured.

Benchmarking is a systematic, scientific method adopted by the organization to measure its performance against the best industry practices. Through the process of benchmarking, the organization learns the best practices from the best in its class, evaluates the difference between the best and its own performance and then implements changes to bridge the gap, thereby resulting in superior performance.

Benchmarking focuses on establishing a leadership position in the market. The organization can also look for benchmarking in specific areas of 'throughput', 'a product attribute', 'servicing' or any other business processes or the product itself.

The benchmarking process identifies the world-class organizations, products (both goods and services) and business practices. It then evaluates the reasons for their being world-class. Benchmarking systematically and continuously integrates that knowledge into the organization's products and services as well as its processes. Benchmarking is for world-class leadership.

The objective of benchmarking is to understand the competitors' strengths and how they operate and wherever it is beneficial, to adapt and build upon their excellent practices for our company's use. The benchmarking process can extend beyond the competition also for a particular product and/or service attribute.

Identify companies renowned as functional leaders. These organizations can be picked up for the process of the benchmarking. The benchmarking process focuses activities towards the customer satisfaction and market leadership. It is a continuous process and it leads to openness to new ideas. Benchmarking can be applied to both the manufacturing and the service industries.

3.7.1 Types of Benchmarking

We will now discuss the various types of benchmarking, viz., internal benchmarking, benchmarking against the competition, benchmarking outside the industry, functional benchmarking, and business process benchmarking.

Internal benchmarking

The internal benchmarking process is benchmarking against a particular department and function which is excelling compared to the other departments or functions. Internal benchmarking could be against a process or individual performance under a certain category which can be implemented in other areas also.

Benchmarking against the competition

This is the most common benchmarking exercise mandatory to be carried out for the organizational survival and performance excellence. As per Michael Porter's theory of 'competitive advantage', benchmarking against the competition in terms of the value advantage, product differentiation or the cost advantage for the market leadership and saleability of the product or the services is mandatory for an organization. This is the normal practice of benchmarking in most of the industries.

Benchmarking outside the industry

On a particular attribute applicable to a product, the organization may go outside the boundary of competition and benchmark itself against the best in that particular sector. For example, internationally a world leader in the field of entertainment electronics, particularly the 'colour television' sector, benchmarked against 'Bose' for the sound system. One of the benchmarked criteria of Xerox Corporation was against a courier company.

Functional benchmarking

This is the most common benchmarking process which is concerned with the product performance vis-à-vis the competition. Quality is defined by Dr. Joseph Juran as "the fitness for use" and by Mr. Philip B. Crosby as "the conformance to requirement". Dr. Edward Deming stated that 'quality performance by a product is key factor for the market leadership'. If we combine the theories of all these management gurus, we shall come to the conclusion that functional benchmarking is not only essential but also mandatory for an organization to survive and excel in its performance.

Business process benchmarking

The benchmarking process pertaining to the various business processes like customer satisfaction, market leadership, order fulfillment, maintenance of machines and services, billing and collection, financial management, asset management, information technology, human resource development, etc., is termed as business process benchmarking. The best practices from the same group of industries as well as the best in each class is taken up as the benchmarking partner for attaining perfection in the respective business operations.

3.7.2 Reasons for Benchmarking Competition

The reasons for benchmarking competition have been discussed below:

Stay in business

The benchmarking process enables an organization to assess its position in a particular market segment vis-à-vis the competition. The organization has to offer the products and services at least in line with what is being offered by its competitors in order to survive in its business in that particular market segment. The organization has to do the gap analysis in product and services feature by feature with reference to its competition and bridge the gap. This is the bare minimum effort that the organization has to make for surviving in its business.

Delight the customer

When the organization can bridge the gap and go beyond it in providing the products and services better than the competition at the same price to the customers, the customer will be delighted and switch over to the organization's products and services consumption, thereby ensuring the organization to have a market leadership in that particular market segment.

Become a world-class leader

After having attained the position of the market leader in a particular market segment, the organization can extend the network to other potential areas of its product and service usage. By steadily following the practice of the benchmarking process in the various market segments and learning from the best in each respective area and combining the knowledge gained from each area to be reflected in practice in the organization's products and services will gradually upgrade the organization to an invincible position at the world-class level. This process being monitored and practiced continuously will make the organization invariably a world-class leader.

3.7.3   Elements of Benchmarking

The elements of benchmarking could be anybody who is superior to the organization in any particular area. The benchmarking process could have the benchmarking partner as one of the following organizations:

Direct competitor

The most common benchmarking partner is from the direct competition and it is the bare minimum requirement of an organization to survive in the today's global business environment. The basic benchmarking process with the competition is the product related features and after-sales service or the distribution services. This practice of the benchmarking process is followed when the organization is a follower or laggard in the industry.

Admired company in the same industry

When the organization attains a powerful position in the industry it shifts its focus of the benchmarking process from the competition to the best in the same industry as it is thriving to go beyond the competition. It is of course assumed that the admired company in the same industry has similar customers and it has attained the position of admiration by better understanding of the market and obviously the consumers and customers.

Admired company in any industry

The benchmarking process pertaining to the business processes looks for a benchmarking partner who has attained a position of being the admired company in any industry and excels in its performance in one or more business processes. It is much easier to benchmark processes of an admired company outside the competition as the flow of data and relevant information can be collected easily with the help and cooperation of the benchmarking partner as his business interest does not clash with that of the organization. This will also help the organization to go beyond the competition in best business practices as the choice of selecting the benchmarking partner is wide and from a much better breed of organization to choose from.

Best of breed on different aspects

When the organization has attained a very high level of performance in terms of its products and processes, it needs to progress further and now has to increase the level of its benchmarking partner to the best of breed on a particular aspect. The fine tuning of the benchmarking process will lead the organization to an all-round, excellent performance level.

Chasing multiple competitors

When the benchmarking process reaches a very high level of standard and maturity over the years, the organization may have had different benchmarking partners for different attributes of the product or for each different business process. The objective of the organization is clear. It wants to attain world-class performance level in each individual segment of the product or the process vis-à-vis the world's best in each individual segment, and ultimately wants to attain the best position on an overall basis which is better collectively than any of its benchmarking partner individually.

The organization starts with the process of benchmarking against an organization which is better than it at the moment. After some time the organization bridges the gap and reaches the same level or beyond by activities of continual improvement. Now that the organization has reached a performance level beyond the originally benchmarked organization, it then looks for a new benchmarking partner whose performance is much beyond the earlier benchmarking partner (refer to Figure 3.6).

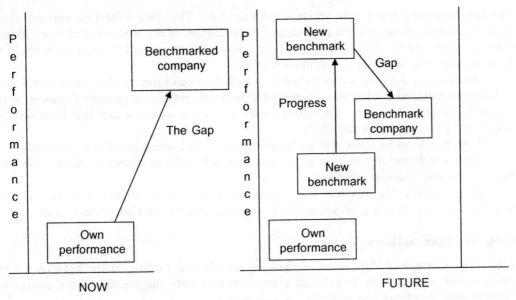

FIGURE 3.6

3.7.4 Benchmarking Measurements

3.7.5 Process of Benchmarking

The benchmarking process consists of four distinctive steps, which follow successively in a systematic and scientific manner, highly structured and oriented towards the specified and well-defined objectives. These steps have been discussed below.

Step 1: Prepare to benchmark

The benchmarking process starts with the top echelon of the organization accepting the fact that its performance in various sectors of products and processes needs to be improved at the earliest. Once the above objective is accomplished, involve the Chief executive officer and the heads of the functions and build the quality council support. Decide 'what to benchmark' and the 'scope of benchmarking' i.e., whether it is broad and shallow or narrow and in-depth. The benchmarking topic could be either the products and processes that are the critical success factors for the organization either by way of market leadership or the financial parameter or both.

Now assign the change agent for the benchmarking process and assemble the team for benchmarking. The benchmarking team now prepares to collect data and understands its own operation. It then documents the data collection procedure and communicates it to all concerned. The benchmarking team now meets periodically on a fixed day and time and devotes enough time. It is extremely important for the benchmarking team to thoroughly understand and document the current product and the current process.

Step 2:   Discover facts

The benchmarking team now starts collecting data. The data collection process starts with the identification of sources of data, determination of the method of data collection, sharing of information and finding the right contact for the data. Data collection could be done through the direct or the indirect method.

The indirect data can be collected by visiting as customer to the competitor's shop or selling outlet, purchasing the competitor's products, reverse engineering, survey of the competitor's suppliers, etc. The direct data collection sources are the mail survey, telephonic interviews and site visits.

Now decide as to what will be benchmarked? And who should we benchmark?

After benchmarking, decide as to how the data will be collected. Now collect the information and analyze the result.

Then analyze the reasons for performance gap with reference to the process practice, business practice, organizational structure and the market environment.

Step 3:   Take actions

After the collection of data, data analysis, synthesis and finding of the reasons for the performance gap in various focused areas, communicate the results to the concerned departments, functions and officials.

Now establish the goals in terms of 'where are we?' 'Where is the benchmarked company?', 'After a chosen time where will be the benchmarked company and where we want to be?'

Now develop an action plan to attain the goal in a time-bound manner and implement the change. Every change has other related consequences. The adverse consequences have to be pre-empted and suitable actions taken so that only the required end objective is achieved without any other negative fallouts or reactions.

Step 4:   Monitor and recaliberate

After the actions are implemented and results obtained, monitor the progress. The benchmarking process continues with the measurements being identified and results being communicated to the concerned departments including the senior management. Monitor the progress of the satisfactory implementation of the action plan. Now update the benchmarks against a better competitor, a better process, technology, etc.

The stages of the benchmarking are detailed in the Figure 3.7. The process starts with the selection of the weak areas or the benchmark areas which are critical for the business success as well as the areas where there is substantial scope for improvement in the performance. Then the benchmark organizations and the areas of benchmark are decided. The performance of the organization vis-à-vis the benchmark organization is compared in the next stage.

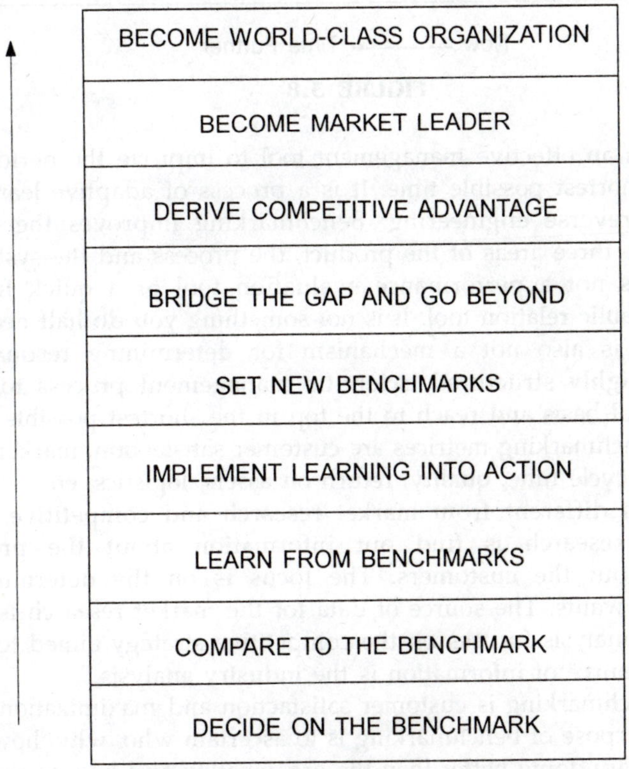

BECOME WORLD-CLASS ORGANIZATION
BECOME MARKET LEADER
DERIVE COMPETITIVE ADVANTAGE
BRIDGE THE GAP AND GO BEYOND
SET NEW BENCHMARKS
IMPLEMENT LEARNING INTO ACTION
LEARN FROM BENCHMARKS
COMPARE TO THE BENCHMARK
DECIDE ON THE BENCHMARK

FIGURE 3.7 Stages of benchmarking.

Benchmarking is an adaptive learning process. The organization learns from the best, i.e., the benchmarked organizations and implements the learning into the action to bridge the gap in performance and the knowledge. Once the benchmark parameters are achieved, the benchmark is revised to the next higher order and new benchmarks are set.

The organization again attempts bridge the gap and go beyond. Then it may go for multiple benchmarking on multiple products and business process attributes and reach an overall higher performance level. It may derive competitive advantage and become the market leader. The organization needs to upgrade on a continual basis and attain the level of a world-class organization as depicted in Figure 3.8.

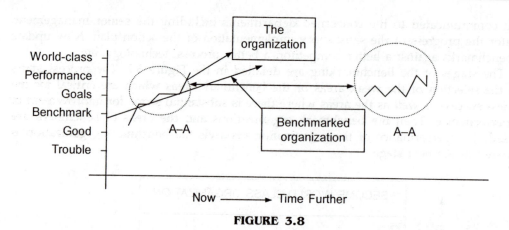

FIGURE 3.8

Benchmarking is an effective management tool to improve the performance of the organization in the shortest possible time. It is a process of adaptive learning from the best and a case of reverse engineering. Benchmarking improves the organizational performance in all the three areas of the product, the process and the system.

Benchmarking is not a performance evaluation tool or a quick fix program, a panacea, a fad or a public relation tool. It is not something you do half heartedly or in a sporadic manner. It is also not a mechanism for determining resource reduction. Benchmarking is a highly structured, scientific management process to continuously improve on a continual basis and reach to the top in the shortest possible time.

The common benchmarking metrices are customer satisfaction, market share, cost as a percent of revenue, cycle time, quality, return on assets, logistics, etc.

Benchmarking is different from market research and competitive analysis. The purpose of market research is find out information about the product/service requirements and about the customers. The focus is on the determination of the customers' needs and wants. The source of data for the market research is the customer himself. Competitive analysis focuses on the competitive strategy aimed to ascertain the competition and the source of information is the industry analysis.

The focus of benchmarking is customer satisfaction and maximization of the return on investment. The purpose of benchmarking is to ascertain who, why, how and in what areas the benchmarks are doing better than the organization and how to reach quickly to their level of performance by learning from them. Benchmarking involves the original research work based on internal and external data.

Xerox, AT&T, Motorola, Ford, Toyota, etc., are world-class organizations that use benchmarking as the common element of the quality standard. Malcolm Baldrige National Quality Awards has the mandatory requirement that the applicant organizations benchmarks external organizations. Benchmarking is the systematic search and adoption of the best practices, innovative ideas and highly effective operating procedures from the experience of others and the application of it for the improvement of the organization. AT&T has a twelve-step benchmarking process and the Xerox corporation has a ten-step benchmarking process. All the processes of benchmarking are similar to each other.

3.8 BUSINESS PROCESS RE-ENGINEERING

Mr. Hammer and Champy in their business bestseller *Re-engineering the Corporation* defined re-engineering as 'the fundamental rethinking and radical redesign of business process to achieve dramatic improvement in critical contemporary measures such as cost quality, service and speed'.

From the definition of the 'Business Process Re-engineering' (BPR) it is apparent that the activity focuses on the fundamental purpose of the organization's existence, i.e., it concentrates on what the company should be and not what it is. This is achieved by the 'radical redesign' of business process by getting to the root of the things. BPR looks for dramatic and not marginal or incremental improvements.

The entire business process re-engineering hovers around the 'business process' which can be described as a collection of activities that take one or more kinds of inputs and creates a output that is of value to the customers. All activities are process-oriented and not task or jobs or structure oriented.

The characteristics of BPR are the customer focus and its view of the business as a system with sub-systems organized around the processes with common goals for the entire organization.

The companies that undertake business process re-engineering are either the companies that find themselves in deep trouble or the companies that are not in trouble at present but foresee trouble in future. BPR is also equally important for those companies that are on peak but are facing a threat from the competition to dislodge them from the leadership position.

3.8.1 BPR Process

Amongst the many methodologies adopted for the business solutions, BPR has emerged as one of the vital management tools. The concept of radically changing business practices promising significant performance improvement makes business process re-engineering an effective management tool which solves management problems. This concept has received both acclaim and criticism as corporations worldwide have geared their processes to meet the challenges of the intensive global competition.

In BPR several jobs and operations are combined into one wherever feasible. The workers are empowered to make the decision. The work is performed at the point where it makes the most sense. Rejection, reconciliation and rework are minimized. The checks and controls are reduced as the focus is more on controlling the process rather than the product.

When the BPR results started coming in, the companies were disappointed as their expectations were much higher from this exercise of BPR. A survey of Fortune 500 companies and top 100 U.K. companies was carried out by Pricewaterhouse. According to the survey, 67% of the companies reported that "increased speed with which new products and services were developed and brought to the market" was the strongest motivation for BPR. Apart from the above, the following five objectives were met. These objectives accomplished by the BPR were the streamlining of business processes, increase in productivity, reduction in the cost of manufacturing, reduction of manpower and increasing the efficiency of the workforce as well as eliminating low value work.

A few myths pertaining to BPR need to be cleared before we move further. BPR is not the panacea for all the problems prevalent in the company which may be caused by poor management practices or unhealthy business practices. It is not organization wide computerization even if I.T. has played a major role in many success stories of BPR implementation.

BPR involves changes that may impact existing functions and egos. The involvement of the CEO is likely to be intensive during the process.

Re-engineering has worked well in many Indian companies like Mahindra & Mahindra Ltd. For the effective implementation of BPR there must be eagerness to tackle the vital critical issues that leads to the quick and effective fulfillment of the customers needs. BPR challenges the old mindsets and creates an interest in using the technology available.

Information technology plays a critical role in the implementation of BPR. Business process re-engineering refers to the industrial engineering principles and practices enabled by the information technology. It makes use of information technology to transform the work procedures in an effective manner rather than merely hastening the office work.

Time has now come for business processes and technology to be integrated in order to function effectively in real time world. An example of this is the airline and railway reservation system. The system is updated and the status is made available to all the terminals on transaction to transaction basis. The implementation of supply chain management is the ultimate manifestation of the integration of business processes and information technology for the effective and efficient operation of the business enterprises. Information technology should enable simplification of the business process and the business process should be perfected by the use of technology.

3.8.2 Implementation of BPR

BPR is implemented in four phases. These phases have been discussed below.

The focus phase

The quality council decides to implement BPR in the organization and defines the objectives for implementing the same. It then set up a cross-functional core processing re-engineering group. The team conducts a 'pareto analysis' and identifies the key processes that are of high priority for re-engineering. The focus phase considers the following factors.

The business vision and goals are normally customer-driven and contain in them the survival values and critical success factors of the enterprises. They also include actions for maximization of the return on investment. Achievement of the business vision may involve re-engineering of one or more processes. The BPR process decides the vital process attributes like cost, quality, time, wastages and the process measures. BPR examines these processes critically for their improvements in terms of quality, reduction of the cost and time. The probable benefit realization opportunity of these processes decides the focus area and works out a rough cut implementation plan along with the details of activities and resources requirements. The process looks for the radical examination of re-engineering with the resultant likely benefit to justify such changes and related efforts to be taken.

The design phase

The organization makes a serious effort to measure the performance of the existing processes on the identifiable and well-defined attributes. First the chosen existing process and its enabling technology is analyzed and its assessment made. Now the viable alternative processes are designed and a prototype of the alternative processes is built up. A comparison is made of the alternative process with the existing one and its benefits and drawbacks are both assessed. The one alternative which satisfies all the musts and maximum number of the wants related to the products and the services in the least cost is the chosen solution to the BPR Process.

Implementation phase

The new solution and processes as an outcome of the BPR process needs proper change management. First of all, the top management and quality council members have to give their concurrence to the findings and go ahead for the implementation. This acceptance will be followed by the massive training of the workforce, staff and managers both from the concept point of view as well as individual training to operate the new process by the respective individuals. The control points and the units of measurement of the new process have to be established. Once all this is done, BPR process can be implemented as the plan along with the focus in the key areas. The periodic measurement of the performance as per the plan and correction of deviation, if any, will complete the implementation phase.

Benefit realization phase

The new process is now actually implemented in the pilot situation and eventually into full stream implementation. The implementation of the BPR process takes about couple of years but its start coming in from the end of the third month.

The final stage needs a lot of business acumen and skill for all the companies as it involves issues that are multidimensional in nature relating to technology, attitudes of the people, creating new organization structure, etc.

Such issues are highly enterprise specific, and the methods to be adopted depends largely on the organizational climate prevailing at that time. The BPR implementers have to be cautious of not imposing too many change programmes with too many goals competing with each other. Involvement of the key individuals, coordinated and integrated effort, careful and optimum- resource planning and allocation are the important aspects of the smooth benefit realization of the BPR process. The effective communication within and outside the organization is a critical element of approach.

There must be a shift from a defensive to an offensive approach which not only encompasses the cost-cutting approach but also gives a strong thrust to customer satisfaction.

Hence the following six lever approach as suggested by Pricewaterhouse should be adopted:

(1) Markets and Customers
(2) Product and Services
(3) People and Culture
(4) Technology
(5) Business Processes
(6) Structure and Facilities

The first two are at strategic level while the other two are at operational level. Such a methodology will not only re-design the business but most importantly will evaluate the shareholders, products, markets, services, etc.

Despite all the publicity and enthusiasm surrounding re-engineering many organizations remain in the state of confusion and misunderstanding. BPR in India is yet to take off and the question is whether it will.

Many companies have realized the importance of the BPR process. The organizations which have implemented it are ITC, L&T, M&M, Siemens, Crompton Greaves, etc.

The main hurdle in implementing BPR is that the benefit of re-engineering is realized after many months of painstaking efforts for which normally the management may not agree to wait. The consultants and information system managers may be tempted to unnecessarily load the organization with costly I.T. hardware and software much more than what is required. In order to bring everything under BPR, the organization may lose focus on the key issue of marketing and human resource management which are low cost areas to generate revenue and reduce the cost of manufacturing.

Hence to make BPR successful, a clarity about the scope and objective of the re-engineering should be attained at the beginning of the activities and all the wrong notions must be removed.

Business process re-engineering, if implemented as a sporadic activity without well-defined focus and long term planning, may not yield the desired result in many organizations. However, India is a developing country, growing at a fast rate. The transfer of technology globally is taking place at a tremendous speed and low cost. The scope of implementing BPR in India is fantastic and the returns from the same are also likely to come much faster than the global standards since there is so much re-engineering of business processes to be done in such a short time for business survival and performance excellence.

3.8.3 Case Study

The organization is one of the top twenty manufacturing companies in India. This company is engaged in the business of manufacturing sports utility vehicles (SUVs) and tractors. Around mid-eighties, the organization had been facing intense competition from the new entrants and multinationals, leading to a reduction in its market share. Hence the organization decided to go for the BPR. The organization hired a costly consultant from U.K. However, the first 3–4 years went only in the process planning exercise. The company faced the problems of reduction in market share, higher inventory, large amount of non-value adding activity, low productivity level, frequent change in production planning and idle machine capacity. The organization further had the problem of multi-tier organization, poor communication, strong departmental orientation, centralized control system and lack of process ownership.

After identifying all these problems, the CEO of the organization kept a ten-year target to achieve the following parameters. (This is an example of areas of concentration of BPR.)

- To reduce customer complaints by 90%
- To increase sales per employee by 175%
- To reduce price of vehicles by 15%
- To reduce cost of material as percentage of sales by 10%
- To improve the stock turnover ratio to 4 times a year
- To reduce the lead time by 70% and
- To achieve 100% schedule adherence.

However, the target could not be achieved as per stipulation and it was extended further by an year and half.

Some of the good results achieved due to this effort of BPR were inventory reduction the axle division by almost 50% in these eleven years. Unloading time came down from the 48 years to 2 hours. The modvat credit was available on the same day. Lead time was reduced from 45 days to 30 days. Rejection was lower by 25%. However, the organization could not show any significant improvement in its bottom line. Even if there was some improvement in selected areas, was the long duration of eleven years and the heavy investment in BPR justified?

Questions

1. Explain the high points of the case.
2. Is BPR a success or failure in India?
3. What are the areas where you can get easy success through BPR?

EXERCISES

1. Define and explain 'Value Analysis' and 'Value Engineering'. Describe in detail the phases of value analysis.
2. What are the benefits of value analysis? What are the areas of value analysis? Explain the method of value analysis.
3. Write short notes on:
   a. Brainstorming.
   b. Nominal group technique.
   c. Whole brain thinking.
   d. Ergonomics.
4. Explain the process of 'Quality Function Deployment'. How will convert the 'Voice of Customer' into the production planning process?

5. Explain the 'House of Quality' in QFD. What are the advantages and disadvantages of QFD. How will you implement QFD in an organization?

6. Explain the concept of the 'Single Minute Exchange of Dies' and its significance in the manufacturing industry. Explain the SMED process.

7. Elaborate the concept and process of the 'Total Productive Maintenance'.

8. Define 'Benchmarking'. Explain the concept and process of benchmarking in detail.

9. Define 'Business Process Re-engineering'. Explain the concept and process of BPR in detail.

10. Out of the total quality management practices discussed in this chapter, explain which of them can be applied to an automobile manufacturing industry and how?

Chapter 4

*Holistic Management System for World-class Performance and Leadership**

CHAPTER OBJECTIVES

In this chapter, we will discuss the following:

- Holistic management system for world-class performance and leadership and its three-step module of foundation, infrastructure and total quality management.
- The various components of foundation, infrastructure and TQM
- The results of the holistic management system for world-class performance and leadership.

India was a closed-door shielded economy for a long time right through the fifties, sixties up to the late eighties. All through this period, Indian industries had a comfortable time due to 'License Raj', which in other words meant that the supply of a product in the market was always lower than the demand. This enabled even a junk product to have a customer. The industries followed a 'push' strategy, i.e., they produced a product to maximize the utilization of the plant capacity and then looked for the customer. The customer-orientation was totally missing, leading to an ever-widening gap between the customers' needs and the products provided. The industry environment was stagnant with no innovation and no improvement in product, service, technology, modernization, etc. Following of socialist economic and labour policy led to a non-productive lethargic workforce. The result was that India developed a conglomerate of private and public enterprises with outdated technology, lower productivity, poor product quality and stagnant industry.

Mukherjee, P.N., "Theory of Holistic Management for World-class Performance and Leadership", Rubber India, Vol. VIII, No. 11, November 2005.

In the meantime, Japanese industries followed the path and guidance of Dr. Juran and Mr. Edward Deming and followed the total quality management principles and by mid-seventies became the world leader in most of the industries and consumer product segment. 'Sony' in consumer electronics, 'Toyota' and 'Honda' in four wheeler automobile sector, 'Honda' and 'Yahama' in two wheeler industry, 'Seiko', 'Citizen' and 'Ricoh' in watch industry and 'Mitsubishi' in heavy vehicles represent the world leader status of Japan.

Gradually the concept of TQM spread to most of the world's industries in Korea, Europe and USA and it was accepted as a 'universal mantra' for world-class performance and excellence in individual fields of operations. The concept of 'big Q' overlook 'small q' and TQM became a way of life for most of the progressive industries in the world. The importance of product quality as well as associated services was universally accepted. The result was that while Japan had a revolutionary rate of growth in the sixties and the seventies; Europe, USA and some of the Asian countries like China, Taiwan and Korea also had similar fast paced progressive production and growth in late seventies and eighties.

When the floodgates of liberalization and globalization were opened in India in the early nineties, a wide gap had developed between the products produced by the Indian industries and those produced by the above stated countries. The Indian industry was caught as sitting duck and on the top of it, the inertia of lethargic working settled down so much over the years that the Indian industries just could not successfully face the global competition. The conventional Indian industries were unable to face the international competition which entered in the country along with globalization and liberalization.

The TQM principles started getting appreciated in the Indian industry as well. But its understanding was very little, particularly at the top management level. Industries tried to implement the TQM principles in loosely coordinated, sporadic manner without the involvement of the top management. A new branch of management consultants emerged who hardly understood the subject of TQM and probably knew only bits and pieces of it. Somebody spoke about 'SQC', somebody about 'JQI', somebody else about 'Kaizen' and some other on 'quality circle'. This bits and piece practice of TQM without the involvement of top management gave miniscule benefit as the 'holistic approach of TQM' was grossly missing. What was needed by the industry was acceptance and implementation of the TQM principles in totality. Juran's theory of TQM and 'Juran's Trilogy' were hardly understood by the industry and was reduced to the sporadic mindless adoption of 'JQIP' in the areas selected at random. The result was obvious; most of the existing Indian industries could not face the stress and strain of globalization, liberalization and international competition and closed their shutter. Whereas a new group of Indian industries who practiced TQM principles like customer focus, continuous improvement, employees empowerment, ISO 9000 Quality Management System adoption, adoption of knowingly and unknowingly quality planning, quality control and quality improvement emerged as winners compared to others. Even many of the existing Indian industries who adopted and practiced TQM principles, survived and gained success even in this challenging industrial environment.

During 1960s and 70s, selling of goods from one state to another in India needed permits and licenses. Post 1970s, the country as a whole was united from the point of view of trade and commerce and there was free trade without any inhibition within the country. With the crumbling of U.S.S.R. and Eastern European Socialist and Communist blocks, the world became unipolar. This coupled with the information technology revolution led to a movement of globalization all over the world. The country restriction in the movement of goods and services started withering. India too followed the suit. With opening up of economies and current liberalization scenario, India has opened its floodgates to international competition. Everyday, with new steps towards liberalization and globalization, like reduction of import duty, full convertibility of rupee on trade account, abolition of license raj, signing of WTO, being taken, the market is becoming increasingly difficult. The Indian industry has enjoyed monopoly for a long time. The market was a seller's market. For simple items like a scooter or a car, the customer had to wait for years. The product quality was much below the international standards. Even for the items of regular day-to-day use like soaps, detergents, kitchenware, electronic items, the options were limited and were of poor quality. Every sub-standard product also had a customer since the government ensured that the demand was always more than the supply. Today the consumers have the entire world at their disposal. The latest designs and models of almost all the products are freely available, giving consumers a wide choice. Under the circumstances, only the 'Best' can survive.

Today the Indian industry has learned to live in the 'buyer's market' where customer satisfaction has become the key word. The customer is said to be satisfied when his/her stated and implied need gets fulfilled by the use of the product and associated services. The simple word 'customer satisfaction' has changed the whole complexion of not only the Indian industry but also of the world industrial scenario. The key to the success of Japanese industry has been their orientation towards customer satisfaction. All these factors combined together have made it imperative for the Indian industry to adopt successful management practices to survive and compete globally.

With liberalization, signing of WTO and convertibility of rupee, the world is the market and India is one small part of the world market. There is nothing like Indian or domestic market anymore. Today's mantra for business success is 'think globally but act locally'.

The key to customer satisfaction is to go beyond the concept of product quality or 'small q'; it is the adoption of the 'big Q' or the concept of TQM. ISO 9000 is only a part of TQM. It is an international standard on 'quality system' aimed towards customer satisfaction. TQM, a part of which is ISO 9000, goes much beyond the quality control department or product quality and embraces in its fold all functions including marketing, production, materials, personnel and even finance.

In fact under the TQM theory, the marketing department assumes a critical function where the TQM activity begins and ends. As far as the organization is concerned, marketing becomes the internal customer for the organization and a channel of communication with the external customer or the actual customer. Operation/production department's function is 'value addition by conversion' and all other departments' function is to support the operation. For each product there were at least 3 to 4 dominant players in each country. Considering that the implementation of WTO was round the corner and the fact that more than 120 countries had signed the agreement, these 3 to 4 dominant players in each of the countries were replaced by 3 to 4 dominant players internationally, thereby leading to a situation wherein 3 or 4 players out of 360 to 480 players were going to survive in each product category. Today in the post-liberalization stage and unipolar world, there are only 3 to 4 dominant players in each category all over the world. This survival rate is less than one percent, indicating that only the best is going to survive. The TQM model for world leadership is the hypothesis of the author's research work. The model is partially based on Juran's theory of quality management process backed up by the infrastructure and a sound foundation. The model's nomenclature is 'The Holistic Management Practice for World-class Performance'.

With my initial exposure to TQM, the all-embracing 'big Q' covering all functions influenced me. The subject interest grew further leading to reading of various books, theories and practices propagated by various management gurus like W. Edwards Deming, Armand V. Feigenbaum, Kaoru Ishikawa, Peter Drucker, Micheal Porter, Philip B. Crosby, Sheigo Shingo, Micheal Hammer and Champy. The interest in this new avenue of world-class management systems and TQM grew further with reading more and more in this field. However, the greatest influence was exerted on me by Dr. Joseph M. Juran and his associates like Mr. Frank Gryna, Mr. A. Blanton Godfrey, and so on. I have meticulously gone through most of the writings on the subjects consisting of thousands of pages. Based on my theoretical knowledge and the influence of various writings on the subject, including case examples, and backed up by over twenty years of industrial experience in senior positions like General Manager and Chief Executive Officer, the initial hypothesis model focused on TQM and the relevance of Dr. Juran's theory of quality planning, quality control and quality improvement. This was at the beginning of my research work.

As I went deeper into the subject and visited a good number of industries and participated myself as a leader of Juran quality improvement project, got involved in the working of various organizations as consultant, studied the cases in depth, the thinking horizon widened further. There are many success stories of TQM but majority of them are cases. There are quite a lot of failure stories at organizational level. Hence TQM is not an all-embracing solution for eliminating all ills and meeting current challenges from globalization and liberalization. These are the reasons why I thought of the hypothesis model of 'holistic management practice for world-class performance', which is depicted in Figure 4.1.

This is a three-step module of Foundation, infrastructure and total quality management. Each consists of further three sub-divisions each, as stated below:

Foundation: Customer focus, continuous improvement and strategic quality planning.

Infrastructure: Total organization involvement, logistics and supply chain management and quality management system.

Total quality management: Quality planning, quality control and quality improvement.

The results are delighted customers, empowered employees, higher return on investment and all-round performance excellence.

4.1   FOUNDATION

For establishing any system, a foundation needs to be built first. The foundation should be strong enough to see through the organization in turbulent times. It should be able to

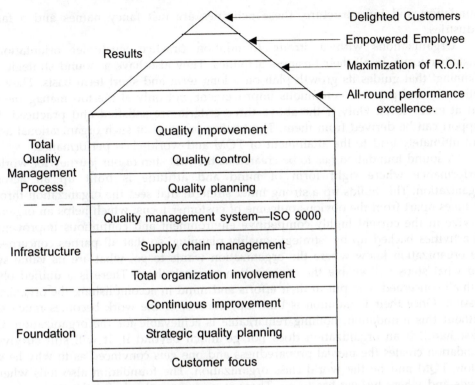

FIGURE 4.1   Dr. P.N. Mukherjee's theory of holistic management system for world-class performance and leadership.

sustain the infrastructure and growth on an ongoing basis. Without the foundation, one can neither build an infrastructure nor an organization or a system. A castle cannot be built in the air. This can be at the most a fad or dream that wouldnot sustain at all for any period of time or otherwise.

This is the primary mistake that has been committed by most of the organizations studied. Without building a strong foundation, they jumped into the journey for TQM with a partially built infrastructure. This obviously has taken them nowhere. There are some common complaints: the company is an ISO 9000 certified company, still it is not doing well; we have more than fifty or hundred JQIP to our credit, still we are struggling; or we practice Gemba Kaizen, still we are in trouble. There is an endless list of the organizations who caught hold of just one or two isolated branch of TQM and thought they are great or doing fine. This is a mirage with the organization which does not last long. They have got some benefit out of it, but not enough to sustain in tough period.

Hence long before undertaking such fads of TQM or little understood fancy names like 'Kaizen Gemba', 'LSCM', 'Juran's Trilogy', 'TPM' 'BPR', 'ERP', etc., the foundation has to be laid down for the organization to understand and absorb such activities in the real sense so that they can derive benefits out of it. All their TQM activities are excellent and give tremendous benefit, provided they are administered properly at the right time and right place and fit properly in the entire system of TQM. Without laying a proper foundation and infrastructure, these activities are just fancy names and a fad with industries.

Organizations with a strong foundation practice 'customer orientation' and 'customer focus' in all their business activities. They also have a 'sound strategic quality planning' that guides its growth plan on a long term and short term basis. They always believe in and practice 'continuous improvement' not only at the top management level but at every level. Only if the above three criteria are satisfied and practiced, further support can be derived from them. The further progress of such organizational activities will ultimately lead to the attainment of TQM and world-class performance.

A sound foundation has to be created as the first step of our journey for world-class performance where right form of mind and attitude is built up all across the organization. This builds up a strong inner strength that sees the organization through at all times apart from the obvious outcome of customer focus, which helps an organization survive in the current highly competitive environment and continuous improvement in all activities backed up by 'strategic quality planning' so that all parties concerned with the organization know where the organization wants to go, what are its value systems and what steps will enable the organization to reach there. There is a unified objective with all concerned who put in their efforts and mind in accomplishing the organizational mission. Once their foundation is built up, the rest of the work becomes much simple. Without this foundation, nothing remarkable is achievable for the organization. On the other hand, if an organization does not go much beyond it, it will still survive. The foundation creates the mental preparedness and one gets convinced as to why he should follow TQM and be the world-class organization. The foundation also tells where one stands and where he/she has to go. There is no universal rule for the time required for building this foundation. It is peculiar to the organization's present status, its size, educational and training level of its employees, number of units, top management and business practices followed. The building of the foundation is extremely critical and may need a lot of patience and counseling. Building of the foundation is a total metamorphosis of the organization and involves attitudinal change from negative or neutral frame of mind to positive thinking and ultimately becoming pro-active. As one can understand, this transformation takes time. Continuous improvement, customer focus and the mental discipline to understand and follow strategic quality plan should enter into the 'habit' cycle. Once this is accomplished, we can certify that the organization is now ready to go to the second phase of infrastructure development. We shall now be elaborating on the three aspects of foundation building, i.e., customer focus, continuous improvement and strategic quality planning.

4.1.1   Customer Focus

This is fundamental requirement of an organization to survive. It is the customer who pays for the salary of the employees of an organization by paying for the products manufactured by the organization or the services provided by the organization. The customer is the engine which pulls an organization. Hence customer focus and his satisfaction is the mandatory requirement for an establishment to survive under any circumstances whatsoever. The customer focus is created by value analysis, new product development, market research to understand customer's stated, implied and latent needs and by practicing customer relationship management and mass customization, if feasible. The process involves identifying and understanding the customer's stated and implied needs and developing the products and services which fulfil the same by way of right quality in right quantity, right place, right time and right price.

4.1.2 Continuous Improvement

Continuous improvement lays out the strong foundation for an organization aspiring to be world-class as continuous growth and improvement should be a way of life for such an organization. The adoption of Deming's P-D-C-A (Plan-Do-Check-Act) cycle for day-to-day running of the organization leads to self-renovating institute, continuously improving its performance by elimination of mistakes (Pokayoke). The implementation of the 'Kaizen' culture of small improvements in day-to-day working in manufacturing, waste elimination, housekeeping, product features and customer satisfaction leads to an environment of continuous improvement. Organized quality improvement projects for converting weaknesses into strengths should be a part of the day-to-day activity of the organization. Quality improvement or problem-solving teams like 'Kaizen Gemba', 'quality circle' at the operator's level, 'Juran's Quality Improvement Projects (JQIP)' at the middle level management and 'quality council' at the top level management with ISO 9000:2000 quality management system forms an organization of continuously self-renovating culture. This organization always remains ahead of the competition and is a leader in its class.

4.1.3 Strategic Quality Planning

It gives direction, values and guides the organization to a level of world-class performance and world leadership. The strategic quality plan bridges the gap between where the organization is and where it wants to reach in the long run. The process starts with defining the 'mission' and the 'vision' statements. The mission defines the organizational value system. The vision is the long term objective of the organization. The vision should be 'SMART', i.e., specific, measurable, attainable, realistic and time bound. The vision is broken into annual 'objectives' or the short-term plans. The next process is to identify customers who will enable the organization to achieve its vision. A detailed market research is done to understand the customer's perception about the products and services leading to the fulfillment of his/her needs and resulting in customer satisfaction. The strategic action plan is based on 'SWOT analysis'—which is an analysis of the strengths, weaknesses, opportunities and threats—and 'PEST analysis' which is an analysis of the politcal, economic, social and technological environment—to ascertain the opportunities and threats. The strategic action plan consists of sensitizing the customers about the strengths of the organization, inducing him to buy the organization's products and services, and converting the organizational weakness into strength through internal research and development with product improvements. It also consists of a strategy to capitalize on its strengths and convert the threats into opportunities by taking suitable action plan. The strategic action plan is implemented and reviewed annually to ensure proper implementation and continuous improvement as per changing market factors or other environmental factors.

4.2   INFRASTRUCTURE

Infrastructure builds up a solid foundation which enables an organization to survive in this turbulent environment of globalization, liberalization and intensive international competition. The infrastructure enables the organization to face competition on equal footing, hold the gains of continuous improvement, retain the existing customers and create a ladder for continuously going up in the performance level, thriving for the leadership in whatever area the organization chooses to be in. The infrastructure consists of total organizational involvement (TOI), logistics and supply chain management and quality management system.

4.2.1   Total Organizational Involvement

Total organizational involvement or TOI includes a process of involving in the organization not only the employees and the management but also the suppliers, customers and society as a whole. It goes much beyond total employee involvement (TEI). The employee involvement is brought about by identification of their training needs, offering need-based training, working out a sound wage and remuneration system based on scientific job evaluation employing time study, motion study and method studies. It should recognize good performance and suitable reward system distinguishing performers and non-performers. The entire workforce should be converted from a negative or neutral state of mind to positive, active and ultimately proactive state of mind. The top management should involve the head of the functions in decision-making and ensure effective implementation of decisions by forming a quality council where all important decisions are taken. The members of the quality council are the head of the functions with the CEO as the chairman. The middle level management is involved through participation in quality improvement and problem-solving teams like value analysis, Juran's quality improvement projects (JQIP), suggestion scheme, empowerment and process orientation with its measurement of value addition. The operational level workforce is involved through quality improvement and problem-solving teams in their work area through quality circle activities, Kaizen Gemba, suggestion scheme and total productive maintenance. The suppliers' capabilities are leveraged through their involvement in product and process development at their end, asking for their suggestions, organizing their factory visit and periodic need-based training program.

   The customers are involved in the organization by conducting market research on their perceptions on the product and services with respect to their quality, quantity, time, place and price, by organizing customer or dealers' meet, etc. The entire process has to be properly planned, integrated and organized in proper perspective to create effective total organizational involvement.

4.2.2   Supply Chain Management

Integrating your supplier, customer and the entire business process on line in a single unified business process is oriented towards maximizing customer satisfaction and minimizing the inventory and lead time of processing a customer's order and the cost of such execution. Logistics and supply chain management involve demand management and coordination of the same with the supplies. First, it is the systematic management of dependant demand items that goes into assembly of the finished product in 'Material Requirement Planning (MRP-I)' from the suppliers' end to the organization. Then controlling and coordinating the entire process of conversion of incoming raw materials and components into the finished product through the process of 'Manufacturing Resource Planning (MRP-II)' and 'Capacity Requirement Planning (CRP)'. The final process in supply chain management which consists of 'Distribution Requirement Planning (DRP)' by arranging to deliver the finished products to the end users through the distribution channels so that the end objective of providing the customers products and services of right quality, in right quantity, and at the right time, right place and right price is accomplished. This process leads to the achievement of the business objective of maximizing customer satisfaction as well as the return on investment.

4.2.3 Quality Management System

A sound quality management system (QMS) like ISO 9000:2000 holds the organization together at all times. It creates root strength in an organization from individualistic-oriented performance to the team-oriented or rather the organization-oriented performance. QMS creates a customer-oriented organization with process-orientation and focus on continuous improvement. Every failure is analyzed to find out the root cause and take corrective and preventive action so that it is never repeated again. The quality management system holds all the gains out of the improvements and does not allow the organization to slip back to the old inferior performance. QMS creates an excellent infrastructure to retain the performance at its existing level and continuously improves the same in accordance with the organizational objective and its value system defined in its vision and mission statements. It creates an environment in the organization where its customers as well as the employees are fully satisfied. It creates an infrastructure where both the business objectives of the maximization of the customer satisfaction and the return on investment for the entrepreneur is assured.

4.3 TOTAL QUALITY MANAGEMENT

After creating a sound foundation and strong infrastructure as stated above, the organization is now ready for the implementation of total quality management to attain the best in its class or be a world-class performer in whatever industry it is in. Here we are going to broadly base our theory similar to Dr. Juran's trilogy of quality planning, quality control and quality improvement which has to be followed together and not in isolation or individually to achieve the desired effective result. Total quality management establishes a 'world-class management system' in an organization. Once the foundation and the infrastructure is established, then only TQM can deliver the desired result catapulting an organization to the world-class performance level, enabling it to attain a leadership position as per its vision. Without establishing a sound foundation and the infrastructure, the sporadic directionless implementation of the TQM tools will not give the desired result of world-class performance excellence. It may give some benefit here and there but not enough to be a leader in its class. TQM has three successive tools of quality planning, quality control and quality improvement which have to be integrated with proper coordination to achieve world-class performance.

4.3.1   Quality Planning

The organization's mission defines the value system of the organization to attain its long term strategic position or the vision. The annual quality plan is drawn in line with the strategic quality plan. The quality plan benchmarks in all areas against the best and draws a quality plan for all functions, including operations/production, marketing, materials, human resources, technology and R&D, Finance, etc. It defines the specific objective in each functional area in line with the overall business plan. Each milestone on the path to attain the respective objective is well-defined on a time scale with details of the performance measures. The resources required to attain the quality plan are defined and arranged in advance to make it available just in time. The alternatives are analyzed and the best alternative for the achievement of the end objective in time is chosen. The one which satisfies all the musts and maximum number of the wants is chosen as the best course of action. It obviously consumes the least resources to achieve the end objective in time. The quality plan gives a definite direction to the entire organization and integrates all its efforts without any wastage to achieve its individual as well as overall organizational objectives in time.

4.3.2   Quality Control

The quality plan is executed as per laid out norms and guidelines. However, in spite of all efforts and precautions deviations may take place, leading to disruptions of the attainment of the end results. Quality control periodically measures the performance and identifies the deviations. It focuses more on the control of processes and produces periodic appraisal report on adherence or deviation to the quality plan at predetermined intervals and locations controlling the critical success factors. Quality control also rectifies and corrects these deviations found to put the process back on line with the expected result of the quality plan. It ensures that the performance of the organization remains at the specified level and does not deteriorate below it. The quality control activities also take care of the adherence of performance as per the plan.

4.3.3   Quality Improvement

The quality council assesses the weaknesses of the organization, its products, services and input resources like men, machine or material as well the impending threats to the organization. It also develops systematic measures of all the wastages and opportunities lost under the heading of the 'cost of poor quality (COPQ)'. The quality council then lists all these factors together and conducts a pareto analysis to prioritize the factor which, if solved, will give maximum benefit to the organization. The two factors to be considered for Juran Quality Improvement Project (JQIP) are that the problem should be chronic in nature and under normal circumstances must appear to be unsolvable. The organization takes up JQIP in these areas and converts the weaknesses into strengths and threats into opportunities. The other objective could be to solve a major problem or a major wastage.

The JQIP team is cross-functional with representatives from each function and the leader is chosen from the most effected function. If the project is pertaining to increase in sales, the leader is the head of marketing and if the project is for product development, then the leader is normally the head of manufacturing or R & D. There are other quality improvement projects undertaken under various other theories like 'Quality Circle', 'Kaizen Gemba', 'Bottleneck Theory' or 'Theory of Constraints' or 'Kepner, Tregoe's Problem-solving Technique'. Deming's P-D-C-A cycle also leads to continuous improvement in day-to-day working of the organization. Quality improvement leads to a near perfect working of the organization and the world's best performance in its area of operation. It leads to continuous improvement and elimination of problems, resulting in a revolutionary rate of growth, taking the organization to the market leadership position and world-class performance.

4.4 THE RESULT

If this model is implemented step by step as indicated above, it will enable the organization to achieve its end objective, i.e., its vision or the long term strategic position that the organization is aiming to achieve. The practicing of this model will ensure the organization to attain 'total quality' in every sphere of its working, i.e., to attain the ultimate in its performance which is the best in its class in the world. This performance which we term as the world-class performance and leadership is the sum total of delighted customer, maximization of the return on investment, empowered employees and all-round performance excellence.

4.4.1 Delighted Customer

The identification and fulfillment of the customer's stated, implied and latent needs will result in customer delightment, leading to global market leadership and maximization of sales and revenue with customer loyalty and support and a long term enjoyable relationship between the customer and the organization.

4.4.2 Empowered Employees

The total employee involvement will gradually lead to a situation where employees will progressively take more responsibility. This will develop a situation of employee empowerment leading to a relaxing, tension-free work environment where everyone is enjoying his/her work, has job satisfaction and is ever-ready to give his/her best for the organization with practically zero labour turnover or labour conflict.

What differentiates a world-class organization from an ordinary one is its people and their involvement in the organizational activities.

4.4.3 Maximization of Return on Investment

An entrepreneur or a businessman goes into the manufacturing or service sector basically because this is the only sector which promises him the highest return on their investment than any other form of investment, like fixed deposit, investment in gold or real estate or the share market, with relatively lower risk. The maximization of the return on investment comes from desired level of sales, lesser product failure and better market share. Dr. Juran has proved through his research work that the top management is unilingual and understands only the language of money. The top management is also fully satisfied by this model as its objective of maximizing the organizational revenue is also achieved.

4.4.4 All-Round Performance Excellence

Following the model of holistic approach will lead to increase in all-round excellence in performance due to reduction in wastages, rework, external failure at customer's end or internal failure at final inspection or loss of order due to delayed delivery, etc. This saving is substantial. This will lead to committed delivery, zero defect, customer satisfaction, maximization of return on investment, increase in employee moral, excellent quality of products and services.

From the above analysis and validation of the model for the 'holistic management practice', it is now proved conclusively that the practice of the same leads the organization to the level of world-class performance and attainment of market leadership. The step by step approach begins with first building up the foundation which by itself makes the organization strong, resilient and performance-oriented with a focused approach for the attainment of the organizational goal. The infrastructure enables the organization to give a consistent performance which will help it survive even in bad times. The infrastructure is good enough to lead the organization to performance excellence. The foundation along with the infrastructure makes the organization so strong and result-oriented that its level of performance is retained and consolidated at all times and under all circumstances. This coupled with the TQM approach of quality planning and quality improvement takes the organization to a new height of performance excellence beyond the reach of its competitors. This will accomplish world-class performance, resulting in delighted customers, empowered proactive employees, maximization on return on investment and all-round performance excellence. All these features make the organization the best in its class and clearly a global leader in the relevant areas.

Dr. P.N. Mukherjee's model of 'holistic management practice for world-class performance and leadership' is explained in brief above. However its implementation needs elaborate knowledge and application of the relevant subjects as described in the model. Chapters 5, 6, 7 and 8 describe each module and its applicability in detail to get the desired result of world-class performance in this regard. The application of the 'holistic management practice for the world-class performance and leadership' is a step by step process of implementing the management tools in a systematic manner. Unlike the other theories, all the three main activities of creating a sound foundation, infrastructure and total quality management can start simultaneously with everybody's involvement. However, there should be a focus group formed under each activity to steer the implementation of the respective activity. The preamble for the success of the entire model depends on the adequate education and training on each of the subjects with an action plan for implementation. Unlike the other models, this model can start delivering result from the second month of its implementation.

EXERCISES

1. Explain in detail Dr. P.N. Mukherjee's theory of 'holistic management practice for world-class performance and leadership' in the current highly turbulent and competitive global business environment.

2. Design and apply the theory of 'holistic management practice for world-class performance and leadership' to the following industrial sectors:

   (a) Automobile car manufacturing unit.
   (b) Textile industry.
   (c) Pharmaceutical industry.
   (d) Two wheeler manufacturing industry.
   (e) Computer hardware manufacturing industry.
   (f) Software development industry.
   (g) Travel and tourism industry.
   (h) Steel manufacturing industry.

Chapter 5

Foundation

CHAPTER OBJECTIVES

In this chapter, we will discuss the following:

- The concept of foundation
- Customer focus and its various aspects
- Step-by-step approach to the strategic quality planning process
- Continuous improvement

For establishing any system, the foundation needs to be built first. The foundation should be strong enough to see through the organization in turbulent times. It should be able to sustain the infrastructure and growth on an ongoing basis. Without the foundation, one can neither build an infrastructure nor an organization or a system. A castle cannot be built in the air. This can be at the most a fad or dream that would not sustain at all for any period of time or otherwise.

This is primarily the mistake that has been committed by most of the organizations studied without exception. Without building a strong foundation, they jumped into the journey for TQM with a partially built infrastructure. This obviously has taken them nowhere. Some of the common complaints are that the company is ISO 9000 certified company and still it is not doing well; or we have more than fifty or hundred JQIP to our credit and still we are struggling; or we practice 'Gemba Kaizen' and still we are in trouble. There is an endless list of organizations who caught hold of just one or two isolated branches of TQM and thought that they are great or doing fine. This is a mirage with the organization and this mirage does not last long. The organizations do derive some benefit out of it, but not enough to sustain it in tough period.

Hence long before undertaking such fads of TQM or little understood fancy names like 'Kaizen Gemba', 'LSCM', 'Juran's Trilogy', 'TPM' 'BPR', 'ERP', etc., the foundation has to be laid down for the organization to understand and absorb such activities in the real sense so that they can derive benefits out of it. All their TQM activities are excellent and give tremendous benefit provided they are administered properly and at right time and right place and provided they fit properly in the entire system of TQM. Without laying proper foundation and infrastructure, these activities are just fancy names and a fad with industries.

A classic example is a leading air conditioner manufacturer in India who was a market leader in the pre-liberalization era. It practiced so many TQM activities but without a foundation. Hence all activities went waste. The moment international competition came in, the organization struggled for its survival. Another classic example is of a leading industrial group in textile and pharmaceutical industry with a few thousand crore turnover where detail research exposure was prevalent. Many such TQM activities like Kaizen Gemba, JQIP, etc. had been followed without giving thought to building a sound foundation or infrastructure. Hence the organization derived miniscule benefit in limited areas. Except pharmaceuticals, in all other areas of textile and engineering, they are not doing well at all.

On the contrary, Reliance Industries does not practice all these and just recently they have started opting for the TQM techniques. But they have over the years built up a sound foundation as propagated in my hypothesis model. They strongly practice customer orientation and customer focus in all their business activities. They also have sound strategic quality planning that guides its growth plan on a long term as well as short term basis. Reliance also always believed in and practiced continuous improvement not only at the top management level but also by all its employees at every level.

Hence the foundation for world-class performance has to be very strong and sound and it should be a way of life for everybody working in the organization. All activities have its base in three things. Everything is based on the three basic principles of 'Customer Focus', 'Strategic Quality Planning', and 'Continuous Improvement'. Only if the above three criteria are satisfied and practiced further support can be derived from them. The further progress of such organizational activities will ultimately lead to the attainment of TQM and world-class performance.

A sound foundation has to be created as the first step of our journey for world-class performance where the right form of mind and attitude is built up all across the organization. This builds up a strong inner strength that sees the organization through at all times, apart from the obvious outcome of customer focus which helps an organization survive in the highly competitive environment prevailing, continuous improvement in all activities backed up by strategic quality planning so that all parties concerned with the organization know where the organization wants to go, what are its value systems and what steps will enable the organization to reach there. There is a unified objective with all concerned that put in their effort and mind in accomplishing the organizational mission. Once their foundation is built up, the rest of the work becomes much simple. Without this foundation, nothing remarkable is achievable for the organization. On the other hand, if an organization does not go much beyond it, still it will survive. The foundation creates the mental preparedness and one gets convinced as to why he should follow TQM and be a world-class organization. The foundation also tells where one stands and where he/she has to go. There is no universal rule for the time required for building this foundation. It is peculiar to the organization's present status, its size, educational and training level of its employees, number of units, top management and business practices followed. The building of the foundation is extremely critical, and may need a lot of patience and counselling. Building of the foundation is a total metamorphosis of the organization and attitudinal change from negative or neutral frame of mind to positive thinking and ultimately becoming proactive. As one can understand, this transformation takes time. Continuous improvement, customer focus and the mental discipline to understand and follow strategic quality plan should enter into the habit cycle. Once this is accomplished, we can certify that the organization is now ready to go to the second phase of infrastructure development. We will now be elaborating on the three aspects of foundation building, i.e., customer focus, continuous improvement and strategic quality planning.

5.1 CUSTOMER FOCUS

A conventional organization neither has a quality policy nor a quality objective. They are running the organization without a specific mission and vision. The only objective is to produce goods. This worked only when there was a license raj restricting the supply and ensuring it to be always less than the demand. Hence in such situation, any junk good will also have a customer since demand is more than the supply. This was typical situation prevailing in India and East European countries including Russia in 1960, 1970 and even part of 1980. We used to pronounce customer in Hindi, i.e., Cust-Se-Mar, i.e., die out of pain. Till middle of 1980s, Premier Automobiles Ltd. was selling a car model, which was withdrawn by Fiat, Italy in 1957. Our friendly Ambassador is a 1957 model car—updated marginally till mid-1980s. For simple things like scooter, you had to wait for 5–7 years after paying a booking amount. Every product was substandard and much below the international standard. The focus was on optimization of plant capacity and quality took a back seat. The customer orientation was totally missing. A scooter would give 24 km./litre and lousy pick up and another scooter of the same organization will give 40 km/litre and good pick up. Definitely the first one is of extremely bad quality, but since it ran on the road, it was still sold in the market. Similar things were happening all around for all the products. In running of an organization the focus was on departmental objectives which could be quite diverse and opposite to each other. No investment was taking place in the technical upgradation, employee's training, technology of manufacturing, plant layout, worker's skill level, raw material quality, etc. All were at the same status when the organization was incorporated 30–40 years ago. The products and services in the meantime have been upgraded around the world, particularly Japan, China, Korea and the West. Establishments in these countries have moved at a revolutionary pace during 1960s, 1970s and 1980s, whereas we in India were almost 30–40 years behind them in terms of the product quality, services associated with the product, the technology and productivity. In terms of customer satisfaction, i.e., fulfillment of the stated and implied needs, the gap between our industries and the rest of the world was substantially high. Hence for Indian industries to develop a customer focus is a total change in attitude and culture, more so with the top management than the workers. Juran's contention that 80% of problems are related to upper management is absolutely correct in this context. There has to be a total change in the attitude of the top management towards the customer satisfaction to begin with.

To create a customer focus we have to take various steps. The first and foremost change is warranted in the organizational structure. In the absence of a quality policy or objective, the departmental objectives take precedence over organizational objectives. We call this type of working as 'vertical chimneys'. Here the ideas flow vertically upwards and are not shared between departments. There are watertight walls between departments. The objective of each department is different and at times it may neutralize each other, like between the marketing and production departments. The marketing department's common argument would be "They are most competent and efficient, but due to incompetent production department, producing products of lower quality and at higher cost, they are unable to sell". On the other hand, the production department says, "They are producing world-class products and as the marketing department cannot sell due to its incompetence, the organization is unable to meet the target. Hence to give excuse, they are blaming the production".

The marketing department backs-up its statement by 'field failures' and its focus gets shifted more towards collection of field failures than making efforts to eliminate them by finding the root causes. On the other hand, the production department backs up its statement by showing evidence of in-house trial against world-class products. Their focus gets shifted to manipulating their trials rather than improving the product performance. It is like two sides of the same river looking at each other all along throughout their entire life, but never meeting at a common point. All the energies and efforts get wasted in inter-departmental fights and the end result on output from such organization is zero or negative. The various departments within the organization are busy fighting amongst each other while the competition is progressing at a revolutionary rate of growth all round the world. When the final curtain of globalization and liberalization was lifted 1992 onwards, Indian industry neither had the culture nor the spirit to fight the world competition, with few exceptions. They were like a flock of sheep before large predators of international organizations. The foundation was of quick sand.

5.1.1 Horizontal Quality Thinking

The only way to survive in the market is to create the customer focus. The more such types of organizations tried to understand the philosophy of 'customer focus', the more they realized that their entire style of work culture had to be drastically changed in real sense. Since time has come, not to make one plus element into zero by introducing one minus element, but of an organization which has a common objective and all resources are pulled together for the attainment of this common objective. Here the role of the departments is to stand next to each other, supplementing and complimenting one another, creating a situation of 1 and 1 as 11 (and not +1 and −1 into zero). This creation of customer focus can come only from a unified objective—a mission statement which is quantifiable and measurable. This can also be broken into lesser measures of 'quality objectives' or 'goals'. To achieve this mission, we need a vision or a way of life and a value system or an overall 'quality policy' which will enable the organization to attain its mission. We transform business into a process including manufacturing activity with varied objectives and end-to-end connection of various processes to attain the same.

We also introduce the concept of 'internal customer'. Every following process becomes the internal customer for the preceding process. Hence marketing becomes the internal customer for the production department, which in turn becomes the internal customer for the materials, human resources and maintenance department as shown in Figure 5.1.

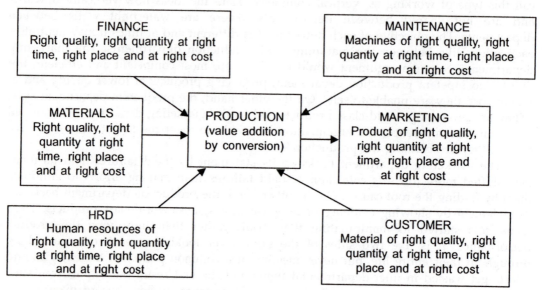

FIGURE 5.1   Internal customer orientation to create a customer focus.

The end objective of 'customer focus' is the 'customer satisfaction'. A customer is said to be satisfied when his/her stated and implied needs are fulfilled. Principally a customer's stated and implied need is fulfilled by use of products and services that are of right quality, in right quantity and made available at the right time, right place and at the right price.

By this concept, the external customer becomes customer to the organization in general and marketing function in particular. Marketing becomes a customer to manufacturing, which becomes a customer to materials and so on.

For a manufacturing industry, the input is the raw material and the output is the value added raw material known as product and services.

For a service industry, the input is the customer and the output is the value added customer. Every employee of the organization and every function is oriented towards customer satisfaction. The departmental objectives are no more as important as the unified organizational objective of 'customer satisfaction'. This concept is known as the 'horizontal quality thinking', as shown in Figure 5.2. This has already been explained in detail in Chapter 1.

5.1.2   Customer Satisfaction

Customer satisfaction is talked about much but never practiced by the Indian industries. Whereas in Europe and USA, almost everyday a consumer would receive a number of salesmen trying to give him free samples, asking for his opinion on some product or the

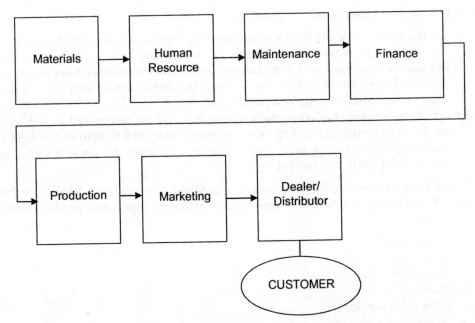

FIGURE 5.2 Horizontal quality thinking.

other. An Indian consumer never experiences even one such sales call in the whole year. Indian industries rarely make an attempt to understand what the customers need. They assume the customers' requirements, thereby making an ass of both the market as well as themselves. In the current situation of liberalization and globalization leading to intense competition, the organization with poor knowledge of customers' needs and wants has no option but to close down. Customer satisfaction is the key parameter to business success in this contemporary environment.

The root to customer satisfaction begins with training on topics like

- The need to satisfy customers
- Accurate demand measurement and sales forecasting
- Buyer seller dyad and various selling theories
- Market research
- Customer relationship management (CRM)
- Technology management
- Environment scanning
- Marketing in post WTO environment
- Value analysis
- Logistics and supply chain management (SCM)
- Excellent customer response (ECR), etc.

It will be followed by conducting a market research by breaking up the product into various attributes and asking customers to rank the attributes as per the hierarchy of his preference in selecting a product. This is followed by asking his opinion on their preferential attributes, and the performance of the company's product vis-à-vis the competitors' products on these attributes.

It will be two-pronged action plan:

(a) On the preferential attributes where the organization scores over the competitors, to design an advertising campaign sensitizing the customer about the organization's edge over the competitors. If this attributes happens to be the preferred attribute number one or two, the organization definitely has better competitive edge than its competitors.

(b) Attributes on which the company scores low will be recognized as the weakness of the organization. The organization must benchmark against the best in the market and develop product features improving over the present status and be one of the best in the market.

To elaborate on this, let us take an example of a colour television set. I have conducted a number of workshops on this. We first break up the product into product feature as attributes, i.e.,

- Picture quality
- Price
- Aesthetics
- Sound
- After-sales service
- Number of functions
- Number of channels
- Weight
- Trouble-free performance
- Reliability
- Dealership network

Out of these eleven features, the customer invariably chooses picture quality and sound as the most sought after attributes leading to firming up the decision to buy or use a particular brand of CTV. This is the first part of the action plan.

In the second part, ask the customers whom they think as the world's best in this category of picture quality and sound. The feedback collected from the sample population in the workshop, rate Sony as the best in picture quality and Bose in terms of sound. Now if a manufacturer of CTV comes out with product with picture quality as good as Sony and sound system as good as Bose, it will definitely dominate the market, as this is the correct interpretation of the word right 'quality'.

The manufacturer has to buy best quality of raw materials and develop a process producing this highest level of picture quality and sound system which has to be the world's best to gain market leadership and world-class performance. Now along with this, the organization has to compile and find out the right quantity and make the CTV available at the right time, right place and at the right price to maximize customer satisfaction.

5.1.3 Value Analysis

Value analysis is an extremely important management technique which achieves both the organizational key objectives of 'maximization of the customer satisfaction' and the 'maximization of the return on investment' by reducing the cost of production. In short, value analysis provides the customer 'value for money' for the product or the services that the customer uses.

After the feedback about customers' requirement, conduct a critical analysis of the product by 'value analysis' and look for the possibilities of cost reduction retaining the same customer satisfaction or try to enhance the customer satisfaction at the same cost. Value analysis has been discussed in detail in Chapter 3.

The procedure of value analysis is detailed below:

- Eliminate the parts which do not add any value to the product
- Look for combining functions of two or more parts into one and eliminate the other
- Substitute the existing part with a part of cheaper and better material
- Try to standardize
- Try to simplify
- Try to relax the tolerances
- Try to reduce the specified dimensions
- Eliminate the dimensions that are not critical
- Add parts that add to product feature and add maximum value than the cost of introducing it
- Reduce the number of operations required to manufacture the parts
- Eliminate super finishing operations if not required

5.1.4 Maximization of 'Customer Service'

The organization should also look for 'maximization of customer service' by proper strategy and steps to make the product available at right time, right place, of right quality, right quantity and right price. This is possible only when the organization understands the customers' needs and if it can speedily react to change as per the customers' needs. In fact the organization should be proactive in assessing the customers' service requirements and position the products and its back-up services accordingly. In this respect, logistics and supply chain management play a lead role in maximizing the customer services at least cost, thereby maximizing the return on the investment also. Compression of the supply chain leads to not only reduction of cost and enhancement of margin but also maximization of customer satisfaction.

The customer focus will enable the organization to become the market leader in its operational segment. The organization should consolidate and retain the position of market leadership by constant customer feedback, change in technology, development of better substitute product, cutting down on 'cost of poor quality' and reduction in wastage, compression of the supply chain, etc. on a continuous basis. The next step for the organization is obviously to extend its network in other market segments as well. However, the process should be step by step and steady, that is retaining the current position, consolidating the same and then improving it on a continual basis.

5.2 STRATEGIC QUALITY PLANNING

This is the strategic point for an organization to create the foundation in its journey towards TQM and world-class performance leading to world leadership. While the other two steps of customer focus and continuous improvement are organization wide activities involving everybody, strategic quality planning is a management activity where the top management gets involved from the very beginning. The outcome of strategic quality planning is a well-defined mission statement and the guiding principle and value system for the organization, i.e., the vision statement. The mission statement indicates where the organization dreams to be in the long run ultimately. The output of strategic quality planning is a well laid out action plan which is focused, systematic, scientific and oriented towards the end objective. Where the organization will rise up to will largely depend on the activity of strategic quality planning and how well it is done and in what depth. The steps of the strategic quality planning process are shown in Figure 5.3.

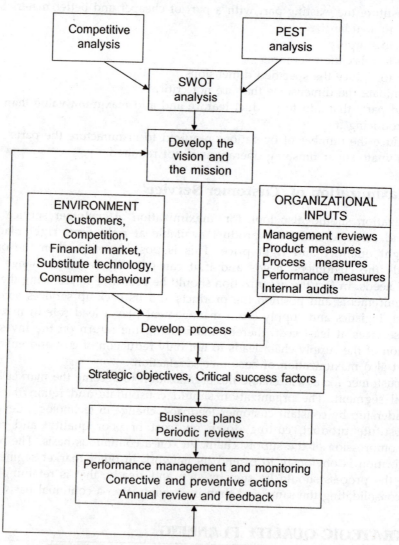

FIGURE 5.3 Strategic quality planning process.

5.2.1 SWOT Analysis

The term 'SWOT' is an acronym for 'strength, weakness, opportunity and threat'. Whereas accessing the strength or weakness is vis-à-vis the competition, i.e., the opportunity or threat is vis-à-vis the environmental factors, i.e., outcome of the PEST analysis. The SWOT analysis provides a body of knowledge that is needed to undertake the strategic planning process. The organization should work out internal corrective steps to overcome the weaknesses and develop proper planning to counter the threats. Whereas the proper marketing effort of advertising and sales promotion sensitizes the customers about the strengths of the organization, the weaknesses have to be eliminated by undertaking 'Quality Improvement Projects' and converting the weaknesses into the strength. The strategic plan should maximize the exploitation of opportunities and effectively avert the threat.

Competitive analysis

To determine the company's strength and weakness vis-à-vis the competitors, a competitive analysis is mandatory. According to Michael Porter, "a little bit extra in key product attributes than the competitors gives an organization competitive advantage". Here, by competition, we not only look at the existing competitors, but also threat from low cost and better substitute products, threat from new entrants and the technological innovators in the same product category. However, competitive advantage in the vital few product attributes, which the customers prefers maximum, decides the leadership position in the market.

The outcome of competitive analysis is the identification of the strengths and weaknesses of the organization.

Identifying organizational strengths: The organizational strength is 'any capability or characteristic giving the organization competitive advantage'. It could be:

- Financial strength
- Market reputation
- Higher quality of products
- Higher quality of services
- Wide product range
- Cost leadership
- Strong management team
- Efficient technological process
- Talented workforce
- Faster time to market
- Excellent customer relationship
- Ease of availability

There could be many more strengths identifiable in different situations.

Identifying organizational weakness: An organizational weakness is 'an inadequate characteristic or lack of capability which puts the organization in a disadvantageous position'. The organizational weaknesses could be any of the following factors:

- Obsolete plant and machinery
- Obsolete process
- Inadequately trained workforce
- Poor working condition
- Narrow product line
- Poor image in market place
- Weak financial management
- Poorly managed organization
- Higher cost of production
- Poor quality in products and services

The strength and weakness assessment is always carried out vis-à-vis the competition existing in the market. The strength and weakness is a dynamic criteria to some extent. It could be also a certain market segment specific or a customer specific. While the strength and weakness of a product attribute of one manufacturer vis-à-vis the other is fairly stable, their relative importance varies depending on the market segment. For example, a food product with high calorific value has an advantage to a competitor's product for the market segment of growing children in the age group of 5–20 years and sick whereas the same product is at a disadvantage in the market segment of middle-aged affluent class where obesity is common. Hence for correct analysis of strength and weakness, the preferred market segment of the organization has to be kept into the purview.

'PEST' analysis

To ascertain the opportunity and threats to an organization, the correct assessment of the environment, or environment scanning, is must. The environment factors are influenced by four situations, i.e., political, economic, social and technological factors. Popularly known as 'PEST analysis'. The political factor involves Govt. Stability, Govt. Policies, political situation etc. The economic factors are signing of WTO, member of Economic Block, buying power of consumers. Economic factors influence the environmental factors of opportunity and threat. The social factors include cultural influences, social influences on the buying behaviour, preferences, food habits etc. The technological factor of environment analysis is a key to success of an organization. The technological innovation keeps an organization ahead of the competitions.

PEST analysis helps identify the external opportunities and threats.

Identifying external opportunities.   These are the opportunities in the organization's business environment that gives scope for growth and/or for gaining a sustainable competitive advantage. Some examples could be:

- Availability of new customers
- Growing market for existing or potential/planned products
- Ability to diversify into related products/services
- Removal of growth-inhibitive barriers
- Failure of competition
- New productivity or quality enhancing technologies coming on line
- A new government regulation, increasing demand of product

Of course, there could be many more opportunities existing in a particular situation.

Identifying external threats. An external threat is a factor in an organization's business environment that is detrimental to the organizational growth and is likely to put it at a disadvantage. The threats could be:

- Technological invention of a new substitute product
- A foreign government's adverse economic policy affecting the company's products
- Diversification by a high profile organization into the company's existing products
- New regulation putting some of the company's advantageous resources unusable (e.g., use of child labour)
- Slowdown in market growth
- Introduction of costly new regulatory requirements
- Incompetent supplier base
- Change in taste and habits of consumers
- Potentially damaging demographic changes

The threats can emerge from change in any of the four factors, viz., political, economic, social or technological. This criteria of opportunity and threat is again a dynamic factor depending on the market segment in purview and the organization's focus on that particular market segment.

5.2.2 Developing the Vision

Vision can be defined as 'the organization's guiding force', the dream of what it wants to become, and the reason for being there should be apparent. A vision is the force which keeps an organization moving. A vision statement defines the desire, the value system, the future state of the organization and the entire organization's structures, policies, processes, resources, culminating into the realization of the mission. A vision can be viewed as the ultimate goal, one that may take 5 years or more to achieve. Some examples of the vision statement of companies are given below.

DuPont. Our vision is to be the world's most dynamic science company, creating sustainable solutions essential to a better, safer and healthier life for people everywhere.

Compaq. To be the leading supplier of PCs and PC servers in all customer segments.

Nokia. LIFE GOES MOBILE!
Ten years ago, Nokia had a vision that seemed revolutionary for the times: Voice Goes Mobile! As history shows, this vision became a reality in an incredibly short amount of time. With more than 1.6 billion mobile phone subscriptions globally – and more mobile phones than fixed-line phones in use—we see that mobility has transformed the way people live their lives.

Today, Nokia sees mobility expanding into new areas such as imaging, games, entertainment, media and enterprises. There are new mobile services already taking our industry forward and creating new opportunities. At the same time, major opportunities still exist in bringing mobile voice to completely new users. So today Nokia's vision can be 'Life Goes Mobile'.

This is an excellent example of a critical role played by the vision statement for the world leadership of an organization.

ERICSSON.   To be the Prime Driver in an all-communicating world.

Maruti.   The leader in the Indian Automobile Industry, Creating Customer delight and Shareholder's Wealth; a pride of India.

P&G.   Be, and be recognized as the best consumer products and services company in the world.

K.J. Somaiya Institute of Management Studies and Research. To be among the top 50 management schools in Asia by the year 2015.

From the above example, it can be observed that vision statements have the following characteristics:

- It is simple and easily understood by all stakeholders
- All the vision statements recognize quality
- Is a guiding force setting a target, which is challenging but attainable
- Performance against the vision is measurable
- It is exciting yet tangible
- It deals unity of purpose among all stakesholders

The vision of an organization should be 'SMART', i.e., specific, measurable, attainable, realistic and time bound.

5.2.3   Developing the Mission

'Mission' is the next step and a good mission statement has the following characteristics:

- It describes 'who' the organization is, 'what' it does, and 'where' it is going. 'Who' describes the organization and its customers.
- Mission statement should be brief and comprehensive.
- Words should be simple, easy to understand and descriptive.
- A company must avoid 'how' statements.

A mission is defined as a 'statement of the organization's purpose and scope of its operations, i.e., 'the business we are in'. It describes the organization's value system. The mission statement tells the organizational philosophy and value system with which the organization is going to achieve its vision. The concept of a mission statement has been illustrated below with the help of examples of mission statements of some of the leading corporates.

NOKIA: Connecting People.
By connecting people, we help fulfill a fundamental human need for social connections and contact. Nokia builds bridges between people—both when they are far apart and face-to-face—and also bridges the gap between people and the information they need.

Intel.   To do a great job for our customers, employees and stockholders by being the preeminent building block supplier to the worldwide Internet economy.

Sudaram fasteners. The company's mission, driven by quality and technology initiatives, is of becoming a vibrant, dynamic, customer-oriented global company. The major initiatives of growth will be through strategic acquisitions and diversifications into new product areas which will help the company in placing itself in a position of strength in various parts of the world in delivering value to its customers.

The company is committed to increasing the stakeholders value and wealth by consistent performance year after year and giving maximum return on their investment.

The company considers human resources as its invaluable asset and provides a platform to its employees to improve their performance and grow as the company grows.

K.J. Somaiya Institute of Management Studies and Research

- To impart state-of-the-art education and skills in management to students and working professionals.
- To conduct research and consultancy in the field of management, thus benefiting society, industry and students.
- To cultivate and practice integrity and principles of good governance in all activities.

The mission statement sets forth what an organization is doing today and based on that, i.e., the organization's core competence, examine and analyze the external and internal environment and think strategically for the future success in business. The objective in mission statement is on the basis of current quality culture and current quality system, to develop and deploy a strategy to improve the market standing on quality, reduce the cost of poor quality and thereby excel in 'company wide assessment in quality'.

The recent trend in the industry is to have a common mission and vision statement and rather the content of both the vision and mission statements is combined into one statement so that the statement becomes simple, integrated and easily understood. This is a better and more effective trend as it removes the jargon of the vision and the mission statement and make it easily acceptable and easy-to-implement by even the ordinary workers.

5.2.4 Environmental Factors

Prior to strategy formulation, certain external and internal data input analysis is carried out. The external inputs are with regard to the following aspects:

Customers

The customers' stated and implied needs are ascertained through sample survey, market research questionnaire and personal interview. These stated and implied needs are categorized into the 'vital few' and 'trivial many' in order of importance towards the fulfillment of customer needs leading to customer satisfaction. It is apparent that focus will be to excel on the vital few parameters as compared to the competition.

Competition

The rating of the company's performance as 5 or 6 or any other number does not indicate anything; what matters is that whether this number is better or worse than the competition. If it is better, the company will get business and if it is worse, the company will lose business. This differentiation on the positive side is termed as 'competitive advantage', the reverse is the competitive disadvantage. In this regard the feature strategy of the competitors and the new entrants, including substitute products, are of critical importance.

Financial market

The financial viability of the existing enterprise as well as the new diversification and/or expansion, government fiscal and monetary policies, RBI regulations, banking norms, return on investment, fund flow and cash flow positions with reference to the economic environment prevailing in the country are all taken into consideration and analyzed for formulation of the strategy. The favourable mix of financial parameters maximizing the return on investment will be what the strategy has to take into consideration.

Substitute technology

It is most difficult thing to predict about the future. Most of the technological innovations are kept confidential till the last moment and predicting technological advancement on long term basis is practically impossible. The best that can be done in this regard in keeping oneself abreast of the latest technical innovations in the world pertaining to the company's current products as well as the substitute products. The technological innovations puts a sudden stress on the company's market standing as it needs longer than the other factors to handle and even out the disadvantage. This effort may put a lot of financial pressure on the organization's financial resources as technological upgradation is a slow process and returns are slow to come. Hence it is wise to provide a continuous effort and provision of fund for technological innovation on an ongoing basis.

Consumer behaviour

The consumer's behaviour is changing at a fast rate due to availability of multiple product options and easy availability at affordable price. Let us take any example of dental care system. About three to four decades ago people were using mainly neem tree branches known as 'datuns' or coal ash as a means of cleaning teeth. The consumer behaviour shifted to the use of tooth powder a couple of decades ago. Then the consumer behaviour changed to the use of dental cream as a dental cleaning system. Today at least 50% of the consumers have switched over to the use of 'gel' type of tooth care system.

A similar example can be given for the changing consumer behaviour in almost all areas including cosmetics (from chemical to herbal products), automobile sector (from scooters to motor cycles), textile (from cotton to nylon to polyester and back to cotton fabrics), entertainment (from cinema to television), classroom presentation (from chalk and talk to overhead projectors to LCDs).

5.2.5 Organization Inputs

The internal inputs are equally important in ascertaining the correct status as well as for further advancement with reference to the competition and market. The internal inputs are the inherent strength of the organization and they decide the capability and competence of the organization to reach to the level of world-class performance and market leadership. The organization should continuously measure its performance vis-a-vis the organizational goal and thrive for improvement in its all-round performance excellence.

Management review

The periodic review of the company's performance at least once in a month in ascertaining its performance vis-à-vis the quality plan, market position vis-à-vis the competition, financial performance, progress of new expansion, successful corrective and preventive action, and the future plan's focus are useful internal requisite for formulation of the strategy. The following of Deming's P-D-C-A cycle is extremely important for the organization's excellent performance. Management review is the C (Check) and A (Analyze and Act) of the Deming's cycle.

Performance measures

Various parameters of company's performance are measures of customers' satisfaction, return on investment, reduction in cycle time, reduction in wastage, increase in profitability, better cash flow management, etc., which gives indication of the current and future health of the organization and forms the foundation for development of the strategy plan.

Product measures

The vital factor for an organization's survival and performance excellence is the customer satisfaction which can only be attained through the product and associated service. The product attributes only satisfy the customer's stated and implied needs. The product design and performance determines the extent to which the customer is satisfied after the use of the product. If the customer is satisfied, he will patronize the product and the organization will gain the market share and ultimately market leadership, which is the key to organizational survival and world-class performance.

Process measures

Customer satisfaction is an outcome of the fulfillment of the customer's stated and implied needs, which is accomplished by the use of the products and services. The consistent good performance of the products and services depends on process control. Hence process measures inculcating how much the processes are under control is an important element for strategy formulation.

Internal audit

Periodic evaluation of the performance against plan and its concurrence or deviation is noted in the internal audit report. This indicates the health of the organization in terms of the top management's and employees' commitment to the business goal, their competence and need for training and additional resources in accomplishment of the strategy.

5.2.6   Developing the Guiding Principles

An organization's guiding principle lays down the framework within which it has to pursue its mission. Each guiding principal indicates an important organizational value. All the guiding principles together form the organizational value system—the foundation of its corporate culture. These guiding principles should be dynamic, contemporary and innovative enough to deliver the results as desired by the organization. An organization's guiding principles establish the parameters within which it is free in pursuit of its mission. A common example of the guiding principles may be as follows:

- Freedom from control. The organization will uphold the highest ethical standard in all its operations.
- Customer and inspection is the highest priority.
- The company will make every effort to deliver the highest quality products and services in the business.
- The company will treat all its stakeholders as partners in business.
- In the company, employee input will be actively sought, carefully considered and strategically used.
- In the company, continued improvement of products, processes and people will be the norms.
- The company will provide employees with a safe and healthy work environment that is conducive for consistent peak performance.

The guiding principles are normally formed by the company's top management. However, inputs are sought from all levels before formulating the guiding principles.

5.2.7   Developing Strategic Objectives

Strategic objectives translate the organization's mission into measurable terms. They indicate actual targets that the organization aims at and for the achievement of which it will allocate resources. Strategic objectives are more specific than missions but at the same time broad enough to last for a reasonable period of time. Strategic objectives have the following characteristics:

They are broad enough to last for some time.

- They are specific enough to be measurable but not in terms of numbers
- Each objective is focused on a single issue
- They are linked with the mission of the organization
- They are in accordance with the organization's guiding principle
- They clearly indicate what the organization wants to achieve

- The strategic objectives should be few in numbers. The general norm is 3 to 5
- They must be simple, clear and easily understood by all employees
- All strategic objectives should be tried together to be in line with the mission and the vision
- Strategic objective should not restrict performance but form a base for enhancement of the same
- All employees should be able to relate to the strategic objectives
- Good objectives will challenge an organization without being unrealistic

The specific tactics for accomplishing the broad strategic quality are important as number of tactics together enable an organization to accomplish the strategic quality. Specific tactics are well defined, projects are finite and activities are undertaken to achieve specific defined desired outcome.

The tactics are:

- Specific in nature
- Measurable
- Quantifiable
- Linked to a strategic objective
- Assigned to a specific individual or group
- Achievable within a specific time frame.

The strategies are generally targeted towards increasing either the 'operational effectiveness' or the 'competitive advantages'. Quality activities go much beyond reducing waste and the cost of poor quality. Strategies are the engine for quality success. These strategies must then be supported with goals, operational plans and projects.

Operational objectives

The operational objectives can be summarized in the following points:

- Reduce costs and cycle time through waste reduction using six sigma approach
- Institute formal cross-functional process management
- Decentralize decision-making through employees trained in problem-solving
- Realign reward and recognition systems to focus on quality
- Pursue ISO certification.

Competitive advantages

The competitive objectives can be summarized in the following points:

- Pursue customer loyalty and retention
- Focus on the product development process
- Build a learning organization

Development of goals by competitive benchmarking

A goal is a dream with a deadline. It is a desired result to be achieved in a specified time.

The overall long-range organizational goal is called the 'mission'. Medium range company goals (say for five years) are called 'strategic goals'. Short range goals (say one year) are 'tactical goals'. The goals at various levels may be called as 'business goals', 'objectives' or 'targets'.

The popular key areas where goals are fixed are as follows:

- Product performance
- Competitive performance
- Quality improvement
- Cost of poor quality
- Performance of various business processes
- Customer satisfaction
- Customer retention and loyalty

All the statements on quality goals are quantified and have a specific date to attain the target. They cover both product characteristics and tasks in overall company quality programme.

(a) The quality goals formulation inputs could be:
  - Cost of poor quality
  - Market standing on quality
  - Part analysis of repetitive external alarm signals (field failures, customer complaints, returns, etc.) and internal alarm signals (scrap, rework, rejection, sorting etc.)
  - Proposals from suggestion scheme and employees
  - Feedback from consumers/customers
  - Data on performance of products versus that of competitors from users' feedback and from laboratory tests
(b) These inputs are analyzed and quality assessment is done
(c) Then competitive benchmarking is done. Competitive benchmarking is the continuous process of measuring products, services and practices against the company's toughest competitors or those companies known as industry leaders.

A benchmark is simply a reference point that is used as standard of comparison for actual performance. The benchmark organization may be the 'best in our industry' or 'best in any industry'. For example, Xerox Corporation used IBM and Kodak as benchmark organizations to evaluate many Xerox operations. But for warehousing and distribution activities, Xerox chose, as a Benchmark, the C. C. Bean Company, a catalog sales distributor of clothing and other consumer products. Benchmarks serve not only as a standard of comparison but also as a means of self-evaluation and subsequent improvement.

The criteria for benchmarking can be any of the following:

- Specification
- Customer desires
- Competition
- Best in our industry
- Best in any industry

The steps in benchmarking are detailed below.

- Identify the benchmark subjects. They are normally related to products, customer services and internal processes
- Select the benchmarked organization and its relevant process being benchmarked
- Collect and analyze data of the benchmarked organization as well as own organization
- Determine the gap and conduct gap analysis
- Project future performance of organization as well as industry
- Communicate the results
- Establish the functional goal and measures
- Develop action plans to breach the gap
- Implement plans and monitor results
- Recalibrate the benchmarks periodically.

The benchmarking procedure and application modalities are explained in detail in Chapter 3 under the topic of benchmarking.

5.2.8 Formulation of Strategic Action Plan (Business/Budget Plan)

After carrying out the detailed SWOT analysis, i.e., ascertaining our strengths and weaknesses vis-à-vis the competition and opportunities and threats vis-à-vis the environment, i.e., political, economic, social and technological environment, we come to a conclusion and list out the above four key attributes of an organization. The formulation of action plan is two-pronged.

The first part of the action plan concentrates on sensitizing the customer about the organizational strengths and telling him how it is capable of fulfilling the customers stated and implied needs better than the competitors so that not only the existing customers are retained but also it opens up new vistas of growth and prosperity in line with the attainment of the organization's mission and vision. The second outlook of the first part of the strategic action plan is to exploit the favourable changes of environment emerging as an opportunity and making the best of the same in the strategic action plan.

If an organization is not at the level of world class and is at the beginning of its journey for TQM, the strains may be too few, that also may be in the area of trivial many in the perceptional analysis of the customer as well as the internal process management of the organization. In such a kind of situation the opportunities also may not be much. Hence, the second phase of planning of the strategic action plan becomes of more relevance, challenging and mandatory for attainment of results. Starting with the vital few weaknesses determined as an outcome of the pareto analysis and keeping in the mind the strategic goals for attainment of the mission and the vision, quality improvement projects are selected on a time frame along with annual business goals. The objective will be to work hard and convert the weaknesses into strengths. For this we will have to select the weak attribute, identify the benchmark organization, do a gap analysis and again form a specific time-bound action plan to breach the gap. This will ensure that over a period of time all the weaknesses are converted into strengths. However, for this all the employees in the organization, including the top management, should have the 'customer focus' and continuous improvement must be a way of life in the organization. The second phase of the second part of strategic action for formulation will examine critically the threats to the organization in terms of emerging unfavourable changes taking place in all the four areas of environment, namely political, economic, social and technological environment. The strategic action plan will take into consideration each of these as unfavourable factors and try to convert these threats into opportunities. The pertinent example in this respect in the current industrial scenario can be given as follows.

For an Indian garment exporter one of the main market has been the USA market. Being a developing country it was enjoying certain tariff concession of substantial amount in USA which made the business profitable. Recently these benefits have been withdrawn and there is a big threat to the very survival of the Indian garment exporters due to economic unviability. Our neighbouring country Bangladesh still enjoys the special duty concession from USA. Bangladesh being a SAARC country and having a bilateral treaty with India, any product imported from India in Bangladesh for some nominal operations and for deemed export does not attract any duty. The Indian garment exporters have now started routing the garment export to USA through Bangladesh and have eliminated this threat. Not only that, they have converted this into an opportunity while many of its competitors from other countries have gone out of business due to the same USA legislation.

5.2.9   Execution of the Strategic Plan

Equal care should be taken with the same amount of seriousness to implement the strategic action plan as that formulation of the plan itself. For successful implementation following care should be taken.

- Communicate through proper communication and ensure that all stakeholders understand the plan and are aware of their role with authorities and responsibilities and where they fit into it
- Build capabilities by proper training and develop the skill needed to carry out the assignment
- Arrange for all the resources needed to carry out the plan in terms of men, machine, material, money, technology at proper time, proper places, and of proper quality and quantity
- Establish suitable environment, stimulus, rewards and recognition for carrying out the strategic action plan.
- Remove administrative barriers of the old administrative process to accommodate the new business plan
- Identify advocates and resisters of for implementation of the action plan. Take help of the advocates to implement the plan and remove the resisters
- Gear strategic leadership among managers and workmen for execution of the plan
- Adopt a flexible and open attitude for implementation of the plan. Accept suggestions for improvements in parts of the plan
- Monitor, analyze and adjust the plan as and when and where needed to improve the performance
- Convert the organization into a 'learning organization'

Once goals have been set and further divided into sub-goals, business plans and projects, the key measurement is established for all such activities and the strategic level measurement is developed for each strategic goal defined in the strategic plan. The measurement pertains to areas like product performance, competitor performance, quality improvement, and cost of poor quality, performance of business processes, customer satisfaction and customer loyalty and retention. The measurements from financial customer internal processes, learning and growth areas in to a balance scorecard. This scorecard is used along with the formal management process. The four management processes are translating the vision, communicating and linking strategy deployment and individual strategies integrating business and financial plans and modifying strategies to reflect real time learning. Creation of a 'learning organization' inside the organization for creating, acquiring and transferring knowledge and modifying the behaviour to reflect new knowledge and insights the learning organization is an evolving concept.

5.3 CONTINUOUS IMPROVEMENT

The one thing which is constant in life and business is 'change'. A human being changes every day and transforms from a baby to a child to a youth to middle age to old age. If this is the process of life and everyday our body undergoes some change, why should our mind and efforts be static? It also has to change. However brilliant we may be at childhood, we cannot remain there forever and act in a childish manner at our youth or at the middle age. We shall just be obsolete, outdated and would not survive for long. The same analogy applies to a business organization where business focus improves everyday, becomes fiercely competitive and the technology is constantly getting upgraded. Hence the entire organization, including the top management, the workers as well as the suppliers, must accept the fact that they have to adopt the change. Obviously we are looking for a change for the better, i.e., improvement. Hence 'continuous improvement' should be a way of life for a world-class organization. The most popular way of continuous improvement in the industry is the practice of Deming's P-D-C-A cycle that is the Plan-Do-Check-Act cycle. This concept is fundamental to the working of the world-class management system. Even ISO 9000:2000 has made it compulsory for the organizations going for certification to have evidence that they are practicing the Deming's P-D-C-A cycle, as this practice inculcates the habit of continuous improvement in all the activities in an organization. Deming's P-D-C-A cycle has been explained in detail in Chapter 1.

5.3.1 Continuous Enhancement of Productivity

The prime objective of continuous improvement is the continuous 'enhancement of productivity' in all aspects of a business enterprises, like 'men', 'machine', 'technology', 'process', 'meeting environmental challenges', 'material', 'supply chain', 'logistics', 'financial management', etc. This continuous improvement should be a habit for everybody in a world-class organization. However, it needs a structural approach.

The enhancement of productivity can be brought out by the reduction in wastages also. Hence the other main objective in continuous improvement is reduction in COPQ or the cost of poor quality. They fall in category of:

- Reduction in rejection
- Reduction in rework
- Reduction in errors
- Savings in material consumption
- Savings in power fuel consumption
- Savings in man hours of work
- Reduction in customer complaints
- Savings in cycle time
- Savings in machine hours
- Reduction in accidents
- Improved working condition
- Better design of the workplace

This has been explained in detail in Chapter 2 under the topic of '3M practices'. The wastage is known as the 'muda' in the Japanese system on management. What are the nine 'mudas' and how to reduce them has been explained in the same chapter.

5.3.2 Training Needs

Continuous improvement is a structured activity where certain tools and techniques of improvements are deployed to get efficient and effective success. First of all, the all employees would be explained and convinced about the necessity for improvement. They should be changed from negative or neutral thinking to positive thinking and ultimately converting them into proactive employees always striving to do better than what they have done yesterday. They are all aware that competition is increasing, and technology and methods of work are changing. For mere survival they should adapt to these changes and improve. The continuous improvement should be the only way of life. To bring in the continuous improvement in an organization, the employees have to play a lead role in a structured scientific way. To accomplish this objective, training is must.

The training can start in subjects like:

- TQM
- Problem solving techniques
- Benchmarking
- Business process re-engineering
- Productivity improvement techniques
- Quality circle
- Kaizen gemba
- ISO 9000, ISO 14000, QS 9000
- Dr. Juran's Trilogy"
- Juran quality improvement (JQI) project
- Whole brain thinking
- Brainstorming and nominal group technique (NGT)
- Kepner Tregoe technique for problem solving and decision making, etc.

All these concepts have been explained in detail in Chapters 2 and 3.

5.3.3 Quality Improvement Tools

All the improvement techniques like Kaizen Gemba, quality circle and JQI are good approaches and need substantial improvement in their adoption to a specific organization. These tools and techniques have been explained in detail in Chapter 2. The same techniques and principles can be applied here also. However, I would propagate a two-pronged approach for continuous improvement.

Approach I

It is basically an intra-departmental improvement approach with section head/department head as the leader. The workers are members of such quality improvement teams. It aims at improvement of process, method, quality improvement, house keeping, safety, maintenance and other improvements in the department including wastage and savings. They are small improvements together leading to large benefits to the organization.

Here the popular effective tools of improvements are 'quality circle' and 'Kaizen Gemba'. The 'quality circle' was most powerful tool of continuous improvement in 1960s till 1980s. The concept of quality circles was modified by Masaki Imai and the technique of Kaizen Gemba was introduced. 'Kaizen Gemba' in Japanese means 'workplace improvement'. The common principles of both quality circle and Kaizen Gemba are as follows:

1. A group of 10–12 workers from the same department is chosen as the team.
2. The leader is the hierarchical supervisor of the department.
3. They periodically meet for at least once in a month.
4. The individual workers suggest improvements and execute the same.
5. The improvement is in routine day-to-day work.
6. The best three improvements of the month are publicized heavily by putting on notice board, publishing in in-house journal, presenting in quality council etc.
7. The objective is to motivate workers to work with their brain along with their Brawn.

The difference between quality circle and Kaizen Gemba is as follows:

1. In Kaizen Gemba, day and time of meetings are fixed whereas in quality circle they are flexible.
2. Attendance is compulsory in Kaizen Gemba whereas in quality circle it is voluntary.
3. Every member has to speak in Kaizen meeting whereas some members may keep quiet in quality circle meetings.
4. The gain out of the improvement is measured and shared equally by management, workers and customers in quality circle. In Kaizen Gemba, all the gain goes to the management.

The key to success of both the movements is as follows:

1. It leads to total employee involvement by motivating them to use their brain along with their business.

2. It leads to empowered employees.
3. Its success comes for satisfaction of 'ego needs' of the employees.
4. It makes continuous improvement as habit and way of life.

Both 'Kaizen Gemba' and 'quality circle' have been discussed in detail in Chapter 2, including the principles, concepts and application.

Approach II

This in inter-departmental organizational improvement technique aimed to solve chronic problems otherwise thought to be unsolvable and in case it gets solved, it would give major substantial benefit to the organization. The team is cross-functional constituting senior officers and the leader is the departmental head of the most affected department. It is discussed in detail in the Juran Quality Improvement (JQI) methodology.

- It needs a facilitator for both the types of projects to measure their success and measurable quantum gain in performance of the organization as a whole.
- Each member of the first few quality control teams can act as a leader and the facilitator for further quality improvement projects teams.
- Ultimately quality improvement will be a habit for everybody and it will start an organization wide revolutionary improvement where every function like finance, production, process, technology, materials, maintenance, and human resources will be continually improving the respective function's performance as also every individual will develop a habit of doing things better the next day.
- However, it takes a long time depending on the size of the company, structure of the company and the number of quality improvement projects going to cover all employees under the umbrella of the training programme. The value of each employee generating at least one idea for improvement per year is great.

For years many companies made statement that 'their strength is the people who work for them'. But this turns out to be a hollow statement. The companies still blindly follows Taylor's systems of few planners, few engineers and managers planning all steps of every process, defining carefully worked job descriptions and enforcing the unthinking to follow the instructions. This attitude has to change with immediate effect. The draft of such process has to be circulated among the employees, who have to carry out the process, ask for their opinion, and seek improvements, ask suggestions and then finalize the final process with the involvement of all concerned. That is the way matured world-class organizations functions efficiently and effectively. Making continuous improvement a habit cycle is yet to mature in industry. In an advanced country like United States, the average number of implemented ideas per employee per year is still only 0.16, that is one idea implemented per year for every six employees. Ideally it should be for a benchmark, i.e., in Toyota's George town plant, it is an average of over 46 implemented ideas per employee per year.

Apart from ideas contributed for improvement, other participation in continuous improvement are participation in quality improvement and quality planning teams, membership on business process re-engineering teams, work on statistical quality control, self control of their own work processor and working as a member of high performance on self-directing work teams.

Continuous improvement has a direct relation with continuous learning. This concept includes both incremental and 'break through' improvement activities in every operation, function and work process in the company. Improvements are made through enhancing value to customers, reducing errors, defects and waste, improving responsiveness and cycle time performance, improving productivity and effectiveness in the use of all resources and improving the company's performance and leadership position in fulfillment of its public responsibilities and corporate citizenship. Learning and improvement are need to be embedded in the way the organization operates..

The topics like the 'Kaizen Gemba', 'Quality Circle', 'Kepner Tregoe problem solving technique', etc. have been explained in detail in Chapter 2 of this book

EXERCISES

1. Explain the significance of building a solid 'foundation' for a business enterprise.

2. How would you create a 'customer focus' in the organization? Explain with respect to a food product manufacturing organization.

3. Explain the process of the 'strategic quality planning' for an organization. Select a manufacturing sector and a service industry of your choice and work out a 'strategic quality plan' for the organization.

4. Elaborate why an organization should go for 'continuous improvement'?

5. Explain the various continuous improvement tools discussed in the first five chapters till now.

6. How will you build up the foundation of a composite rubber industry in the non-tyre sector?

Chapter 6

Infrastructure

After laying the foundation for world-class performance wherein everybody in the organization, including its suppliers, have undergone an attitudinal development of thinking and taking all actions with a customer focus and continuous improvement, in the backdrop of a sound strategic quality plan the infrastructure is laid out of:

- Total organization involvement
- Supply chain management
- Quality management system

The infrastructure deployment is the enabler for attainment of world-class performance and world leadership through the TQM process. All the three above stated activities are mandatory to develop to attain the end results. This infrastructure makes the TQM process more effective and efficient. In fact implementation of ISO 9000:2000 system is the first step for establishing a total quality system. The ISO 9000 certification by an internationally reputed certifying agency in the first external audit and confirmation of a world-class quality management system. The result or output from the TQM process of quality planning, quality control and quality improvement is enhanced to a great extent. If the steps are correct, the result has to come. If the foundation is sound and infrastructure is well developed, the result from TQM is bound to give revolutionary growth as well as performance to the organization.

The development of all the three infrastructure facilities is extremely important before we start the first step of TQM, i.e., quality planning. The infrastructure holds the 'quality gains' without allowing it to slip back to the original position. It is the infrastructure that holds the 'quality gains'. Also, all quality improvement results will be sporadic and not systematic unless there is a sound infrastructure. Unless there is a sound fort, an emperor cannot dream of expanding his kingdom. Similarly, in business an establishment has to consolidate and protect its position in a competitive environment, marketplace and in house before it can spread its activities internationally or in the foreign land. It is the infrastructure that builds the impregnable sound fort of business, which holds it at all times of favourable or unfavourable business environment.

The infrastructure only holds the organization together giving it a platform to venture into unforeseen terrain and extends its hold in the new terrain in a firm manner. It ensures that a step taken in forward direction is never required to be withdrawn and that continuous increase in growth, profitability, return on investment, employees' empowerment and motivation and reduction in cost of poor quality are not happening by accident and not in a sporadic manner but as part of a solid strategic plan and infrastructure which holds all such gains in an integrated manner. The infrastructure gives the inherent strength to an organization and stability in its performance. The infrastructure also gives a consistency in the performance of the organization.

6.1   TOTAL ORGANIZATIONAL INVOLVEMENT

Total organizational involvement (TOI) goes beyond the total employee involvement and it brings under its purview apart from the involvement of all the employees, the top management as well as the suppliers to the organization. The total organization involvement tends to get the customer involved in its business if it works out to be feasible. It is the most important of the infrastructure development activity of an organization. It is the people that differentiate an ordinary organization from an extraordinary organization. This vital 'extra' can come only from the people. The people process involves not only the organization's employees, but also its suppliers and the customers. Hence the total organizational involvement consists of the total involvement in the prosperity and growth of the organization as well as maintaining the same by its employees, suppliers and the customers alike.

6.1.1   Total Employees Involvement

Total Employee Involvement (TEI) consists of both the top management of the organization as well as its employees. For the growth and prosperity of an organization to a world-class level, both the top management and the employees should by bound by the single objective and form a united force totally involved in achieving the organizational goals and objectives.

Current industrial scenario indicates that successful organization has one thing in common, i.e., the involvement of the top management. Top management is involved in defining the mission and the vision as well as the value system of the organization and formulation of the strategic plan. The top management has also arranged for the resources needed by the organization.

The process of TEI starts with imparting training on relevant subjects to the employees leading to the change in their mindset from negative and neutral to active and proactive. This training is often extended to the suppliers also.

The subjects for training here are:

- Time management
- Leadership and motivation
- Effective communication
- Habit control
- TQM
- Introduction to result oriented management techniques
- Stress management
- Delegation
- How to plan and control
- Productivity improvement techniques
- Environment scanning and SWOT analysis
- Management by objective
- Knowledge management
- Technology management, etc.

Conduct a psychometric analysis of the supervisory and managerial employees through a set of well-designed questionnaires and follow it up with a psychosomatic counselling for their total involvement in work, identification of their personal goal and goal integration with that of the organizational goal.

Now install a TEI (Total employee involvement) result-oriented system by bottom-up approach.

Workers should have well defined target of:

(i) Quantity
(ii) Quality and
(iii) Improvement

These three key activities should be 80% subjective measurement of his key result area (KRA).

Every person at manager/supervisor or officer level should have a

(i) Pending work (to-do) list.
(ii) Time log for the day with hourly planning schedule of activity.

This will ensure that routine day-to-day work—which is the key to organizational success—is carried out by the persons concerned with their own responsibility.

Every employee is responsible for his own work and target. He is not waiting for the boss to tell him as to what he has to do and makes full use of his productive time.

Opportunity in target must exist for good performers to earn a bit extra for good performance by way of incentive. The bad performers should be reshuffled with transfers to find out their suitability in the right area.

This bottom-up approach will ensure total employee involvement with committed focus on their own performance and measurable result leaving the top management to concentrate on expansion, innovation, policy making and continuous improvement.

The top management must show their involvement in participation in quality council activities, pareto analysis for selection of problem to be solved on priority and so on.

Ultimate in total organization involvement is 'employee empowerment' which can be elaborated as the creation of a culture 'where people have the knowledge, skill, authority and desire to decide, act and take responsibility for the results of their actions and for the contribution to the success of the company'.

The implementation of this clear working of empowered management is made more effective by providing just-in-time training where employees are susceptible to make mistakes or likely to take wrong decisions. Also pre-emptive steps are taken where the workers are likely to lose with improvement projects by providing them with alternate value-added job than the previous one or already selected. Quality work facilitators provide direct support back on the job for ease of absorption of new or innovative techniques.

It is proven beyond doubt that business success and quality both go together and TQM is the sound business strategy to achieve both. The General Accounting Office (GAO) of the US government conducted a study of 20 of Malcolm Baldridge National Quality Award winners, which was given for excellence in TQM. The study proved that increased quality and improved financial performance were both associated with the introduction of quality. If we consider leadership also within the paradigm of total organization involvement's outcome and suppliers an integral part of the organization, the percentage weightage given for TOI in Malcolm Buldridge Quality Award is 31.5% (315 points out of 1000) and that in European Quality Award in 28% (280 points out of 1000).

Employees' empowerment as discussed already is an advanced form of employee involvement. TOI is possible only with total employee empowerment wherein the employees to take actions in response to the needs and opportunities regarding the customer satisfaction, operational success, safety, quality and value addition to the products and services, business results and continuous improvement of products, process and people.

Under employee empowerment in total organizational involvement, employees align their goals with higher organizational purpose, have the authority and responsibility to maximize their contribution by maximization of opportunities available, are capable of taking proper actions and are committed to the organization's purpose and have the means to achieve it.

Hence total organizational involvement covers out the following factors:

1. Employees and suppliers are aligned with organization's mission and vision.
2. The management, employees and suppliers know the needs of customers and are aware of their contribution and its effectiveness in fulfilling the same.
3. Organizational strategies, goals and subjective plans are the outcome of the total involvement of all stakeholders.
4. Individual authority, responsibility and capability are consistent, stable and measurable.
5. Barriers to successful exercise of authority have been removed.
6. The cordial environment of mutual help among management, all employees and suppliers are existing where each one supplements and complements the others' effort.

7. It is recognized that all business results are the outcome of well-coordinated team effort.

8. The necessary tools, supports and resources are existing to avoid diversion in effort and the entire focus is on the attainment of the mission, vision and business goals.

9. To develop the capability of employees and suppliers, continuous training in the relevant subject as discussed later is mandatory to make TOI effective and fruitful.

10. Commitment is the key to success of TOI and it is what makes an ordinary person giving extraordinary results. Commitment is a state of mind, which is in evidence when the employee assumes responsibility for creating success and takes initiatives to achieve that success. The organization must earn the commitment of employees by continuously demonstrating that the employees are valued members of the organization and by appropriately reorganizing and rewarding them.

11. The immediate objective of total organizational involvement is to attain healthy human relationships throughout the organization, including the suppliers. Healthy human relationships are open, positive and efficient. Healthy human relationships leads to employees and suppliers developing a feeling of ownership and a sense of belonging which motivates them to give their best. This is bound to create exceptionally good business results. This is in short what Mr. W. Edward Deming described as 'joy in the workplace'.

12. Communication and transparency in communication is a key feature of total organization involvement. The employee has full knowledge of mission, vision and quality objectives and what performance is expected against the strategic quality plan on individual basis as well as on collective basis and how will it contribute to the organization's business result. Hence the transparency and clarity in communication is a must to achieve total organization involvement. Let everyone know the key scorecards including financial performance and contribute towards the enhancement of the performance of same.

13. Communication must be clear, timely, believable and supported by data and facts. Empowered employees are supposed to be decision-makers. Unless one has information, how can he/she take decision?

14. 'Freedom from fear' is mandatory for TOI. Two of Deming's fourteen points are 'driving out fear' and 'eliminate fear' so that everyone could put in his best performance unafraid of consequences.

15. Ideas and feedback from employees are essential. This will flow freely only when the employees know that for their feedback and ideas which may fail, they will not be blamed, punished, ridiculed and reprimanded. Fear can also lead to people to avoid giving suggestions or actually bringing out improvement on a continuous basis.

16. The best way to put forward the facts is in the reliable written form of data. Unless employees have knowledge of facts and data such as quality goals, quality plans and their performance against the same like COPQ, defect rates, production capabilities, wastages, service capabilities, etc., they cannot work effectively towards customer satisfaction and continuous improvement. The first

step of any quality improvement project is data collection and analysis. Data orientation makes decisions objective and impersonal. Employees need training on methods of data collection, their interpretation and decision-making. Data-oriented concepts like finding out causes of variation, common causes, special causes and root causes are at the very heart of total quality systems.

The best measure of the employees' involvement in their work and result delivered can be both achieved and assessed by the process of the 'management by objective' or 'MBO' where each employee's job assignments are clearly defined. The total job is divided into sub-processes known as the 'key result areas' or 'KRAs'. The total points given to the entire job to be executed by the respective employees are out of 100. The marks for each sub-process are given based on its relative importance in achieving the employee's main objective which is integrated with the organizational objective. For example, a sales executive's 100 marks can be divided into 50 marks for achievement of his sales target, 20 marks for realizing the payment from the customers in time, 15 marks for getting new customers, 10 marks for intensive and periodic coverage of his assigned territory customers and solving their problems and 5 marks for the timely submission of various sales reports. MBO is a very powerful tool of objectively measuring the employee's involvement in his work and the organizational activities as well as his effectiveness and efficiency.

6.1.2 Supplier's and Customer's Involvement

How important is the involvement of the customer in the success of an organization has been explained in Chapter 2 as well as in Chapter 5. The key objective for any organization's survival and performance excellence is customer satisfaction. It is the customer who pays for the salary of the employees of an organization. The only source of income for an organization is the customer. To ensure customer satisfaction, the organization has to understand the customer's stated and implied needs and produce products and services which satisfy the same. It is but natural that to accomplish this objective the organization has to ensure the customer's involvement in the organization. This is done by the regular feedback from the customer about the products and services produced by the organization. For the ancillary units, parent organizations like Maruti, Tata Motors, Mahindra & Mahindra and Bajaj Auto regularly deputes its engineers and representative to help the suppliers in their effort on process control and identification of vendors to them. This ensure the presence of the required level of the product and service performance of the parts and components supplied by the ancillaries.

The organization also ensures suppliers' involvement for the reduction in the cost of the parts and the components supplied by the organization to its customers. Sometimes the supplier supplies the technology for development of a key component or a part which is critical for the performance of the end product. The suppliers' involvement can only ensure implementation of just-in-time system for an organization by ensuring timely, defect-free supply. The suppliers' interest has to be defended by the organization. The suppliers' involvement can come only if the organization considers the suppliers as its integral part and the supplier in turn knows that he will grow along with the organization. TOI integrates the entire supply chain as per the customer's requirement and fulfillment of his needs by integrating suppliers at the back end and the customers at the front end and employees of the organization in the middle during the processing of products and services.

6.1.3   Benefits of Total Organizational Involvement

The following are the benefits of TOI:

1. It encourages the development of mutual trust and confidence among all the stakeholders, mainly between the top management, employees and suppliers.
2. It helps develop a customer focus and a culture of customer satisfaction both internal as well as external.
3. Employees' empowerment and involvement fosters a climate of continuous improvement in all areas of business.
4. Transparent, open and consistent communication leads to the development of an environment of honesty, integrity, respect for opinion of others and fairness in dealing, thereby permanently eliminating rumours, isolation of people, failure in keeping commitments etc.
5. It leads to employment stability wherein the technology and knowledge developed in an organization by years of hard work, dedication and training remains with the organization, thereby making it sounder and technically more competent than the competitors.
6. TOI leads to all-round increase in competitive advantage and value addition to the products and services of the organization.
7. Apart from customer satisfaction, TOI leads to employee satisfaction and employee development.
8. TOI leads to all-round reduction in COPQ and reduction in wastages, rework, errors apart from savings in resources like material, manpower, cycle time, power and fuel, etc.
9. TOI leads to the shared leadership between both operators and managers wherein operator takes charge of running and solving problems of day-to-day operations while managers concentrate on the more important function of quality plan, etc.
10. All these factors combined together lead to the development of an excellent team concept including empowerment, control of variance at source, sharing of leadership, cordial relationship, accountability for performance of products and services and fairness in reward and recognition.

TOI leads to optimum satisfaction of employees, management, suppliers and customers alike, leading to a world-class organization. However, the top management has to play a leading role in creating TOI. They have to set the ball rolling by first deciding the target in terms of the mission, vision and strategic objectives and then structurally aligning the organization along with the allocation of resources. TOI takes over from here by communication of the above stated information, discussing the needs of the organization and its stakeholders and finding out an optimum solution for the same, reinforcing positive thinking and ultimately ensuring that the organization attains its mission, vision and related quality goals, thereby making it a world-class organization where all the stakeholders are fully satisfied.

6.2 SUPPLY CHAIN MANAGEMENT

Supply chain management (SCM) is probably the most talked about subject in the management of the organization but least understood. The topic is always discussed in part with many misnomers like inventory management system and inclusion of suppliers in the organization structure. Supply chain management is in a way extension of the porter's theory of 'value chain management'. However, it goes much beyond either of these two concepts.

Let us give below the description of the supply chain as given in ISO 9000:2000 edition clause no. 3.

"The following terms used in this edition of ISO 9001 to describe the supply chain have been changed to reflect the vocabulary currently used".

Supplier ⟶ Organization ⟶ Customer

However, this definition as given in ISO 9001 has been modified into an updated and a much more advanced definition of the supply chain as elaborated in a simplistic, comprehensive manner in Figure 6.1.

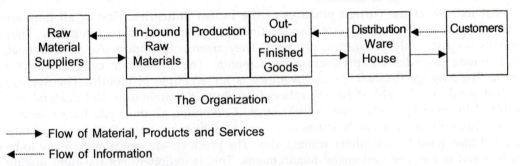

— ▶ Flow of Material, Products and Services

◀ ······· Flow of Information

FIGURE 6.1 Supply chain management.

6.2.1 Logistics and SCM

In the conventional organization and in the situation where, through license raj, the demand was more than the supply, manufacturing was always based on maximization of plant capacity. After manufacturing the product, the organization looked for the customer and tried to 'push' the product in the market. However, in the current scenario of elimination of the license raj through liberalization, signing of WTO and globalization leading to intense global competition and shortened product life cycle, the 'push' strategy does not work due to fast product obsolescence, non-competitive product features and ultimately no buyers for the product.

Hence the only way to survive in the current business environment is to switch over to the 'pull strategy' wherein the customer pulls the entire supply chain. Only products and services that are capable of providing customer satisfaction by fulfillment of customers' stated and implied needs survive. This, in short, is the need and objective for supply chain management. The main objective of SCM is the maximization of customer satisfaction by providing the right quality of products and services, in right quantity, at right time, at right place and at right price. The internal objective is to maximize the return on investment (ROI) by compression of the cycle time. Both the objectives are attained by compression of cycle time and producing only the goods that are needed to fulfill the customers' requirements.

Concept of 'RIGHT QUALITY'

The definition of quality has already been discussed time and again. However, two definitions are more pertinent. The first definition is given by Dr. Joseph Juran and also accepted by W. Edward Deming, the two fathers of TQM.

Quality of products and services is defined as 'fitness for use and free from product non-conformities'.

ISO 9000:2000 defines quality as 'the degree to which a set of inherent characteristics fulfils requirement'. This product feature fulfilling customer requirement is changing today at a fast rate due to intense global competition, more focus by manufacturers on R&D, technological innovations, development of additional product features, shorter product life cycles and fast changing consumers' preferential lifestyles. If an organization cannot adapt fast to all these changes, its products or services become obsolete and it goes out of business.

Let us look at the current practices of the Indian industries. First of all they are extremely poor in deploying resources for finding out customers' requirements. They normally do a monthly production planning. They arrange for inputs like raw material, etc. Planning precedes the production by a month. The production cycle is about a month. The average finished goods inventory is for a couple of months. The average finished goods stock held at branch offices/distribution warehouses and dealers' end combined together is another two months stock. Combining all this cycle time together, the consumer always get the products and services which are more than seven months outdated than what the consumer wants today. The products are hence more likely to be obsolete and not as per customers' requirements. This is definitely not the right quality we are talking about. International organizations today like Zaras, a Spanish firm dealing in readymade garments for teenagers, has compressed this cycle time to 15 days from the market research to market delivery.

There are many more examples in this context. For instance, United Colours of Benetton, an Italian garment manufacturer having thousands of retail outlets spread over hundred countries, has the cycle time from ordering by the franchisee at the retail outlet to the goods replenished from the central warehouse at Italy to the outlet with customs duty paid completed in less than a week.

Concept of 'RIGHT QUANTITY'

Consumer has a buying habit in terms of quality of the products. If you feel thirsty you will buy a bottle of cold drink and not consume three bottles just because there is a quantity discount, unless you have somebody else to share it with.

Normally you purchase soaps, toothpastes, shaving creams in unitary mode. The retailer purchases the same from wholesalers in boxes having 100 units of them packed together. The wholesaler purchases in containers while the distributor may purchase a full truckload. The packaging as well as storing has to be done accordingly for compression of cycle time, ease of handling and economics of transportation cost, storage space, etc. Hence the primary packing should be done in an attractive packet in which it is sold to consumers, as the distributor receives a full truckload goods stacked in a container.

When the container is opened by the distributor, goods are available in crates to be delivered to next stage of wholesalers. The distributor needs material handling equipment and storage space for storing of the containers and crates. The wholesaler has material handling arrangement and storage space for crates and boxes. When crates are opened, material is duly packed in boxes to be delivered to retailers, where storage space again is designed to store boxes and when he opens the boxes, goods are available in packets to be sold to consumers.

Various powerful products have failed to take off in the market or sales promotional scheme failed since the company tried to sell in more quantity than the buying behaviour of the consumers. Various soap sellers' scheme of giving one soap free with six soaps failed but when the same scheme was given as one free with two soaps, it succeeded as consumers had to buy one month's requirement at the most and not more than that. Jyoti laboratory's sales promotional scheme of giving one 'Ujala' free with six bottles failed to take off due to the same reason. The shirt sellers' scheme of one shirt free with purchase of two shirts failed as a promotional scheme since consumers do not have a habit of buying three shirts at a time.

Concept of 'RIGHT PLACE'

The customers have a buying habit for purchasing products. One does not travel ten kilometres to buy sugar, soap or toothpaste, i.e., products of day-to-day need, even if it is available there at a cheaper rate. We all know that these products are available at a cheaper rate at a wholesale market a few kilometres away, but still we prefer to buy at next door shop.

This is place utility and is mainly created by dealers and retailers. Coca-Cola Ltd. was smart enough to foresee the importance of place utility and entered in the takeover of 'Parle Soft drinks'—makers of the popular 'Thumps Up' brand of cola with a wide distribution network and thereby gained in the market share. Its competitor Pepsi Foods Ltd., in spite of having heavy television, newspaper and other advertisements popularizing the brand, could not gain market share even in a premium market like Mumbai. This was due to lack of place utility as for this kind of products the customer would not even visit the next shop for Pepsi if both brands are available. Hence it was forced ultimately to enter into a strategic alliances with Dukes Ltd., to gain market share. Similar is the case with P & G and Godrej alliance. The place utility is created by proper supply chain management only.

Concept of 'TIME UTILITY'

Every product demand peaks at a certain time. The sale of every product is seasonal to some extent. Hence the supply chain management, keeping in mind the seasonal cycle time, should immaculately plan and ensure that the product and services are available at the right time for the customer needs. This does not happen automatically but needs to be managed and controlled.

For example, sales of fans, refrigerators, air conditioners, water coolers and coolers pick up in the months of April and May. An organization manufacturing these products had scheduled its peak sales in mid-May. Due to delay in receipt of raw material by ten days and delay in transit time due to transporter's strike by seven days, the consignment arrived in the market by mid-June. The entire goods will remain unsold at company's distribution godown for next six to ten months. By this time the consumer's preference may change and the products may themselves become obsolete. Also, the cash flow will be disturbed and minimum loss will be 10% to 15% due loss of interest alone. Then there is a chance of some defect developing due to environmental effect of moisture, etc.

Apart from the above example, many times it has been seen that the company advertises for a new product being launched or a sales promotion scheme immediately as the product leaves the factory, without considering the goods in transit and other element of cycle time. All efforts including lakhs of rupees in advertisement are wasted. When the consumer visits the dealers' shop, the products are not available. The effect of the advertisement is lost as human beings have short memory. This is due to the fact that the time utility has not been created.

Concept of 'PRICE UTILITY'

All other four utilities, i.e., quality, quantity, time and place being equal, price plays a dominant role in customer satisfaction and better saleability of the product. In short, the product available with same features and utility but at a lower price means better value for money. Same quality product getting a higher price due to esteem value associated with a brand has totally disappeared in case of an industrial product and the same trend is becoming visible in case of consumer durables and non-durables.

6.2.2 Benefits of SCM

1. Getting higher return on investment due to effective supply chain management and multiplying the same is the main benefit for the management. Please refer to the example given under concept of right quality. Over this cycle time of seven months, add another three months as outstanding debtors and the working capital cycle time becomes ten months. 20% is the average profit and we earn one profit per completion of one working capital cycle, i.e., from the time we pay and procure raw materials and convert the same to finished product, sell it to the customer and receive the money. On this we earn only $12/10 \times 20\%$ profit, i.e., 24% over completion of one working capital cycle which is ten months in the current case. To quantify, if one month's sale is Rs. 1,00,00,000, our working capital involvement would be roughly around Rs. 9,00,00,000 assuming cost of raw material and WIP is 50% value of sales and money blocked in excise and sales tax is equal to 20% bridge of profit. Our net earning is only Rs. 24,00,000. Hence the ROI is 2.6% on our working capital investment, which is marginal.

Now if we can compress the cycle time by proper supply chain management to 7 days production cycle instead of monthly production cycle, the resultant raw material inventory will be one week, production cycle time will be one week, finished goods inventory two weeks and compress goods in transit time for one month (four weeks) to two weeks and stock at distribution houses of two weeks and debtors as one month, i.e., four weeks and retain profit at same level of 20%. The cycle time now becomes 12 weeks, i.e., 3 months. Hence now the organization earns 20% on a month's sale every three month. Hence in a year it will earn 12/3 × 20 = 80% of a monthly sale, i.e., Rs. 80,00,000 per annum. The blocked money is Rs. 2,75,00,000. The return on investment is 29%, which is more than ten times than the earlier case.

2. Benefits that are derived out of proper supply chain management are substantial and manifold.
3. In today's competitive world, increase in earnings by price increase is rarely possible. Cutting down the COPQ and reducing the cost of production thereby increasing the profit also takes substantial effort and time. On the contrary, SCM is the fastest method of increasing the earning within the shortest possible time.
4. Return on investment (ROI) = Profit × No. of working capital cycle turnover

   While the profit cannot be increased by supply chain management, it can either be increased by price increase or reducing the cost of production. Both have marginal effect. Proper SCM increases the working capital cycle turnover in multiple times. One working capital cycle completion means one profit. A normal organization to remain healthy should have 4 working capital cycle turnovers, thereby earning the profit four times. Hence ROI can be increased many times by proper SCM only.
5. It maximizes customer satisfaction by providing goods and services of right quality, in right quantity, at right time, right place and at right price. Achieving all these above five parameters by SCM is a tremendous achievement for customer satisfaction.
6. It gives competitive advantage in the marketplace.
7. It avoids product obsolescence. Decreasing the cycle time to market, it always provides contemporary products in the marketplace, thereby preventing product obsolescence.
8. It helps the organization enhance its market share and attain leadership position.
9. It leads to practice of customer relationship management (SCM) and excellent customer response (ECR).
10. It leads to reduction in blocked capital and hence improves the cash flow and fund flow situation.
11. It adds more value to the organization and system in least cost.
12. SCM principles can be applied universally and are bound to give benefits.
13. Proper supply chain management is mandatory in a world-class organization and is a basic infrastructure requirement.
14. SCM can cater to customers' delivery requirements.
15. It integrates the entire system from suppliers to customers online with a single unified objective of maximization of customer satisfaction externally and maximization of return on investment internally.

6.2.3 Pre-requisites for Effective SCM

1. Regular updating of the entire network by all concerned parties is mandatory.
2. Correct feeding of data in the system is important for SCM to function properly.
3. Uniform software package interacting to each other's system through Internet should be there to make the system operative. Normally Visual Basic at front-end and Oracle at back-end makes a good support system for this database management system (DBMS) of computerization for SCM.
4. Proper education and training on operation and day-to-day servicing of the equipment and system must be imparted to all concerned in the supply chain for making the system effective and properly working.

6.2.4 Flow in the Supply Chain and Logistic Management

What flows backwards in the supply chain is the flow of information. Customer is the driver of the engine of the entire supply chain. The flow of information means the customer's requirements and demands. His purchase orders origin, order acknowledgement, technical clarifications and subsequent realization of the purchase order is the flow of information.

In response to this flow of information what flows forward are the raw materials, finished goods and numerous products and services. This flow is from the supplier to the organization. This makes the raw material to flow within the organization. Value is added to this raw material by converting it into finished product. The finished product flows from the finished goods store to the customer.

This backward flow of information from the customer to the manufacturer to the supplier is on line and integrated. In response to this information of customer's requirement of goods and services, the supply chain management ensures flow of raw material from supplier's end to the manufacturer's end and conversion of raw material to finished goods inside the manufacturer's organization and ultimately to the customer.

6.2.5 Logistic Management

Supply chain management and logistic management go hand in hand. Logistics is the support for the supply chain. All the concerned members of the supply chain, including the suppliers, the organization, its branch offices/distribution houses and the dealers, should have internet facility with e-mail, i.e., they must have telephone line, computers with modem, internet connection and a uniform software package as detailed earlier. This is the logistic support needed for the flow of information through the supply chain in backward direction.

The logistic support needed for the flow of raw materials products and services are as follows:

Transportation management

The cycle time for the goods-in-transit has to be minimized at the least cost. In transportation management, the latest trend is the 'multi-model transportation' to economize the cost, increase the speed and have effective transportation. Another trend which is emerging in this arena is the 'specialized logistic managers' with tremendous amounts of infrastructure back-up which even a large size organization cannot afford. Examples are Airfreight Ltd., DHL Ltd., Sembium SemCop., American President Lines, Dynamic Logistics Ltd., Gati (TCI Ltd.), etc.

Warehouse management

The storage of materials in safe, secure manner at various storing points of stocking and distribution is another important aspect of logistic management. Safe and secure storage, minimization of storage cost and time, keeping proper records, required retrieval, prevention of deterioration during handling and proper material handling are all part of warehouse management in the logistic area.

Proper packaging

Primary, secondary and tertiary packaging are also the subjects of logistic management. Simultaneously, the statutory requirement pertaining to the packaging and leveling has to be taken into consideration for packaging. A detailed study to keep goods in safe and secure condition without deterioration at the least cost during storage and transportation has to be done.

Flow of information

Proper status of the processing of the raw materials into the finished goods, stock availability, status of goods-in-transit, etc. are important information for the customer. He will be interested to know at what time, what place and in what quantity the products and services will be made available. This again is possible through proper computerized network of system with common interactive software. A good logistic manager may not provide mobile phones with roaming facility to his executives but will provide it to the truck driver who is carrying goods worth lakhs of rupees.

Logistic management cost is very important for the products which has a lower price/kg of the raw material, i.e., weight of the material like cement, salt, steel, etc. Here the transportation and handling cost forms a good percentage of the selling price and economizing on the same through proper multi-model transportation and least warehousing is the key to success of the organization in the marketplace.

The main cost involved in supply chain management is holding of more inventories than required and holding the inventory longer than the required time. Here the required time and quantity is decided by the customer and the organization so that there is no shortage or rather the concept of right time, right quantity and right place is fulfilled.

6.2.6 Inventory Management

Inventory can be defined as all the movable items held in temporary storage for subsequent processing and/or converting ultimately into finished products, the final product itself as well as those items which are held in stock for smooth running of production operation and the related plant and machinery.

The inventory does not add any value to the product, i.e., inventory is a non-value adding activity. Therefore, inventory has to be minimized. At the same time, we have to maximize the customer service by making the product and services available at the right time, right place in the right quantity and at the right price. This objective is accomplished only by proper supply chain management or control of raw material, finished goods (products) and the related services.

Inventory classification

Inventory is a broad-based term. It covers a wide spectrum of entities, which are summarized below:

1. **Raw material.** They constitute the basic raw materials like steel, aluminum, rubber, plastic granules, etc. which are processed further and converted into components which are useful in final assembly of the products. Its location could be at the ancillary's place or at the manufacturing units itself.
2. **Work-in-progress (WIP).** They are the in-process inventory during various stages of conversion process of raw material into finished products. They could be semi-finished and awaiting assembly into the final product.
3. **Bought-out items.** They are the items which are sourced from outside. They are those parts which are either

   (a) technically not feasible to manufacture in-house,
   (b) economically not viable for in-house manufacturing, or
   (c) to meet customers delivery priorities.

   They are sourced from outside even if they can be made in-house but not in the time when required. These products could be raw material, semi-finished product or finished product.
4. **Finished goods inventory.** They are the final assembled products lying at the finished goods store, at central warehouse, at regional warehouse and at dealer's showrooms. They are the finished goods, i.e., final product and services, which should be made available to the customer when he needs, where he needs and in required shape, form and quantity to attain customer's satisfaction.
5. **Goods-in-transit.** It can be shown separately or it can be shown by adding to the raw material in transit, which is paid by the organization. Similarly, it is paid bought-out items. The bulk value of the goods-in-transit is the finished goods on its way from the manufacturing factory to the dealer's sales outlet via various warehouses. The logistic support plays a vital role in minimizing goods-in-transit. The quantity of goods-in-transit is always to trade-off between cost and time.
6. **Indirect and/or other inventories.** They can be broadly classified into four categories:

   (a) Manufacturing Aids, which constitutes the stock of tools, jigs, fixtures, inspection gauges, dies and moulds, cutting oil, etc.
   (b) Maintenance spares like V-belts, bearing, electrical items, lubricants, etc.
   (c) Servicing spare parts to supplement the after-sale service at dealer's outlet or service outlets.
   (d) Fuels for boilers, generators, etc.

6.2.7 Dependent and Independent Demand

A component's sub-assembly or assembly is classified as 'dependent demand' when the demand for that particular part, component's sub-assembly or assembly is directly proportional to the number of finished products sold. It is normally all the components that are used as standard feature of a finished product. For example, each motor cycle will need two wheels. If a firm produce 10,000 motor cycles, it will need 20,000 tyres, and 20,000 tubes. The requirement of the tyres and tubes are items of dependent demand. On the other hand, the motor cycle offers an optional feature of push button start for which it needs a battery. Since every motor cycle is not offering push button start, the requirement of batteries is not dependent on the number of motor cycles sold. It is classified under independent demand.

Every pen needs a refill; hence the demand of a refill is a dependent demand. The standard feature of a product and related components, all fall under the category of dependent demand. Inspite of such a large category of items falling under the category of independent demand items, it constitutes only 3–5% of the inventory items whereas dependent demand items constitute the other 95–97% of the inventory.

Since the dependent demand items follow logic, it can be easily computerized which gives tremendous amount of flexibility and speed in data handling. The dependent demand items are handled under various computer-based modern techniques of inventory handling, like material requirement planning (MRP-I), manufacturing resource planning (MRP-II) and distribution requirement planning. The independent demand items are handled by the conventional inventory management systems like the concept of order-reorder model and economic order quantity (EOQ).

6.2.8 Inventory Cost

The inventory and related cost could be broadly divided into two categories: the cost of material, and the cost on material.

Let us assume that '100' is the value of sales. Then as per industry norm, the component of this '100' will be 20 as profit and 80 as the cost of production (including direct and indirect). This 80 can be sub-divided as:

1) 50 material-related cost (2/3rd of 50, i.e., 33% as cost of material and 17% as cost on material).
2) 7–8% as labour cost (wages).
3) 7–8% as cost of power, fuel and consumables.
4) 8–12% as marketing, selling, and administrative overheads.

It is interesting to mention that the average cost of labour for Indian industry is 7–10% of sales value whereas the international norm for the same is 5–7% contrary to the belief that Indian labour cost is cheap. The actual fact is that per unit head Indian labour is cheap, but it also happens to be the least productive. An average Indian worker works for 3 to 3.5 hours per shift of 8 hours whereas an average worker as per international norm in Europe, America, Japan and Korea works for atleast 6.5 hours per 8-hour shift. These workers also handle more than one machine whereas in India workers are reluctant to handle more than one machine. The reason is over-protective labour laws and socialist type of government's working.

Whether this kind of working will sustain in today's globally competitive environment is a big question to be answered. This topic may be out of place to discuss under the topic of inventory cost at first look but we should not forget that the major portion of cost on material is related to human productivity.

Nevertheless we cannot do much towards reducing cost of material, we can definitely reduce substantially and even can make it near to zero the cost on material, which is as high as 17% of sales value and is nearly as much as the total profit (20%) of the organization. This is one of the major reasons attributed to current focus on SCM with an objective to reduce bulk of this cost on material. Let us now understand what are the elements of cost of material and that of cost on material.

Cost of materials

Cost of materials is about 33–35% of sales price and it consists of the following:

1. **Basic price:** This is the consideration payable to the supplier. This is approximately 60% of cost of material and 20–21% of the sales price.
2. **Government duties:** It constitutes of excise duty, custom duty, sales tax, local tax (Octroi), etc. This is approximately 35% of cost of material and about 11–12% of sales price.
3. **Packing:** Primary as well as secondary packing cost for safety, preservation and presentation of the product.
4. **Transportation:** This is the cost of transporting materials and products in least time and at minimum cost.
5. **Clearing and forwarding:** The custom clearing and forwarding agents, the octroi clearing agents, all charge their fees for clearing and forwarding of the goods.
6. **Insurance:** To protect the goods-in-transit against loss, theft, spoilage, accidents, etc., the goods are insured at cost.
7. **Material handling:** At every transit point, the material needs to be handled, i.e., loading and unloading charges.

Cost on material

Cost on material, also known as inventory carrying cost (ICC) is approximately 33% of material related cost and about 16–17% of the sales price. It consists of the following elements:

1. **Cost of capital (interest cost):** The investment in inventory is a hidden cost. Lot of capital gets blocked in inventory. Money as a resource cost interests about 15% p.a. as per current trend. The ROI depends upon the speed with which the working capital turns round. The inventory constitutes the major component of working capital.
2. **Storage space (warehousing) cost:** The additional inventory requires additional space for storage, thereby incurring investment on land, building, storage racks, watchman, clerk for record-keeping and incidental expenses.
3. **Insurance cost:** Raw materials and the products when kept in stock need to be insured against various calamities like fire, earthquake, flood, riots, etc.

4. **Inventory risk costs:** The inventory risk cost constitutes product obsolescence, pilferage, loss, damage and deterioration.

Eight areas of INVENTORY CONTROL SYSTEM

- Accurate demand forecasts.
- Selection of inventory models, i.e.,
  - Dependent demand items model—MRP-I, MRP-II, CRP and DRP (97% of inventory).
  - Independent demand items model—ABC, HML, FSN, SOS, GOLF, etc. (absolutely 3% of inventory)
- Measurement of inventory cost
  - Inventory carrying cost
  - Ordering cost (EOQ)
- Method to record and accounts for items.
- Method for receipt, handling, storage and issue of items.
- Information procedure to report exception.
- Safe and secure primary and secondary packaging of the product.
- Safe and speedy transit of raw materials and products at respective demand points.

6.2.9 Material Requirement Planning (MRP–I)

Material requirement planning (MRP-I) is a computer based planning and control system used to plan and control effectively the internal production and material flow.

The objective of MRP-I is to minimize inventory and to maintain delivery schedules. This is achieved by forecast of needs derived from a 'master plan (MSP)' and 'bill of material' required which can be used to project, release and control orders.

The MRP system has the following four elements, as shown in Figure 6.2.

1. The bill of material file containing product structure record.
2. The inventory status file.
3. The master production schedule.
4. The MRP package.

The 'MRP LOGIC' is that demand for materials, parts and components depend on demand for an end product.

Bill of material

MRP-I is the first stage of supply chain management. It can only be applied to the dependent demand items, which forms the basic raw material, work-in-process and finished goods inventory. The first stage of the MRP-I is compilation of the bill of materials (BOM). Each product is exploded using the 'product tree concept' as shown in Figure 6.3. We keep on exploding the product into major assemblies, and sub-assemblies till we arrive at the basic raw material or the bought-out part to be sourced from outside.

Each stage of explosion has a separate stage number sequentially from zero onwards. Product at zero level is the final assembled product which can be used by the

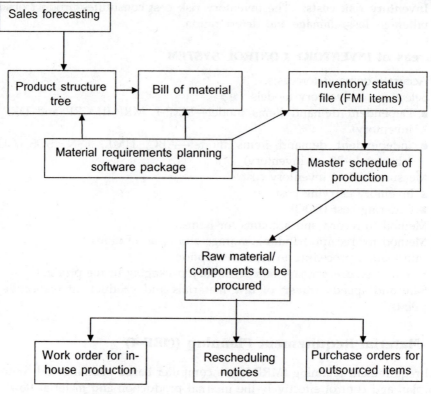

FIGURE 6.2 Material requirement planning.

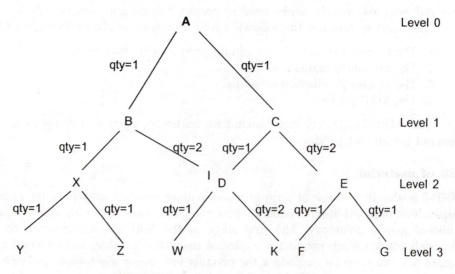

FIGURE 6.3 Product structure tree.

customer. At the end of the process of explosion, similar parts are segregated and aggregated to form the final list of materials and components to be procured for manufacturing the final product. This consolidated list is known as Bill of material which is given to the material department for sourcing.

Another statement known as 'multi-level bill of material' is released to the shopfloor production department to indicate components and materials related and required at each level of sub-assembling and assembling.

Inventory status file

This gives an indication of raw material and components in stock, in process and how many of them are reserved against the previous order and how much is available in free stock. Normally for production planning and control an FSN analysis is done. 'FSN analysis' means segregating the items into the fast moving, slow moving and normal moving items. The production capacity is filled up to 80% of the components and parts against the actual customer orders. The balance 20% of the plant capacity is filled in by the fast moving items. These 'FMI' items are normally available in the stock. These are the items which are shown in the inventory status file.

Master production schedule

The master production schedule is derived from the customer demand and gives the quantity required under each product category. The basic data fed in to the bills of material file is the quantity of raw material and components required to produce one number of final assembled product which can be used by the customer. The final list of bills of material is worked out based on the master production schedule and the quantity required under each product category. This consolidated requirement is noted in bills of material for the month. From this statement, the MRP package deducts the free inventory available and produces the final list of 'planned order release'.

This planned order release is divided into two categories:

1. Items to be produced in-house and
2. Items to be bought from outside.

At the stage of MRP-I, we release purchase order for those items for which the organization does not have the technological ability to produce in-house.

MRP-I package

The material requirement planning package is the centre of processing the entire inventory and parts and components with the procurement right from the suppliers to the point of receipt in the raw material store and issue to the shopfloor for the manufacturing of the particular product. The product tree structure is already fed into this software package. The most successful software package for supply chain management consists of Visual Basic at the front-end and Oracle or SQL at the back-end. The moment the product wise sales forecast for the month is fed into the system, the MRP software package works out the bill of material and the requirement of the parts and components to meet the market demand. The MRP-I software package checks automatically with the inventory status and deducts the parts/components available in the inventory and produces the final list of parts/components either to be produced in-house or to be sourced from outside. The MRP-I package also balances the requirement by issuing the rescheduling notices in case of shortages or the excess inventory available.

6.2.10 Manufacturing Resource Planning—(MRP–II)

Manufacturing resource planning (MRP-II) takes care of the balance items which are verified against the organization's manufacturing capability. The MRP package has all the information regarding various workstations, machines and their capacity and capability. This list of items is verified against their capacity known as 'capacity requirement planning' and further two final lists are prepared:

1. One list is for the items which are economically and technically viable to be manufactured in-house up to the full plant capacity utilization.
2. The balance items are to be procured from outside. These items are either not economical to produce in-house or even if economical, the organization cannot produce the item in the required quantity within the stipulated delivery period.

This is known as manufacturing resource planning or MRP-II. The output from MRP-II is either a work order for in-house production or a purchase order for bought-out items, as shown in Figure 6.4.

While booking the capacity for in-house manufacturing, the normal industrial practice is to fill up the capacity by 80% with the planned order releases and 20% with the open order file which consists of the fast moving items. Now the capacity is filled in, keeping in mind the load profile for each machining centre and production routing file. MRP-I links the supplier to the organization and extends from the supplier to the receipt of the goods and parts at the incoming raw material stores. MRP-II extends from the incoming raw material to the finished goods store.

6.2.11 Material Requirement Planning and Manufacturing Resource Planning

The features are detailed and elaborated in the following points:

1. It contains the necessary logic to operate the system.
2. The system tied together becomes a tool for planning and controlling a great number of inter-related parts and products.
3. MRP considers the current and planned quantities of parts and products in inventories in addition to the time element in order to incorporate long and short run changes for inter-related parts and products.
4. MRP needs all records and files to be updated on a continuous basis and containing accurate information.
5. It is also vital to have all necessary records in good database form for computer application.
6. MRP can be applied for inventory control of items that have a discontinuous, non-uniform and dependent demand.
7. It is suitable for assembly, production, manufacturing or fabrication operations and not suitable for wholesalers and traders.

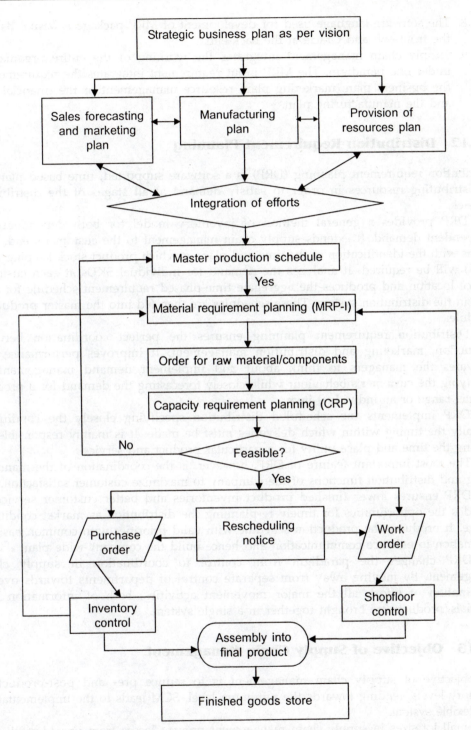

FIGURE 6.4 Manufacturing resource planning (MRP-II).

8. The software language used for development of MRP package is Visual Basic at the front-end and Oracle at the back-end.

9. Supply chain management integrates the working of the entire organization under one paradigm. The MRP input requirement integrates the requirement of the business plan, marketing plan, resource management or the financial plan and the manufacturing plan.

6.2.12 Distribution Requirement Planning

Distribution requirement planning (DRP) is a software supported, time based planning of distributing resources in order to satisfy demand at all stages of the distribution channel.

DRP provides a general method of inventory model for both dependent and independent demand. It extends supply chain management to the customer's end. DRP begins with the identification of the time and place at which product stock keeping units (SKU) will be required. It analyzes the demand for individual SKUs at each customer service location and produces the aggregate time-phased requirement schedule for each level in the distribution system. These schedules are then fed into the master production schedule.

Distribution requirement planning ensures the perfect coordination between production, marketing and distribution management. It improves performance and motivates the managers to think about and implement demand management by modifying the customer's behaviour while closely forecasting the demand for a product, product range or an individual item.

DRP implements the scheduled distribution specifying closely the conditions, specially the timing within which deliveries must be made. It is mainly responsible for creating the time and place utility for a particular product and service.

The most important feature of DRP, however, is the coordination of the manufacturing and distribution functions of the company to maximize customer satisfaction.

DRP ensures lower finished product inventories and better customer service. It provides the opportunities for timely re-planning the distribution as market conditions change. It produces the production schedule with valid priorities with common basis of information to enhance communication and hence build the company-wide plan.

DRP changes the paradigm from control to coordination in supply chain management. By moving away from separate control of departments towards overall coordination of effort, all the major movement activities, both of information and materials/products are brought together in a single system.

6.2.13 Objective of Supply Chain Management

The objective of supply chain management is to reduce pre- and post-production inventory levels, tending towards the minimum level. SCM leads to the implementation of a flexible system.

Small lot sizes in supply chain management prevent losses from unsold stock and allow flexibility through accommodating small changes. SCM prevents product obsolescence in today's shorter product life cycle. It ensures maximum efficiency in using labour, capital and plant throughout the company. It provides a scope for flexible planning and control procedures and also ensures controlled customer service performance. It leads to a system of performance with minimum variances due to the reduced uncertainty.

Supply chain management creates an organization which incurs minimum total cost. It also ensures product quality by preservation of added value by faster delivery to the point of consumption from the point of manufacturing. This is particularly true for the food products and pharmaceutical products.

6.2.14 Prerequisites for Success of MRP, DRP and SCM

The following points needs to be kept in purview for the success of MRP, DRP and SCM:

- For all these systems to be effective, accurate information and control to the extent of at least 98% is mandatory.
- The full proofing of the system is necessary.
- Adoption of methods like bar coding, Kanban or JIT, computer communication and linkage for ordering and billing, cycled stock-taking, statistical expertise and education and training are must.
- All the parties including the supplier, materials, stores, production, marketing, logistics, distributors, branches and dealers are to play well-coordinated and well-versed role for making the above activities successful.
- The security of the system implementing supply chain management is extremely important since the system will provide limited access to the network to so many of its vendors and dealers apart from the organizational offices.

6.2.15 Just-In-Time

Just-in-time (JIT) is defined as a highly integrated production, sales and distribution system leading to continuous flow through the entire supply chain.

The finished goods inventory of one department becomes the raw material inventory for the next downstream department requiring that particular part.

Core Japanese practices of JIT

The ultimate manifestation of supply chain management as well as the implementation of total quality management is reflected in the Toyota production system or TPS. JIT is an integral part of the Toyota production system which is designed and practiced by Mr. Taichii Ohno.

The core practices followed by the JIT are the use of the Kanban system or the card system in production which ensures that the items are manufactured only against an actual customer's order and not otherwise. To achieve this, production is adapted to accommodate the demand change. The set-up time is reduced by employing techniques like SMED and computer integrated manufacturing to reduce the production time and the operations are standardized to attain line balancing.

For the implementation of JIT, the machine layout is the group technology or the cellular manufacturing technique. The machine operators are multifunctional for the flexible work concept. There is implementation of activities by the small group and the suggestion scheme to reduce the workforce and increase the worker's morale. The visual control system is installed to achieve the autonomation concept, i.e., integrating the quality control and the production together. The organization should be practicing total quality management and a functional quality management system to promote company-wide quality control.

All employees of the organization should be JIT oriented. The organization should promote practices that promote continuous flow manufacture. It should eliminate wastage or the 'muda', i.e., any activity that adds cost and no value like rejection, rework and wastage, etc. These practices are described in detail in Chapter 2. The organization should make efforts to improve activities that add value.

It should also reduce activities that add cost, i.e., it should reduce inventory, reserve stock, lead time, discourage over production and reduce machine set-up times. The organization should also ensure negligible order processing or changeover costs.

The just-in-time activities belong to four categories of people, process, planning and the quality.

The JIT system should opt for the mixed model scheduling as per the production rate and demand by flexibility of production lines to allow concurrent assembly of different models on the same line. This enables the JIT system to achieve synchronized scheduling and regularity in end product scheduling and delivery as per the market demand. It should incorporate frequent deliveries, small lot size production and buffer stock removal and it must manufacture the products only as per the market and the customers' demand.

The JIT system eliminates the inspection of incoming goods and outgoing goods by opting for the six sigma system of production process control and standardized container so that there is no need to count the products or the parts produced.

JIT enablers

We can now try to summarize the main factors which enable the implementation of the JIT system. They are detailed below:

1. Housekeeping: The use of 4 S for good housekeeping can be suggested here, viz.
   - Seiri: orderliness.
   - Seiton: tidiness.
   - Seiso: clarity.
   - Seiketsu: cleanliness.
2. Problem solving techniques: It includes implementation of pareto analysis, ishikawa diagram and brainstorming backed up by techniques like quality circles, Kaizen Gemba and Juran's quality improvement.
3. Waste reduction: Use of 3 M practice
   - Muri: unreasonableness.
   - Mura: unevenness.
   - Muda: waste.

4. Visibility: The visibility and transparency in the production as well as in the entire organizational operation is mandatory for success of JIT.
5. Standardization: It includes standardization of parts, processes, dies and mould sizes.
6. Total productive maintenance: It refers to shifting of routine maintenance to operators and focus on preventive maintenance.
7. SMED: Reduction of set-up times to single digit minutes makes small lot size production feasible.
8. Statistical process control (SPC): SPC is an important aspect of quality control and quality management. It leads to process orientation and zero defect.
9. Autonomation: This helps in automatic defect control, prevention of poor quality in production.
10. Total employee involvement (TEI): This is a JIT prerequisite. This is achieved through teamwork, education, training, job enrichment, quality improvement project, etc.
11. Design: Design of modular manufacturing technique and simplicity is an integral part of JIT.
12. Flexible process and equipment.
13. Management control.
14. Others including high level of technical support and production engineering.

Just in-case (JIC) stock

The JIT system can be implemented step by step over a number of years by successive reduction in the inventory. Every time the inventory is reduced, new problem surfaces needing immediate action to prevent any stock-out of raw material and production stoppage or stock-out of the finished products leading to their shortage in the market.

The four factors which are responsible for such occurrence of stock-out and failure of the JIT system are late deliveries, rejections, sudden increase in the market demand and the machine breakdown, as shown in Figure 6.5.

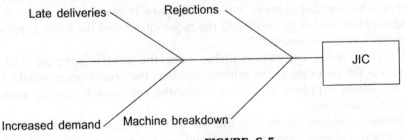

FIGURE 6.5

The problem can be eliminated progressively by finding out the root cause through the 'Ishikawa' or the 'cause and effect' diagram followed by a brainstorming session. Once the root cause is determined, suitable corrective and preventive actions are taken for the elimination of these four factors responsible for the just-in-case stock which is a measurement of the inefficiency of the entire system. The objective in the JIT system is to reduce the JIC stock to zero over a period of time.

JIT systems

The just-in-time system consists of two major parts, that is the just-in-time purchase and the just-in-time production or the Kanban system. We shall first discuss just-in-time purchasing which is primarily responsible for the vendor management system and raw material and components inventory.

JIT purchasing

In the just-in-time purchasing system, quality has superseded price to become the primary consideration in the selection of supplier. The word 'quality' implies both the quality of the components and parts supplied by the vendor as well as the reliability of timely supply.

The goals of just-in-time purchasing is to filter out the wastes in the production processes and to improve upon the quality of the product and the services. Just-in-time purchasing should be able to satisfy consumer demand in an efficient and reliable manner. It should ensure that value is added to the products.

The Just-in-time purchasing system should look into the following aspects of the organization in order to be efficient:

1. **Inventory:** The objective of just-in-time purchasing is to have only the correct part in the correct place at the correct time. To achieve this objective, approach is to remove bottlenecks and have only as small inventories as possible. Just-in-time purchasing is possible only if the suppliers have fast set-ups and small lots size for production and frequent delivery. The just-in-time purchasing system should have flexible labour and equipment. At the management level there should be consensus management and integrated technical support. Just-in-time purchasing always challenges as-usual attitude and looks for improving everything.

2. **Suppliers:** The JIT purchasing system has few suppliers, preferably one or two supplier per component, as per Mr. Edward Deming. JIT purchasing should give preference to the nearby suppliers and repeat business with the same suppliers.

    It should make active use of analysis to enable desirable suppliers to be price competitive. The supplier who is better of the two is rated as 'A class' or the 'preferred supplier' and is given 70% of the requirement and the other supplier is given only 30% of the business.

    If all certain items are not available with the nearby supplier and the organization is forced to go to the remote supplier, the organization should form a cluster of remote suppliers at a place where the company is already sourcing some of its requirements.

    'Competitive bidding' is mostly limited to new items and the commercial terms are discussed only once in a year and an annual rate contract is signed between the organization and its suppliers.

    The suppliers are encouraged to extend JIT buying to their suppliers. The organization ensures that all its suppliers are implementing statistical process control.

3. **Quality:** The JIT purchasing system imposes minimum product specifications on the supplier. The parent organization helps the suppliers to meet quality

requirement. There is close relationship between buyers' and suppliers' quality assurance procedures. The suppliers are encouraged to use control charts and to implement statistical process control so that the parts are of zero defect and do not need any inspection at the organization level. The suppliers are also required to supply the components in standardized containers so that no time is wasted in counting the parts supplied.

4. **Quantities:** The JIT purchasing system expects a steady output rate and frequent delivery in small lot quantities from its suppliers. The system has long-term contract agreements with the suppliers and there is minimum or zero paperwork.

   The JIT purchasing system fixes the delivery quantities variable from release to release but fixed for whole contract term between the buyer and seller organizations. It does not allow any 'overage' or 'underage' of receipts in term of the quantity and the suppliers are encouraged to package in exact quantities in the standardized containers. The suppliers are encouraged to reduce their production lot sizes.

5. **Deliveries:** The JIT purchasing system schedules the in-bound deliveries. The organization gains control of the delivery time by the use of company-owned or contracted transportation system. The delivery and storage of the components and parts are kept under the control of the organization whereever possible.

JIT production.   After the execution of the JIT system of purchasing, the JIT system of production has been deployed. The system is also known as the Kanban system.

There are two types of Kanban system:

1. Production Ordering Kanban (POK) and
2. Withdrawal Kanban (WK).

These two together execute pull type of JIT production. It produces only that much which is needed for the customers. The output from the previous process becomes the input to the succeeding process without any delay or being held in stock. Similarly, when the product reaches the final stage, it is immediately dispatched to the customers as products are produced only against customers' orders.

Kanban

1. Kanban system is an integral part of the JIT production system.
2. It is designed to produce only the number of units needed by a 'pull' or demand feeding process.
3. It leads to smaller set-up times, small production lots and reduced in process inventories.
4. Kanban is a card of two types, as shown in Figure 6.6.
5. A withdrawal Kanban shows the quantity of items that the subsequent process should withdraw from previous or proceeding one.
6. Production ordering Kanban shows the quantity that proceeding process should produce.
7. The Kanban system provides an additional close link between operations, reinforces previous linkages that lead to improved quality and productivity.

KANBAN

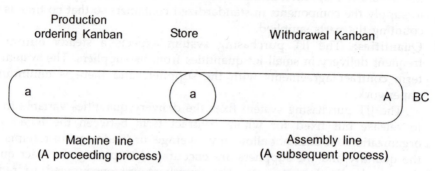

Flow of two Kanbans

FIGURE 6.6 The flow of two Kanbans.

8. The Kanban system of inventory control works well in situation with standardized parts and products cycled in the manufacturing system.
9. It goes well with MRP and inventory control.
10. The Withdrawal Kanban (WK) details the quantity that the subsequent process should withdraw. Refer to Figures 6.7 and 6.8.
11. The Production Ordering Kanban (POK) shows the quantity which the preceding process should produce.
12. Carrier of subsequent process goes to the store of the preceding process with necessary number of WKs and empty containers.

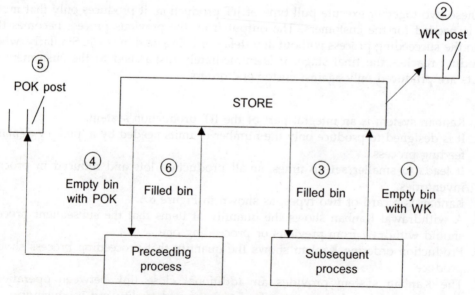

FIGURE 6.7 The Kanban process.

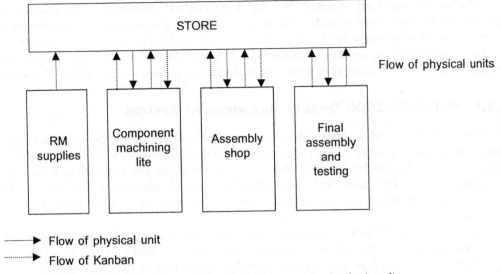

FIGURE 6.8 Chain of Kanbans and physical unit.

13. When this process carrier withdraws the parts from store, he detaches the POK attached to physical units in pallets and deposits this in Kanban receiving post. He also leaves behind the empty pallets.
14. Each POK he replaces with his WK after checking the quantity.
15. When work begins in subsequent process, WKs are put in WK post.
16. In the preceding process POKs are withdrawn with empty pallets.
17. The POKs are reproduced as per original sequence.

The JIT production system and the Kanban system are integral parts of just-in-time manufacturing. This is a demand pull system of manufacturing where the products are manufactured only that much as required by the customers. This process ensures zero wastage and minimum lead time for processing from the raw material to the finished product. The just-in-time system ensures zero inventory and maximum efficiency in the manufacturing.

6.3 QUALITY MANAGEMENT SYSTEMS

There are several quality management systems prevalent depending upon the ultimate objective of the quality management system and its orientation and focus. The quality management system ensures a structured, systematic way of working of an organization making it to thrive for world-class performance. The most prominent among them and the basic quality management system based on world-class total quality management system is the ISO 9001:2000 quality management system. This standard is devised by the International Standard Organization and accepted worldwide as a TQM system, mandatory to prove by a third party audit that the organization is a world-class organization fit to supply good quality products and service consistently at the competitive price.

The other standard devised by the International Standard Organization and accepted worldwide as a quality management system focused on the environmental aspect of an organization is the ISO 14000 standard. There are other internationally accepted standards on quality management system similar to ISO 9000 standard as applicable to the automobile component manufacturing industry is the QS 9000 standard.

6.3.1 ISO 9000:2000 Quality Management System

ISO 9000:2000 is a world-class quality management system giving the certified organization the status of a world-class organization. It takes the mystery out of the quality. It defines quality chapter by chapter and verse by verse. In the current globalized and liberalized era, the ISO 9000:2000 certification has become mandatory for entry into the global as well as the local market and getting the firm registered with a reputed organization.

Due to various different standards existing in various countries, a need was felt to have one unified standard to facilitate international trade. This was the first organizational standard in quality management consistent in terminology as well as content for international trade. ISO 9000 standards had great impact in international trade and quality systems implementation by organizations worldwide. The standard has been adopted as national standard by more than 120 countries. This is applied through a wide range of industry, economic, service and government regulatory areas. The ISO 9000 standards deal with the management system set by organization to design, produce, deliver and support their products. The standard applied to all generic product categories: hardware, software, as well as processed materials.

Definition of ISO 9000:2000

The ISO 9000 standard defines the formal quality management system necessary to assure that the technical, administrative and human factors affecting the quality of an organization's products or services are under control.

Further this formal system must be implemented such that its effectiveness can be demonstrated to the organization's management, to the customers of the organization and to an independent third party for the purpose of verification and certification.

Purpose of the quality management system

The purpose of the quality management system is to enhance customer satisfaction through effective application of system. The entire organization should be customer-oriented, continuously assessing the customer's stated and implied needs. Based on this feedback the organization is generating the products and services leading to continual customer satisfaction. The quality management system also includes processes for continual improvement. QMS also results in maximization of return on investment along with the total employee involvement.

QMS follows a process-orientation with Deming's P-D-C-A cycle. The organization must have a main process for value addition by conversion and break it up into linkages of sub-processes. At every stage the system measures the input, output, the value addition and efficiency and effectiveness of the process management with quantitative measurement of the effectiveness in terms of generation of surplus as per schedule.

Due to different standards existing in various countries, a need was felt to have one unified standard to facilitate international trade. This was the first organizational standard in quality management system containing the terminology as well as content for international trade. ISO 9000 standards had great impact in international trade and quality systems implementation by organizations worldwide. The standard has been adopted as national standard by more than 118 countries. This is applied through a wide range of industry, economic, service and government regulatory areas. The ISO 9000 standard deals with the management system set by organization to design, produce, deliver and support their products. The standard is applied to all generic product categories: hardware, software and processed materials. ISO 9000:2000 edition gives a fundamental quality management system for an organization.

ISO 9000 series and related standards

The earlier standard ISO 9000 series was first introduced in 1987 and revised in 1994. It focused on quality assurance system and consisted of standards, viz. ISO 9000, 9001, 9002, 9003 and 9004. The current revision published in December 2000 consists of only three standards:

1. ISO 9000:2000—Quality management system—Fundamentals and vocabulary.
2. ISO 9001:2000—Certification standard for quality management systems process approaches in design, development, production, installation and servicing. It has a provision for certification with a single exclusion limited to requirement within Clause 7 for product realization where such exclusion does not affect the organization's ability or responsibility to provide products that must meet customer's and applicable regulatory requirements.
3. ISO 9004:2000—Gives guidance for wider range of objectives of a quality management system than what is given by 9001. It gives guidelines particularly for continual improvement of an organization's overall performance.

The main improvization that has been done in ISO 9000:2000 edition compared to 1994 edition is that the 2000 edition introduced a process approach to business and an organization's working rather than the product approach. While the 1994 edition was more of a quality assurance system, the 2000 edition is on a quality management system.

The ISO 9000 family does not deal with any technical specification for a product and is complimentary to any technical specifications, standards or regulations applicable to the organization's product or its services. The standards in ISO 9000 family are produced and maintained by technical committee 176 of the international standard organization (ISO). The first meeting of ISO/TCI 176 was held in 1980. ISO 8402, the vocabulary standard was introduced in 1986 and the initial ISO 9000 was published in 1987.

Evolution of ISO 9000

The evolution of the ISO 9001:2000 is explained in Figure 6.9. The need for standardization for consistency in performance was strongly felt by the US army. A big percentage of the bombs dropped from the aircraft could hit the target but failed to explode. They faced a similar problem with the performance of the other war arsenals

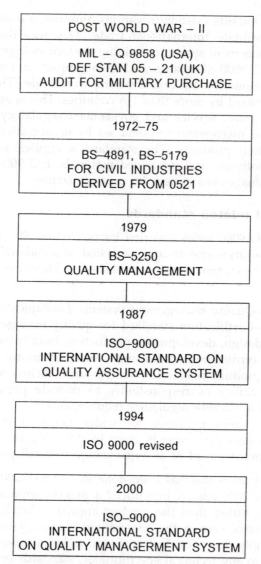

FIGURE 6.9 Evolution of ISO 9001:2000.

and the vehicles. To overcome the problem they brought forward a standard known as US Military Standard MIL Q 9858. The United Kingdom followed suit by bringing a similar standard STAN 05–21.

A similar need was felt by the United Kingdom's civil industries and the standard BS 4891 was brought in 1972 and for all the industries in general by BS 5179 in 1975. The first official standard on the quality management system was brought by the British Standard Institution in the year 1979 as BS-5250.

BS-5250 was accepted as the first organized standard on the quality management standard and it was adopted by the International Standard Organization as a standard on the 'quality assurance system' and first time the ISO 9000 series of standards was published in 1987. The standard had gone minor changes in its revised edition in 1994.

The ISO 9000:2000 was published with major changes in December, 2000 so that all the lacunas of the standard were removed. The standard was more demanding in continual improvement and preventive action as well as warranted a process approach following Deming's P-D-C-A cycle. In short, the standard was upgraded from the 'quality assurance system' to the 'total quality management system' or TQM.

Apart from ISO 8402, 9000, 9001 and ISO 9004, the other members of the ISO 9000 family of international standard are:

1. **ISO 14000:1996**—It is an international standard on the environment management system. The two international standards ISO 9000:2000 and ISO 14000 are synchronized in the recent 2000 version of ISO 9000.
2. **ISO 19011**—Guidelines on quality and environmental auditing.

Difference between ISO 9000:1994 and ISO 9000:2000

The shift from quality assurance standards, i.e., ISO 9000 to 9003:1994 to the latest ISO 9000 and 9001 standard 2000 is on quality management system. The difference can be summarized as given in Table 6.1.

TABLE 6.1 Quality management system vs. quality assurance

1. Achievement of quality related result.	1. Demonstration of achievement of requirements of quality.
2. Motivated by stakeholders both internal, i.e., management and external, i.e., customer.	2. Motivated by organization mainly customers.
3. Process oriented.	3. Product oriented.
4. Goal is satisfying all stakeholders.	4. Goal is satisfying customers.
5. Superior overall performance is intended.	5. Confidence in the product is the intended result.
6. Scope covers all activities that impact the total business result of the organization.	6. Scope covers activities that directly impact product results.
7. Continuous improvement is mandatory.	7. Continuous improvement is not mandatory.

Quality management principles

The present versions of ISO 9001 and ISO 9004 have been based on eight-quality management principles, which reflect best management practices. In order to manage an organization successfully, it should be managed in a systematic manner. The requirement for any organization to remain successful is to continually improve performance by addressing the needs of all interested parties.

The following eight principles should be taken into account when developing a quality management system to meet the requirements of ISO 9001:2000. By applying the following eight principles, organizations will produce benefits for customers, owners, people, suppliers, local community and society at large. Each of the major clause of ISO 9001:2000 is based on these eight principles.

A quality management principle is a comprehensive and fundamental rule or belief for leading and operating an organization aimed at continually improving performance over the long term by focusing on customer while addressing the needs of all other stakeholders.

Customer focus. Organizations depend on their customers and therefore should understand current and future customer needs, should meet customer requirements and strive to exceed customer expectations.

Customers play a major role in the future profitability of an organization. In order to retain customers, the organization must understand the current requirements and potential future requirements of their customers.

Applying the principle of a customer-focused organization leads to the following actions:

- Understanding the whole range of customer needs and expectations for products, delivery, price, dependability, etc.
- Ensuring a balanced approach among customers and other stakeholders' (owners, people, suppliers, local communities and society at large) needs and expectations.
- Communicating these needs and expectations throughout the organization.
- Measuring the customer satisfaction and acting on results.
- Managing customer relationship.

Leadership. Leaders establish unity of purpose, direction and internal environment of the organization. They should create and maintain the internal environment in which people can become fully involved in achieving the organization's objectives.

The management of an organization must provide direction, leadership, and provide a suitable environment for the organization to function. By doing this, the management provides the opportunity for people to become fully involved in achieving the organization's objectives.

Applying the principle of leadership leads to the following actions:

- Being proactive and leading by example.
- Understanding and responding to changes in the external environment.
- Considering the needs of all stakeholders, including customers, owners, people, suppliers, local communities and society at large.
- Establishing a clear vision of the organization's future.
- Inspiring, recognizing and encouraging people's contributions.
- Setting challenging goals and targets.
- Implementing strategy to achieve these goals and targets.

Involvement of people. People at all levels are the essence of the organization and their full involvement enables their abilities to be used for the benefit of the organization.

People at all levels of an organization have the ability to influence the organization in its ability to achieve its objectives.

By involving people, using their skills and knowledge, the organization provides an environment where people can assist and be involved in achieving its objectives.

Applying the principle of involvement of people leads to the following actions by the people:

- Accepting ownership and responsibility to solve problems.
- Actively seeking opportunities to make improvements.
- Being innovative and creative in furthering the organization's objectives.
- Deriving satisfaction from their work, and being enthusiastic and proud to be part of the organization.

Process approach. A desired effect is achieved more efficiently when related resources and activities are managed as a process.

Any activity that receives input and converts them into output can be considered a process. For an organization to be effective, it must manage all processes in the most effective manner. The systematic identification and management of the process employed within an organization and the interactions between such processes may be referred to as the process approach.

Applying this principle leads to the following activities:

- Defining the process to achieve the desired results.
- Identifying and measuring the inputs and outputs of the process.
- Evaluating possible risks and impacts of process on customers, suppliers and other stakeholders of the process.
- Establishing clear authority, responsibility and accountability for managing the process.

System approach to management. Identifying, understanding and managing a system of inter-related processes for a given objective contributes to the effectiveness and efficiency of the organization.

Managing the inter-relationship between all the identified processes will assist in achieving the end objective. The output from one process may become the input for next process. This area of the organization activity must be managed.

Applying the principle of system approach to management leads to the following actions:

- Defining the system by identifying or developing the process that affects a given objective.
- Structuring the system to achieve the objective in the most efficient way.
- Understanding the interdependencies among the processes of the system.
- Continually improving the system through measurement and evaluation.
- Establishing resources constraints prior to action.

Continual improvement. Continual improvement in the organization's overall performance should be a permanent objective of the organization.

Improvements refer to the actions taken to enhance the features of product and/or to increase the effectiveness and efficiency of processes used to produce and deliver them.

Applying the principle of continual improvement leads to the following actions:

- Making continual improvement of products, processes and systems should be an objective for every individual in the organization.
- Applying basic improvement concepts of incremental and breakthrough improvement.
- Using periodic assessment against established criteria of excellence to identify areas for potential improvement.
- Continually improving the efficiency and effectiveness of all processes.
- Promoting prevention-based activities.
- Providing employees with appropriate education and training on methods and tools of continual improvements, such as:

  (a) The Plan-Do-Check-Act (P-D-C-A) cycle.
  (b) Problem solving methods.

- Establishing measures and goals to guide and track improvements.

Factual approach to decision-making. Effective decisions are based on the analysis of data and information.

Managers at all levels within an organization are required to make decisions that will influence the direction of an organization with regard to the achievement of its objectives.

Applying the principle of factual approach to decision-making leads to the following actions:

- Taking measurements and collecting data and information relating to the objective.
- Ensuring that the data and information are sufficiently accurate, reliable and accessible.
- Analyzing the data and information using valid methods.
- Understanding the value of appropriate statistical techniques.
- Making decisions and taking action based on the results of logical analysis balanced with experience and intuition.

Mutually beneficial supplier relationships. An organization and its suppliers are interdependent and a mutually beneficial relationship enhances the ability of both to create value. The products received from suppliers are an important element of the final product delivered to the customer. By improving the relationship between the organization and its suppliers, customers can benefit in the areas of quality, reliability and consistency.

Applying the principle of mutually beneficial supplier relationships leads to the following actions:

- Identifying and selecting key suppliers.
- Establishing supplier relationships that balance short-term gains with long-term considerations for the organization and society at large.

- Creating a clear and open communication.
- Initiating joint development and improvement of products and processes.
- Jointly establishing a clear understanding of customers' needs.
- Sharing information and future plans.
- Recognizing supplier improvements and achievements.

Importance of ISO 9000

The internal significance of ISO 9000 is as follows:

- Vehicle to hold quality improvement gains.
- Provides good platform for continuous quality improvement.
- Provides method for involving non-manufacturing areas in quality and quality improvement.
- Keeps employees' morale high and ensures their total involvement.
- Helps in reducing the wastages and reduction in the cost of production.
- The organization has a sound world-class management system for all-round performance excellence.

The external significance of ISO 9000 is as follows:

- Ensures customer satisfaction.
- Generates customer confidence through world-class products and services.
- Ensures confidence with all stakeholders in the organization including suppliers, investors, shareholders, etc.
- Fulfills commitments to society and country as a whole.
- Fulfills the mandatory requirement of entry as a supplier to export market and many domestic organizations.

ISO 9000 expectations

- Is the organization's quality system adequate?
- Does the organization follow its quality system?
- Is there a process-orientation in the organizational activities?
- Is there a platform for holding the gain and for continuous improvement?
- Does the organization audit itself?
- Is there an evidence of documented quality system audits with evidence of resulting corrective action?
- Are management reviews of the quality system conducted and acted upon?

Development of the quality management systems

ISO 9000 system has become mandatory and popular all over the world due to the phenomenon of globalization. The total management approach in the standard leads the organization first to understand and analyze the customer's needs and expectations keeping in mind the customer requirements as well as the requirements of all other stakeholders including the management.

The ISO 9000:2000 quality management system establishes the quality policy and quality objective of the organization. It then defines the products and services which are acceptable to the customer as well as are in line with the attainment of the quality objectives. The system then should have a sound quality control. This means that there should be an ongoing measurement of the effectiveness of the processes.

The quality management system then establishes a documented quality management system to attain the quality objectives. Then measure the effectiveness of the processes towards attaining quality objectives. After measurement, analysis and review of the effectiveness and efficiency of processes, the quality management system finds out the deviation and takes the corrective and preventive actions for continuous improvement and the feedback loop is completed by giving this feedback to the beginning of the quality management system. The quality management system is shown in Figure 6.10.

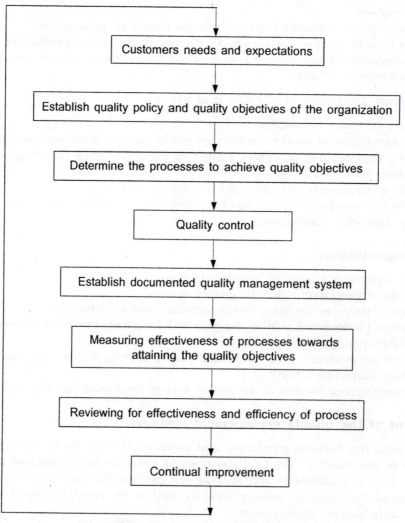

FIGURE 6.10 Quality management system.

Overall objectives of this QMS is prevention rather than deviation and continual improvement of the system and therefore the continual improvement of the product and/or service supplied which result in customer satisfaction. The requirement of this standard is generic and can be applied to all organizations regardless of size, type and products and services offered.

ISO 9000:2000 specifies requirements for a QMS where an organization needs to provide products that meet the customers' regulatory requirements and aims to enhance customer satisfaction through processes for continual improvement of the system.

The adoption of the QMS should be strategic decision and part of the organizational need. Requirements specified in this standard are complimentary to the requirements of the products. The basic purpose is to prove the organization's ability to meet the requirements of the customer and the organization.

The present editions of the ISO 9001 and ISO 9004 are developed as a consistent pair of quality management system standards complementing each other. They can also be used independently.

This QMS is based on the process approach, which believes that if the processes are correct the product cannot go wrong, and has to be correct and consistent in performance.

The process approach

The adoption of a quality management system should be a strategic decision of an organization. The design and implementation of an organization's quality management system is influenced by varying needs, particular objectives, the products provided, the processes employed and the size and structure of the organization. It is not the intent of this international standard to imply uniformity in the structure of quality management system or uniformity of documentation.

QMS requirements specified in this International Standard are complementary requirements for the product. Information marked 'Note' is for guidance in understanding or clarifying the associate requirement.

Internal and external parties, including certification bodies to access the organization's ability to meet the customers' regulatory and organization's own requirements can use this international standard.

The quality management principles stated in ISO 9000 and ISO 9004 have been taken into consideration during the development of this International Standard.

The International Standard promotes the adoption of a process approach for developing, implementing and improving the effectiveness of a QMS to enhance customer satisfaction by meeting customer requirements. For an organization to function effectively, it has to identify and manage numerous linked activities. An activity using resources and managed in order to enable the transformation of inputs into outputs can be considered as a process. Often output of one process becomes the input for another process. A model of process-based quality management system is shown in Figure 6.11.

An advantage of the process approach is the ongoing control that it provides over the linkage between the individual processes within the system of processes, as well as over their combination and interaction. Such an approach emphasises the importance of:

(a) Understanding and meeting requirements.
(b) The need to consider processes in terms of added value.

(c) Obtaining results of process performance and effectiveness.

(d) Continual improvement of processes based on objective measurement.

The model of a process-based quality management system, shown in Figure 6.11 illustrates the process linkages presented in clauses 4 to 8. This illustration shows that customers play a significant role in defining requirement as input. Monitoring of customer satisfaction requires the evaluation of information relating to customer perception to whether the organization has met the customer requirement. The model shown in the figure covers all the requirements of this International Standard but does not show processes at a detailed level.

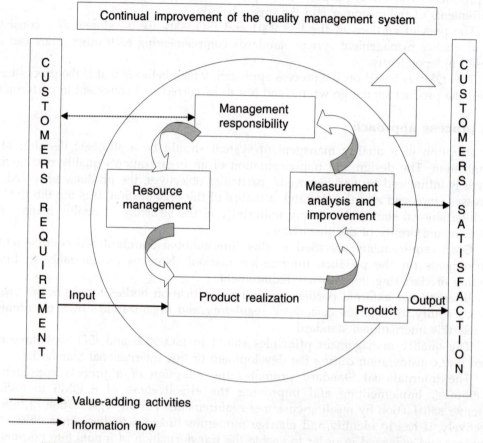

FIGURE 6.11 Model of process-based quality management system. (IS/ISO 9001:2000 page no. (ii) and page no. (iii)).

Note: In addition, the methodology known as 'Plan-Do-Check-Act' (P-D-C-A) can be applied to all processes. P-D-C-A can be briefly described as follows:

Plan: Establish the objectives and processes necessary to deliver results in accordance with customer requirements and the organization's policies.

Do: Implement the process.

Check: Monitor and measure processes and product against policies, objectives and requirements for the product and report the results.

Act: Take action to continually improve process performance.

Figure 6.11 shows the input as the customer's requirement and the output is the customer's satisfaction which mainly comes from the product realization (clause 7).

The important supportive functions are determined as management responsibility (clause 5), resource management (clause 6) and the measurement, analysis and improvement (clause 8). The figure also clearly indicates that all these activities should be continuously improved along with the overall improvement of the quality management system.

The entire organization has the flow of the value adding activities and the flow of information.

Details of the quality management system

The main section of ISO 9001:2000 are as follows:

4.0 Quality System Requirement.
5.0 Management Responsibility.
6.0 Resource Management.
7.0 Product Realization.
8.0 Measurement Analysis and Improvement.

Each one of the section is broken into further subdivisions.

Section 4.0—Quality management system.   The organization shall establish, document, implement and maintain a quality management system and improve its effectiveness.

The organization shall identify processes needed for the QMS and determine sequence and interaction of these processes. It should develop critical methods to operate and control these processes and ensure the availability of resources and information for these processes. The QMS should monitor, measure and analyze these processes and implement action to achieve planned result and continuous improvement of these processes. The organization should also have control over outsource processes [Clause no. 4.1].

Clause 4.2—Documentation requirements: The quality management system will have a certain amount of documentation in the form of procedures, work instructions and quality records. This will depend on size, complexity and skill level of the employees and the organization. Additional requirements will be from contractual, statutory and management requirements.

Clause 4.2.1—General requirement: The QMS should have a documented system, including quality policy, quality objective, six mandatory documented procedures, quality records and any other relevant documents for planning, operation and control of processes. Similarly, all the records should also be controlled. It should all be included in the 'Quality Manual'.

Clause 4.2.2—Quality manual: The quality management system will have a quality manual to include the scope and exclusions, sequence and interaction of the processes, procedures, work instructions and quality records. It should be controlled.

Clause 4.2.3—Control of documents: There should be written procedure for this clause. All the documents should be approved, reviewed, updated, easily available and readily identifiable, i.e., all the documents should be adequately legible and controlled. All the obsolete documents must be removed and only the current documents with revision status should be available.

Clause 4.2.4—Control of records: There should be written procedure for this clause. The quality records should be legible, readily identifiable, protected during storage. The quality records should have a defined retention time and system for its disposition.

Section 5.0—Management responsibility

Clause 5.1—Management commitment. The top management shall provide its commitment to the QMS and continually improve its effectiveness by communication on importance of meeting customers and regulatory needs, establishing quality policy, quality objectives, conducting management reviews and ensuring availability of resources.

Clause 5.2—Customer focus. Top management shall ensure the fulfillment and continuous enhancement of customer satisfaction. The entire organization should be customer focused and the top management has the responsibility to create a suitable structure for the same.

Clause 5.3—Quality policy. The top management will establish the quality policy, which is appropriate and committed to the QMS. At the same time it should be communicated and understood by everybody in the organization. The quality policy should provide a framework for establishing and reviewing quality objectives, their attainment and continued suitability.

Clause 5.4—Planning.

Clause 5.4.1—Quality objectives. The top management will also decide the quality objectives which should be measurable and consistent with the mission, vision and the quality policy. The organization should have a proper planning to achieve these quality objectives.

The quality objectives should be 'SMART', i.e., specific, measurable, achievable, realistic and timely. There should be evidence of their progress to the set objective and that of continual improvement.

Clause 5.4.2—Quality management system planning. The documented quality planning must include the processes of the quality management system, the resources needed and the continual improvement of the quality management system. The changes to the quality management system must be in a controlled manner so that the quality objective can be maintained and continual improvement of the management system is achieved.

Clause 5.5—Responsibility, authority and communication

Clause 5.5.1—Responsibility and authority. The top management should ensure that responsibility, authority and communication are defined and communicated within the organization to show how they are inter-related. The inter-relationship of different job function can be depicted as an 'organization chart' or described it as part of various job descriptions.

Clause 5.5.2—Management representative. The top management shall appoint a management representative (MR) to establish and monitor the QMS. The management representative should ensure that the processes are established, implemented and maintained. The management representative should report on the performance and improvement and promote awareness of the customers' requirements throughout the organization.

Clause 5.5.3—Internal communication. The management should ensure the establishment of appropriate communication process within the organization for effectiveness of the QMS.

Clause 5.6—Management review.

Clause 5.6.1—General. The top management should establish a process to review the QMS at planned intervals to ensure its continuing suitability, adequacy and effectiveness and maintain records for the same.

Clause 5.6.2—Review input. The management review input consists of results of audit, customer feedback, product and process performance, corrective and preventive actions status, follow up actions from previous reviews and any changes that would affect the quality management system.

Clause 5.6.3—Review output. The review should have the minutes and it should include improvements in the management of products, processes and the quality management system and need for any further resources.

Section 6.0—Resource management

Clause 6.1—Provision of resources. The organization shall determine and provide resources needed for implementing, maintaining and continuously improving the effectiveness of QMS and to enhance customer satisfaction by meeting customer requirements.

Clause 6.2—Human resources

Clause 6.2.1—General. Personnel performing work effecting product quality shall be evaluated for competence and imparted periodic training for skill development.

Clause 6.2.2—Competence, awareness and training. The employees should be trained, educated, skilled and experienced and have proper training of the job to be performed. The training should be based on competency need; the right kind of training should be provided and its effectiveness must be evaluated.

Clause 6.3—Infrastructure. The company should provide and maintain infrastructure like building, work space, process equipments, hardware, software and support services.

The organization shall determine, provide and maintain infrastructure including workplace, process equipment and support services needed to achieve the product conforming to requirements.

Clause 6.4—Work environment. The organization shall also create and manage the work environment needed to achieve conformatory product requirement.

Section 7—Product realization. Exclusions are permitted only against clause no. 7. However, the exclusions need to be justified.

Clause 7.1—Planning of product realization. The organization shall plan and develop process for product realization in line with quality objectives and allocate resources for the same. It should have specific criteria for product acceptance and will have recorded evidence for the same.

Clause 7.2—Customer-related processes

Clause 7.2.1—Determination of customers' requirement related to the product. The above stated process should be customer related and meeting the statutory requirement.

Clause 7.2.2—Review of requirements related to the product. The customer shall review the requirement related to the product. In case of any difference, it will be resolved with the customer and suitable record of the review will be maintained.

Clause 7.2.3—Customer communication. There should be the evidence of customer communication with reference to product information, contracts and customer feedback complaints.

Clause 7.3—Design and development. Those earlier organizations who had gone for ISO 9002 as per 1994 edition opted for exclusion for this clause. The organization should have evidence for the following:

- A systematic plan for design and development of the product.
- The responsibility and authority for the same.
- Design and development inputs related to product, performance and regulatory requirements should be determined and recorded.
- Design and development outputs should meet input requirements as well as defined product acceptance criteria. It should provide relevant information for purchasing, production and service and specify characteristic for safe and proper use of the product.
- There should be documented systematic review of design and development.
- There should be proper verification of design and development and results of the record should be maintained.
- Design and development validation will be done as per the plan.
- Any change in design and development should be identified, reviewed, verified, validated and approved before implementation and records for the same will be maintained.

Clause 7.4—Purchasing

Clause 7.4.1—Purchasing process. Organization should have defined purchasing process, ensuring that purchased products conform to specified purchase requirements. The suppliers should be evaluated and selected as per established criteria worked out by the organization and record of the result of such evaluation will be maintained.

Clause 7.4.2—Purchasing information. The organization shall ensure that purchase information describes the product and, whereever required, the relevant processes, procedures, equipment, personnel and its QMS.

Clause 7.4.3—Verification of the purchased product. The organization shall ensure the adequacy of specified purchase requirements and communicate to the supplier. The organization shall establish and implement specified activity for verification and acceptance of the purchased product.

Clause 7.5—Production and service provision

Clause 7.5.1—Control of production and service provision. The organization shall plan and carry out production and service under controlled conditions as per work instructions as necessary and by using suitable equipments, monitoring and measuring devices and finally implementation to realize delivery and post-delivery activities.

Clause 7.5.2—Validation of processes for production and service provision. The process for production and service provision shall be validated and recorded in terms of qualification of processes, equipment, personnel, methods and procedures.

Clause 7.5.3—Identification and traceability. Product should be identified and traced. The test status of product pass, fail or on hold should be indicated on the product.

Clause 7.5.4—Customer property. Proper care will be taken with reference to the customers' property being kept and/or used by the organization and record should be maintained for that.

Clause 7.5.5—Preservation of product. During internal processing and delivery to the customer, organization shall preserve the conformatory of the product.

Clause 7.6—Control of monitoring and measuring devices. All monitoring and measuring devices used by the organizations should be calibrated, identified and suitably protected to ensure observed results consistent with the monitoring and measurement requirements of the products.

Section 8—Measurement, analysis and improvement

Clause 8.1—General. The organization shall plan and implement the monitoring, measurement, analysis and improvement processes needed to ensure conformity and continuous improvement of the product as well as the QMS.

Clause 8.2—Monitoring and measurement

Clause 8.2.1—Customer satisfaction. The organization shall measure and monitor customer satisfaction and establish a system for the same. This information should be used as a measure of performance of the QMS.

Clause 8.2.2—Internal audit. The organization shall conduct internal audits at planned intervals to ensure the conformation, implementation and effectiveness of the management system. The audit criteria, scope, frequency and methods shall be defined along with responsibilities. The result of the audit should be recorded. The audit should be followed up for elimination of the detected non-conformities. A procedure has to be compulsorily written for the internal audit.

Clause 8.2.3—Monitoring and measurement of process. The organization shall have suitable method for monitoring and measurement of processes to confirm the continued suitability of the processes.

Clause 8.2.4—Monitoring and measurement of product. Finally monitoring and measurement of the products and the evidence of conforming with the acceptance criteria shall be recorded, including product release and revised delivery.

Clause 8.3—Control of non-conforming product. Non-conforming product should be identified and controlled to prevent its unintended use and delivery. The non-conforming product can be disposed of by eliminating the non-conformity, acceptance under concession by an appropriate authority or by the customer or to preclude its original indented use. Records of non-conformatory as well as all such action shall be maintained. A procedure has to be compulsorily written for this.

Clause 8.4—Analysis of data. The organization shall determine, collect and analyze appropriate data to demonstrate as well as the suitability, effectiveness and continual imprcvement of the quality management system. This analysis should provide information related to customer satisfaction, confirmation of product requirement, characteristics and trends of processes and products, including preventive actions. The above will apply to the suppliers also.

Clause 8.5—Improvement

Clause 8.5.1—Continual improvement. The organization should have a process of continually improving the effectiveness of QMS. The means are quality policy, quality objectives, audit reports, data analysis, corrective and preventive actions and management review.

Clause 8.5.2—Corrective action. The organization should take corrective action on the non-conformities and their elimination. A procedure has to be compulsorily written for this.

Clause 8.5.3—Preventive action. The organization should also take preventive action to eliminate the causes of non-conformities and/or potential non-conformation to prevent their occurrence and reoccurrence. A procedure has to be compulsorily written for this.

To an ordinary employee ISO 9000 quality management system unfolds the mystery of quality and TQM phrase by phrase and stanza by stanza. The ISO standard is simple, clear and step by step approach of implementing the quality management system. It is the bare minimum requirement for attainment of TQM and the first step towards it. The latest addition ISO 9000:2000 breaks up the entire business into certain basic fundamental process. ISO 9000 system implementation ensures proper implementation and organized approach towards conduct of business enterprise. It ensures consistency in performance, in terms of products and services offered by the organization. It guarantees minimum assured world-class performance by an organization. The ISO 9000 registration has become a mandatory requirement for exporting to Europe and America as well as most of the reputed organizations. ISO 9000 ensures a structure for holding the gains as well as for continuous improvement. It also audits for involvement of top management, education and training to all employees, process control & customer satisfaction as part of the total quality system.

The current ISO 9000:2000 edition puts additional focus on continuous improvement apart from customer satisfaction. The achievement of this is professed by the International Standard Organization by switching over to process orientation for product orientation. This advancement is bound to strengthen the infrastructure by a more sound, effective and efficient quality management system.

Eleven steps of ISO 9000:2000 implementation

- *Training program on awareness of ISO 9000.* The first step of implementation of the ISO 9000:2000 quality management system is to train all the employees of the organization on the standard as well as the 'quality policy' and individual's role in the organization towards the fulfillment of the organizational objectives, that is, its quality goals.
- *Writing of the procedure, work instruction and the quality manual.* The next step for the implementation of the ISO 9000:2000 quality management system is to write down the working of the organization in terms of the work instructions and the work procedures. The quality manual must be written as per the standard's requirements and clearly specify the quality records to be maintained as conformance to the following of the work instructions and the work procedures. The principle of writing the quality manual is simple 'Do what you say and Say what you do'.
- *Adequacy audit of the quality manual.* Once the quality manual is written, it is given to a third party expert, mainly the certifying auditor, to evaluate whether it is written as per the ISO 9000:2000 quality management system. The standard specifies certain guideline for writing the quality manual which has to be adhered to. The ISO 9000:2000 quality management system specifies minimum six work procedures to be written against the following clauses as detailed below:

Sr.No.	Clause No.	Description
01.	4.2.3	Control of documents
02.	4.2.4	Control of records
03.	8.2.2	Internal audit
04.	8.3	Control of non-conforming product
05.	8.5.2	Corrective action
06.	8.5.3	Preventive action

The organization implementing the ISO 9000:2000 quality management system can write more than these six mandatory procedures as it deems fit for its convenience and world-class performance.

- *Training on the implementation of the quality manual.* Once the quality manual is written and adequacy audit and the related corrections are over, the ISO 9000:2000 quality management system with reference to the quality manual is explained to the entire organization with focus on the individual's work area and his duties and responsibilities in the accomplishment of the standard and its working.

- *Training of internal auditors.* It is mandatory as per the ISO 9000:2000 quality management system to periodically audit the entire organization for the compliance of the quality manual in practical working conditions. The internal auditor has to be trained by a certified lead auditor on the ISO 9000:2000 quality management system as well as on the internal audit. The trained internal auditors along with the management representative play the lead role in the implementation of the ISO 9000:2000 quality management system.

- *Implementation of the quality manual.* Now the approved quality manual is implemented all over the organization. The ISO 9000:2000 quality management system can be implemented by adherence to the written down work instructions and work procedures. The quality records must be properly maintained. The organization has to ensure its working as per the written down manual and look for opportunities for the continual improvement and modifying the work instructions and procedures accordingly. The quality records could be a sample, an evidence of good performance, etc. The quality manual and records can be the soft copies also.

- *Periodic internal audit for implementation.* The periodic internal audit is a mandatory activity for the ISO 9000:2000 quality management system implementation. The internal audit principally ensures the compliance to the ISO 9000:2000 quality management system. The internal auditor can officially audit another function or department and not his own department. The internal audit identifies the conformance or the non-conformance of working with the quality manual. In case any deviations found in the working, a 'non-conformity report' is raised. The 'non-conformity report' has to be closed within a specified period by taking suitable corrective and preventive actions. The internal audit reports are submitted to the quality council and reviewed in the management review meeting for continual improvement.

- *Certification audit.* After the ISO 9000:2000 quality management system is fully implemented and a couple of round of the internal audit completed, all the 'non-conforming reports' are closed by taking suitable corrective and preventive actions. The organization is confident that the ISO 9000:2000 quality management system is implemented. Now any of the third party auditors like the 'Bureau Varitas Quality International (BVQI)', 'TUV', 'DNV', 'BIS' etc. are called for conducting the external certification audit. If everything is found to be conforming as per the quality manual and the the ISO 9000:2000 quality management system standard and all the non-conforming reports are closed, the third party auditor recommends the certification to be awarded to an internal certifying agency like the 'UKAS' of United Kingdom or the 'ANSI' of USA.

- *Awarding the certificate.* After all the procedures as stated above are satisfactorily completed and recommendation received from the third party auditors, the certifying agency releases the certificate valid for three years with a condition that the periodic audit will be carried out to ensure continued compliance of the ISO 9000:2000 quality management system. Normally the receipt of the the the ISO 9000:2000 quality management system certificate is heavily advertised as it is a confirmation of world-class performance standard of the certified organization.
- *Efforts for continuous improvement.* The ISO 9000:2000 quality management system certified organization has to provide evidence of continual improvement and should have well defined vision, mission and quality objectives ensuring that the quality management system has an in-built system for the continuous improvement. Activities like 'quality circle', 'Kaizen Gemba' and 'JQI' should be implemented as evidence for continual improvement. The Deming's P-D-C-A cycle oriented towards continual improvement should be implemented with a process approach.
- *Surveillance audit.* The surveillance audit is the periodic third party audit once in six months or a year to ensure that the ISO 9000:2000 quality management system is being followed by the organization. The surveillance audit should also ensure that the evidences are available for the continuous improvement of the ISO 9000:2000 quality management system. The re-certification audit is carried out after three years of certification.

6.3.2 ISO 14001:1996 Environmental Management System

The ISO 14001:1996 is a part of the quality management system of an organization pertaining to environment management. All the organizations have to control the impact of their activities, products and services on the environment. Most of the countries' governments have got stringent regulations to protect the environment as the worldwide concern about the protection of the environment and control of the pollution is increasing. The organizations have to undertake environmental reviews and audits to assess their environmental performance and ensure that the same is as per the legal as well as the company's environmental policy requirements. To achieve this the organizations must have a structured management system integrated with the overall management system of the organizations.

This international standard on the environmental management system specifies the requirements of an effective environmental management system applicable and adaptable uniformly to all types and size of the organizations. The basis of the approach is shown in Figure 6.12.

The environmental management system should have commitment from all levels and functions and establish convincing evidence of the conformance to the environmental policies, objectives and procedures. The overall aim of this environmental management system is to protect the environment and prevent pollution in balance with the socio-economic needs. The environmental management system may address many of the requirements concurrently or revisited at any time. The environmental management system encompasses a full range of issues including the strategic, competitive or the key survival issues.

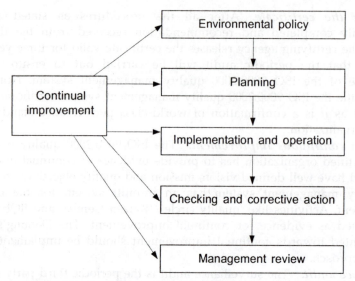

FIGURE 6.12 Environmental management system ISO 14001:1996.

The complementary standard for detail and further guidance on the environmental management system is the ISO 14004:1996, environmental 3.0 management systems-general guidelines on principles, systems and supporting techniques. The ISO 14001:1996 environmental management system is a certification standard.

The clause-wise details of the standard is given below.

Clause 1.0 Scope

The environmental management system should enable an organization to formulate the policy and objectives taking into account legislative requirements and information about significant environmental impact which the organization can control and over which it has an influence. The environmental management system standard is applicable to any organization concerned with the environmental management system.

Clause 2.0 Normative references

Nil.

Clause 3.0 Definitions

All the definitions are taken from the international standard ISO 14001:1996.

Continual improvement. Continual improvement is process of enhancing the environmental management system to achieve improvements in the overall environmental performance in line with the organization's environmental policy.

Environment. Surroundings in which an organization operates, including air, water, land, natural resources, flora, fauna, humans and their interrelation.

Environmental aspect.   Element of an organization's activities, products or services that can impact the environment.

Environmental impact.   Any change to the environment, whether adverse or beneficial, resulting from an organization's activities, products or services.

Environmental management system audit.   A systematic and documented verification process of objectively obtaining and evaluating evidence to determine whether an organization's environmental management system conforms to the environmental management system audit criteria set by the organization and for communication of the results of this process of management.

Environmental objective.   Overall environmental quantifiable goal arising out of the environmental policy.

Environmental performance.   Measurable result of the environment management system related to an organization's control of its environmental policy, objectives and targets.

Environmental target.   Detailed quantifiable performance requirement applicable to the organization or the parts thereof that arises from the environmental objectives and that needs to be set and met in order to achieve those objectives.

Interested party.   Individual or the group concerned with or affected by the environmental performance of the organization.

Organization.   Company, corporation, firm, enterprise, authority or institution, or part or combination thereof, whether incorporated or not, that has its own functions and administration.

Prevention of pollution.   Use of processes, practices, materials or products that avoid, reduce or control pollution, which may include recycling, treatment, process changes, control mechanisms, efficient use of resources and material substitution.

Clause 4.0   Environmental management system

The environmental management system includes organizational structure, planning activities, responsibilities, practices, procedures, processes and resources for developing, implementing, achieving, reviewing and maintaining the environmental policy.

Clause 4.1   General requirements

The general requirement of the organization is to establish and maintain an environmental management system.

Clause 4.2   Environmental policy

The environmental policy is a statement by the organization of its intentions and principles in relation to its overall environmental performance which provides a framework for action and for the setting of its environmental objectives and targets. The organization should declare its environmental policy.

Clause 4.3 Planning

Clause no. 4.3.1 Environmental aspects. The organization shall establish and maintain procedures to identify the environmental aspects of its activities, products or services and control them. The organization has to ensure that the aspects related to these significant impacts are part of its environmental objectives. This information should be uptodate.

Clause 4.3.2 Legal and other requirements. The organization should have a written procedure to identify and have access to legal and other requirements which the organization has to follow and that are applicable to the environmental aspects of its activities, products or services.

Clause 4.3.3 Objectives and targets. The organization shall establish and maintain documented environmental objectives and targets at each relevant function and level within the organization.

When establishing and reviewing its objectives, an organization shall consider the legal and other requirements and its significant environmental aspects, its technological options and its financial, operational and business requirements, and the views of interested parties.

Clause 4.3.4 Environmental management programme(s). The organization shall establish and maintain programme for achieving its targets and objectives. It shall include the formulation of the designation and the responsibility for achieving objectives and targets at each relevant function and levels of organization. The means and time frame for this has to be defined.

For the new developments and modified activities, products or services, the programme will be amended suitably to ensure that environmental management applies to such projects.

Clause 4.4 Implementation and operation

Clause 4.4.1 Structure and responsibility. Roles, responsibilities and authorities have to be defined, documented and communicated in order to facilitate effective environmental management.

Management shall provide resources essential to the implementation and control of the environmental management system. Resources include human resources and specialized skills, technology and financial resources.

Clause 4.4.2 Training, awareness and competence. The organization shall identify the training needs. It shall require that all personnel whose work may create a significant impact upon the environment, have received appropriate training. The organization should write a procedure for its employees or members at each relevant function and level aware of:

(a) The importance of conformance with the environmental policy and procedures and with the requirements of the environmental management system.
(b) The significant environmental impacts, actual or potential, of their work activities and the environmental benefits of improved personnel performance.

(c) Their roles and responsibilities in achieving conformance with the environmental policy and procedures and with the requirements of the environmental management system, including emergency preparedness and response requirements.

(d) The potential consequences of departure from specified operating procedures.

Clause 4.4.3 Communication. With regard to its environmental aspects and environmental management system, the organization shall establish and maintain procedures for both the internal communication between the various levels and functions of the organization as well as from the external interested parties.

The organization shall establish the processes for external communication on its significant environmental aspects and record its decision.

Clause 4.4.4 Environmental system documentation. The organization shall write a procedure and establish and maintain information by way of a 'hard copy' or 'soft copy'. Environmental system documentation describes the core elements of the management system and their interaction and provides direction to related documentation.

Clause 4.4.5 Document control. The organization should have a written procedure for the document control. All the documents should be approved, reviewed, updated, easily available and readily identifiable, i.e., all the documents should be adequately legible and controlled. All the obsolete documents must be removed and only the current documents with revision status should be available.

Clause 4.4.6 Operational control. The organization should identify and control the operations and activities with significant environmental aspects in line with its policies, objectives and targets. A procedure has to be compulsorily written for this.

Clause 4.4.7 Emergency preparedness and response. The organization should identify the potential areas of accidents and emergency situations. The organization should establish, maintain, review periodically and revise, if the need be, the procedure for its response and emergency preparedness for the accidents and emergency situations and for preventing and mitigating their impact on the environment.

Clause 4.5 Checking and corrective action

Clause 4.5.1 Monitoring and measurement. The organization should establish, maintain, review periodically and revise, if the need be, the documented procedure for regularly monitoring and measuring the key characteristics of its operations and activities that has a significant effect on the environment as well as requirement of the legislation.

The monitoring and measuring equipments have to be calibrated. The records for this process shall be retained.

Clause 4.5.2 Non-conformance and corrective and preventive action. The organization should establish, maintain, review periodically and revise, if the need be, the procedure for defining authority and responsibility for handling and investigating non-conformance, taking actions to mitigate any impacts caused and for initiating and completing the corrective and preventive actions.

Clause 4.5.3 Records. There should be a written procedure for this clause. The quality records should be legible, readily identifiable, protected during storage. The quality records should have a defined retention time and system for its disposition.

Clause 4.5.4 Environmental management system audit. The organization shall conduct periodic environmental management system audits at planned intervals to ensure the conformation, implementation and effectiveness of the management system. The audit criteria, scope, frequency, methods shall be defined along with responsibilities. The result of the audit should be recorded. The audit should be followed up for elimination of the detected non-conformities. A procedure has to be compulsorily written for the internal audit.

Clause 4.6 Management review

The top management should establish a process to review the environmental management system at planned intervals to ensure its continuing suitability, adequacy and effectiveness and maintain records for the same.

The ISO 14001:1996 is an environment management system aimed at the improved environmental performance of an organization and continual improvement in the same. The objective is to make the industrial organizations more responsible to the society and to prevent environmental disaster like the Bhopal gas tragedy at the Union Carbide factory or the pollution in Ganges or the metro cities in India. Internationally the recent release of harmful industrial wastage on one of China's major river has caused panic and discomfort to thousands of inhabitants by the side of the river.

There is another popular quality management system known as 'QS-9000' which is a derivative of the ISO 9000:1994 standard. This was first brought out in August 1994 followed by the second edition in February 1995 and the third edition was brought out in March 1998. This quality management system standard is typically applicable to the suppliers of the automobile industry. The quality management system is divided into two sections. The first section is typically the ISO 9000 based requirements. The second section is the 'customer specific requirement'. In the second section the specific requirements of the three major automobile manufacturers of the world, i.e., Chrysler, Ford and General Motors, is given in detail. At the end of the standard a passing reference is made to the reference standard of the other global automobile manufacturers like 'Mack Trucks', 'Navister', 'Paccar', 'Toyota—Australia, Mitsubishi Motors- Austrialia and Volvo Standards.

The Chrysler/Ford/General Motors developed the supplier quality requirement task force. This supplier quality requirement task force developed the quality system requirements QS-9000. Previously each of these companies had their own expectations for the supplier quality system and the corresponding assessment document. In 1988, the purchasing and the supply Vice Presidents of these companies charted the task force to standardize the reference manuals, reporting formats and technical nomenclature. Accordingly the task force published the quality system requirements QS-9000. The standard has been well received by the supplier community.

In the end of 1992, the vice presidents, as stated above, directed the task force to harmonize the fundamental supplier quality system manuals and assessment tools. It was decided that the company-specific, division-specific and commodity-specific requirements will be handled by each company separately.

QS-9000 implemented the spirit of the continuous improvement, enhanced the performance of the quality system by eliminating redundant requirements and thus reducing the cost. This is an additional exercise of value analysis. The task force encourages the suppliers to suggest how the documentation and its implementation can be improved.

The goal of the quality system requirements QS-9000 is the development of fundamental quality systems that provide for the continuous improvement, defect prevention and the reduction of the variation and waste in the supply chain.

The quality system requirements QS-9000 defines the fundamental quality system expectation of Chrysler, Ford, General Motors, truck manufacturers and other subscribing companies for the internal and external suppliers of production and service parts and materials. These companies are committed to work with their suppliers to ensure customer satisfaction beginning with the conformance to the quality requirements, and continuing with reduction of variation and waste to benefit the final customer, the supply base and themselves.

EXERCISES

1. Explain the significance of building a strong infrastructure for a business enterprise.

2. How will you ensure 'Total Employee Involvement' in an organization?

3. Explain the process of 'Total Organizational Involvement'.

4. Explain the process of 'Supply Chain Management'.

5. How will you implement 'Logistic Management' in an organization. Discuss all the five arms of logistic management.

6. 'Logistics and supply chain management maximizes both the customer satisfaction and the return on investment'. Discuss in detail.

7. What are the various 'quality management systems'? Explain their significance to an organization and its performance.

8. Explain the correlation of various quality management systems.

9. Explain your awareness about the quality management system ISO 9000:2000 in detail.

10. How will you implement the ISO 9000:2000 quality management system in (a) a manufacturing industry, and (b) service sector. Select a specific organization in both the sectors for discussion.

Chapter 7

Holistic Quality Management

CHAPTER OBJECTIVES

In this chapter, we will discuss the following:

- Holistic Quality Management
- Various quality awards like the European Quality Award, the Deming Application Prize and the Malcolm Baldridge National Quality Award
- Quality planning and its process
- Quality control, its process and tools
- Quality improvement

In the context of understanding the concept of 'total quality management', it is yet to be understood and defined in a matured and universally accepted manner. Every famous management guru of current times, including W. Edwards Deming, Joseph M. Juran, Armand V. Feignbann, Philip Crosby and Kaoru Ishikawa, has spoken and written so much about TQM. This is one concept which the industries were unanimous in adopting worldwide. But still it has remained a little understood subject as no two people have defined the term 'TQM' in an identical manner and come to consensus regarding its definition and meaning even if the end point or objective of TQM has been universally interpreted by all concerned as the same, i.e., 'customer satisfaction', 'continuous improvement' and 'employee involvement'. However, there is so much confusion about the methodology to reach the end point as end only has the correct concept widely accepted. The same confusion is reflected in the writing of either Joseph M. Juran who has written so much on the subject for so many years (approximately 50 years) or that of W. Edward Deming.

While keeping in mind the theories and practices adopted by all these management gurus as mentioned above as well as studying so many case studies and practical experience with practicing TQM organizations, let us try to build up the concept in the right manner step by step so that it is properly understood without any confusion. Then only the concept of 'TQM' can be implemented in an effective and efficient manner, balancing all factors simultaneously. This is vastly different from uneven, sporadic and haphazard manner in which TQM is applied in bits and pieces to industry.

Let us critically analyze and understand TQM. At the centre of this concept is quality. Father of scientific management, F.W. Taylor, entirely focused on productivity, which was many times at the cost of quality. A similar approach was also adopted by Henry Fayol, Frank and Lilian Gilbreth. They were all productivity-oriented people. Here the meaning of the word quality was inspection of the product and declaring whether or not it is fit for use. As long as there were buyers for the product, the companies were satisfied and were least bothered what happened to the product after it was sold. However, the great recession of 1930s and the second World War, taught the industries all over the world a great lesson. The marked leadership drastically changed the economic scenario upside down and there was realignment of economic and industrial power of countries and industries.

This is the time when the consumers, customers and producers started going beyond the product and looked at subtle difference between two products, like cost of production, competitiveness, after sales service, more product features, etc. and the concept of quality was born. Hence 'small q' which is product quality got replaced by 'big Q', i.e., process quality. The foundation work on quality was done in the 1930s by a statistician named Walter Shewart, whose concept of PDCA cycle, control chart and statistical quality control is still the backbone of TQM.

While Walter Shewart of Bells Laboratory was the creator of great theories, he had a dynamic disciple in W. Edward Deming who was responsible primarily for converting the war-ravaged demolished economy of Japan in post World War II to become an economic superpower in the world by the mid-seventies. The dominance of Japanese industries in the manufacturing sector continues even today. Deming was advisor to Japanese industries and he played a pivotal role with the vision of the Union of Japanese Scientist and Engineers (JUSE). In 1956 Deming was awarded the 'Shewart's Medal' by the American Society of Quality Control. By 1960s Deming was spearheading Japanese industries' growth and putting them on the path of top industrial businesses. The emperor of Japan awarded him 'the second order of the sacred treasure', one of the highest Japanese civilian awards. The highest quality award for TQM given by JUSE is named after W. Edward Deming as 'Deming's Award'.

Along with Deming, another gentleman who pioneered the quality revolutions of 1955–70 in Japan was Joseph M. Juran. He was the first writer of the *Quality Control Handbook* published in 1951. He was the first person to popularize the concept of the 'economics of quality', which implies that higher quality actually costs less. He arrived in Japan in 1954 on invitation from the Union of Japanese Scientist and Engineers (JUSE). The seminars and lectures given by him converted the simple word 'quality' into 'quality management'. He believed that things cannot happen by accident but they have to be planned, controlled and managed. His famous trilogy of quality planning, quality control and quality improvement gave an organized approach to the concept of TQM. He believed that majority of quality problems (80%) are management related and only the remaining (20%) are related to poor workmanship on the shopfloor. Dr. Juran is perfecting his theories and practices all over the world even today at the age of 98 years.

Inspired by the teaching of Deming and Juran, professor Kaoru Ishikawa (1915–89) contributed to the quality revolution in Japan by pioneering and popularizing the famous 'quality circle' movement of 1960s in Japan of quality improvement. The quality problem solving techniques of 'pareto analysis' and 'cause and effect diagrams' (popularly known as Ishikawa diagrams) is still the most efficient and effective way of quality improvement and managerial breakthrough in the world. Mr. Ishikawa pioneered the concept of company vide quality control (CWQC) involving all business processes and every individual of the organization.

In the western countries of USA and Europe, apart from Juran's contribution, Mr. Philip Crosby's starting of a quality college and his efforts with western industries on quality front was appreciable. Another gentleman, Mr. Armand V. Feignbann, who was the worldwide Director of General Electric company made substantial contribution to the field of quality control—principles, practices and administration. He looked at quality control as a business method rather than a technical method. Mr. Armand V. Feignbann advocated that quality control is seen as the activity into all phases of industrial production process, for customer specification and sale through design, engineering and assembly and ending with shipment of product for customers who are happy with it. He always propagated the total quality programme.

By looking at Japan's success of converting itself into the world's most advanced country in the field of economic growth and industry and commitment to quality leadership by western and American successful industries, the world forum has came to a consensus regarding the usefulness of this quality consensus of modern management gurus as stated above. To have an organised effort in 'quality management system' guidelines in 1972, the British Standard Institution published BS 4891 'A guide to quality assurance' and BS 5179 'Guide to Quality System' in the year 1975. However, the purview of these standards excluded customer requirement or the assessment of suppliers' quality system and hence a single combined national standard BS 5750–1979 was issued. Following the success of the standards and increasing international awareness in quality management led to the developing and publishing of ISO 9000 reviews of quality system in 1987. This was further reviewed and reissued in 1994. The current version of ISO 9000:2000 was issued on 15th December, 2000 in its modified version as a 'Process Oriented Quality Management System'.

The backdrop of above paragraph which gives is, in the nutshell, the evolution as well as the concepts of TQM and the contributions made in this field by various management thinkers and pioneers. Let us build up the understanding and interpretation of TQM. Let us understand first the interpretation of 'total quality'. As explained, the conventional interpretation of the word is 'small q' or product quality alone. The word 'total quality' or 'big Q' interprets much beyond product quality, like handling of order, timely delivery, service quality, etc. The 'big Q' has to meet the customer's stated and implied needs along with the obligatory needs specified by the law of the land. The end objective is delighted customers, maximization of internal returns and high employee's morale.

The dictionary meaning of the word 'quality' is 'degree of excellence with respect to the relative nature or land of character'. We will now look at various interpretations of the word 'quality'.

"Quality is not only product and services but also includes *processes, environment and people*".—Stephen Uselac

Quality is *"performance to the standards expected by the customers."*—Fred Smith, CEO, Federal Express

Quality is *"meeting the customers needs first time and every time."*—General Service Administration (GSA)

Quality is *"provide our customers with products and services that consistently meet their levels and expectations."*—Boeing

Quality is *"doing the right thing right first time, always striving for improvement and always satisfying the customers."*—US Department of Defence (DoD)

Quality is "fitness for use".—Joseph Juran

Quality is *"the conformance to requirements"*.—Philip B. Crosby

Quality is "the degree to which a set of inherent characteristics fulfils requirements".—ISO 9000:2000

Although no two definitions of quality are identical, there is a basic similarity among definitions with common elements as:

- Quality involves meeting or executing customer's expectations.
- Quality not only applies to product but also to services, people, process, environment, etc.
- Quality is a dynamic concept and is ever-changing.

However, we will go by the definition of quality universally accepted in ISO 9000:2000 as "quality is the degree to which a set of inherent characteristics fulfills requirements".

Here the inherent characteristics are the distinguishing features of the product and they could be:

— Physical
— Sensory
— Behavioural
— Temporal
— Ergonomic
— Functional

The rather formal definition is often shortened to:

Fitness for purpose or quality = Conformance to requirements.

Here the requirement implies customer's stated, implied and obligatory needs. In short, the customer received what was ordered to a set of specifications implied and stated on time and at an agreed price. It also means that product or service will be reliable and fit for the intended purpose in all respects.

Deming is of the view that perception of good quality varies according to the needs of the individual consumer and under different situations.

Customer satisfaction is his perception about fulfillment of his requirements, i.e. stated, implied and obligatory needs. Grades of quality control can be different. Dr. Juran clearly explained the danger of accepting any shorter definition of such an important organization wide activity. According to him, any short phrase of the definition of quality is a trap.

Management can be defined as "the process of creating an environment conducive for performance of a group of people working together for attainment of a common objective in time."

Quality management as defined in ISO 9000:2000 edition is "coordinated activities to direct and control an organization".

The objective is to spread the 'quality policy' to all areas within the organization so that it is implemented. Quality management is the responsibility of all levels of management. In order to implement quality management, a formal system should be placed detailing the 'what we do, who does it and how we do it', i.e., a quality system which is a set of inter-related or interacting elements or processes".

Quality management is defined in ISO 9000 as "a management system to direct and control an organization with regard to quality."

An effective quality management system must ensure that all activities from receipt of inquiry to the delivery of the final product and services are appropriate and adequate to comply with the requirement of total quality and meeting set quality objectives.

Quality objective is something aimed for, related to quality. The quality objective must be measurable.

Now that we understand in totality TQM and its various aspects, we may define TQM as:

"A set of activities with total involvement of all concerned, inter-linked into continuously improving processes, producing products and services fulfilling customers' stated and implied needs with maximization of internal revenue towards attainment of quantifiable and measurable quality objectives in time."

Any definition shorter than this would be a trap and would be in a truncated form, not fulfilling the end objectives.

TQM is a way of life in the organization where constant endeavours improve the activity on measurable scale. It is everybody's business and everyone is involved in TQM. However, all these activities are well linked in a set of inter-linked processes whose final output is product and services which are world-class, the best in its category and consistently fulfill the customers stated, implied and latest needs leading to customer's delightment. All these work as per schedule at proper time. In fact in TQM activity, it is proven that higher quality actually cost less by reduction in wastage. Hence TQM also maximizes value addition or return on investment for an organization.

To sum up, the evaluation of TQM from inspection over the years is detailed below.

The quality management system matured from inspection to quality assurance to total quality control and finally to total quality management. The individual features of the each activity are given in Figure 7.1.

Inspection is mainly concerned with declaring whether or not a product is ok, after it has been manufactured. The corrective actions are grading, rework and salvaging. The system does not improve or the rejection does not reduce by this exercise.

Quality assurance shifts the focus from the product to the process and implements statistical process control (SPC). The philosophy is that if the process is under control, the product cannot be defective. This ensures a consistency in the product performance.

The next level is total quality control which concentrates apart from the process approach in taking the corrective actions and spreading the quality concept of performance excellence all over the organization in all the functions and makes extensive use of the seven quality tools for problem solving.

The ultimate maturity of performance excellence of the organization will lead to the implementation of the total quality management which primarily focuses on three vital

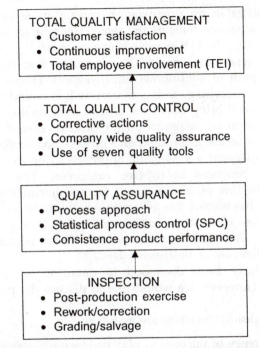

FIGURE 7.1 Four levels in evaluation of TQM.

aspects of world-class performance, i.e., customer satisfaction, continuous improvement and the total employee involvement.

There are two towering personalities, W. Edward Deming and Joseph M. Juran, who pioneered the TQM movement. We have already discussed the work of Joseph Juran and his trilogy.

Let us now examine the pioneer work of W. Edward Deming. The fundamental to W. Edward Deming's work is the Deming cycle of PDCA, now adopted by ISO 9000:2000 series of quality management standards.

Demings PDCA cycle completes its process in totality. The quality 'plan' takes care of all input resources, its optimum deployment, and the flow process chart and control points. Every care is taken to make it foolproof and error-free. The objective is defined in a measurable manner as quality objective moving around customers' satisfaction and maximization of return on investments.

The next step is 'do' or the execution of the plan, which means to go ahead and implement. However, more often than not there is a gap between the plan and actual performance.

The 'check' activity measures this gap and finds out the point of deviation. It also measures the extent of deviation and the damage caused by the deviation. This is measured in quantifiable terms as the cost of poor quality or COPQ.

The next step of 'act' is to find out the root cause of such deviation by a systematic and scientific approach, i.e., pareto analysis and Ishikawa or cause and effect diagram. This is followed by a brainstorming session to eliminate such deviations in the future by taking corrective and preventive actions (CAPA).

Most of the things in an organization remain more or less static with minor deviations. The product range remains the same. The people, the motives, the processes all are more or less static. The PDCA cycle keeps on rectifying the errors and assures that they do not repeat again and again. This ensures that the PDCA cycle puts an organization on the path of continuous improvement. Hence at the beginning if one measures deviations in percentage today, tomorrow it is bound to come down to PPM or part per million. This will bring down the cost of poor quality (COPQ) or wastage, etc. for an organization, improve its return on investment, ensure customer satisfaction by timely delivery and reduction in product and process non-conformities.

Deming has propagated a systematic approach to business success and separated business forces and practices in to two categories. The first category takes an organization down the line of disasters and factors detrimental to the progress of an organization. Deming has named this as 'seven deadly disasters'. The second category of factors leads to progress of an organization and makes it world-class. These points are popularly known as 'Deming's fourteen points'. These points are necessary for the survival and competitiveness of business today.

Both of these have been discussed in detail in Chapter 2 under Deming's philosophy on TQM. However, we would like to discuss the points again in the Indian context.

Deming's seven deadly disasters are as follows:

1. Lack of consistency of purpose to plan product and services that have a sufficient market to keep the company in business and provide jobs.
2. Emphasis on short term profits; short term thinking that that is driven by a fear of unfriendly takeover attempts and pressure from bankers and shareholders to produce dividends.
3. Personal review system for managers and management by objectives without providing methods or resources to accomplish objectives. Performance appraisals, merit rating and annual appraisals are all part of these disasters.
4. Job hopping by managers.
5. Using only visible data and information in decision-making with little or no consideration given to what is not known or cannot be known.
6. Excessive medical costs.
7. Excessive cost of liability driven up by lawyers that work on contingency fees.

Out of these seven deadly disasters, the point number 6 and 7 are practically a matter of concern to US and Japanese companies, peculiarly to the environmental factors of these countries, and not of much relevance to the Indian organizations. The first five points are of the matter of keen concern to the Indian organizations. However, we can replace point number 6 and 7 with another two points in Indian context. They are as follows:

1. **High cost of finance.**   The borrowed money from banks, finance institutions and private financing companies consumes a lot of time during sanction as it involves an elaborate procedure.

Cost of finance for business enterprises is more than twice as that of comparable foreign multinational companies (MNCs) in other countries. Apart from the high cost, the finance availability is scarce and procedures are time-consuming and lengthy, contributing to a lot of lost opportunities.

2. **Lack of infrastructural facility.** The seventh factor added is the lack of infrastructural facilities. Basic input to industries, like electricity and water, is not only excessively costly but also scarce. Most of the Indian states have average power cuts of around 30% to 50% during January to the month of June, i.e., almost six months in a year.

High cost of transportation and slow movement of vehicles increases cost of transportation as well as is a cause for huge blockage of capital in goods-in-transit. Excessive government control with lot of corruption and too many inspectors make the day-to-day running of industry extremely cumbersome and frustrating.

These two factors being environmental may not be cased by total quality management efforts and have to be tackled on business footing.

However, Deming s concept of negative factors detrimental to the organization's growth and prosperity is still applicable under all circumstances, particularly the first five points. This is more pertinent for the Indian organizations that have refused to adapt to the new era of business challenges thrown by liberalization, globalization and international competition. These seven factors have to be tackled by the individual business enterprises, business associations, and above all the Government of India should come forward to accept and admit the lacunas and find out the solutions for the same. All these have to be taken in time right away without any delay whatsoever. Over the years, Dr. Deming has developed 14 points to be acted upon for business to survive and be competitive today. These points have been modified by Deming himself over the years. However, these 14 points are at the heart of Deming's philosophy and essence of all his teachings. They are listed at random and work together and form a quality organization. Understanding and implementing these 14 points forms a new attitude towards work and work environment that will foster continuous improvement. These points are as follows:

1. Create constancy of purpose towards the improvement of products and services in order to become competitive and stay in business.
2. Adopt the new philosophy management. Must learn that it is a new economic age and awaken to the challenges, learn their responsibility, and take on leadership for change.
3. Stop depending on inspection for quality. Build in quality from the start.
4. Stop awarding contracts on the basis of low bids.
5. Improve continuously and forever the system of production and service to improve quality and productivity and thus constantly reduce the cost.
6. Institute training on the job.
7. Institute leadership. The purpose of leadership should be to help people and technology to work better.
8. Drive out fear so that everyone may work effectively.
9. Break down barriers between departments so that people can work as a team.
10. Eliminate slogan exhortation and targets for the workforce. They create adversarial relationship.
11. Eliminate quotas and management by objectives. Substitute leadership.

12. Remove barriers that rob employees of their pride of workmanship.
13. Institute a vigorous program of education and self-improvement.
14. Make the transformation everyone's job and put everyone to the work.

The above points have been explained in detail in Chapter 2.

The TQM movement gained so much momentum post-1980s that Juran went so far to state that "just as the 20th century was the century of productivity, 21st century will be the quality century." In global competitive market, TQM became the most important single factor for success.

The President and the US Department of Commerce paid personal attention and support to quality, promoting it to the national agenda. In 1991, the GAO (US general accounting office) studied carefully and established relationship between quality management activity and success and profitability.

In 1995 the national institute of standards and technology of US Department of Commerce studied and established greater success stories of the Malcolm Baldrige national quality award winning companies compared to average companies. The Malcolm Baldrige national quality award is issued by the US government as recognition of outstanding contribution in the field of quality management.

The European foundation for quality management was created in 1988 as recognition of understanding of quality management as a leadership issue and competitive tool. In 1992, the European Quality Award was introduced for recognition of excellence in TQM by European organizations.

However, the Union of Japanese Scientists and Engineers (JUSE) was the first to introduce an award for TQM activity in the year 1951, the 'Deming Application Prize'. However, with the passage of time, it also opted the concept of company wide quality control (CWQC). In 1997, JUSE formally changed the term 'total quality control (TQC)' to 'total quality management (TQM)'. The objective was to adopt a more internationally accepted term and provide the opportunity to revisit the origin of quality control and rebuild the concept to meet the new environmental challenges in business management.

The TQM committee 1997 a, b, c, and d of the Union of Japanese Scientists and Engineers (JUSE) explained the TQM concept in four publications.

In the view of the Union of Japanese Scientists and Engineers (JUSE), TQM is a management approach that strives for the following in any business environment:

- A strong top management should lead by personal involvement.
- The organization should have clear, established long term and mid term vision and strategies.
- Properly utilize the concept, values and scientific methods of TQM.
- Regard human resources and information as vital organizational infrastructure.
- Operate a quality assurance system under a suitable management system.
- Simultaneously operate other cross-functional management systems such as cost, delivery, environment and safety.
- The organization should be supported by fundamental organizational powers like core technology, speed and vitality.
- The organization should have sound relationship with all customers, employees, society, suppliers and stockholders, etc.

- Continuously realize corporate objectives in the form of achieving its mission, building the organization with respectable presence and continuously securing profits.

7.1   RESULT OF TOTAL QUALITY MANAGEMENT

The world has recognized that managing quality goes beyond the conformance to specifications and requirements. Quality actually means meeting or exceeding the needs and expectations of the consumers. Quality also includes having the correct documentation. It implies delivery in time of the product and services of right quality, in right quantity and at the right time and place.

Lower cost

Higher quality means lower cost by reducing errors, reducing rework and reducing non value-added work. The cost of correcting errors in designing stage is much lower than that of the production stage error correction or correction at final inspection stage. Cost of poor quality reduces cost in five categories, viz.

- Traditional poor quality cost
- Hidden poor quality cost
- Losts in income
- Customer's cost
- Socio-economic costs

Higher revenue

Higher quality means satisfied customers, increased market share, improved customer retention and increasing sales. We may even get a premium price for reliability and production excellence. All these factors combined together will lead to an enhancement in sales revenue.

Delighted customers

Delighted customers buy the company's products and services over and over again, advertise the company's products and services to others and act as an opinion leader. They also act as good ambassadors for promotion of company's goods and services. They being neutral have tremendous impact in the market, not only in terms of retaining the market but also gaining new customers and enhancement of the business.

Empowered employees

For many years organizations viewed empowered employees as a means for achieving lower costs, higher revenues and delighted customers. Now most of the leading organizations have realized that creating such employees is also a major goal of TQM. These organizations not only aim to solve the problems of today but also want to create an organization that can solve or even avoid the problems of tomorrow.

The concept of empowered employees embraces many new ideas. They have the means to measure the quality of their own processes and compare this measurement of goals to take corrective actions. They can also play the role to improve the process performance plan for quality.

The three strong forces or the primary drivers are as follows:

1. **Alignment.** To achieve all-around excellence in performance and breakthrough results, it must work out focused organizational goals, a sound and correct strategy and activities aligned with the strategy. A clear definition of a small number of key objectives and translating of the same into individual activities or jobs. Hence the company achieves its goals. This alignment of all associates with the top priorities or objectives of the company is absolutely critical. This strategic planning process should align all layers of workforce, customers, suppliers, environmental factors and even the competitors.

2. **Linkages.** The organization must also understand and incorporate the cross-functional linkages across the organization. This is called as 'system thinking' or 'process thinking'. This understanding of the way work is done is crucial. The process linkage is a complete end-to-end set of activities that create the end value for a customer. Hence the activities across all the functions and departments in the company must be linked together in series to achieve the end objective. The steps to manage the critical linkages and make dramatic and continuous improvement to key processes responsible for business success have to be well-designed and controlled.

3. **Replication.** Associates in the organization must be able to replicate success quickly. A small improvement may be worth a few thousand dollars; but replicated 50 or 100 times in different areas may become major contribution to the organizational success. Replication is the most powerful way to dramatically accelerate the result of quality and productivity improvement efforts. The result of quality improvement project is made known widely throughout the organization. Those with similar problems or opportunities will start the project and look into the possibility of replicating the same in these areas. Active sharing system force the issue at Hondas annual facilitator network meeting attended by over 3000 people worldwide, participants is expected to share one completed improvement project and study its replication in their own area when they get back to their plant.

The three critical processes of TQM, i.e., quality planning, quality control and quality improvement are dealt in detail subsequently.

7.2 QUALITY PERFORMANCE EXCELLENCE AWARDS

The international quality awards on total quality management have created a worldwide awareness and benchmark of organizational performance. One of the most important trends in TQM is a benchmark both on personal level and organizational level. These are the yardsticks, indicating strong points of the organization as well as where they lack in performance. The oldest among them as indicated in the Demings Application Prize awarded by the Union of Japanese Scientists and Engineers (JUSE) since 1951. A similar award given in the United States is the Malcolm Baldrige Award and in Europe the award is known as the European Quality Award.

7.2.1 Deming Application Prize

Deming Application Prize (DAP) was established by the Union of Japanese Scientists and Engineers (JUSE) in 1951. These are of two types:

1. Deming Prize for individual, and
2. Deming Prize for companies and divisions.

Deming Application Prize is awarded to organizations that have achieved outstanding results through application of CWQC companywide quality control based on statistical methods and are likely to do so in the future.

CWQC companywide quality control is defined as 'the activity of economically designing, producing and supplying products and services of the quality demanded by customer focused principles and with full consideration of the public welfare.'

Deming Application Prize is non-competitive and there is no restriction on the number of companies that can receive the Demings Application Prize in a year. Due to worldwide interest, the Deming Prize Committee created new regulations in 1989 to make it possible for companies outside Japan to apply for the prize.

Floride Power and Light, an American company, became the first organization to win the Deming Prize outside Japan in 1989. We are giving below the first level deployment and second level deployment for the assessment model of the Deming's Application Prize (DAP).

Assessment model of the 'DAP'

- Policy
  - Management and quality policy
  - Policy creation
  - Consistency of policies
  - Use of statistical methods
  - Policy transmission
  - Review of policies
  - Relationship between policies and plans
- Organization and its management
- Education and dissemination
- Quality information management
- Analysis
- Standardization
- Control/management
- Quality assurance
- Result/effects
- Future plans

Role of management

- Leadership
- Definition/dissemination quality policies
- Creation/management of quality system
- Definition goals/strategies and strategic planning
- System audits
- Creation of values
- Management team unity
- Responsibility v/s bodies/society/environment

Corporate values/culture

- Customer-orientation
- Excellence and continuous improvement
- Team spirit/matrix mentality
- Management by facts
- Respect for the individual
- Participatory management

Infrastructure

- Management goals, means and vertical alignment
- Process management/horizontal integration
- Information/data collection/analysis
- Customer satisfaction measurement
- Strategic improvement
- Improvement organization/teams
- Assessment/audits
- Involvement of external partners
- Standardization
- Benchmarking organization
- Product/service quality assurance

Involvement/Use of resources

- Motivation/involvement
- Communication
- Team work
- Internal supplier-customer relation
- Empowerment/participatory management/decision-making processes
- Policies/standards/procedure
- Job rotation
- Education and training
- Reward system

Adequacy/Use of technical resources

- Diffusion/application of statistical know-how
- Process management methodologies

- Problem solving methodologies
- Policy deployment
- Quality function deployment diffusion/use
- Information technology diffusion/use
- Standardization methodologies/tools (SDCA)

The Union of Japanese Scientists and Engineers (JUSE) awards the prestigious Deming's prize to a company or its division based on the application of companywide quality control (CWQC) and attaining very high level of performance through continuous performance improvement.

7.2.2 European Quality Award

The European Quality Award (EQA) put heavy emphasis on self-assessment. They give equal importance on 'enablers' as well as the 'results', assigning 500 points to each, making it a total of 1000, as shown in Figure 7.2.

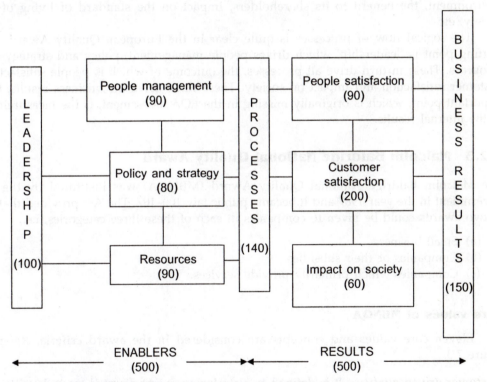

FIGURE 7.2 European Quality Awards: Scoring process.

The European Quality Award is also an important measure and acknowledgement of the contribution by a particular industry in the field of the quality. In the 'enablers', maximum weightage is given to the *processes* followed by the organization as 140 marks followed by the *leadership* as 100 marks. The importance given by the European Quality

Award to the other three factors are the *resources* (90 marks), *people management* (90 marks) and *policies and strategies* (80 marks). It is apparent from the above marking procedure that the maximum importance for the award in the *enablers* is given to the *management* of the organization which is responsible for all the five factors of providing the leadership to the team, designing sound processes, arranging the resources, human resource or people management as well as designing and declaring the policies and strategies of the organization.

Equal importance given to the *results* where maximum importance is given to *customer satisfaction* (200 marks) and *business results* (150 marks), i.e., 70% weightage is given to these two parameters; 40% importance is given to customer satisfaction which is responsible for running the wheel of an organization, its survival and prosperity. Dr. Joseph Juran has clearly stated that the top management understands only the language of money. Hence the business result means actually the *return on investment*. The balance parameters of the results are the people or *employees satisfaction* (90 marks), i.e., 18% of the result and the *impact on the society* (60 marks), i.e., 9% of the result. The impact on the society could be the effect of the company's product and processes on the environment, the benefit to its shareholders, impact on the standard of living of the society, etc.

The logical flow of processes is quite clear in the European Quality Award. The starting point is 'leadership' which drives people management, policy and strategy and resources. These in turn drive all processes, the outcome of which is people satisfaction, customer satisfaction and impact on society. These three drive the business results. One important point, which is originally missing in the EQA assessment, is the measurement of the internal results.

7.2.3 Malcolm Baldrige National Quality Award

The Malcolm Baldrige National Quality Award (MBNQA) was instituted by the US government in the year 1987 and it became public law 100–107. The Act provided that up to two awards could be given to companies in each of these three categories, i.e.,

(a) Small business
(b) Companies or their subsidies
(c) Companies which primarily provide services.

Core values of MBNQA

Eleven core values and concepts are considered in the award criteria. Refer to Figure 7.3.

Customer driven quality. It is defined as a strategic concept directed towards customer retention and market share gain. Hence focus is on product and service attributes that contribute value to the customers' satisfaction and preferences over the competing offerings.

Leadership. Focus is on senior executive leadership, emphasizing on such activities as planning, communication, and creation of clear and visible quality values with customer-

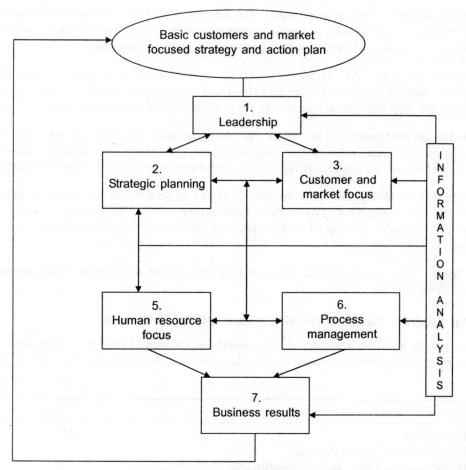

FIGURE 7.3 Information and analysis.

orientation and high expectation, review of quality performance, recognition serving as a role model.

Continuous improvement and learning. Continuous improvement and learning has to be embedded in the organization's normal working involving all employees for both incremental and breakthrough improvements, enhancing value to customers as well as reducing wastage towards improving company's performance and leadership position.

Valuing employees. Improving employee's involvement, quality and skill level by continuous education, training and opportunities for continuous growth will lead to overall organizational performance.

Fast response. Short-term cycle time leading to faster and more flexible response to customer has become the key to business success.

Design, quality and prevention. Design, quality and prevention based system is a primary driver of downstream quality.

Long range outlook of the quality plan. The fundamental TQM process is always long-term customer-oriented as well as keeps in view the interest of all stakeholders, including long term development of employees, suppliers and management interest.

Management by fact. All decisions must be made based on reliable factual data, information, and its analysis. Customers' feedback, employees' feedback, stakeholders and society are also reliable, accurate and properly analyzed to take decisions.

Partnership development. The need to develop the internal partnership with employees and external partnership with suppliers, customers and strategic alliances with competitors are all important factors for performance excellence of an organization.

Corporate responsibility and citizenship. It refers to leadership and support to such areas as education, resource conservation, community service, improving industry and business practices and sharing of non-proprietary quality related information, tools and concepts.

Result focus. The award criteria stress results throughout. Performance measurement need to focused on key results.

Malcolm Baldrige National Quality Award (MBNQA) Criteria

The core values and concepts already explained are embodied in seven categories. The dynamic relationship between these seven categories and their sub-divisions are detailed below:

Categories/Items	*Point Values*
1.0 Leadership	125
1.1 Organizational leadership—85	
1.2 Public responsibility and citizenship—40	
2.0 Strategic planning—85	
2.1 Strategy development—40	
(a) Strategy deployment—45	
3.0 Customer and market focus	85
3.1 Customer and market knowledge—40	
3.2 Customer satisfaction and relationship—45	
4.0 Information and analysis	85
4.1 Measurement of organizational performance—40	
4.2 Analysis of organizational performance—45	
5.0 Human resource focus	85
5.1 Work system—35	
5.2 Employee education, training and development—25	
5.3 Employees well-being and satisfaction—25	
6.0 Process management	85
6.1 Product and service proceses—55	

6.2 Support processes—15
6.3 Supplies and partnering processes—15

7.0 Business results   450
7.1 Customer focused results—115
7.2 Financial and market results—115
7.3 Human resource result—80
7.4 Suppliers and partner result—25
7.5 Organizational effectiveness result—115

TOTAL POINTS   1000

The MBNQA process follows several carefully defined steps.

The first is the annual improvement of the criteria, the guidelines and the entire award process.

The next step is the completion of the eligibility determination forum for the applicant company. The applicant must have the eligibility approved before applying for the award. Each applicant then completes and files the application. The award application goes through the following four stages of review:

Stage 1—Independent review by at least five members of the Board of Examiners.
Stage 2—Consensus review and evaluation of application that score well in Stage 1.
Stage 3—Site visits to applicant that score well in Stage 2.
Stage 4—Judge's review and recommendations.

7.3 QUALITY PLANNING

7.3.1 Quality

The word 'quality' has multiple meanings, out of which the key issues which define quality can be summed up as the three important attributes, viz.

- Product performance oriented towards customer satisfaction.
- Freedom from deficiencies.
- Fitness for use.

Product performance oriented towards the customer satisfaction

The principle meaning of quality is product performance. Product performance results from product features that create customer satisfaction and lead customers to buy the product.

Here the word 'product' can be tangible or intangible, i.e., it can be a tangible physical product or it can be a service. The word 'customer' means all persons who are impacted by our process and our products.

Hence the customer can the consumer of the products and services, the dealer, distributor, wholeseller, franchisee or the opinion leader (like a doctor prescribing a medicine) and above all the society at large.

They could also be external customer or internal customer. The term 'external customer' means persons who are not part of the company but impacted by the products and services. The internal customer means persons working in the organization or who are a part of the company. The products attribute performing as per the customer expectation fulfill her/his stated, implied or latent needs leading to customer satisfaction or rather customer delightment, which is key to business success. This business success comes from:

- Increased customer satisfaction vis-à-vis the benchmarked competitor.
- Making the product saleable.
- Meeting and exceeding competitor's performance.
- Enhancing market share.
- Better customer contact.
- Building of a strong brand.
- Enhancing sales income.
- Better value addition to customer.
- Securing premium prices.
- Satisfying the customers' stated, implied and latent needs.

The major effect of this is on the sales and increase in the market share leading to market leadership. Higher quality usually costs less due to elimination of wastages, reduction in overheads due to increased sales with the same effort and the product carrying the price premium due to better product performance. Hence product performance is directly related to customer satisfaction.

Freedom from deficiencies

The other meaning of quality is 'freedom from deficiencies'. Here the word deficiencies could imply bad product quality, late deliveries, field failures, incorrect invoices, cancellation of order, scrap, rework, design changes not communicated or unaccepted, deficiency resulting in complaints, claims returns, rework and other damage. All these lead to product dissatisfaction. It should be clear that product satisfaction and dissatisfaction are not opposite words. Product satisfaction is why a customer buys a product and product dissatisfaction is why they complain. All such deficiencies can be classified under the category of COPQ, i.e., cost of poor quality. Here higher quality enables companies to:

- Reduce error rates
- Reduce rework
- Reduce wastage
- Reduce scrap
- Reduce field failures
- Reduce warranty charges
- Reduce customer dissatisfaction
- Reduce inspection and testing
- Shorter time to introduce new products in the market
- Increase productivity
- Enhance value addition

- Increase yields capacity
- Improve delivery performance
- Shorten order-processing cycle
- Reduce the 'value chain'
- Better supply chain management (SCM)

The Japanese way of calling this is Muri—Unreasonableness, Muda—Wastage and Mura—Unevenness. The above three concepts of Muri, Muda and Mura have been explained in detail in Chapter 2.

The major effect of this effort is on freedom from deficiencies, leading to reduction in cost. Here 'higher quality means reduction in cost'.

Fitness for use

The third arm of the triangle of quality can be defined as 'fitness for use'. 'Fitness for use' takes the definition beyond the paradigm of 'product conforming to the specification'. It implies all products, goods and services suitable for operational and notional performance associated with the product, whether for sale or not. It brings in the concept of big 'Q' engulfing all the business processes like marketing, manufacturing, materials, human resources under one umbrella guided towards the unified objective of making the product and associated services usable by the customer to his fullest satisfaction. The customer's concept of use of the product and associated services changes its concept of 'fitness for use' with time, environment, spatial convenience, customer profile, geographic centralization of habits, income group, sex, age, etc. Hence 'fitness for use' is a concept which is an ongoing process of constant monitoring, adaptation, feedback, alteration and suitability to unique situation for a class or category of customers under a given environment. There are many uses that the user looks for at various steps of the same product or service. Each user can be categorized as an internal or external customer. Dr. Juran has tried to refer these steps of uses and users as the 'the spiral of progress in quality'.

Planning can be defined as the process of selecting the best alternative which leads to consumption of the least amount of resources giving the maximum output or result. Therefore, quality planning consists of developing the products and processes capable of meeting customers' needs. Quality planning consists of an invariable series of specified, well-defined planning activity. These activities are interlinked. This interlinking can be done by interlocking the input-output chain or common units of measure or common objectives/means of evaluating quality. As is already explained 'managing for quality' is carried out through a trilogy of managerial process, i.e., quality planning, quality control and quality improvement.

7.3.2 Application of Quality

- Establish 'quality policy'.
- Establish 'quality goals'.
- Immaculately create a 'quality plan' and provide resources to carry out the 'quality plan'.

- Establish quality controls to evaluate progress against quality goals and to take appropriate actions.
- Provide motivation to stimulate the personnel to meet the quality goals.

Now we will see what we mean by 'quality policy' and 'quality goal'.

Quality policy is a guide to the managerial action published. Quality policy usually relates to cost relations, quality competitiveness in improvements and relations with internal and external customers.

Quality goal is aimed at attaining the quality target, an achievement towards which the efforts are deployed. Corporate quality goal should be deployed and divided to sub-goals at lower levels. Such deployment identifies specific deeds to be done along with assignment of specific responsibility for doing the deed. Quality goals should extend to all functions. It should cover not only the organization but also its suppliers and clients. Normally joint goals are worked out with the suppliers and customers. Quality goals must be synchronized with the quality policies.

Company wide quality management (CWQM) is a system approach for setting and meeting quality goals throughout the company. It is an integral part of TQM. It parallels closely the approach of setting and meeting the financial goal. It needs personal leadership by the top management. Companies that have opted for CWQM have outperformed the companies that are following the conventional method of management. CWQM creates an organization for quality management. The members are the functional heads and the leader is the CEO. This apex body is known as the 'quality council'. CWQM involves planning for meeting quality goals and it provides the necessary essential resources. CWQM includes establishment of controls for evaluating performance against quality goals. It also involves accessing the deviations and taking suitable actions for eliminating the same. In case solving the problem is not feasible, it is subjected separately to a cross-functional quality improvement team. CWQM also provides scope for occasional business-oriented quality audit by upper management. A standardized package of report similar to financial reports is evolved to serve the quality functions institution of CWQM. However, it has an impact on the traditional autonomy of departments and functions. It needs to be resolved by joint participation to avoid any resentment.

Corporate mandates occasionally meet with cultural and social resistance. To overcome the same, behavioural scientists make use of the rules of the road to introduce change into a going culture and adaptable to the new situation. The steps are as follows:

1. Provide participation to suitable representatives in planning and execution of the change.
2. Provide enough time to:

   (a) evaluate the merits of the change in relation to their habit's status and belief.
   (b) find accommodation with the advocates of change.

   This is facilitated by starting the change in a small way with proper communication. This should be carried out with no surprises and by having patience for the right time.
3. Keep the proposal free from cluttering with irrelevant matters.

4. Work with the re-organized leadership of the culture. Convincing the leadership is a significant step in getting the change accepted.
5. Treat the people with dignity to get the best out of them.
6. Reverse the positions. Go into the role-playing to stimulate understanding of the other person's position.
7. Look at the alternatives and choose the best one acceptable to all concerned.

There is a need for quality planning to bring under its gamut the entire organization along with all its operations, i.e., fundamentally the processes and ultimately the products. The fundamental objective of quality planning is to avoid creating deficient products and processes. There must be planning for all such activities that lead to increase in output in terms of both products and services, i.e., the value addition with related least consumption of resources or rather their optimum utilization. Anything that enhances the unwarranted consumption of input resources is categorized under the heading of 'cost of poor quality'.

Therefore, quality planning should be an integral part of the basic management process for running an organization, i.e., deciding in advance the various management processes for attainment of its end objectives. Quality planning is a part of the company wide quality management activity involving everyone in the organization and involving all the functions. Quality planning should ensure the consistency of performance of all the functions along with its continual improvement.

The quality crisis evolves from the following basic areas, viz.

- Loss of sales due to quality of product.
- Loss of sales due to competition in quality. A competitor understand the customers' stated and implied needs better than the organization and the product features of the competitors' product are better suited for a particular market segment.
- Cost of poor quality. Customer complaints, liability lawsuits, rework and salvaging defective work, scrap, excess consumption of any input resources, i.e., utilizing more machine capacity, more material consumption, etc., all contribute to the cost of poor quality. This constitutes the major part of the cost.
- Threat to the society. People in industrial society live behind protective quality dykes. Substandard product quality can be an element of hazard in all walks of life. Substandard quality of medicine may play with the life of an individual. Any engineering product from automobiles to domestic fans can really cause safety hazards if the performance is below the designed or claimed level. Any day-to-day chemicals in the form of detergents, soaps, perfumes and toiletries can play havoc if not of a proper quality.
- Threat to the employees. Inadequate facilities, poor condition of the machines, inadequate maintenance of the machines and building and electrical wiring, improper housekeeping, inadequate lighting and poor ergonomics are responsible for accidents and other occupational hazards leading to threat to the life and well-being of the employees.

Substandard process quality not only produces deficient product but by itself creates grave danger to the society. The instances are the three mile island nuclear reactor, the deadly gas clouds at Bhopal, the space shuttle challenger, the carbonyl nuclear reactor and the recent release of extremely harmful industrial wastages by Chinese factories to the rivers. Detailed investigation about the root cause of these quality crisis has always been pointing at a singularly most important factor that 'quality was not planned' in all these cases. Therefore, we can conclude that the quality needs to be planned to avert quality crisis.

7.3.3   Planning for Quality

The planning for quality follows a scientific, systematic procedure as is described below. Here the word 'quality' means world-class performance of the products, processes, each individual employee, etc. Planning for quality is a long drawn process. Dr. Juran had said that if you have one hour to chop down a tree, you may spend seven hours sharpening your axe. This highlights the importance of the planning in real life situations to accomplish the attainment of the end objective.

1. The entire activity starts with creating an awareness regarding the dangers of quality crises and the role of quality planning in averting the same. Basic approach is to bring about a change in the mindset of all employees that everyone would 'do it right the first time'.

2. Quality planning should have a well-defined objective to remove any ambiguity regarding the focus on the end result. Once the objective is defined and accepted by the organization and the concerned team for its implementation, the quality plan is worked out in detail with the resource allocation and assignment of responsibilities to the team members. On achievement of the end result, a suitable, fair and just reward system should be prevalent linked to the end result and the gains out of it.

3. Now ensure to achieve the quality plan through proper execution. This consists of providing training in how to plan for quality, an orientation towards the proper execution of the quality plan along with ability of the team members to handle any eventualities. The team members should assist company personnel to re-plan existing processes to be void of quality deficiencies. Ultimately the quality plan must be institutionalized so that the company personnel should be able to execute and achieve the quality plan without creation of any new chronic problems.

7.4   THE QUALITY PLANNING PROCESS

Quality planning develops the products and processes required to meet the customers' needs. Hence quality planning has three definite steps to attain the end objective. It starts with the identification of the customers and their needs. The next step in quality planning is to develop a product that fulfills their needs. Once product development has settled down, quality planning develops a process capable to produce the product.

7.4.1 Identification of Customers' Needs

The quality planning process starts with the existing products and their end uses. The quality planning team should identify the customers and find out their needs by a suitable market survey and customer perception analysis. Follow the 'quality function deployment' technique as described in Chapter 2 and convert the customer needs in the company's language, i.e., in terms of the product features and how it can be developed.

Identify customer

Input to this process is the organization's existing products and services. The intermediary and end user's identification is part of the process and the output of this exercise is the list of the customers.

To make it happen systematically, first clearly define the products, i.e., goods and services offered by the organization. Then draw a 'flow diagram' of the entire process of the usage of these goods and services till the end. Look at the scope for improvement for your 'process' as well as the efficient utilization of the 'processor team'. To identify customers, follow the products, i.e., persons/agencies impacted by the goods and services offered by your organization. The categories of customer could broadly be five, namely:

- **Customer.** They buy from us and are source of our income.
- **Consumer.** Consumers are the end users of the company's products and services. Their feedback on use of the product strongly influences the buying decisions.
- **Investors.** They buy the company's securities or finance against them.
- **Regulators.** The regulators are normally the government bodies. Their rules are a form of mandated needs to be met.
- **The public.** They influence the environment of our operation.

Out of these five categories, obviously the first two play a vital role. Companies and clients interface in multiple ways. We have to identify and focus on the key interface important to our business.

Once we have identified the customers, we have to conduct a 'pareto analysis' of the customers and the sales volume. Then identify the vital few–20% of the customers who give 80% of the sales volume. Hence the primary focus for need fulfillment should on these vital few customer. These customers expect the organization to understand them in depth and contact them with careful planning by regular visits, in-depth review of proposals and regular feedback on their needs. The organization can practice customer relationship management (CRM) with them and categorizes them as the 'platinum' customers and has closest interaction with them. Many customers may also give useful feedback regarding their perception of future buying pattern, suggestions for improvements, product usage, etc. Vital few customers include principal buyer, upper management of the organization, union leader, government registry body representative, etc. Customers include consumers, merchants, workforce, processors, investors, public, etc.

Needs of the customers

From the input as the list of customers, here the process involves discovering the customer needs in terms of stated needs and implied or real needs as well as the perceived need. The output of the entire process is summarizing and stating the customer needs in their language.

Clients may state their needs in terms of goods they wish to buy. The real or implied needs however may be far from the services these goods can provide, e.g., client's stated need could be food but the real need in satisfying hunger and the pleasant taste of the food. The client's stated need could be a house but the implied need is a comfortable living place. Similarly, the stated need could be buying a pen but the implied need is writing.

Customers normally state their needs best on perception. These are known as perceived needs, which normally originate from the cultural pattern. These perceived needs could also be categorized as latent needs. Customer may have haircut either one from a barber in a barber's shop, from a hair stylist in a saloon or from a specialist in a beauty parlour, what differs is the cost, sense of comfort and his perception.

Many times product fails because it is used in an unintended manner or used by untrained workers. This is a difficult area as precautionary measures are hypothetical, not focused and normally taken care by adding a factor of safety during quality planning that is over design that adds costs. The customer needs are normally collected and noted in terms of primary, secondary or tertiary needs. Obviously more attention is paid towards the fulfillment of the primary needs. The processes for discovering customer needs are the following:

- Be a customer.
- Communicate with customers.
- Simulate customers use.

All the three activities can be carried cut simultaneously. However, the main focus should be drawn understanding the stated, implied and perceived needs of the vital few clients. It should always be remembered that customer needs keeps on changing and it is a moving target. Communication with customer should be an ongoing process. Normally the communication on product dissatisfaction is at the customer's initiative and the communication on product satisfaction is usually at the organization's initiative, i.e. through market research.

Market research to discover customer needs requires as bare minimum an answer to the following questions:

- Which product features are most important to customer?
- On these key features, how does our product compare to that of competitors?
- What is the significance of these quality differences to the customer in monetary or any other way whatsoever?
- Customer's suggestions on changes, alteration in product and/or product features to make him/her accept this product as the preferred one.

Market research should be product-specific and kind of customer-specific. While for communication, customer feedback is an ongoing process for 'vital few' customers, for 'useful many' customers market research is carried out by sampling. It is a cost-effective way of securing information.

Translation of customer's needs into the units of measurement

In this process, input is the customer's needs in his language. This is to be translated, converted and adopted to the customer's need fulfillment requirement in organizational language. This is the desired output from this process. The objective here is not mere translation of customer need from his language to the company's language, but also to make all concerned in the organization understand the same. The organizational ladder has multiple dialects. While the upper management only understands the 'language of money', the operational level workers and lower management understands the 'language of things'. The middle management is 'bilingual'. After understanding the customers' need in own company's language, it should be accepted by standardization and a common understandable unit of measurement. It is advisable to use the same quality planning spreadsheet where customer's need has been noted for translation into customer's need in understandable company's language. The following are the common steps taken for easy understanding of this interface:

- Glossary.
- Samples.
- Special interface committee for translation.
- Standardization and common units of measurement.

Now the 'units of measurement' need to be established. The objective here is to establish the units of measurement for the translated customer needs. These units of measurement should be universally understood at all levels of the organization as well as at the customer's end. A common language is must for quality planning. This interface is vital to the success of the entire process. Precision in matter of this common language and case of understanding is to quantify the measurement, i.e., state in specific scale or numbers. To accomplish this, for each quality features, there should be a specific unit of measurement and sensor. Hence we add another column to quality planning spreadsheet, i.e., 'units of measure'.

There are multiple 'key performance indicators (KPI)' to be measured. For instance,

- Technological
  E.g., degrees for heat, hour, minute, seconds for time.
- Product performance
  E.g., km./litre of fuel efficiency of an automobile.
  0–100 km/hr speed attainment in seconds for performance indicator, etc. In hours, days for timeliness of service to customer.
- Product failures
  E.g., number of errors and failures, percent defective of field failures of product, percent error in billing accuracy, etc.
- Functional performance measures
  E.g., months required to launch new product for product development, cost of poor quality per Rs. 100/- of manufacturing cost.

- Corporate performance
  E.g., cost of poor quality to sales, return of investment, etc.
- Managerial performance
- Percent of error-free product
- Cost of poor quality versus the cost of operation

It is apparent that for all units of measure there should be a precise definition. Units of measurement for abstractions can be established by:

- Counting the violations, and
- Breaking the abstractions up into identifiable realities.

Units of measure form a pyramid starting with technological units at the base and ending with financial units, indexes and ratios at the top. An ideal unit of measure should possess the following characteristics:

- Provide a mutually agreed base and interface between customer and the organization.
- Provide a mutually agreed performance measurement indicator at all levels and at all functions.
- Provide a uniform agreed base for decision-making in the organization at all levels.
- Be easily understandable to all concerned.
- Apply broadly to all aspects of management and functions.
- Be susceptible to uniform inter-relation.
- Be economical for application and implementation.
- Be compatible with existing designs of sensors.

Now 'establish the measurement'. After establishing the units of measurement and quantifying, the process is to establish the means of measuring accurately and precisely the units.

A sensor is a device specially designed to evaluate the presence and intensity of specific phenomena. For technological performance measurement, it is invariably a measuring instrument, e.g., a voltmeter measures voltage and an ammeter measures current; a measuring tape measures distance while for financial performance measurement it is a ratio on key figure. The precision of sensor has its ability to reproduce or repeat the result on repeat test.

The accuracy of a sensor is the degree to which it is correct. Sensors are used to measure the performance at all levels of the company, i.e., technological performance, product performance, and departmental, corporate and managerial performance. There is more reliability, accuracy and precision in using an instrument as sensor rather than human beings that could be at times major a source of error. Various human errors can be reduced by using certain methodology and a systematic approach.

Misinterpretation errors can be reduced by focused and accurate definition of commonly understood and universally accepted terminology, simple sequential instruction, check list, examples, models, training and certifying.

Inadvertent errors can be minimized by aptitude testing, reorganization of work and by use of fail-safe technique. Errors due to lack of technique can be eliminated by proper training. Conscious errors can be reduced by creating a constructive environment for error reduction rather than shifting of the blame to others. Error due to bias can be restricted by design review of the data collection plan.

Overall error can be reduced by taking suitable action on reports of human sensors and establishing a system of measurement, which is more objective-oriented than subjective. Sensing is done in three time frames relative to operations, i.e., before, after and during the operation. The endeavour is to secure early warning signal for the quality planners so that deviation from quality planning can be detected early and corrected accordingly. To make the system effective and for obtaining early warning signal, the following techniques are used:

1. **Using the planner as sensor.** The planner makes frequent rounds to gain the first-hand information on operation so as to detect the early warning signal.
2. **Design review as sensor.** A team is formed of managers, operator and specialist who are drawn from those operating areas heavily impacted by quality planning. The team continuously monitors the implementation of quality planning, detects early warning signal for any deviation and takes suitable, corrective action.
3. **Formation of joint quality planning team.** A joint quality planning team is formed, including the representative of the operating department to ensure continuous monitoring of quality planning. The spreadsheet is further modified to include the sensor.

Quality affects company in two major ways, viz.,

(a) **Effect on costs of production.** A factor known as COPQ, i.e., cost of poor quality, is introduced to quantify and measure all such available losses during production. These are eliminated by undertaking quality improvement projects.
(b) **Effect of quality on sales income.** Higher quality necessarily means lower cost of production (due to less wastage) and more product attributes, conformance to standards and defect-free products. This results in higher sales, more margin of profit, higher market share and customer satisfaction.

7.4.2 Product Development

Once the customers' needs are identified and interpreted in terms of the technical language, the design and development function and manufacturing assists the team in developing the prototype product. The prototype can be an alteration and modification of the existing product or an altogether new product, as the case may be, depending on the market feedback.

After the prototype product is developed, it is tested extensively in the laboratory to identify any potential flaw in the product design or the performance. Simultaneously, the feedback is taken from the test market for product performance and product validation. Once the feedbacks are obtained, they are consolidated and suitable alteration is made in the product to incorporate the new features warranted and remove the unwarranted ones. Now the product development is more or less complete in the first stage. It is to be remembered that product development is a continuous process during the entire life cycle of a product as per the changing perception of the customer in the market.

The input to the process of product development is customers' needs expressed in the units of measure. The output is well-defined product features responding to customer needs. Product development means development of product features that respond to the customers' needs. There are two distinct quality functions with responsible persons assigned the task to carry out the same:

(a) Quality engineers, whose functions were associated with product quality in the factory.
(b) Reliability engineers, whose functions were associated with product quality in the field.

These two functions play a lead role in the quality planning team in terms of product performance and development of product features. Customer needs are met through product features. Each customer need is unique and requires a matching of unique, product feature, and every such product feature should fulfill certain criteria like

- Meet the needs of customer.
- Meet organizational need.
- Meet competition.
- Minimize the combined cost of customer and the organization.

Subsequent to this, the product development cycle starts, which consist of following sequential development steps. Nomination of the scientific technological conceptual principle is to be employed (e.g., electronic, hydraulic and optical).

- Study of technical feasibility.
- Economic evaluation and feasibility study.
- Decision on conceptual principle.
- Model design and testing under controlled condition.
- Draw conclusion, compare with competition and evaluate.
- Modify, if required.
- Now launch the product test marketing under actual operating condition.
- Collect feedback and improve.
- Scale up and launch the product under operating conditions.

A complex product contains numerous product features to satisfy numerous customer needs. The more the number of product features, the greater is the need for a structured and formal quality planning. The structured approach makes use of a variety of planning and analysis tools, including:

- Spreadsheets.
- The phase system.
- Product sub-division.
- Criticality analysis.
- Competitive analysis.
- Saleability analysis.
- Analysis to avoid failures.
- Value analysis.

Accordingly, the spreadsheet will be modified to include the product features against fulfillment of customers needs.

The next stage of product development is the 'Product Design'

The input to the process of optimizing product design in the product features resulting in product development and output is the final product design that meets both the customer's needs and the organization's needs and at the same time minimizes the combined cost. As has already been discussed, a product could be tangible or intangible and consists of both goods and services.

The product should be in line with the quality goals or targets and satisfying the quality standards. The quality goals should be:

- Optimal as to the overall results. Any sub-optimization of any activity may damage the overall performance.
- All inclusive.
- Maintainable.
- Modular and
- Economic.

These factors together comprise setting of the quality goal. However, to the operating forces implementing the quality goal, it should be:

- Legitimate.
- Attainable.
- Understandable.
- Applicable, i.e., fit the conditions of use as well flexible and adaptable for the condition of use.
- Worthwhile from deriving benefit out of meeting the quality goal.
- Equitable as a standard of evaluation.

The basis of establishing quality goals could be:

- Historical reason.
- Engineering study and its input.
- Market acceptability as a basis.
- Decreed quality standard.

Goals based on history are attainable but may lead to on outdated poor performance. Goals based on engineering study produces better-focused, attainable results than empirically based goals. However, it has to be supplemented and complemented by a market-based goal in a competitive society. The goals should be set on a participative manner having representatives from all departments. Internal monopolies on goal-setting lead to unilateral creation of problems for other related functional departments.

Sub-optimization is a serious obstacle to the attainment of the optimization of product design both within the organization as well as at the customer's end. The chief remedy of sub-optimization is joint planning and participation. To attain participation, the organization is specially designed and supplemental with coordinators and interdepartmental teams. The participants should be able to provide several kinds of input to goal-setting and goal attainment, viz.

- Early warning of upcoming problems.
- Data to aid in optimizing.
- Challenge to theories.
- Remove internal and external obstacles.
- Ensure smooth operation of the system.

Resolving differences within the organization and between the customer and the organization is vital for the attainment of the optimal solution. In case of external customers, the differences are mainly focussed on the technological and economical aspects. In case of internal customer, additional forces of behaviour and nature may come into play. To resolve difference it is advantageous to identify the specific decisions and actions that are at issue.

The steps to reduce conflicts are as follows:

1. **Specialties and broad planning.**   Clearly a distinction should be made between areas of expertise of experts and the broad planning of their areas.
2. **Compromise.**   It reduces abrasion, but never finds the optimum. It satisfies none and lacks the basic spirit of teamwork.
3. **Constructive conflict.**   It is a team approach to discover the optimum and the epitome of progress.
4. **Publication of standards and goals.**   It makes them clear without ambiguity, easily understandable and authenticates the parameters to be adhered to.

Thus, optimizing the process consists of jointly finding the optimum meeting point of the needs of both the customer and the organization alike at the minimum combined cost. All differences and conflicts needs to be resolved totally to workout the 'optimum'.

7.4.3   Process Development

Quality planning lays out the next stage as 'process development' after optimizing the product design, and developing and finalizing the product goals. The principal focus of process development is to achieve the required product features as per product design at the least consumption of resources like men, machine and material at the least cost in time. The main focus of process development is the development of the process capability with least cost and the least time of conversion for the required value addition to the end product. Now the process is standardized and put into practice to prove the process capability. Once this exercise is over, the process is ready to be transferred to the shopfloor for regular running of the commercial production. Now with the minor adjustments, if any, the commercial production starts on a regular basis and the quality planning objective is achieved.

The quality planning steps are overlapping and form a chain where the output of preceding activity becomes the input to the next activity. Every activity plays the simultaneous role of customer, processor and the supplier. The entire process must be evaluated in terms of well-defined common performance measures. The control and evaluation points should be pre-determined and accurately assessed to enable the organization to convert quality planning as a foolproof process.

After the product has been developed and optimized, a suitable process is developed that is capable of meeting the product goals. A process can be defined as:

"A systematic series of actions directed to achievement of a goal"—Dr. J.M. Juran

Some of the features of a process are as follows:

1. The process should be 'goal-oriented', i.e., directed towards attainment of product goals as well as the quality goals.
2. The process should also be systematic with all the action being sequential, interconnected and interdependent.
3. The process should also be capable of achieving the end result comfortably.
4. The process must be legitimate, acceptable and understandable by all concerned.

The entire business activity consists of interlinked series of processes. If the processes are right and under control, the product has to be correct and of 'zero defect'. Process includes manufacturing as well as non-manufacturing activities, interlinking and optimum utilization of human resources as well as physical facilities. To develop a systematic approach, the process itself needs to be planned. The aim is to provide the operating forces with the means for meeting the quality and product goals.

The final result of process planning consist of the following:

1. The software, i.e., the description of process and its ability to meet the goals under operating condition.
2. The word ware, i.e., physical facilities needed to carry out operations.
3. The information needed to provide instruction, explanation and clarification for use of the hardware and/or software. Process capability is a quantified measure of the ability of a process to deliver the end results. This concept can be applied to all manufacturing as well as non-manufacturing organizations. The process capability is evaluated from operating data and is a measure of what a process can do and process performance is what the process actually does.

Process performance is always below inherent process capability due to influence of significant causes of variation. Hence we take help of normal distribution curve and other statistical inputs like mean (x), Range (R) and standard deviation (σ).

$$X = \frac{X_1 + X_2 + X_3 + \ldots + X_n}{N}$$

$(x_1, x_2, \ldots x_n)$ are individual readings, and n = number of readings taken)

$$R = x\ max - x\ min = \text{Maximum deviation}$$

$$\sigma = \sqrt{\frac{(x_1 - x)^2 + (x_2 - x)^2 + \ldots + (x_n - x)^2}{n}}$$

Some statistically significant differences in performance are economically important, others are not. They may impact other non-tangible areas. All processes, human or non-human manufacturing or non-manufacturing, exhibit variability. This variability should be measured and controlled.

A frequency distribution or normal distribution curve is a graphic way of presenting this variability. Standard deviation (σ) is a measure of such variability. Refer to Figure 7.4.

Population of product produced as a result of a process shows the following tendency in a normal distribution curve:

- 68.26% products lie within range of $+\sigma$
- 95.57% products lie within the range of $+2\sigma$
- 99.97% products lie within the range $+3\sigma$

This implies that if the control limits of a process is fixed at $+3\sigma$ limit, the chances of a product going outside this limit is only 3 in 10,000, i.e., 3 p.p.m.

The deployment of this principal of process control is popularly known in industry as statistical process control (SPC).

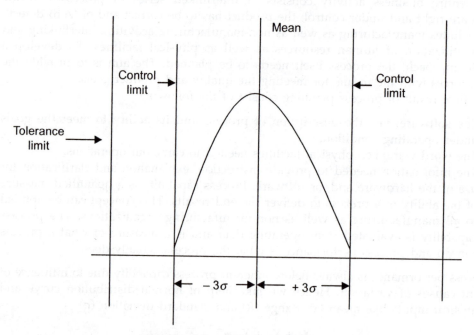

FIGURE 7.4 Statistical process control.

Since tolerance limits are beyond control limits, CP will always be more than one for process under control.

Hence we can conclude that:

Process capability $> 6\ \sigma$, standard deviation, i.e., the Six Sigma.

To ensure that the process is capable to produce the product, the tolerance limit should be atleast beyond this $+3\sigma$ limit or $6\ \sigma$. Here for quantitative measurement we introduce a factor known as 'process capability index' or CP.

$$\therefore \qquad CP = \frac{\text{Product tolerance}}{6\sigma}$$

For a process to be capable, CP > 1.

Preferred minimum for process capability index is one and ideally it is 1.33.

Here I would like to introduce another index over and above what is suggested by Dr. Juran, i.e., 'process capability index factor' or Cpk. The need for this index is to measure the centrality of the distribution curve. If the Mean of the tolerance specified does not coincide with the Mean of the products produced, the process may be capable, but it will still produce defective parts. Refer to Figure 7.5.

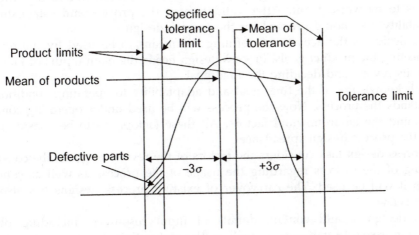

FIGURE 7.5 Process capability factor.

Hence coincidence of centrality of the mean of tolerance and mean of process is mandatory to produce product with 'zero defect'.

$$\therefore \quad Cpk = \text{Minimum of} \left(\frac{\text{Upper tolerance limit} - \text{Mean of process}}{3\sigma} \right)$$

and

$$\left(\frac{\text{Mean} - \text{Lower tolerance limit}}{3\sigma} \right)$$

If these two indexes are equal to one, the chance of producing a defective part is 27 in 10,000.

To ensure zero defect, the tolerance limits are beyond the control limits. A suitable mechanism at control limits will ensure that no product is allowed to go beyond them. If proper process designing is done as stated above, it will ensure a system of 'zero defect' and the possibility of producing a defective product will be nil.

The quantification of process capability serves multiple purposes, viz.,

- Evaluate ability to meet specified tolerances.
- Judge relative merits of alternative process.
- Communicate needs to various member/suppliers of process.
- Ultimately ensure to install a cost-effective, optimum zero-defect process.
- Databanks help to tabulate process, particularly more so with the non-manufacturing planning. Such databanks help both the operating managers as well as quality planning.

For creation of databank, an organized approach is needed. The sequential steps are to first form a team and determine the scope of the product and the process.

Now establish input data, units of measure, method of evaluation, sample size, etc. Organize the training for the team selected to carry out the activity. The data is collected on the data collection form by the primary survey. Establish the form of measurement and the method of analysis. Now the procedure for the establishment and working of the databank has to be worked out. After validation of the process and establishing the process capability, we should proceed for the process design.

Process design is the activity of defining the means to be used by the operating forces for meeting the product goals. Process design needs the main inputs of knowledge of the goals, its review and deciding the final goal.

Through knowledge of the final goal and adaptability to operating conditions, the user understands the process. Now the process will be used under operating conditions keeping in mind the environmental factors. All these factors are to be considered and reflected in the process design spreadsheet.

The process design task considers the factors of the review of goals, the consumer's understanding of the process regarding the usage of the process as well as conditions under which it will be used. The carryover of existing process designs has also to be taken into purview.

Process design should contain details of input resources, including physical equipments, the associate software as well as the instruction details of operating this equipment and the required skill level of operator. All these should be reflected in a process design spreadsheet. We should also establish relation of process variables to products results.

The process control system should possess the following:

- A program of periodic measurement.
- Establish the measurement capability.
- Design the process controls.
- Evaluate the actual performance of the process.
- Compare actual performance with goals.
- Take action on difference by eliminating the same through adjustment capability as detailed below:

  (a) Each product feature should be linked to a single process variable.
  (b) Means should be provided for convenient adjustment of the process setting for the variable.
  (c) There should be a predictable, precise relationship between the amount of change in the process setting and the amount of effect on the product feature.

We should undertake quality improvement projects to eliminate and solve chronic problems. Quality planning should evaluate process capability of proper product features before carrying over to the next product design. This is aided by process capability data. However, in the absence of this data quality planning may seek information from (a) similar process, (b) test of alternative, (c) data from other uses or databanks and (d) simulation.

Quality planning should focus on dominant process variable and bring it under control in terms of set-up, component, time, operator, and information on any other factor. However, the control activities follow a systematic sequence called 'quality control' where the flow of information proceeds as is given in Figure 7.6.

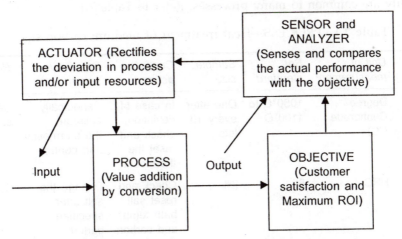

FIGURE 7.6 Quality control and feedback loop.

There is an input to the organization in terms of input resources of men, machine and material. The basic input to the manufacturing industry is the raw material and to the service industry is the customer himself. The objective of an organization is the conversion process of the input raw material into the finished product through value addition or in case of the service sector, of the customer into a value added customer. The output of the organization is as per the organizational objective.

The sensor senses the output of the process. The sensor is aware of the goal and standard. The analyzer takes the output from the sensor and evaluates the actual performance, i.e., the output with reference to the set objective. In case the output is as per the planned objective, the analyzer does not activate the 'actuator'. In case there is a deviation, the analyzer reports on performance deviation to the actuator.

The actuator evaluates whether the deviation is due to the input resources or the process itself and accordingly the actuator triggers the corrective action to eliminate the difference. The actuator undertakes such adjustment which rectifies and eliminates the difference.

This ensures to bring the performance in line with the goals.

Since human errors forms a vital element of product or process variable, it is advisable to counsel workers and put them in a state of self-control for which they should be provided with:

- The means of knowing his actual performance.
- The means of knowing their targeted performance.
- The means of adjusting the process to meet the targeted performance.

Assigning responsibility for planning process controls depends on the criticality of the process. In the spreadsheet, horizontal rows are the process control subjects, the vertical column consists of elements of corrective measures plus other features needed by the operating forces to meet the product goals. Some elements of vertical column may be unique to process features. Certain vertical elements like unit of measure, type of sensor, goal, tolerance, frequency of measurement, sample size, criteria for decision-making and responsibility are common to many processes. Refer to Table 7.1.

Table 7.1 PROCESS—Heat treatment of medium carbon steel.

Control parameter	Unit of measurement	Set standard	Sample size	Corrective action	Preventive action	Responsibility
Salt bath temperature	Degree Centigrade (°C)	1050°C to 1100°C	One after every 10 lots	In case of deviation, check and reset the thermostat	Periodically calibrate the thermostat and control	Departmental supervisor
Hardness	HRC	60	2%	Check and reset salt bath temp. and carbon % in steel.	Change the salt after specified period. Analyze RM composition	QC Inspector

Process control can take place at several stages of progression, viz.,

- **Set-up/startup control.** Controls before and during starting of the process.
- **Running control.** It takes place periodically during operation of process.
- **Product control.** It takes place after some amount of product has been manufactured. It is done by understanding the product goal, make, measurement and determining the difference.
- **Facilities control.** This refers to verification and assessment of physical facilities, i.e. equipments, machines, tools, instruments, etc. Product's quality depends mainly on these facilities. Procedure of facilities control is established. A schedule for periodic availability and control of these facilities leads to formation of a checklist for maintaining each facility and assigning of clear responsibility for adherence to schedule.

7.4.4 Optimization of Process and Proving the Process Capability

The input is process features to this Process of optimizing of Product features and proving the process capability and the output is the process ready to transfer to operation. Optimization has already been done in following areas:

- In developing the product goals, we have optimized organization and customer needs.
- The needed functions must be optimized at minimum cost. One of the means of doing this is by value analysis.
- Product and process performance have been optimized through specific designed experiments.

Pertaining to the relationship with external customers, we can optimize the cost of ownership of long-life product by life cycle costing. Also we can introduce specific design experiment to optimize product performance additionally to other areas of operating forces.

Optimized with external suppliers requires close teamwork relationship with them.

Internal optimization requires balancing situation between planning and subsequent work of operations. Two principal activities that help to strike the balance are design review and joint planning.

Design review is an early warning device during product development, and is carried out by a design review team consisting of representatives from customers, manufacturing, product development department, production, quality control and servicing. The design review concept involves identification, creation of a team and review by the team at various stages of planning. The result is early warning identification of problems ahead and pre-emption of the same by suitable change in the plan or other actions.

Another form of optimizing internal joint planning is to establish team responsibility for the final plan. This ensures full participation and contributes to proof of process capability. Human error is measurement of source of failures of process and product. Quality planning should include provision to reduce human error. Checking for human error should be planned in an active manner.

Foolproofing, i.e., guarding against human error, includes the following steps:

- Elimination of error-prone operations.
- Replacement of error-prone human workers with automization or mechanical devices.
- Provision of aids and training to help human workers reduce error.
- Detection of error at an early stage.
- Pre-empting precautionary steps to minimize/eliminate the damage caused by human error.

The human errors could be due to lack of training, lack of perceptions, lack of memory, lack of momentary or occasionally physical and mental fitness and finally due to negligence.

The critical processes are those which present dangers to human life, health, the environment or risk the loss of large sum of money. Such process must be planned with ample margin of safety to the structural integrity, fail-safe provision, redundancy, multiple factors and all possible safeguards. The basic quality planning must include planning for operating quality control system. It should provide:

- Time for operating force to respond to a crisis.
- Criteria for qualification of operating personnel.
- Adequate training to operating personnel
- Opportunity for rehearsals.
- Criteria for maintenance.
- Systematic feedback.
- Prior identification of problematic areas and undertaking pre-emptive steps.

Process planning is aided by access to data on process capability.

7.4.5   Proof of Process Capability

Transfer of operation includes transfer of responsibility from planners to the operating managers who will definitely demand proof of process capability. Cases where direct method are available for quantifying and arriving at the process capability figures, i.e., CP and CPK more than one, the capability of process is proved beyond doubt. In the absence of such data on direct measurement, planners rather resort to other not so sound methods like dry runs, pilot testing, process validation and simulation.

Dry runs

Dry runs is a test process under operating conditions. The resulting product need not be sent to the customer. The aim is to produce enough number of products to demonstrate that the process and the product will meet quality standard under operating conditions.

Pilot testing

The approach is to introduce a scale-up stage between planning and full scale operation. The approach could be:

- A pilot lot to test manufacturing process
- A test town for trying out new market plan.

Process validation

Process validation a documented programme which provides a high degree of assurance that specific process will consistently produce a product meeting its predetermined specifications and quality attributes. A principal aspect of quality assurance is a review of all quality-related process features to assure that they do conform to the process specification.

Simulation

Simulation is an imitation of the real thing. Our planning may contemplate a new process that involves considerable investment. Since the process is new, such an investment is at risk; we have no proof that it will be able to meet our goals under operating conditions. This risk is reduced by simulation, i.e., designing and testing scale down process. The result from such test is used to predict the result of full scale operation. A special form of simulation is through the mathematical models. The world of simulation differs extensively from the world of full-scale operations. Discovery of process incapability even in an advance planning stage increases the range of option available for dealing with such incapability. However, the full proofing of process and establishment of process capability is ensured before transferring to the operational stage.

7.4.6   Transfer to Operations

The input to the process of transfer to operations is the process ready to transfer, i.e., its process capability is established and that the process is controllable.

The output we are expecting is the process ready to produce under guidance and responsibility of the operating department. Transfer to operations includes transfer of know-how gained during the planning process. The system approach for transfer of know-how includes:

- Product goals. Knowledge about customers' needs, product features and product specification should be known to all concerned.
- Process specification and process goals must be conveyed and known to the operating force.
- Procedures should be simple, easily understandable and in written form. Forms are the reference base. This also may include written instruction, cautions, etc.
- Briefings are meetings specially set up for transfer of information. Quality planning makes presentation supplemented by visual aids and built around written statement, manual and drawings.
- On-the-job training is must for effecting transfer of technology and know-how to the operating department. This is done during overlapping period between quality planners and operating department personnel.
- Formal training courses are needed when the new process is radically different from the old process. It also increases organization wide training, knowledge, teamwork, etc.
- Prior participation. This form of transfer of know-how is a mixture of transfer before the fact and transfer after the fact. Both forms are needed. The formalities of transfer of operation from planning to operation are structured and formalized. An information package is prepared with standardized essentials.

7.5 QUALITY CONTROL

Quality planning develops products and process to meet the customers' needs and quality control ensures that the execution proceeds as per the quality planning without any deviation. Therefore, quality control determines the control points at progressive stages of planning, measures actual performance against the quality planning and notes the deviation or the difference.

The further step of quality control is to take suitable steps to correct this difference and take pre-emptive measures to prevent the occurrence in other areas as well as in future. Quality control also tries to detect and generate early warning signals. As customer needs are fulfilled by the uses of the products or rather by the product features and the product is an output of the process. Hence the main focus of quality control is the control over processes.

The attainment of quality goals is achievement of the company wide sub-goals. The control should be company wide and quality control proceeds in three steps:

- Evaluating actual performance
- Comparing actual performance to goals
- Taking action on the deviation

An essential element of control is evaluation of actual performance. While discussing quality planning we have discussed in detail on the units of measure and establishment of measurement in detail. This forms the main activities in quality control. Under the quality planning we have also discussed the measurement of process capability. These are the main measures of quality control. Fundamentally, for Quality Control we need:

- A unit of measure
- A sensor that can evaluate performance in terms of units of measure
- In case of deviation, taking the corrective action
- To put the process back onto the original course

For technological and product performance measures, we make use of measuring instruments. For other type of measures like errors and failures, departmental, corporate and managerial performance measures are results of data analysis and mathematical calculations. The same is true in case of process capability evaluation. The entire topic, including measurements, sensors, human errors, etc., has been discussed in detail under quality planning of units and measures and measurements. However, the key measures are on product performance, competitive performance, performance on quality improvement, performance of managers relative to quality and financial performance.

An additional element of quality audit is introduced to have an independent review of quality performance. The audit should be from a different knowledgeable functional department. The audit could be of two types: function wise and product wise. It mainly consists of evaluation of adherence to quality methods and procedures. This is known as procedural audit.

Evaluation of product conformance to product specifications is accessed under product audits. Customers for audit in performance are the managers who are not closely involved with operations but have a need to know. Audits at managerial level mainly focus on product satisfaction to customers, competitive quality, reduction in cost of poor quality and proper cohesion among functional departments. The top man or the president also conducts audit to assess the competency of the systems. The quality report package generates various useful reports for further processing and needful actions.

7.5.1   Quality Control Process

Quality control is defined in ISO 9000 as 'part of the quality management focused on fulfilling quality requirement'.

A quality requirement is a need or expectation that is either stated, implied or obligatory by the customer.

The three processes of the quality planning, quality control and quality improvement are linked together to form the fundamental managerial process. It becomes apparent that stability in this managerial process comes basically from quality control activity or from the control over process. The vital secret to business success is reviewed as a string of interrelated process in which each process plays predominantly three roles—that of supplies, processor and customer.

In the beginning, the process is stable and under control, but operating at an high level of wastage or the COPQ is high. Therefore, it is more important here to improve than to control. But once you improve and bring it to the acceptable level of performance, quality control becomes more important to retain the gains at current level as well as to prevent deviations. This often needs new level of control.

Let us understand and interpret correctly the term 'quality control' and its relation with other related terms. Basically the concept of quality control was introduced to broaden the concept from 'inspection' to 'defect prevention'. 'Statistical quality control' is only a tool of quality control and does not represent the entire quality control activity.

The 'Reliability Movement' confined the quality control activity only during the test and not to its service life.

In USA, 'TQM' is used as an all-embracing term, of which 'quality control' is a part. In Europe the term has the same interpretation. Hence to give it broader perspective, 'European Organization for Quality Control' has been renamed as 'European Organization for Quality'. However, in Japan the term has a broader meaning as their TQC has the same meaning as TQM. In 1997, the JUSE adopted the term 'TQM' to replace 'TQC'.

The input-output diagram for quality control process emphasizes clearly the main function of quality control. The input is 'operating process feature' developed to produce the product feature required to meet the customer needs. The output consists of a system of product along with process controls. The main objective here is to provide stability and reliability to the operating processes not only during testing but also during the actual production.

Quality control and quality assurance are understood as the same. But their actual interpretation is quite different from each other.

- Quality control's objective is to maintain 'control' whereas the main objective of quality assurance is to verify the 'control' and its suitability.
- In quality control, the performance is evaluated during operations whereas in quality assurance the same thing is done after operation.
- In quality control, the performance is compared to the goal during the operations and the feedback is given and used by the operating forces. In quality assurance, the performance is evaluated after the operation and feedback is given to both operating forces as well as to the top management for overall corrective actions.

The phenomenon is taken care of during quality planning including the 'feedback loop'. The 'feedback loop' plays an important role in quality control, as shown in Figure 7.6.

The feedback loop works on the concept that 'products are the outcome of the process'. Hence it correctly concentrates on the process and verifies its consistency through a sensor. The sensor constantly measures the process and feeds it to the mechanism or human source known as umpire, which constantly compares with the standard goals of performance. If the umpire finds that the performance is varying substantially, he actuates the 'actuation' which corrects the deviations in process parameters and puts it back to the desired level of performance. Thus the process is kept under control and resultant products are also as per the required level of reliability. As a result, stable performance fulfilling the customers needs and satisfying them ultimately is achieved. This process control reduces the cost of production as well as provides the required level of service on a consistent basis, thereby leading to maximization of revenue.

Here the development of the concept of 'self-control' is inculcated among the workforce in a systematic manner to make the entire system more effective. Here we need transparency in our business. The workforce should be told about what is expected of the process, what is happening actually and the corrective actions to be taken in case of non-conformance. To enable workers to take corrective actions, the following conditions should mandatorily prevail:

- The process should be capable.
- The workers should be trained for comparing actual with standard performance and corrective actions.
- The workers should have the tools and skills to take corrective action.
- The workers should have the powers to take corrective actions.

Self-control is the ultimate objective to aim for in getting a successful system implemented for quality control.

7.5.2 Choosing Control Subject

The centre point of the feedback loop is the 'control subject'. It can be either related to the product or the process. At worker's level, the control subjects are either product or process related, mainly translated into specification and procedural manner. At the top management level, the focus of 'control subject' is on business-oriented matters. The emphasis shifts to the customer needs and to environmental scanning, including competition in the market.

The control subjects could be:

- Understand customer needs
- Translate customer needs for product feature.
- Conduct pareto analysis and choose the 'vital few' product features that are vital to fulfill the customers' stated and implied needs leading to their satisfaction.
- Technological analysis to convert 'vital few' product features to process parameters.
- Government standards and industry standards should be kept in purview.
- Need to protect environment should also be considered.
- Need to avoid side effect such as irritation to employee or offense to neighbouring community needs to be eliminated.

The control subjects which fall under the 'vital few', to fulfil customers needs can be elaborated with the help of a few examples. A CTV has many product features such as picture, quality, sound, price, functions, after sales service, etc. I have conducted a number of workshops on the subject and found without exception that customers have chosen the two product features of 'picture' and 'sound' quality as 'vital few' characteristics for their satisfaction. Hence the entire process that is involved in the manufacture of the sound system and the picture quality of the CTV, i.e., the process of manufacturing the picture tube, speakers, and the related parts associated with production of the 'vital few' product features happen to be the focus of the control subject.

Similarly, a pen has multiple product features including price, ability to write clearly, flow of ink, life of the pen before needing change of refill, not overflowing of ink, etc. I have conducted pareto analysis and found that the ability to write clearly and smoothly and life of the pen before needing refilling are the vital few characteristics. Both these vital needs are related to the quality of ink and the tip of the pen. Hence control subject becomes the quality of the ink and the tip for the ink manufacturer.

7.5.3 Establish Measurement

The next step is to establish the means of measuring the actual performance of the control subject. For establishing measurement, the following factors need to be considered:

- Specify clear and simple means of measurement on the sensor
- The frequency of measurement
- Way of recording data
- The format for reporting data
- Data analysis
- Conversion of data after analysis into useful information
- Who will make measurement?
- Lastly, the decision-making procedure

7.5.4 Establish Standards for Performance

Each control subject is necessarily a product or process feature. Hence for each control subject there will be a product goal or process goal. Goals are the targets or objectives, which should be attainable and reasonably high standard of performance to be achieved. All the efforts should be directed towards this focus of achievement.

The prime goal for the product is to meet customers' needs. While industrial customers specify their needs with precision, the consumer tends to be vague. Such needs should be defined, understood and translated into the language of the producer to become quality goals or product goals. The other product goals could be related to reliability and durability.

The process goals could be of two types, viz.

- To produce products that meet customers' needs.
- Process conformance should be established, i.e., each product should be under control.

These product or process goals are directly related to cost of producing goods and services. Subsidiary quality goals can be in existence for individual or departments. However, any quality goal should be legitimate, measurable, attainable and equitable to the group in question.

Quality goals are normally based on either technological analysis or benchmarking.

7.5.5 Measure Actual Performance

The vital step in quality control is to measure the actual performance of the product or the process. This measurement is done by a sensor which is normally a technical detecting device (of temperature, pressure, dimension, time, weight, etc.) or human being. The large amount of data collected by sensors is converted into information which is summarized in various useful objective-oriented ways to provide broader measures, detect trends, predict future course and identify the vital few problems known as 'information'. The data analysis could be done by computers also. Most sensors provide their evaluation in terms of a unit of measure.

7.5.6 Compare to Standard

This activity is carried out by an 'umpire', who could be either a human being or a technical device. The umpire has standard quality product or process goals fed into its system. The actual measurement is compared with the standard set goals and the observed difference is interpreted as either conforming or non-conforming. In case of conformance, the system continues on its path. The non-conformance is called exception, which is detected and corrective action is taken to put the process back on its desired path of performance.

7.5.7 Take Action on Difference

In a closed loop quality control system, the most vital part is taking action on difference between the desired standard performance and actual performance. This job is done by an actuator. An actuator could be a technical device, a human being, or combination of the both. He stimulates action to store the conformance.

All the steps combined together form a system of quality control. A vital focus of all these activities is the 'process'— a means to produce the product features, each of which is the control subject.

A process follows Deming's PDCA cycle. It plans the input of machine, material and its sequence. The activity 'Do' executes the plan, i.e., follows a value addition by conversion activity. The 'Check' measures the actual performance against the set goal and notes the difference. The 'Act' takes action on the difference and gives feedback to the 'plan' for improvement since this is a cycle.

The plan ensures that deviations are not repeated. This constant cyclic action forms the system of quality control, which takes the organization progressively on the path of defect reduction on 'zero defect' and on a path of continuous improvement. The PDCA cycle has got currently such universal acceptability that it has become a part of the ISO 9000:2000 series of International Standard on Quality System.

Apart from defect conversion or reduction in non-conformance, it also progressively follows a path of process-orientation. The entire standard of ISO 9000:2000 is a system standard interlinking the vital business/manufacturing processes in an organization from input to output, i.e., products meeting customer's stated and implied needs, leading to customer satisfaction. The philosophy of PDCA is adopted at each step of process monitoring and control.

7.5.8 Levels of Control

The control subjects are far too many. The number of things to be controlled are quite large. Even in a small company employing 100 people, there could be over a lakh parameters to be controlled.

The control level could be at various level of hierarchy. At the machine operation level most of the controls are automated and self-controlled, ensuring flawless performance. At slightly higher level, the controls are at the machine operators level. These are periodic regular controls of high frequency monitoring for mostly day-to-day regular activities.

The periodic controls function wise or department wise are at the supervisor or the managerial level. The major performance evaluation and corrective action control at the organizational level is at the hand of the Chief Executive Officer or the Quality Council. The top level control on major expansions, takeovers, mergers, etc. are at the level of the Board of Directors

This type of control mechanism is popularly known in the industry as the 'pyramid of control' which depicts the delegation of control mechanism. The maximum number of complaints have to be handled by the lowest level, i.e., automated control and minimum number by the top management.

The technological measurement and measurement of lower importance are normally at the bottommost level whereas the business process measurements, human measurements, and measurements of higher importance are at the higher level. The 'vital few' decisions always emerge from the top of the pyramid. Most of the process control are automated or by the workforce where the principle of self-control is employed to a great extent as elaborated earlier.

7.5.9 Tools of Quality Control

Statistic process control and six sigma have already been explained in detail.

The usefulness of statistical process control and statistical quality control in process development is acknowledged worldwide. The six-sigma concept, zero defects and the normal distribution curve with control limits have spelled wonders in process planning and process control. Since the process is the focus of quality planning and quality control, it has done wonders in this field also.

The flow diagram

The flow diagram is the mapping of the 'flow of operating process'. This is also known as the 'flow process chart'. The flow diagram helps in understanding the operating process and is a basic tool for planning of quality control. This helps in breaking the entire process into segments with well-defined control stations. This also depicts clearly the inter-relationship of segment of process and point of decision-making. 'Control subject' and 'control stations' around which the feedback loop is to be built are identified. The flow diagram depicts the progression of events in the operating process. It also suggests which stages will become the centre of control activity.

The control spreadsheet

Summarized output of quality planning is the control spreadsheet. Here horizontal rows are the 'control subjects' and vertical rows are the 'process control features'. The operating forces have to measure these "Process Control Features" for conformance and corrective actions. The control spreadsheet also defines the responsibility of operating force with specific assignments and authorization for taking corrective actions. It is a proven way to find out answers to the long standing but vague question 'who is responsible for quality?' It precisely pinpoints the responsibility on specific individual to take decision and corrective action.

Stages of process control

All stages of process control need a checklist of controls with indication of standard performance and advise on steps to be undertaken for correcting a non-conformance and assignment of responsibility for the same.

The various stages of process control are as follows:

- **Set up (start up) control:** Control to be reviewed and assessed before starting the process.
- **Running control:** This takes place periodically during operation of a process to find out if there is any non-conformance; the decision is whether the process should continue non-stop and if stopped, how to correct the deviations and restart the process.
- **Product control:** It takes place after some amount of product has been manufactured. The objective is to ascertain whether the product conforms to the product quality goals. The product should be able to fulfill the customer's stated and implied needs and lead to their satisfaction. Hence 'in use' experience of the customers and their feedback for its improvement leads to the refinement of the product quality goals and getting additional focus.
- **Facilities control:** The audit and verification is done to find out whether the facilities input for the process, like men, machine, material as well as technology, are of right quality, right quantity, and are available at the right time, right place and at the right price. The weakest link in the control is adherence to the schedule in general and when it comes to introduction of new technology, the weakest link is training.

Concept of dominance

As is already explained, the control subjects are so many that it is always better to have a control on the 'vital few' control subjects more closely and define them clearly. Identification of 'vital few' is the concept of 'dominance'. Identification and allocation of resources and fixing the priorities for the 'dominant variable' leads to easier accomplishment of results. The dominant variable could be:

- **Set-up dominant:** Such process has all the problems while setting up. Once the process is set up, it exhibits high stability and reproducibility of results consistently. For example, printing.
- **Time dominant:** Here time plays a key role in attaining product quality goals on a consistent basis. For example, rubber moulded products.
- **Component dominant:** Here main variable is the quality of the component. The components and the product are basically an assembly of multiple components, which are partly sourced from outside vendors and partly manufactured in-house. For example, the automobile industry.

- **Worker dominant:** In processes where automation is not possible, it is dominantly dependent on the skill, training and aptitude of the worker. For example, dying of cloth in the textile industry.
- **Information dominant:** Here the key variable is primarily dependent on latest knowledge and information. Here process is job-shop type and changes with customer, and has to be adapted to various customers. For example, the IT industry.

Quality control system

The quality control system primarily comprises of measurement, information and decision-making. The quality control system model is depicted in Figure 7.7.

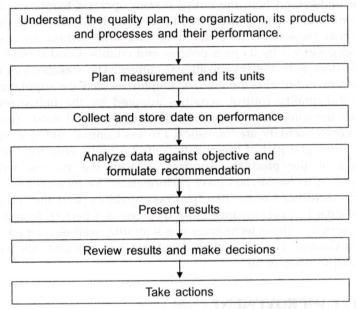

FIGURE 7.7 Quality control system.

The quality control system should start with the in-depth understanding of the organization's vision, mission, business objectives and the business plan. It should also provide a detailed understanding of the company's products, processes and the expectations from them. Once the performance standards are frozen, the next step is to ascertain the performance measurement units and their measurement.

Now the planning phase gives way to the action phase. Collect and store data on the various performance criteria and analyze them against the organizational objectives as stated above. Present the results and find out the deviations for non-performance, if any. Assess the root cause for such deviations and make recommendations for the corrective and preventive actions.

The quality control system now reviews the results and makes decisions. A detailed action plan is prepared for the attainment of the end objectives of the company.

The fundamental question is to ascertain if the process is under control. The measurement act is collection and storage of data whereas 'process of measurement' comprises addition of two more functions, i.e., first plan measurement, then collect and store data and then analyze, and formulate recommendations.

The quality control system broadens the scope of the management process by including at the back-end the understanding of the framework and completes the cycle of quality control by including the final action of making decision and taking action. Ultimately the goal is to help the organization make constantly better decisions and take better actions. Better decisions are defined in terms of results in achieving organizational objectives. Good management system supports a number of organizational goals. It is usually true that 'what gets measured, gets managed'.

The quality control system can be broken into sub-processes of measurement system. For each sub-process, the principal work product and several steps are given. It is important to understand how the entire system operates before we decide what to measure and control and how to measure and control. It is also interesting to note and keep in mind that those who take decisions and take actions are members of the organization and governed by its own policies and culture. Good control system should work in coordination with the organizational culture. The stakeholders are principally not only the customers but also the owners, employees, and the suppliers.

The powerful quality control activities adopted by the industries are basically oriented towards the control of the process. The common and most effective technique for the quality control activity are 'Statistical Process Control' and 'Six Sigma'. Both the techniques are an integral part of the quality control activity, ensuring the consistency in the performance of the products, services as well the process with continuous improvement leading to world-class level performance. The measurement of the process performance in quantifiable terms like 'process capability' and the 'process capability factor' with a standard of performance more than one is a perfect, foolproof tool for the quality control activity. These techniques are scientific, well-developed and elaborate. 'Statistic Process Control' is explained in detail in Chapter 9 and 'Six Sigma' has been discussed in detail in Chapter 10.

7.6 QUALITY IMPROVEMENT

Quality improvement can be defined as 'the change for better performance of the product, process and system in an organization, which is either the elimination of error or for the growth and prosperity of the organization.'

Quality improvement is focused on elimination of error or fault or improvement of the product, process and system of a business enterprise to ultimately give breakthrough improvement in the performance at the world-class level.

Quality improvement is defined as 'part of the quality management focused on increasing the ability to fulfill quality requirements'. Quality improvement is an activity carried out by management to improve areas within the business and thereby increase its effectiveness and efficiency.

Quality improvement is an organization wide activity involving everybody in the organization from the top management to the operators at the bottom level. There are a number of structured quality improvement projects at various levels of an organization. At the operator level for small quality improvement activities to solve the workers' day to-day problem and improve their performance, quality improvement activity like the 'Kaizen Gemba' and 'Quality Circle' is carried out. The team members for the 'Kaizen Gemba' or the 'Quality Circle' projects are normally from the same work area and homogenous. The projects done by them are normally small projects aimed at improving in their day-to-day activities and solving their work-related problems. Taguchi's experimental design is an offline quality improvement activity at the design stage.

Juran's Quality Improvement (JQI) project is carried out for more complex organization wide activities like cross-functional problems or the strategic action plan for breakthrough in the performance of the organization. The JQI projects are normally for longer duration and focus on chronic and vital major problems or growth opportunities. If successful, these projects give a quantum jump in the performance level of the organization. These projects, after their successful implementation, take the organizational performance in terms of the products, process and system to a new height much above the earlier performance level.

All these quality improvement projects have been explained in detail in Chapter 2 and Chapter 3. There are other performance improvement projects in terms of the product and service performance like value analysis and value engineering. There are some other problem-solving techniques for quality improvement like the Kepner Tregoe method of problem solving. These techniques have also been elaborated in detail in Chapters 2 and 3 as well as in Chapter 9.

Hence quality improvement is a beneficial change. Normally there are three types of beneficial changes:

1. **Product improvement.** Product improvement consists of two aspects, i.e., 'product feature improvement' as per the customer's stated and implied needs leading to customer satisfaction. This is income-oriented as it leads to value addition, increase in sales, increased market share and world-class product quality.

   The second way of improving the product is 'freedom from deficiencies' or defects in the product. This results in perfect product performance as per the customer's expectations. This reduces customer dissatisfaction and chronic waste. This is cost-oriented. The product could also be service. 'Service' here refers to pure service from the service industry as well as the service associated with a tangible product.

2. **Process improvement.** The process-orientation eliminates the defect and the product becomes totally of 'zero defect'. The installation of production technique like the 'Statistical Process Control' and the 'Six Sigma' eliminates the errors from the process by ensuring process and machine capability and incorporating computer-aided auto control system in the process as explained in detail in Chapters 9 and 10.

3. **System improvement.** System improvement holds the gains of the quality improvement projects both in process as well as in the product. System improvement only can take the organization to a new height of world-class performance and enable the organization to sustain its leadership and growth at the new height for a long time.

7.6.1   Benefits of Quality Improvement

The benefits of quality improvement are as follows:

1. Structured product development. Structured product development forms part of a business plan. It focuses on the development of those product features which are likely to add maximum value to the product. This is based on market research feedback and customer preferences. Here again the 'vital few' play a decisive role in pareto analysis.
2. Business process improvement. This leads to fewer errors in the entire process and reduction in 'cycle time', providing both service to customer and maximizing the return on investment.
3. Organizational system improvement. This creates a framework to hold the gains of all the improvement activities in terms of the product and the process. System improvement takes the organization to a world-class level, with consistency in the product and the process performance.
4. Reduction in the cost of poor quality (COPQ) or the wastages or the opportunities lost in the various organizational activities leading to better product and process performance and maximum return on the investment.
5. Increase in human safety due to improvement in the process and housekeeping, leading to better working conditions and reduction in accidents.
6. Increase in yield of factory and productivity enhancement due to reduction in wastage of material, no loss of machine hours, reduction in idle time, reduction in rejection, rework reduction, etc.
7. Protection of environment against toxic wastes, resulting in better social commitment and better health and motivation of the organization's workforce.
8. Reduction in errors in office and factory, thereby reducing the cost of production.
9. Reduction in field failures leading to less customer dissatisfaction and also saving in the after-sales servicing cost.
10. Providing better service to the customers. It is achieved by creation of a one-stop shop to reduce customer's frustration and time otherwise spent on dealing with multiple personnel to get service.
11. Structured approach to reduce chronic wastage. By eliminating the root cause, a chronic problem is permanently eliminated. It normally results in substantial irreversible gain.

All these constant endeavours for improvement take an organization to the path of progress. On one hand it facilitates customer satisfaction, leading to increase in income and business and on the other hand, reduction in the cost of production leads to cost leadership position. Hence it is a proven fact that the rate of quality improvement projects decides the market leadership of the organization. The deciding factor in the competition of 'quality leadership' is the ratio of quality improvement. Most of the successful companies follow the path of quality improvement for this purpose. Refer to Figure 7.8.

Company A is the industry quality leader as well as the leader in product saleability. It kept getting better every year at an evolutionary rate of growth and was profitable. Company B being a competitor, was a small player in the market initially. It

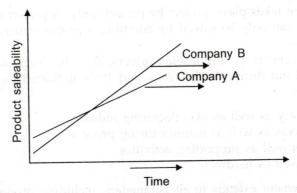

FIGURE 7.8 Two contrasting rates of quality improvement.

opted for a revolutionary rate of quality improvement. Hence its product saleability increased faster than that of Company A. It is threatening Company A with quality leadership.

The similar thing happened to Japanese companies, mainly the automobile manufacturers. They were at an insignificant position in 1950 and were not noticeable in the world market but due to the revolutionary rate of quality improvement, they became world leaders by mid-seventies. Figure 7.9 depicts the estimates of rate of quality improvement in the automobile industry of Japan as against in the West.

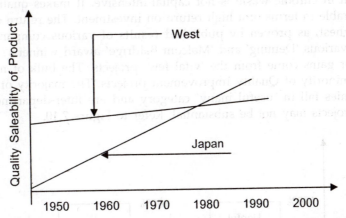

FIGURE 7.9 Estimates of rate of quality improvement in the automobile industry.

7.6.2 Basic Concepts of Quality Improvement

Quality improvement is an integral part of quality planning. Quality control concentrates on retaining the chronic wastage at a certain level by controlling the sporadic spikes.

The chronic wastage may be at a high uneconomical level and quality control cannot reduce the chronic wastage. It is only systematic quality improvement that can eliminate it and bring the process to a new level of performance with the chronic wastage at much lower level. Quality control at the new level should ensure that the performance remains at the renewed level only.

All improvement takes place 'project by project' only. A project or chronic problem selected for solution can only be solved by adopting a proper structural approach with provision of resources.

Quality improvement is applicable universally. The huge amount of quality improvement carried out during 1970s, 1980s, and 1990s indicated that quality improvement is applicable to:

(a) Service industry as well as manufacturing industry
(b) Business process as well as manufacturing process
(c) Operations as well as supporting activities
(d) Software as well as hardware

Quality improvement extends to all parameters, including productivity cycle, time reduction, human safety, ergonomics, environment, field failure reduction, wastage reduction, reduction in internal defect rate, etc.

The backlog of quality improvement projects is high due to non-separation of deficiencies into 'vital few' and 'useful many'. Existing product and process may already have many deficiencies; along with that the new product and project may include deficiencies. Hence a structured approach and prioritizing the quality improvement project are essential. Quality improvement does not come free. It requires structural efforts in several forms, which needs resources costing money. Successful organizations make budgetary provision for quality improvement project. However, all these costs added together does not constitute an exceptionally big sum.

Reduction in chronic waste is not capital-intensive. It makes quality improvement projects favourable in terms of a high return on investment. The return on investment is one of the highest, as proven by published results of various companies. This is also confirmed by various 'Deming' and 'Malcom Baldrige' award winners.

The major gains come from the 'vital few' projects. The bulk of measurable gains come from a minority of Quality Improvement projects. The majority of projects carried out by companies fall in 'useful many' category and are inter-departmental. The gains out of these projects may not be substantial. Refer to Figure 7.10.

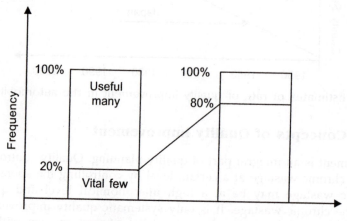

FIGURE 7.10 Pareto analysis.

The interaction of the projects is extremely important in terms of prioritizing the 'vital few' projects which can be taken up to give maximum benefit in the minimum possible time. The vital few projects can be taken up by the multi-functional team consisting of relatively the senior people from the organization. The trivial many projects can be delegated at the functional or the departmental level. Refer to Figure 7.11.

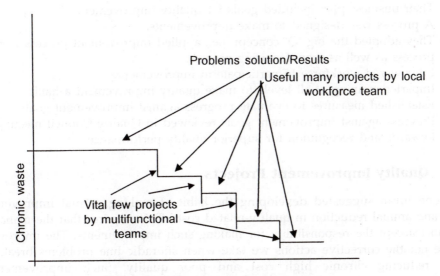

FIGURE 7.11   Interaction of projects.

7.6.3   Inhibitors for Quality Improvement Projects

Any new process, activity or movement takes some time to settle down. Then only you can get benefit from those activities. The inhibitors for quality projects are as follows:

- Disillusion by the failure of the first few or a few projects do not show the correct picture.
- Disillusionment that higher quality costs more has to be removed before quality improvement project becomes successful.
- The disillusion of delegation makes the entire activity de-functional. The top management has to be involved personally to get the best benefit out of these projects.
- Any new movement or change makes the employees apprehensive. The employee's apprehension needs to be addressed diplomatically and with truthfulness and honesty so as to remove the same.

To make everybody in the organization involved with the quality improvement project, this movement has to be addressed and communicated in proper language to be effective and result-oriented.

According to Dr. Joseph Juran, the language of money only will convince the top management to get involved into any activity. The workforce understands the language of things or process on product measures and their improvement. Their efforts should be rewarded with recognition, prizes, promotion, etc. The middle management is bilingual, i.e., it understands both the languages.

The analysis of successful companies—international and domestic during the difficult and competitive phase of 1980s and 1990s shows that most of them carried out many or all of the strategies set out wholly:

- Their business plan included goals for quality improvement.
- A process was designed to make improvements.
- They adopted the big 'Q' concept, i.e., applied improvement process to business process as well as manufacturing process.
- Empowered workforce to participate in improvement.
- Imparted training at all levels to make quality improvement a habit.
- Established measures to evaluate progress against improvement goals.
- Progress against improvement goals reviewed in Quality Council meeting.
- Rewards and recognition for superior quality performance.

7.6.4 Quality Improvement Projects

Dr. Joseph Juran suggested developing the habit of making annual improvement in quality and annual reduction in quality-related costs. This requires that the management team must accept the responsibility for making such improvements. The improvements here are not the corrective actions we take when sporadic line problems break out. It implies reducing chronic high cost and poor quality. Such improvements are breakthrough in to unprecedented levels of performance.

Breakthrough is the organized creation of beneficial change and it follows a universal sequence of events. These sequences are as follows:

1. Proof of the need.
2. Project identification.
3. Organizations to guide each project.
4. Organization for diagnosis—for analysis of projects
5. Remedial action on the findings.
6. Breakthrough in cultural resistance to change.
8. Control at the new level.

The sequence is universal. All breakthroughs follow this sequence. The proof of the need is helped by quantifying the chronic problems into the language of many and presents them as opportunities, which they actually are. This could be losing sales figure or may emerge from awareness of new forces, which has an impact on quality. In order to become specific, we make the use of the project concept, i.e., identifying the specific projects which are to be the subject of cost reduction. All improvements take place project by project and in no other way.

General awareness of opportunities and threats are converted into specific projects for action. This conversion process consist of:

(a) Use of the project concept. A project is a problem chosen for solution. All improvements are achieved project by project. It provides a forum for conductive environment for constructive action. It also helps to secure the needed budgets, facilities, personnel, required data, etc.

(b) Use of the 'pareto principle'. The pareto principle is used to separate the 'vital few' and the 'useful many'. The quality cost figure is a good indicator of whether we have a big problem or not. It also helps to decide whether we should dig in deeper or not. But it does not provide the details needed to nominate the specific projects we should tackle. The pareto principle is useful and for this we find out the highest concentration of cost reduction potential in the fewest number of projects. Such pattern after the greatest potential gain for the least amount of managerial and investigative efforts. The 'vital few' problems are usually automatically nominated to become projects for managers. Whether they are in fact selected as projects depends upon how well they compete against other nominations.

(c) Nominations for projects. The nominations may come from several sources:

1. The pareto analysis of the quality-oriented costs.
2. The pareto analysis of the field complaints, returns and claims. For some of these field returns, it is possible to estimate the quality-related cost.
3. Analysis of other field intelligence, e.g., reports from the sales force or actions taken by competitors. Such feedback, while not easily quantified into money, may be of enough significance to certain nominations for projects.
4. Emerging developments due to the impact on product quality, e.g., new legislation, government regulations, growth of product liability lawsuits, etc.
5. Needs which relate to managerial process and industrial reactions.

(d) Establishing priorities. The priorities are established from upper level management based on the importance and implications of each project to the organization's growth and profitability. The description of projects, time schedule, involved personnel, results expected, urgency and other implications are submitted to the upper management for approval.

(e) Upper management approval. The upper management approval is commonly required for any organized inter-departmental programme involving allocation of significant assets. These approvals are the final step in unifying the minds of the managers. Also these are needed to legitimize the work to be done and to secure the needed funds and personnel faculties.

Securing this approval requires not only a good case but also it requires the art of setting the reason for such inspection and test. The most important inputs to the project are derived from market research. To improve product saleability, close collaboration between the business departments and the technological departments and especially between the marketing department and quality department is required.

(f) The next step is organizing to carry out the projects. This step requires that we establish clear responsibility for three levels of activity:

- Guiding the overall improvement programme.
- Guiding each project individually (as all improvements take place project by project).
- Diagnosing or analyzing each project.

Allocating and establishing such clear responsibilities helps in achieving the planned breakthrough. A specific project is diagnosed or analyzed in stages. Our starting point is 'the symptoms'—it is the evidence that something is wrong or not as per the desired state. Then we want 'remedy'—a solution which will get lead of further type evidence by symptoms. But we cannot have a remedy without properly identifying the 'cause'.

This way we have to undergo two stages:

- A journey from symptom to cause. This could be defined as 'diagnostic journey'.
- A journey from cause to remedy. This could be termed as 'remedial journey'.

These stages are very important and play a vital role. These two are slightly different in their purpose. They are made by different persons and require different skills. Further they differ as to the case or difficulty of the journey.

The stage of cause to remedy is easy as the responsibility is clear and the skills are available. But the stage of symptom to cause is difficult, as the responsibility is vague. Also, the needed skills are not available. While covering the diagnostic journey, one can make use of all inputs available, including those from the workforce.

Remedies can be either irreversible or reversible. For reversible changes, we need to use auditing to assure that we hold the gains. For every project there should be a clear responsibility for guiding and diagnosing the project. The persons or managers held responsible for these projects should be selected or derived depending upon the size of the project, subject of the matter and the state of training in the quality disciplines. The aim helps in getting protection of departmental rights, social and ego satisfaction and for self-development. Appointment to team membership should not be rank-based but based on the ability to contribute usefully to the project.

(g) The next step of the universal sequence for breakthrough is organizing for diagnosis or the diagnostic journey. The journey from symptom to cause is an essential step in the breakthrough. The persons involved in this should have time to conduct diagnosis, diagnostic skills and objectivity.

Time to conduct diagnosis, i.e., the time needed for listing the symptoms, applying the pareto principle, designing plan for data collection and analysis, conducting data analysis, summarizing results, etc. For same projects the time required for the diagnosis is quite modest and it may consume many person years of diagnostic time. Such exclusive blocks of time can be provided only by a full time diagnostician. We can assign the full time diagnostician in following ways:

Diagnostic skills are mostly concerned with scientific testing of theories, how to design a plan for data collection, how to collect the data without bias and how to bring the meaning out of the resulting data.

Forces of objectivity should be present in enough strength to assure a factual approach. This could be done by having a study team comprising of people with varied interests and hence averted biases and by including those people who have no interest in the answer.

Some defects are management-controllable while others are operator-controllable. Each of these two defect classes requires its own unique strategy and tactics for both diagnosis as well as remedy.

We can call defects to be 'operator-controllable' if we have put the operator into a state where it is possible for them to meet quality standards. To reach such a state, the operator must be supplied with all three essentials. viz.

What is expected?

What is their actual performance?

What are the means of regulation of all these needs or ensuring that all the criteria have been met without exception?

We conclude that the operators are in a 'state of self-control'. They have all the means needed and do good work and hence resulting defects are operator-controllable. If any of these criteria has not been met, it is because the management job has not been completed. Hence we call the resulting defects 'management-controllable'.

Three major phases in the management-controllable defects are as follows:

1. Analysis of symptoms. This begins with an understanding of precisely what are the outward evidence of the defect or failure. These evidences came to us in two major forms, viz.
   (a) The words or statements on the rejection tags or in the future reports.
   (b) The autopsies conducted to measure and examine the defects and identify the failure mode.

In some organizations, non-standard language is used in the defect reports. Hence it may convey different meaning and result in high quality cost. The way out of this is glossary. It takes determination for a team to find the meaning of the word used, to reach an agreement and to record the agreement in the form of a glossary. But once glossary is finalized, it will help a lot in diagnosis.

The product units are classified by the team itself. This provides extensive objective knowledge about the symptoms and thereby supplements the information contained in the written report.

The second phase in the diagnosis is formulation of theories as to the causes of symptoms. As all improvements are made project wise, so all progress in diagnosis is made theory by theory, i.e., by rejecting or affirming the specific theory for all the causes.

The theories are secured systematically. All concerned members and diagnosticians are involved in this. An alteration to the tabular listing of theories is the Ishikawa 'fishbone' diagram. As the list of theories grows so does the job of choosing as logical approach for testing the theories. We can:

1. Test all theories simultaneously.
2. Test one group of interrelated theories.
3. Test just one theory at a time.

The team carrying out the project must make a final judgement based on the available facts and in the pursuance of the ideas observed.

Test of things is the final phase of diagnosis. Same theories can be tested and read using the data already in the house. The data may promptly reflect other causes as well, leading to a remedy and ultimately the status of 'case closed'. It can also be tested by study of current operations by cutting new windows or by designing and conducting experiment or by combination of above. In experiments the new or different is done to acquire new knowledge and not to meet current standards.

'Operator controllable' defects are those in which the managers have met all the essential criteria for operator self-control, so that the operator have the means of:

(a) Knowing what is expected from them.
(b) Knowing what they are accomplishing and what is expected of them.
(c) Regulating of the process.

If all the criteria are met, then the means for doing good work are clearly in the hands of operators. These operator-controllable errors are of the following three types:

1. **Inadvertent errors:**   The inadvertent errors are those errors which the workers are unable to avoid because of human inability to maintain attention. These errors are unintentional and unpredictable

   Remedies for these errors involve two approaches:

   (a) Making it easier for the human being to remain attentive.
   (b) Reducing the extent of dependence on human attention by using full proofing tools like safe designs, validation of processes, countdown, etc.

2. **Technique errors:**   These errors arise because the worker lacks some essential technique, skill or knowledge needed to prevent the error from happening. The resulting technique errors exhibit more commonality. Technique errors are specific, consistent and unavoidable.

   The time-to-time trend analysis is used to identify those who are the consistently superior workers and inferior workers. Study of competitive worker usually discovers the knack which enables same workers to do superior work. Once the knack is identified, the way is open to bring all the workers up to the level of the best.

   The three principle tools of analysis for techniques errors are as follows:

   (a) Matrix of errors of workers vs. defect types—it shows the performance of multiple workers with respect to multiple defect types.
   (b) Pareto analysis—this gives the reason for the difference.
   (c) Matrix of errors of workers vs. time—the time-to-time trend analysis gives the extent of consistency in the error over a period of time.

3. **Willful errors:**   These errors exhibit their own unique distinguishing features. These are:

   (a) Willing: At the time of making an error, the worker is aware of it.
   (b) Intentional: The error is made deliberately by the worker.
   (c) Persistent: The worker who makes the error generally wants to keep it up.

The features of willful errors are unique. These are consistent and tend to wide the spectrum of defect types. This could have their origin with management as well as workers.

Management-initiated willful errors are those errors which are intentionally made by the management at the workplace. They are mainly due to the following factors.

(a) **Multiple and changing goals.** Due to changes in the market share, the managers keep shifting their priorities. The priorities of the personnel or the managers are then transmitted to the workforce and this can result in willful violation of one standard in order to meet another.

(b) **Improper communication/communication gap.** There are certain errors which are caused due to improper information and communication between the management and the workers.

Operator-initiated willful errors are those errors which are intentionally made by the operator at the workplace. Workers may have real grievances against the boss or the company. They may try to take revenge by not meeting standards. In some other cases the willful errors seem to be worker-initiated but the responsibility is confused due to inadequate communication.

The following remedies for willful errors emphasize securing changes in behaviour but without special effort to secure a prior change in attitude.

(a) **De-personalizing the order.** It was well-named by a management philosopher, Mary Parker Follet, as the 'law of the situation'. One person should not give orders to other person. Both should take their orders from the situation.

(b) **Establish accountability/responsibility.** The individual should be held accountable for the performance of the job or activity specified to him. The traceability should be established.

(c) **Provide balance emphasis.** Workers are asked to meet multiple standards of quality, quantity, delivery, etc. Sometimes it is not possible to meet all of these standards simultaneously. The major consideration in the workers' order of priorities will be where lies the company's priority. Balance should be maintained in terms of the expected and the reliable.

(d) **Conduct periodic quality audits.** The system of tracebility is not always cost-effective. Quality audits can be designed to provide on a complying basis. The expense to possible audit is itself a form of deterrent.

(e) **Provide assistance to workers.** To provide assistance to the workers' quality 'ques' and quality ques cards could be used. The que card is a presentation of the four or five principle of solving the operator-controllable defects for a specific process. Avoiding each of such defects was a normative description of the knack which could avoid the defect. A que card was prepared for every principle process.

(f) **Improve communication.** Essential quality information should be communicated to workers on matters such as specification, standards, procedure, etc. The company should provide means for workers to communicate their views and ideas. Management actions on quality should be explained to the workers.

(g) **Communicate via quality control circle.** A special opportunity for two-way communication is available through the concept of 'QC Circles'. Workers and managers must communicate on a variety of topics as the project progresses to a conclusion.

(h) **Create competition.** The interpersonal and inter-departmental competition reduces errors count. The associated incentives enhance the motivation level.

(i) **Foolproofing:** This is to avoid the intentional errors by incorporating the method, design and technique which rectifies the individual errors.

(j) **Reassign the work.** Assign the most demanding work to the workers with best quality record. Application of this remedy may require the redesign of the job, separation of critical work from the rest so that selection assignment becomes flexible. In this, the less critical jobs are assigned to the workers with willful errors.

(k) **Use the tools of motivation.** Motivation at various levels also helps in reduction or elimination of willful errors.

There are various diagnostic tools available to take us from symptoms to cause, viz.,

(a) **Tally sheets.** The starting point for diagnosis is data on symptoms. This data is collected on data sheets of all sorts—logs, journals, etc. When facts are to be recorded, it becomes

$$(12 = \mathrm{NJ} \quad \mathrm{NJ} \quad \mathrm{II})$$

correct to design special data sheets. Tally sheets use tally marks.

(b) **Multivariable data sheets.** These data sheets record multiple variables and thereby simplify the job of analysis. A common example is a tally sheet used to record information in multiple defect type and to multiple workers.

(c) **Frequency distribution.** This shows us how many units are there at each value of measurement. It exhibits two main features—central tendency and dispersion. These features of frequency distribution can be quantified and used for various analytical purposes.

(d) **Frequency histograms.** This is made by drawing a block diagram with heights equal to the frequencies. The histogram is easy to interpret.

(e) **Process capability.** For any normal distribution we can quantify process capability once we have calculated the standard deviation. The reason is that all normal distributions exhibit identical scatter of data within any given 'number of sigmas'.

(f) **Pareto principle.** This tool is used to divide any collection of related phenomena in a way which separates the 'vital few' elements from the 'trivial many'.

(g) **Orderly arrangement of theories.** There are two major forms for such arrangement. One is the tabular form—listing all the theories in a vertical order and another is the graphic cause and effect diagram of Prof. Ishikawa (also called the 'fishbone' diagram).

(h) **Process dissection.** In many processes the product goes sequentially through a series of operations. When the entire series has been completed, the product is tested to see whether it conforms to specifications. One tool of diagnosis is to 'dissect' the process in order to discover which of the operations is doing the damage.

(i) **Time-to-time analysis.** Study of time as a variable requires establishing the traceability of defects in relation to time of occurrence. This facilitates the team with the evidence or occurrence of deviations.

(j) **Cumulative failure analysis.** It is a further form of time-to-time diagnosis. It employs cumulative analysis. The data can be represented using the cumulative curve.

(k) **Waybull analysis.** This relates the cumulative percent failures to the amount of use. The horizontal scale is logarithmic. It shows the amount of use, whether in hours, kilometres, and cycles of operation or whatever. The vertical scale is cumulative percent failures and is on probability scale.

(l) **Age reliability patterns.** It is a form of cumulative analysis. This form is used to see whether the cause of failure is related to age of use or to other reasons.

(m) **Concentration diagrams.** It is a plot of the physical location of defects. A simple case was that of the leaks in rubber gloves. The obvious concentration in two areas unified the direction and led to a solution.

(n) **Correlation analysis.** This analysis is conducted to discover the interrelationship among variables. The correlation could be positive or negative.

(o) **Experimental design.** The simplest experimental design consists of dividing a material button and processing it in two different ways—method A and method B.

If material is also to be a variable under study, we can set up a 'two by two' experiment. Analysis of horizontal and vertical sums tells us a good deal about the relative effect of these variables and about their interactions.

7.6.5 The Remedial Journey

The remedial journey is the journey from cause to remedy. This journey involves following steps:

(1) Choice of alternatives
(2) Remedial action
(3) Dealing with resistance to change
(4) Establishing controls to hold the gains.

Choice of alternatives

The diagnostic journey gives a wide variety of dominant causes of the symptoms; weakness in design; inadequacy in the manufacturing process; lack of preciseness in measuring device/instrument; and lack of technical knowledge on the part of workers. We can definitely take direct remedial action for the respective causes. However, there are other alternatives also and some may be preferable. The remedy requires that we take action in one department to secure benefits, which start elsewhere. Hence try to avoid the remedy, which gives lower reduction in quality costs and effect the performance or gain elsewhere.

The common approach to this is the study for optimization of overall cost. This involves optimization of company costs and client's costs rather than reducing the departmental cost. Any one departmental manager will definitely try to improve departmental performance, but in doing so may increase the company's costs. The risk of such damage can be reduced through the interactions among the members of the steering arm.

The choice of alternative is helpful for each alternative; the impact of cost is on a company wide basis. The steering team should quantify the material usage, faulty usage, productivity, energy consumption, etc. The need is to optimize the company's performance and not the individual performance of the department. Sometimes it is also important to include the impact on the client cost and well-being.

Remedial action

Once the alternatives have been weighed, the steering arm makes its recommendation to the concerned department whose responsibilities include the implementation of the type of action recommended. This department then takes the action. The steering arm keeps track on its books until the desired action has been taken and the diagnosticians have tested the remedy for its problem-solving capability. The responsibilities for remedial action are made clear to all concerned.

Many remedies are basically of technological nature as a change in designing tool and instrument. However, many other involve changes of a systematic sort, as changes in policies, goals, plans, organization standards, procedures and emphasis. Such remedies are typically of an inter-departmental character. Hence it is easy for local departmental manager to overlook them. Alternatively, the local managers may be reluctant to be involved due to the appearance of invading jurisdictions of other departments. In such a case, a systematic approach is desired to overcome these problems.

To illustrate the nature of these remedies, we will look at the major phases in the life cycle of a product and identify for each, some of these remedies of a systematic nature.

The life cycle of a product follows a well-known sequence as shown by the model 'the spirit of progress'. The model clarifies that the decisions and actions made early in the life cycle can have adverse effect later on in terms of added cost, delays, waste, recalls, reworks, etc. What emerges is the need for early warning of any such threat so that action can be taken for overall disaster. A major form of early warning is through 'quality assurance'. This prevents the disaster in the later stage by special attention in the early stages. Numerous quality problems are traceable to differences in the product design (research and development, etc.). In many of these cases, the designers sincerely feel that they have done their work properly. Models were made up and these models stood up well under test. Hence, according to designers, all that remains for the manufacturing department, is to make the product as per the design. There could be the possibility of problem due to differences in the systematic approach. These differences could be avoided by:

(a) Designing for actual use rather than for intended use.
(b) Translation of model shop results into production shop prediction.
(c) Training of designers.
(d) Adoption of design review.
(e) Qualification of reliability.
(f) Safety analysis.
(g) Permission of aids to designers.
(h) Having communication in both ways.

In purchase of modern products, we are buying not only the goods but also essential services such as product design and manufacturing capability.

In purchasing, the relevant decisions are:

1. **Policy or vendor relation.** The adverse relationship on quality matters cannot compete with the teamwork relationship.
2. **Qualification of vendor manufacturing capability.** The approach should emphasize technological and personal capability as well as procedural capability.
3. **Evaluating the costs.** The cost of purchased product should reflect the losses due to poor quality.

In manufacturing also, systematic approach is to be applied to reduce or avoid problem in the later stage. Manufacturing involves:

- Manufacturing planning, i.e., activities needed to put the factory in a state of readiness to produce and
- Production, i.e., the execution of the plan.

Manufacturing planning comes first and is the main area which can gain most from early warning signals from the quality assurance. The most fundamental need in manufacturing planning for quality is to assure beforehand that proposed process which will be capable of holding the tolerances. The manufacturing planning procedure should provide for sound assurance. The various approaches are process capability study, process measurement, studying process variables and product results, etc. The training of manufacturing planners for various diagnostic tools for quality is also used.

Fullproofing includes an unflattering evaluation of those human beings that make mistakes. This helps to reduce or avoid the problems at worker level. Beyond this, it enhances the safety and quality. Systematic remedies are also designed to improve inspection and test in various ways such as to avoid defective inspection, detection, to reduce inspection errors, to reduce the cost of inspection and use of active checking for critical cases. Once the defect level has been reduced, inspection costs should also be reduced. The various methods of reducing the inspection cost are as follows:

(a) **Use sampling instead of sorting.** Sorting is needed when the chronic defect levels are too high. Once the chronic defect incidence is reduced to a tolerable level, sorting can be replaced by sampling.
(b) **Reducing the cost of sampling.** The most frequent opportunity is through use of sampling plans, which take advantage of prior knowledge such as process capability and sequence of manufacture.
(c) **Inspect closer to the source.** The inspection of the semi-finished goods at the right location improves the traceability of the defects.
(d) **Go for worker's self-inspection.** Under proper conditions, it is feasible for production workers to take the job of inspecting the product for conformance to specialization. In such cases, inspection by full-time inspector can be abolished while retaining the audit.
(e) **Making use of prior test data.** Sometimes the vendor test data is used to avoid duplicate testing.

(f) Optimize the economics.   Evaluate the cost of finding defects vs. the cost of not finding them. Such studies help to discover where lies the optimum cost for the company.

(g) Conduct value analysis.   Compare the cost of findings with that of the selling price and with the cost of a service call. These figures are helpful for managerial decision-making.

(h) Challenge the standards.   It is suggested to challenge the standards especially on sensory qualities. Discuss the needs and standards in detail with the customers.

(i) Improve inspection methods.   This is done by studying various methods and establishing standards of performance. Such studies are quite similar to those made to improve productivity in other kinds of work.

The most critical defects are those involving safety and health. These defects are expressed using PPM (parts per million) rather than on a percentage basis. To control these defects, updated technology plus automated processes and automated testing, etc. is required. But much of what is needed is a wider application of the quality services or discipline—'that body of quality-oriented concepts, methods, tools, technologies and skills through which we manage the quality function'. For such rare defects, there is no longer any solution through sampling to separate good lots from bad or through 100% human inspection. The remedies suggested are an increase in design margins, improved model testing, improved process capability, etc. We deliberately ignored the 'trivial many' defects in the process of project selection. This collectively involves only a minority of the differences and cost of poor quality. The model shows severally the result of such an attack on the 'vital few' defects. There are 500 defects of which the 'vital few' (50) account for two-third of all the defectiveness.

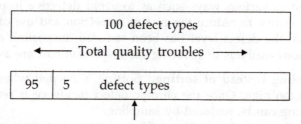

5 Vital few defects tackled by Engineers and Managers

For dealing with 'trivial many' defects, there are two general approaches:

1. **Attack on the trivial many defects collectively.**   This is feasible in those cases where numerous different product types are essentially alike due to having emerged from a process common to all. Hence the order of editing process is common to all of these defects and hence weighs quality as one of the 'vital few' products.

2. **Attack on the Trivial many defects individually.**   This is done on project by project basis and is a totally different matter. The best way to solve the defects is

the QC circle concept. In many organizations, the QC circle has attacked the defects and has carried improvements significantly beyond the levels attained by the managers and engineers.

7.6.6 Dealing with Resistance to Change

We have been following the breakthrough sequence all the way down to providing a remedy for cause of poor quality. On the face of it, all that remains is to apply that remedy. Rather we run into a new obstacle popularly called 'resistance to change'. This refers to delaying tactics or outright rejections of the remedy. The source of the resistance varies—a manager, a supervisor, the worker and the union. What is common is the struggling nature of the stated reasons for the resistance. Beyond this, the cultural factors also play a major role.

A close analysis reveals two types of analysis:

(a) A technological change
(b) A social consequence of the technological change

A social consequence is the troublemaker. It is a sort of uninvited guest who rides in the back of any technological change. Such being the case, if we wish to understand resistance to change, we must first understand the nature of that social consequence. The study of the cultural pattern and the extent of damages to this due to change are required. The measure of impact of the change on the human society should be evaluated. The reasons for resisting change are a mixture of stated plausible reasons and unstated real reasons.

The advocate of change must understand the rule of roads like:

(i) Provide participation both in the planning and in the execution of the change.
(ii) Provide enough time to evaluate the merits of change in relation to the threats to their habits, status and beliefs.
(iii) Avoid cluttering the proposal with extreme matters not closely concerned with getting the result.
(iv) Work with the recognized leadership of the culture. They have their own leadership and this is often informed.
(v) Treat the people with dignity.
(vi) Deal directly with resistance to change.

To reduce willful operator errors, one of the remedies is motivation. We need motivation for quality among all the human forces in the company. Motivation could be taken in three forms:

(a) **Motivation for control.** This involves the constructive approach to identify the forces that mandate various levels/technical people's behaviour and then to help them deal with the same to achieve the results.
(b) **Motivation for improvement.** Sometimes there is lack of clarity or responsibility for guiding the projects. In such case, there should be some motivation for achieving the improvement. The solution must emphasize specific projects and clear responsibility.

(c) **Motivation for involvement.** The progress of managers is strongly correlated with the achievement of the company offering much more opportunity for advancement than a static company. This correlation influences all aspects of motivation for involvement. Motivation of upper management is something special. At this level, the managers themselves are running a business rather than a functional department. This results in selective approach to quality improvement. The quality-oriented programmes are typically proposed by middle managers and these must be sold to the upper management based on the merits as expressed in their business language.

Workers are motivated to do quality work by various methods. The willful errors could be reduced drastically with this approach. There is a decline in worker motivation quality from the craftsman days due to:

(a) The industrial revolution
(b) The Taylor system
(c) Assembly line forms of organization of work.

The most influential force in worker motivation for quality is the company's long-range program of employee relation. Participative programmes are a promising approach towards enabling workers to use their education and creativity on the job. In Japan, the QC circle concept has been spectacularly successful in securing employee participation.

Establishing controls to hold the gains

The final step in the remedial journey is holding the gains so that the benefits of the breakthrough will continue on and on. Holding the gains is by no means assured just because we have found a remedy. Holding the gains requires that we engage in 'control'. In its simplest form, control is a confirming process in which we:

- Evaluate what is our actual performance.
- Compare this actual performance with the standard.
- Take corrective actions if we are 'out of control'.

The number of quality characteristics requiring control is very large. Hence much of the central is built directly into the automated processes and instruments. Most of the rest is delegated to the operating forces—the supervisors and workers in the factories, warehouses and offices. The remaining 'vital few' controls are not delegated; they are retained by the managers as managerial control.

To enable the operating forces to hold the gains, it is required that we:

(a) Make successful transfer of the remedy from laboratory conditions to operating conditions. The main problem of transfer arises because the set of people who discovered the cause and designed the remedies are not going to be in operations forces. Hence it is desired to provide the operating forces with a process capable of holding the gains. Establish operating standards and procedures to serve as a basis for training, control and audit. Train the operating forces to use the procedures and to meet the standards. Establish a system of control to provide for detection and correction of out-of-control conditions.

(b) Provide a process capable of holding the gains. This could be done by establishing a proper system of process control.

(c) Establishing new operating standards and procedures. Standards and procedures help to hold the gains by establishing better operating controls. Standards are defined with respect to input materials, equipments, tools, process variables, etc. Procedures have details of machine maintenance, worker technique, etc.

(d) Training the operating forces. Changes in standards and procedures clearly require training of the operating forces with respect to the impact of those changes. The operating forces should be trained to understand:

  i. What has been changed
  ii. The new product and process standards to be met.
  iii. Which new decisions and actions will be required to make the changes effective.
  iv. Who has the responsibility to make these decisions and take these actions.
  v. How to use the new equipments, tools and instruments.
  vi. What are the techniques, which have been demonstrated to secure the best result.
  vii. What are the consequences of deviating from the specified standards and procedures.

A good transition enables the operating forces to secure the benefits of the break-through. However, these benefits do not first go on and on. What the managers need to do is to provide a systematic means for holding the gains. Control can be exercised before operating by making changes irreversible and through use of the feedback.

Managerial control can be exercised through:

- Direct authority.
- Direct supervision.
- Audits.
- Managerial reports.

Holding the gains requires the skills of troubleshooting, detecting, identifying and correcting adverse changes. Troubleshooting employs many of the same diagnostic tools as are used during quality improvement. We may be sure that once we acquire the habit of improvement, we will never lack for opportunities to exercise that habit.

EXERCISES

1. Explain in detail 'total quality management'. Explain its different facets in detail.

2. Explain in detail the various quality awards with their criteria, with particular reference to the European Quality Award, the Deming Application Prize and the Malcolm Baldridge Quality Award.

3. What is the significance of the 'quality objectives'?

4. Explain in detail the quality planning process.

5. Write short notes on:

   (a) Identification and translation of customer needs.
   (b) Designing the units of measurement.
   (c) Company wide quality management.

6. Explain in detail the quality control process. What are the quality control tools?

7. Elaborate on the types quality improvement. Explain in detail Dr. Juran's methodology of the quality improvement project.

8. Explain the various types of quality improvement projects.

Chapter 8

Results

In this chapter, we will discuss the following:

- Results of Dr. P.N. Mukherjee's "theory of holistic management for world-class performance excellence"
- Customer satisfaction
- Empowered employees
- Maximization of return on investment
- Reduction in cost of poor quality
- All-round performance excellence

If the organization has the right combination of foundation and infrastructure and is following the TQM principles of quality planning, quality control and quality improvement, nobody can prevent it from excelling in its performance in all respects. It will be miles ahead from the rest of the competitors. There is hardly any organization in the world that has the perfect combination of all the three, i.e., foundation, infrastructure and total quality management. The research hypothesis has brought out an ultimate model which is perfect in all respects.

The results can be summed up in the end after discussing the impact of the individual benefits as detailed below. The individual benefits do not have an additive but instead have a multiplicative effect on the organization's end result. The end result is such that the organization following the above stated model can only be at the top of the ladder, i.e., the best in its class internationally. In today's global, highly competitive business environment, the instances of perishing of even good organizations are routine. In this highly challenging environment, only the best will survive. The organization cannot survive by being good in certain sporadic areas. It has to be the best in its class. This is possible if the organization is having a strong holistic management approach towards developing a system in terms of having a strong foundation which cannot be even scratched by the environment and the competition, a sound infrastructure where one and one adds up to eleven in performance and sustainability along with total quality management leading the organization to the level of nothing less than world-class performance and market leadership. The individual benefits can be discussed hereafter.

The results of this model are mainly customer satisfaction, empowered employees, maximization of return on investment and all-round performance excellence.

8.1   CUSTOMER SATISFACTION

Customers focus is developed with the efforts of everybody in the organization, including its workforce, managers and top management. Even the organization's suppliers are oriented towards customer satisfaction. Habit of continuous improvement along with sound strategic quality plan eliminating the weaknesses in the products and services of the organization is bound to lead to a situation wherein the customer's stated and implied needs will be consistently fulfilled. The latent needs will be carefully dug out and suitable solution found out to satisfy the same. All these factors combined together will lead to customer delightment. A sound quality management system, like ISO 9000:2000, will hold the gains made out of continuous improvement in products and services. This will also ensure a consistent performance of products and services fulfilling customers stated and implied needs, leading to customer satisfaction.

The logistic, supply chain management and total organization involvement will together develop a system wherein the customer will pull the organization in terms of his requirements. Only those products will be manufactured which are demanded by the customer. It will also compress the cycle time to market, ensuring that the customer always gets an updated, contemporary and fresh product. It also ensures maximization of customer service by providing the product of right quality, right quantity and at the right time, right place and right price.

Then comes the TQM process. The quality plan enables the systematic fulfillment of quality objectives related to customer satisfaction and delightment. A proper control over process ensures production with zero defects and consistent production performance as per customer requirements. Quality improvement enables the organization to benchmark against the best in the world and convert not only its weaknesses into strengths and threats into opportunities but also devices continuous innovations in all-round performance, making the organization excel its performance in all respects whatsoever.

Delighted customers are the company's real assets. These delighted customers will ensure that the organization grows by leaps and bounds by ensuring continuous patronage, better value for the same products and services, better market share, and lead the organization to remain at the top level. It is the delighted customers and their patronage which can make the company attain the position of the world market leader. It is the customers who run the wheels of an organization and pay for all the expenses of an organization. Without the patronage of the customers, no organization can be successful. The delighted customers will ensure the market leadership for the organi-zation. The organization should have a specific marketing strategy and customized product for every market segment which behaves differently. Technological innovation comes once in a lifetime. What the organization should do is to continue to add new product features or modify the existing ones so that there is continuous improvement in the product and the services, leading to continuous product differentiation and value addition to the product and services. This is the vital factor for market share, customer patronage and market leadership as per Michael Porter's Theory of Competitive Advantage. The practice of the 'customer relationship management' ensures that the 'vital few' customers for industrial marketing and the 'vital few' market segment for consumer marketing will always be with the organization due to the focus created in satisfying their needs and wants. This will ensure that 80% of the market is closely held by the organization due to the delighted customers in this segment also.

The delighted customers are the main asset of an organization which differentiates it from the others. Total quality management or world-class management focuses on customer satisfaction as the main objective of the enterprise. The output, therefore, is bound to be delighted customers which make an organization excel in its performance under all circumstances. The focus of the entire holistic management and total quality management is nothing but the customers and their satisfaction. The customers are the only source of earning for an organization. The rest of the activities need finance. Hence it is but natural that delighted customers will stick to an organization and patronize the same. The delighted customers will also act as the opinion leaders and a nucleus to bring additional customers to the organization. In case the organization as part of its effort on infrastructure development can involve the customers as part of total organizational involvement, the customers will develop a feeling of ownership towards the organization and will strongly back up all the activities of the organization and ensure their success. Customer satisfaction has been dealt with in detail in the Chapter 2.

An organization with satisfied customers and with their involvement will always be the market leader under all circumstances.

8.2 EMPOWERED EMPLOYEES

Customer focus and continuous improvement can only bring results to the organization provided they are practised along with the empowerment of the employees. Empowerment of employees precisely means giving them independent responsibility along with a definite individual goal and also the required authority and power to carry out the responsibility.

The employees will be having an objective which is measurable and quantified. The subject will be broken up into key result areas (KRAs). Each KRA will be given a percentage rating, indicating its importance. Each individual working in an organization from top management to the workers will have an individual objective with well-defined KRAs. In addition, they will have, in a quantified manner, the resources at their disposal, the value addition by conversion, what the employee is supposed to do and the standard of measurement regarding the performance. His efficiency and performance will be measured by his ability to create surplus, i.e., difference between the value added by him to the product and services and the value of the resources consumed by him for this value addition. The surplus generated is also to be interpreted in a different context depending on the relative importance of the KRA and the value added in that respect.

For example, a sales executive has 100% attendance and 100% punctuality in submission of the report in time but out of his objectives, these two KRAs have relative weightage of 5% each, i.e., a total of 10%. The percentage achievement of sales target as KRA is given a weightage of 50%, the realization of payment in time another 25% and the conversion/generation of new customer is given rating as 15%. The sales executive has achieved 50% of his sales target, timely payment realization to the extent of 60% and conversion/generation of new customer 40% of the target. Therefore his total rating is 56%. This is the measurement of totally empowered sales executive.

Compared to this, another sales executive's timely attendance in office is 60% and he is often late in submission of the report due to work pressure and scores a very poor rating of 20%. However, his achievement of sales target is 100%, payment realization is 80% and conversion/generation of customer is 80%. As per the evaluation, he scores 74%. This individual empowerment of individual employee and measurement of performance will lead to a world-class workforce and management and ultimately enable the organization to be the world's best.

What makes a difference between a leader and the laggard is basically the people working in it and not the machines and raw material. You can compel your employees for eight hours of his time, but you cannot ensure his contribution to the organization even for an hour with all your mechanism of pressure tactics. Each employee working in the organization or in the same field for certain years is a warehouse of knowledge. This fact has to be recognized by all concerned, including the top management. Another fact that the organization has to accept is that everybody working in the organization is superior than anybody else in the organization in some way or the other. Even a sweeper in the company; if he does not clean the toilets properly, every employee working in the organization will be uncomfortable and will not be able to give his or her best. The Chief Executive Officer cannot clean toilet just as the sweeper cannot do the job of a CEO. Hence none can say that he is superior in all aspects to another human being and cannot do all the jobs in an equally efficient manner. Once this fundamental logic is accepted, the empowerment of employees and its wonderful benefit for world-class performance can be realized. Then what are we arriving at? We are arriving at the simple fact that the organizational performance excellence to the world-class level is nothing but a team work where everybody has to contribute to the best of his/her might. It is important that in a world-class organization everybody contributes, is involved in the organization and is giving a performance which nothing less than the best in its class. If this is happening, where is the need for close supervision or reminding someone for not performing. The performance automatically comes to the world-class level where everybody is providing a world-class performance. Along with this, if the organization brings in the feeling of ownership of functions and operations, i.e., 'Intrapreneurship' with trust and mutual respect, the employees would feel more committed towards the organization and its goals. If every employee is empowered to carry out the job assignment in a world-class level and provided the resources and of course the training, if required, the job will be executed to the best in its class. The management does not have to worry. It will happen automatically. The organizational work culture will be such that everybody will be enjoying his/her work. The workplace will be free of tension and frustration and no employee will be depressed or stressed. The result is zero labour turnover and an everlasting friendship and healthy relationship will foster in the organization.

After all we want to make our workplace heaven on earth and enjoy every moment of it.

8.3 MAXIMIZATION OF RETURN ON INVESTMENT

The result of Dr. Juran's research work has clearly pointed out that the top management is unilingual, i.e., it understands only the 'language of money'. A businessman takes all the hassles in running an organization because he wants to earn more return on investment (ROI) than what idle money can earn in a Fixed Deposit account of the bank. In short, his return on investment should be more than the bank interest. The increased revenue means the enhancement in the return on investment of the top management. The return on investment is dependent on two factors, viz. profit and turnover of the working capital.

Profit is a difference between the sales price and the cost of production. One working capital cycle means from the time the organization makes the payment to the supplier till the day it collects the sales receipts from the customer. This includes the entire manufacturing cycle, work-in-process, finished goods stock, goods-in-transit, selling of product to customer, invoicing and receiving the money. The completion of one working capital cycle enables the organization to earn one profit. This implies that the more effective the organization is in compressing its supply chain, the more number of working capital cycles the firm can complete per annum. Therefore,

Return on Investment (ROI) = Profit × Working Capital Turnover

On an average, this should be at least four for a healthy organization and minimum two for an organization to survive.

Hence it is apparent that elimination of rejection, efficient logistic and supply chain management, continuous improvement in these areas, customer focus and proper quality planning, etc. will lead to substantial increase in revenue or return on investment (ROI). A major aspect wherein the return on investment can be maximized is reduction in the cost of poor quality. This needs to be discussed in depth for attainment of both the important objective of maximization of customer satisfaction and the return on investment. This concept has been dealt in detail in the Chapter 1.

8.3.1 Reduction in Cost of Poor Quality (COPQ)

The outcome of Dr. Juran's painstaking research on the relevant subject of cost of poor quality (COPQ) shows that even the top companies in the world, i.e., Fortune 500 companies, have an average COPQ as 40%.

Customer focus will ensure that the product and services are always in line with the customer's requirement. This will ensure drastic reduction in external failure or field failure of product and services in terms of quality and delivery. This will make this a principal component for COPQ to be practically zero.

The habit of continuous improvement, a perfect process-oriented QC system involving six sigma will ensure that there is zero defect in product and services provided. This will reduce the COPQ of internal failure in terms of rejection, rework, product salvaging, and conversion to 'B' grade quality. The adoption of Deming's PDCA cycle and continuous improvement will ultimately make the COPQ of internal failure as zero.

As the system matures, the cost of product failure can be reduced substantially as is the case where the JIT system has been implemented. In the organization practising JIT system, like Toyota, there is no inspection of incoming raw material or product as well as outgoing finished goods. This is possible because of the 'zero defect' process-orientation of the organization. The product failure cost can be substantially reduced to practically zero over a period of time by process-orientation. The adoption of statistical process control ensures that if the process is under control, it is impossible to produce a defective product.

The appraisal cost of the cost of poor quality identifies the existing and potential causes of the product and process failure and tries to find out the root cause of the same. The moment a particular defect is occurring, where it is occurring and who is responsible for the same is ascertained; the majority of the defects tends to get resolved by the persons concerned with the defect by taking suitable corrective actions. The appraisal cost of the cost of poor quality has its focus on the specific area of the defect. The defect may be surfacing at the product usage level. But the factor causing the defect may be in the process or the technology or the system of manufacturing itself. The appraisal cost is negligible compared to the external or the internal failure. The appraisal cost of the COPQ is an investment in reducing the product and process failures which are extremely costly. It is observed that with the maturity of the quality management system, there is a substantial drop in the COPQ, with drastic reduction in the external and internal failure of the product and with a marginal appraisal cost. The appraisal cost of the COPQ focuses on the process rather on the product.

The fourth component of COPQ, i.e., the prevention cost of COPQ is the lowest component. The adoption of procedures like 'total productive maintenance', 'proper education and training' builds inherent strength at the roots, strengthening the entire system. The cost of prevention is negligible in a well-coordinated organization following the hypothesis model. The prevention cost of COPQ focuses on finding the root cause of the product failure, process failure or the system failure and takes the preventive measures so that a failure once occurred never gets repeated. The appraisal and the prevention cost of COPQ is negligible as compared to the cost of internal or the field failure which has additional intangible losses like loss of business, wasted opportunities, etc. over and above the cost of poor quality. As the system matures, the overall cost of poor quality drops substantially but the cost of appraisal and preventive measures increases marginally. For a mature quality management system, the external and internal failures tend to become zero. The prevention and appraisal cost remains to control the cost of poor quality at a low level.

Hence there is a reduction in COPQ, which is a major component of the cost in most of the industries and control over the same reduces the cost of production substantially, thereby increasing the profit. As the organization matures in its journey to TQM, the external and internal failure costs tend towards zero .The appraisal cost tends towards first increase and then reduces gradually with the passage of time and with the maturity of the system. The preventive cost remains at the same level almost.

Every rupee saved in wastages is a rupee earned and adds directly to the bottom line.

However, the principal internal objective of the organization is always to maximize the return on investment. Profit is no more an unhealthy word but rather the reverse in the corporate circle. The most respected word in the industry is profit or the return on

Investment (ROI), without which the organization cannot meet its financial commitment to its work force, raw material supplier, the shareholders, the society and the government bodies at large. Hence, out of the two main objectives of an organization, one is the maximization of customer satisfaction externally and the other is the maximization of the return on investment internally.

The ROI is maximized by various arms of the Theory of Holistic Management the World-class Performance. The reduction and elimination of wastages, rejection, practice of the elimination of muda, mura and muri, the logistics and supply chain management, total productive maintenance, the preventive actions of the quality management system of ISO 9000, quality control and quality improvement activities are all aimed at the maximization of the ROI. All the actions that are prescribed in this book for performance enhancement to the world-class level fortunately are basically related to the change in the mindset and application of various proven management techniques, which do not warrant any investment or any major investment. In fact the maximization of customer satisfaction by zero product failure and providing the products and services of right quality, right quantity at the right time, right place and at the least cost also leads to the maximization of the ROI.

The maximization of the ROI enables an organization to pay well in time to its employees and suppliers, invest in the expansion of the plant and machinery, upgrade the product and process technology, spend more on advertising and sales promotion sensitizing the customers about the organization's products and services. The maximization of the return on investment enables the organization to fulfill its commitment to the society by way of rewarding its shareholders and investment in the upgradation of the standard of living of the society by providing better products and services as well as participating in the various social activities. The maximization of the ROI enables the organization to fulfill the government obligation, exporting and earning foreign exchange for the country and above all, maintaining the growth rate of the organization and providing more employment opportunities.

The maximization of the customer satisfaction and the maximization of the return on investment are complimentary activities for a world-class organization.

8.4 ALL-ROUND PERFORMANCE EXCELLENCE

For an organization to be world-class, it has to perform in all the critical areas. The sporadic concentration on certain areas will not sustain the organizational leadership. This is the fundamental problem with most of the organizations. They are good or excellent in certain areas in a sporadic manner. It does give some advantage to the organization but not enough for the organization to excel in today's intensely competitive field. The model of holistic management for world-class performance excellence covers all the aspects of running the organization in a systematic and effective manner.

The strong foundation sustains the organizational performance. The strategic quality planning always keeps the entire organization and the employees focused on the 'vital few' critical areas important for the success of the organization. The critical success factors (CSFs) are never missing. Hence there is an intensive effort in the key performance and result areas. Customer focus keeps the entire organization focused on the main objective of the maximization of customer satisfaction. Only satisfied customers can ensure world leadership. Customer focus actually enables the organization to practically achieve it by even looking into the finer details. Customer satisfaction does not remain a fad but an actual achievement. The continuous improvement effort by all concerned, including the organizational employees, suppliers and its customers, will not only sustain the organizational leadership but will continue to expand its horizon in the other areas as well. Hence the foundation is a critical area contributing to all-round performance excellence.

The infrastructure builds an organization into a formidable fort in a particular segment, defending its market share and market leadership. The total organization involvement brings an attachment and sense of ownership among the employees, suppliers and the company's customers, which is long lasting and impregnable. Supply chain management multiplies the profit of an organization and also maximizes customer satisfaction without any investment. It gives a clear-cut competitive advantage and maximum return on investment. The ISO 9000:2000 Quality Management System holds the gains and never allows an organization to slip back to bad performance. In addition, its focus on the continual improvement and systemization takes the organization to a formidable top position in the industry.

Ultimately having achieved the strong foundation backed by a formidable infrastructure, the organization is now ready to embrace the all-encompassing and all-powerful tool of the total quality management. The quality plan will ensure that the organization is maximizing the use of the scarce input resources for attaining its end objective of world-class performance. The quality plan will ensure the revolutionary growth of the organization. The quality control will ensure that the performance of the organization remains constant as per the quality plan at the world's best level. The quality improvement activity will ensure a revolutionary rate of growth of the organization as well as elimination of all lacunas, problems and reduction/elimination in COPQ. Total quality management will take the organization to a world-class performance level. The model of 'Holistic Management' as described above will take the organization to all-round world-class performance and leadership.

All the four factors are the cornerstones of world-class performance of an organization. If an organization practises all these modes of performance, it will be eternally on the path of growth and prosperity. The organization will have a global benchmark performance. The holistic management theory for the world-class performance is the sure success methodology for attaining world-class performance leading to world leadership in terms of market leadership, employee satisfaction, return on investment and reduction in the cost of poor quality. These factors are not additive but are complementary and supplementary to each other and enable the organization to attain and sustain the top-most world position.

The attainment of the first factor of the result of customer delight will enable the organization to achieve the primary objective of maximization of customer satisfaction. This will invariably lead to increase in the market share and ultimately global market leadership. The more the organization sells in volume, the greater will be its profit and the return on investment. The other factor of the desired result of empowered employees is the key to organizational success. A status of world-class performance can only be attained if the employees are empowered and self-motivated, proactive employees. The employees are obviously at the root of the organizational success of both maximization of customer satisfaction and continuous upgradation of the product and process and elimination of wastages. The third factor of the result of the reduction in the cost of poor quality will definitely reduce the cost of the production. The reduction of production cost will increase the profit and thereby the return on investment. The reduction in the cost of poor quality will also increase the quality and the performance level of the products and service. It will, therefore, increase the delightment of the customer and it will maximize the customer satisfaction leading to continued patronage of the customer and ultimately increase in the market share. This will result in world-class performance and market leadership over a period of time. The fourth aspect of the result is the obvious conclusion of world-class performance where the return on the investment is maximized.

EXERCISES

1. Explain the paraphernalia of a world-class organization.

2. Explain the results of practising the theory of 'Holistic Management Practice for World-class Performance and Leadership'.

3. Apply the theory of 'Holistic Management Practice for World-class Performance and Leadership' to the following industries:

   a. An upcoming two wheeler manufacturing company in India.
   b. A cement manufacturing company with multiple locations in the country.
   c. A conglomerate multinational steel manufacturing unit.
   d. A BPO handling back-office operations of an internationally reputed bank.
   e. An Indian mobile phone manufacturer thriving for a global positioning.
   f. A nationally networked healthcare service industry.
   g. A third-party logistic managing organization. Its clients could be globally sourcing and globally marketing from multiple manufacturing units spread over Asia and Europe.

Chapter 9

Statistical Process Control

Statistical process control is an extremely important element of total quality management or the world-class management system. Statistics believes in the probability theory according to which the inspecting or measurement of a few samples is indicative of the whole lot produced. This statistical sampling inspection of the products. The shifting of the control paradigm from the product to the process has also shifted the focus from the sampling inspection to statistical process control. The original propagator of statistical process control was Walter Shewart of the Bells Laboratory. However, it was popularized all over the world due to its usefulness and was extensively used by both Edward Deming and Dr. Joseph Juran. Statistical process control focuses on the control of the process rather than the product. The philosophy of statistical process control is that if the process is under control, i.e., the process capability figure CP and the process capability factor CPK is more than one and preferably more around 1.27 to 1.33, it is impossible for this process to produce a defective product. This has already been explained partially in Chapter 1. However, the fundamental theory of statistical process control will be built up and elaborated in detail in this chapter.

9.1   SAMPLING

Sampling means drawing a certain percentage of components for inspection from a large-sized batch. The philosophy of sampling is that the sample represents the whole lot. By inspecting a sample lot, we can ascertain the probability of the whole lot being accepted, i.e., we can ascertain whether the lot is good or bad. This is the fundamental principle of statistical quality control. Let us take an example to elaborate the concept.

EXAMPLE 9.1   Assume a batch contains 5000 casting out of which 100 castings are defective. A sample of 5 pins is drawn for inspection.
   The probability for the casting to be defective

$$= \frac{100}{5000} = 0.02 \text{ or } 2\%$$

   The probability for the second, third and fourth pins to be defective lies between $\frac{100}{4999}$ and $\frac{99}{4999}$, $\frac{100}{4998}$ and $\frac{98}{4998}$ and $\frac{100}{4997}$ and $\frac{97}{4997}$ respectively. All these probability values do not differ much from each other. It is more or less constant over the sample drawn. Hence the probability of drawing a defective casting for a large lot is constant for all components of the small sample drawn.
   If p is the probability of a component being defective, and q is the probability of a component being non defective, taking the above example, we get:

$$p = \frac{100}{5000} = 0.02$$

and

$$q = (1 - 0.02) = 0.98$$

and

$$p + q = 1$$

Please note that $p(0) = q^n = (0.98)^5 = 0.904$.
   From the above, it can be concluded that the probability of drawing a non-defective casting is 0.904. It implies that if the random sample of five castings is drawn from the lot on 5000 in separate occasions, a non-defective pin will be found $5000 \times 0.904 = 4520$ times

9.2   FREQUENCY DISTRIBUTION CURVE, BAR CHART AND HISTOGRAM

We will now explain the distribution curve, bar chart and histograh with the help of Example 9.2.

EXAMPLE 9.2.   40 components were manufactured on a machine and their diameters (in mm) were measured. The frequency distribution table indicates the tabulation of the dimensions measured, as shown in Table 9.1.

TABLE 9.1   Frequency distribution table

Dimension (diameter, in mm)	Tabulation	Frequency
5.1	I	1
5.2	IIII	4
5.3	HHÍ HHÍ	10
5.4	HHÍ HHÍ HHÍ HHÍ	18
5.5	HHÍ HHÍ	10
5.6	HHÍ	5
5.7	II	2

The approximate normal distribution curve shows the common pattern of distribution. Depending upon the type of object being measured, there is a pattern of distribution which indicates the way in which a dimension varies.

Figure 9.1 shows a normal curve divided in half and half about the mean size, i.e.,

$$\frac{5.0 + 5.6}{2} = 5.3.$$

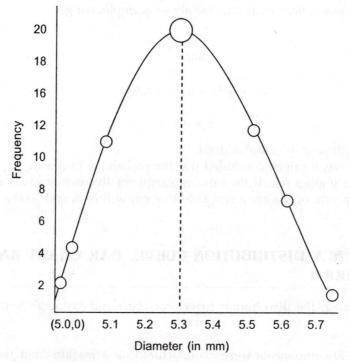

FIGURE 9.1   Frequency distribution curve.

There are approximately equal number of items smaller and larger than the mean size on either side of the normal distribution. The normal distribution curve is also a frequency distribution curve. It is a reverse, bell-shaped curve with the population distributed around the mean line almost uniformly.

Figure 9.2 shows a bar chart prepared from the data given in the frequency distribution table in Table 9.1. A bar chart makes use of the bars. The height of each bar is proportional to the frequency of a particular measured dimension. This is pictorial presentation of concentration of the population on various strata chosen on the scale.

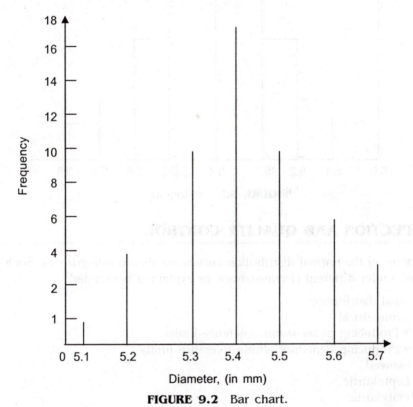

FIGURE 9.2 Bar chart.

Figure 9.3 shows a histogram, which is another way of presenting the frequency distribution graphically. Histogram makes use of constant width bars.

The histogram is the most popular and effective manner in which the data is presented for the suitable analysis for statistical purpose. It helps in stratifying the data in certain group as the need be and depicts accordingly to highlight the particular strata which is occurring for the maximum number of times. In the advanced management tools like the pareto analysis, the frequency of the occurrence of an event in various strata is represented in a histogram in order of their frequency of happening. The stratum which has the maximum number of occurrence is placed on the extreme left side, followed by the next one, and so on. This enables the frequencies to be added up on a different graph on a scale of hundred and the percentage of their occurrences individually and collectively can be shown.

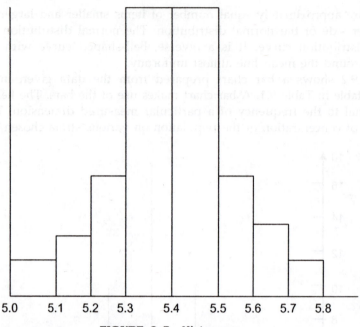

FIGURE 9.3 Histogram.

9.3 INSPECTION AND QUALITY CONTROL

Various patterns of the normal distribution curves are shown in Figure 9.4. Such patterns get generated under different circumstances, as explained hereunder.

1. Normal distribution
    (a) Symmetrical
       • Producing items within tolerance limits
       • Producing items not within tolerance limits
    (b) Skewed
    (c) Leptokurtic
    (d) Platykurtic
2. Multimodal
    Acceptable limits
3. Triangular

1. (a) Symmetrical: This normal distribution curve depicts a stable process. It may be a process of producing items within the tolerance limit, as shown in Figure 9.4 or of a process F which is stable but is not able to produce items within tolerances, as shown in Figure 9.5.

(b) Skewed: The skewed normal distribution curve is inclined more to one side. It shows that there are more number of oversize products than the mean size or more of undersize products than the mean.

Figure 9.6(a) shows a normal distribution curve skewed to the left and Figure 9.6(b) shows a normal distribution curve skewed to the right.

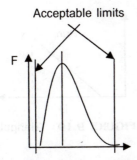

FIGURE 9.4 Symmetrical normal distribution (producing items
within tolerance limits)

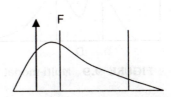

FIGURE 9.5 Symmetrical normal distribution (producing items
not within tolerance limits)

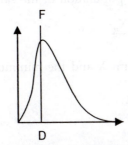

FIGURE 9.6 (a) Normal distribution
curve (skewed left).

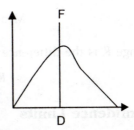

FIGURE 9.6 (b) Normal distribution
curve (skewed right).

(c) Leptokurtic: It has peak higher than a normal curve, as shown in Figure 9.7.

(d) Platykurtic: It has peak lower than a normal curve, as shown in Figure 9.8.

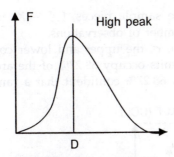

FIGURE 9.7 Leptokurtic.

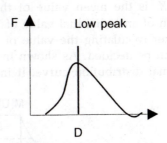

FIGURE 9.8 Platykurtic.

2. *Multi-modal:* It has two or more peaks. Such a distribution pattern indicates that either the products made on different machines have got mixed up or the process is not stable. Refer to Figure 9.9.

3. *Triangular:* This distribution pattern is the result of a defective process or machine whose parameters are changing in one direction with the passage of time. Refer to Figure 9.10.

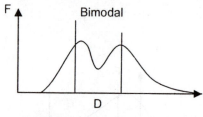

FIGURE 9.9 Multi-modal.

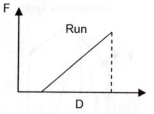

FIGURE 9.10 Triangular.

9.4 MEAN, RANGE, STANDARD DEVIATION AND VARIANCE

The various types of normal distribution curves and the relevant corrective actions are dealt in detail later. Mean value $\bar{X}$ is the mean of the entire population of the samples taken.

$$\text{Mean } \bar{X} = \frac{X_1 + X_2 + \dots + X_n}{n}$$

The range R is the difference between the maximum X and the minimum X.

$$R = X \text{ max.} - X \text{ min.}$$

9.4.1 Confidence Limits

The confidence or control limits are calculated with the help of a statistical measure known as standard deviation, σ, which is given by

$$\sigma = \sqrt{\frac{\Sigma(X - \bar{X})^2}{n}}$$

where $\bar{X}$ is the mean value of the X values for the sample pieces, $(\bar{X} - X)$ is the deviation of an individual value of X, and n is the number of observations.

After calculating the value of standard deviation, σ, the upper and lower control limits can be decided. As shown in Figure 9.12, $\pm \sigma$ limits occupy 68.27% of the area of the normal distribution curve. It indicates that one is 68.27% confident that a random

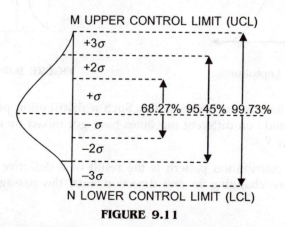

FIGURE 9.11

observation $+3\sigma$ will fall in this area. Similarly, $\pm 2\sigma$ and $\pm 3\sigma$ limits occupy 95.45% and 99.73 area of the normal curve and possess a confidence level of 95.45% and 99.73% respectively. For plotting control charts in statistical process control, generally 3σ limits are selected and they are termed as control limits.

When the control limit is fixed at the $\pm 3\sigma$ limit, the probability of a component falling outside the control limit is 23 nos. in 10000 components. The tolerance limit of the component is normally beyond the control limits. If the process capability figure CP is more than one, the process of manufacturing is said to be capable. CPK or the process capability factor is an indication of the extent the process is uniformly distributed around the mean. Hence for a process to be capable, the CPK has also to be more than one.

The above formulae of standard deviation holds good when the readings given indicate the whole population of the items measured. This implies that this n is the population.

In case of sampling inspection, where n denotes the number of samples taken, the formula for the standard deviation is modified with the denominator becomes $(n - 1)$.

$$\sigma = \sqrt{\frac{\Sigma(X - \bar{X})^2}{(n - 1)}}$$

EXAMPLE 9.3. The dimension for a shaft being machined on a lathe machine is as follows: 8.2, 8.3, 8.3, 8.5, 8.5, 8.4, 8.0, 8.2, 8.3, 8.3. Calculate the mean, range and the standard deviation.

There are ten samples taken.

$$\text{Mean } \bar{X} = \frac{8.2 + 8.3 + \ldots + 8.3}{10} = \frac{83}{10} = 8.3$$

Range $\bar{R}$ = R max. − R min. = 8.5 − 8.0 = 0.5.

Since the readings noted are the entire population, hence

$$\text{Standard Deviation } \sigma = \sqrt{\frac{(8.3 - 8.2) + (8.3 - 8.3) + \ldots + (8.3 - 8.3)}{10}} = \sqrt{(.02)} = 0.14$$

9.4.2 Analysis of Variance

Variance is the square of standard deviation, i.e.,

$$\text{Variance} = \sigma^2$$

Analysis of variance is a useful technique in the field of experimental statistics. Moreover, analysis of variance can be used for analyzing the results of enquiries conducted in the field of industrial engineering, agriculture, etc. Normally there is variance between different treatments and variance between the samples having the same treatment.

9.5   CONTINUOUS SAMPLING INSPECTION

In this system, the existing inspection results help us decide whether to go for sampling inspection or 100% inspection for inspecting the next lot of items.

The principle of statistical sampling inspection is that the sample represents the whole lot and what is normally true for the sample lot is true for the entire lot. For a highly reliable process, single sampling plan of inspection is okay. However, depending on the confidence level of the company, it may decide to go for double sampling or multiple sampling. If the result of multiple sampling plan also shows extremely bad results, the company may decide to go for 100% inspection till the process of manufacturing improves and the results show more reliability. Once the organization regains its confidence level, it may revert back to the statistical sampling plan.

9.5.1   Single Sampling Plan

Under the single sampling plan, a lot is accepted or rejected on the basis of a single sample drawn from that lot. This is the normal procedure of conducting the statistical process control for an organization with a reasonably good performance level.

First a single sample of size n, i.e., of n component parts is drawn. The sample size may either be calculated, or found from tables or decided as per the company's norms.

Then the sample lot is inspected and the number of defective components in the lot is found. If the defective pieces are less than the 'Accepted Quality Level (AQL)' of acceptance number c, the lot is accepted. If defective pieces exceed the acceptance number c, the lot is rejected.

In case the lot is rejected, each and every piece of the main lot size is inspected by 100% inspection or by resorting to the double sampling plan. Now the defective parts are either replaced or the defective parts are salvaged and corrected.

Determination of sample size from the table

The sample size is determined depending on the main lot size as shown in Table 9.2. Depending on the criticality of usage of the product and services, the organization decides the allowable percent defective and also the sample size is determined based on those criteria.

TABLE 9.2

Lot size	Sample size	Allowable percent defective				
		1 c	2 c	3 c	4 c	5 c
Up to 499	75	1	2	3	4	5
500–799	115	2	3	4	6	8
800–1299	150	3	4	5	8	10
1300–3199	225	4	5	8	11	14
3200–7999	300	5	7	10	14	18
8000–21999	450	6	9	14	20	26

For a lot size of 850 and allowable percent defective 3%. Table 9.2 gives a sample size of 150 and acceptance number C is 5.

This means from the lot containing 850 parts, at random pick up 150 parts, inspect them and find out the number of defective pieces. If defective pieces are up to 5, accept the lot; if their number is 6, 7, 8 or more, reject the lot.

The characteristic of the single sampling plan is easy to design, explain and administer. It is the only practical type of sampling plan under conveyor production system when only one sample can be selected.

It involves a lower cost of training and supervising employees. It accurately estimates the quality of the lot. It is more economical than double sampling plan when the lots have their percent defectives closer to the AQL.

It involves a bigger sample size than the double sampling plan. It is simpler and involves lesser record-keeping than that of double and multiple sampling plans. A single sampling plan provides maximum information concerning the lot quality because each sample can be plotted on the control chart.

9.5.2 Double Sampling Plan

If it is not possible to decide the fate of the lot on the basis of the first sample, a second sample is drawn out of the same lot and the decision whether to accept or reject the lot is taken on the basis of the combined results of the first and the second samples.

Double sampling plan procedure

Both the sample lots are drawn as per the laid out norms from the full lot to be inspected. The c_1 and c_2 are the acceptance numbers for the first sample size and second sample size and $c_2 > c_1$.

Inspect a sample of size n from the first lot and find out the defective parts, if any. Now count the defective parts k_1.

There could be three situations:

(a) If $k_1 > c_2$, then reject the lot.
(b) If $k_1 \leq c_1$, then accept the lot.
(c) If $c_1 < k_1 \leq c_2$, then draw another sample of size n_2.

In case of the third situation, the total sample size would now be $n_1 + n_2$. Inspect and now the effective parts are $k_1 + k_2$. If $(k_1 + k_2) > c_2$, then reject the lot.

If $(k_1 + k_2) \leq c_2$, then accept the lot.

The double sampling plan is more expensive than the single sampling plan.

The double sampling plan involves less inspection than that required for a single sampling plan. This plan gives a second chance to a lot before rejecting it.

The double sampling plan consumes more inspection time, is more costly, needs more record-keeping and has more overheads than a single sampling plan.

It does not give that accurate estimation of the lot quality as compared to a single sampling plan. When the level of confidence is lower on the manufacturing process and the level of quality of the finished product, the double sampling plan is recommended to reduce the rejection level.

9.5.3 Multiple Sampling Plan

A multiple sampling plan accepts or rejects a lot upon the results obtained from several sample lots of components drawn from the main lot under inspection.

The procedure consists of inspecting the first sample lot and counting the number of defects found in the sample lot. If this number of defective components is small, then accept the main lot. If there are quite a large number of defective pieces, then reject the lot.

If the number of defective parts is on the borderline and no conclusive decision can be taken, then draw and inspect the second sample. If the number of defects in the first and second samples combined are very small, then accept the main lot under inspection. If the number of defects in the first and second samples combined are large, then reject the main lot.

If the number of defects in the first and second samples combined are on the borderline and no decision can be taken, then draw and inspect the third sample. Count the number of defective pieces in all the three samples combined together. If it is small, accept the lot; if it is quite large, reject the lot; and if it is on the borderline and no decision can be taken, then draw and inspect a fourth sample and continue so on.

The multiple sampling plan involves smaller first samples than single or double sampling plans. A multiple sampling plan is comparatively difficult to design and explain, and expensive to implement. It has higher overhead cost, requires more record-keeping and is less effective in improving the quality standard. It unnecessarily gives too much flexibility for accepting the lot and increases the inspection time and cost substantially. The multiple sampling plan is resorted to when the confidence level pertaining to the product and services is extremely low.

9.5.4 Sequential Sampling Plan

The sequential sampling plan is a plan which undertakes the item by item analysis and acceptance of the main lot. It is a plan in which the sample size is increased by one component at a time till the sample size becomes large enough and contains adequate number of defective pieces to decide rationally whether to accept the lot or to reject it.

It is easy to design, but more expensive to execute than a comparable multi-sampling plan since the steps are more complex to take a decision.

Since sample size is increased by one at a time, the sample results are analyzed much faster than a single or double sampling plan. In the sequential sampling plan, the sampling costs are least but the overhead costs are the maximum.

9.6 $\bar{X}$ CHART AND R CHART

9.6.1 $\bar{X}$ Chart

The $\bar{X}$ chart is the most popular and widely used control chart in the industry. It is the most powerful statistical process control tool. In an organization, everyday a number of sample lots are picked up from the process as per the laid down norms. The mean of each such sample lot is calculated. The norm could be one sample lot of ten pieces per shift of working. These individual means are added together, say for a week, and the mean of all the sample lots' mean is taken during the week. This is the mean of all the sample lot means, i.e., the mean line.

This is $\bar{X}$. Now the upper and lower control limits are calculated after ascertaining the mean range $\bar{R}$ and multiplying it by the constant $A2$.

Normally both the $\bar{X}$ and the $\bar{R}$ charts are used together for the statistical process control exercise.

The $\bar{X}$ chart shows the changes in process average and is affected by changes in process variability. It helps in identifying the process variables by establishing a cause and effect relationship. It is a chart for the measure of central tendency. It shows erratic or cyclic shifts in the process like 'run', 'trend', etc. It detects steady progress changes like tool wear.

This is the most commonly used variables chart and used with the R chart.

The $\bar{X}$ chart tells when to leave the process alone and when to rectify the causes leading to variation.

The $\bar{X}$ chart helps in controlling the quality of incoming material, work-in-process and finished goods and it is a very important tool of statistical process control and statistical quality control.

$\bar{X}$ and R charts, when used together, form a powerful instrument for diagnozing quality problems, taking corrective and preventive actions and also for process control.

9.6.2 *R* Chart

Along with the $\bar{X}$ chart, the R chart is the most popular and widely used control chart in the industry. It is one of the most powerful statistical process control tools and shows the dispersion of the process. In an organization, everyday a number of sample lots are picked up from the process as per the laid down norms. Along with the mean, the range of each such sample lot is calculated. The norm could be one sample lot of ten pieces per shift of working. This individual ranges are added together, say, for a week and the mean of all the sample lots' mean is taken as the mean $\bar{R}$ during the week. This is the mean of sample lots, i.e., the mean line of the R chart.

Now the upper and lower control limits are calculated after ascertaining the mean range $\bar{R}$ and multiplying by the constant D_3 and D_4.

Normally, both $\bar{X}$ and the $\bar{R}$ charts are used together for the statistical process control exercise.

The R chart shows the dispersion or the spread of the process and is affected by changes in process variability.

9.6.3 Plotting of *X̄* and *R* Charts

A number of samples are selected and their average values and range are tabulated for plotting the $\bar{X}$ and R charts. Example 9.4 will explain the procedure.

EXAMPLE 9.4. A good number of samples of items coming out of the machine are collected at random at different intervals of times and their quality characteristics (say, diameter or length, etc.) are measured.

For each sample, the mean value and range is found out. For example, if a sample contains 5 items whose diameters are d_1, d_2, d_3, d_4 and d_5 the sample average $\bar{X}$ is given as:

$$X = d_1 + d_2 + d_3 + d_4 + d_5/5$$

and the range is given by:

$$R = \text{Max. diameter} - \text{Min. diameter}$$

Sample No. (Sample size $n = 5$)	$\bar{X}$	R
1	6.5	2
2	7.0	3
3	8.0	3
4	8.5	2
5	8.0	3
	$\Sigma\bar{X} = 38$	$\Sigma R = 13$

$$\bar{\bar{X}} = \Sigma\bar{X}/n$$

$$\bar{R} = \Sigma R/n$$

Therefore,
$$\bar{\bar{X}} = \frac{38}{5} = 7.6$$

$$\bar{R} = \frac{13}{5} = 2.6$$

For $\bar{X}$ Chart:

Upper control limit (UCL) = $\bar{\bar{X}} + A_2\bar{R}$

Lower control limit (LCL) = $\bar{\bar{X}} - A_2\bar{R}$

For R Chart:

Upper control limit (UCL) = $D_4\bar{R}$

Lower control limit (LCL) = $D_3\bar{R}$

The values of various factors (like A_2, D_4 and D_3) based on normal distribution can be found from Table 9.3.

Here the sample size is 5. Therefore,

$$A_2 = 0.58, \ D_3 = 0 \text{ and } D_4 = 2.11$$

TABLE 9.3

Sample size n (No. of items in a sample)	Limit average A_2	Range lower limit D_3	Range upper limit D_4
2	1.88	0	3.27
3	1.02	0	2.57
4	0.73	0	2.28
5	0.58	0	2.11
6	0.48	0	2.00
8	0.37	0.1	1.86
10	0.31	0.2	1.78
12	0.27	0.28	1.72

Thus,
For $\bar{X}$ Chart:

$$\text{UCL} = 7.6 + (0.58 \times 2.6)$$

$$= 7.6 + 1.51 = 9.11$$

$$\text{LCL} = 7.6 - (0.58 \times 2.6)$$

$$= 6.09$$

and
For R Chart:

$$\text{UCL} = 2.11 \times 2.6 = 5.486$$

$$\text{LCL} = D_3 \times R = 0 \times R = 0$$

These control limits are marked on the graph paper on either side of the mean value (line). $\bar{X}$ and $\bar{R}$ values are plotted on the graph and joined together, thus forming the $\bar{X}$ and the R control charts (refer to Figures 9.12 and 9.13).

Both the $\bar{X}$ chart and the R chart shows that the process is under control.

9.7 *P* CHART

It is a fraction defective chart or the percent defective chart. Under this system, each item is classified as good (non-defective) or bad (defective).

We will now explain the procedure of calculating and plotting a P chart with the help of Example .9.5.

EXAMPLE 9.5. A manufacturing factory's inspection results for five consecutive days are given in Table 9.4. The number of pieces inspected every day is 500 and defective pieces found on each of these days are also given. Calculate the fraction defective and the percent defective and draw a P chart.

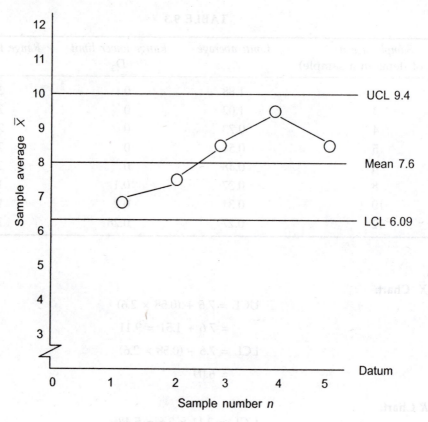

FIGURE 9.12 $\bar{X}$ chart.

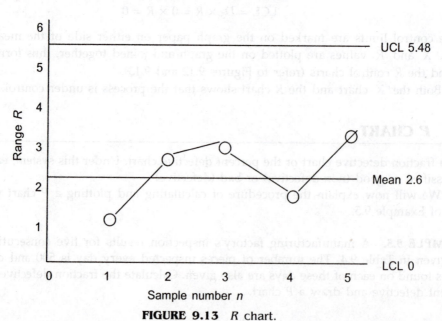

FIGURE 9.13 R chart.

TABLE 9.4

Date	Number of pieces inspected	Number of defective pieces found
July 11	500	10
July 12	500	15
July 13	500	20
July 14	500	12
July 15	500	13
Total number of days = 5	2500	70

The fraction defective and the percent defective have been calculated in Table 9.5.

TABLE 9.5

Date	Number of pieces inspected (a)	Number of defective pieces found (b)	Fraction defective P = (b)/(a)	% defective 100 P
July 11	500	10	0.02	2.0
July 12	500	15	0.03	3.0
July 13	500	20	0.04	4.0
July 14	500	12	0.024	2.4
July 15	500	13	0.026	2.6
Total number of days = 5	2500	70		

$$\text{Upper control limit, UCL} = P + 3\sqrt{\frac{\bar{P}(1 - \bar{P})}{n}}$$

$$\text{Lower control limit, LCL} = \bar{P} - 3\sqrt{\frac{\bar{P}(1 - \bar{P})}{n}}$$

where

$$\bar{P} = \frac{\text{Total number of defective pieces found}}{\text{Total number of pieces inspected}}$$

$$\bar{P} = \frac{70}{2500} = 0.028 \tag{1}$$

and n = Number of pieces inspected everyday = 500

Therefore,
$$\sqrt{\frac{\overline{P}(1-\overline{P})}{n}} = \sqrt{\frac{0.028 \times (1-0.028)}{500}}$$

$$= \sqrt{\frac{0.028 \times 0.9720}{500}}$$

$$= 0.007$$

and
$$3\sqrt{\frac{\overline{P}(1-\overline{P})}{n}} = 0.007 \times 3 = 0.021 \qquad (2)$$

From (1) and (2), we get:

$$\text{UCL} = 0.028 + 0.021 = 0.049$$

and
$$\text{LCL} = 0.028 - 0.021 = 0.007$$

Now let us draw the *P*-chart, as shown in Figure 9.14.

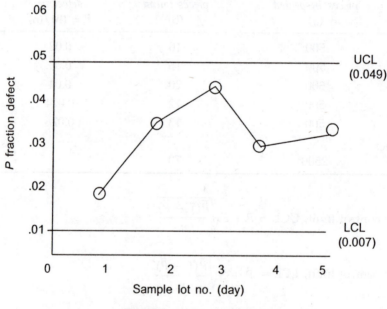

FIGURE 9.14 *P* chart.

The *P* chart is plotted first by calculating the fraction defective and then the control limits. The process is said to be in control if the fraction defective values fall within the control limits. In case the process is out of control, an investigation is to be undertaken to find out the root cause and suitable corrective and preventive actions are to be taken.

9.8 C CHART

It is the control chart in which the number of defects in a piece or a sample lot are ascertained, noted down and then plotted to scale on a graph paper.

The objective is to control the number of defects observed per unit or per sample. Normally, the sample size is taken as constant for the C chart.

The C chart is used where the average number of defects noted are much less than the number of defects which are likely to occur if everything possible that can go wrong actually goes wrong.

While the *P* chart considers the number of defective pieces in a given sample lot size, the C chart takes into account the number of defects in each defective piece or in a given sample. A defective piece may contain more than one defect.

For example, an automobile shaft may be defective on account of:

(a) Diameter of the shaft being oversized.
(b) The shaft may have surface cracks.
(c) The shaft may be oval in shape due to faulty machining.
(d) The run out of the shaft may be outside the tolerance limits.

The C chart is preferred for large and complex parts like automobile crank shaft for a car, LCV or a truck as it has more than 100 simple and relative dimensions.

The C chart is plotted in the same manner as the *P* chart except that the control limits are based on Poisson Distribution which describes more appropriately the distribution of defects. This chart is used to control the overall quality of a component. The objective is to find out if the fluctuations in product quality level are due to chance cause alone or it is men, machine or process related.

It can be used for the variable sample size also, but calculating control limits for each sample is rather cumbersome.

EXAMPLE 9.6.   Ten automobile transmission shafts were inspected in detail. Each of the components was observed to have certain number of defects as given below. Draw a C chart.

Transmission Shaft No.	No. of Defects
1	3
2	6
3	4
4	5
5	4
6	3
7	5
8	4
9	2
10	4
Total sample = 10	Total defects = 40

Solution.

$$\bar{C} = \frac{40}{10} = 4$$

UCL = $\bar{C}$ = $+3\sqrt{C}$

and LCL = $\bar{C}$ = $-3\sqrt{C}$

or   UCL = $4.0 + 3\sqrt{4.0}$ = $4.0 + 3 \times 2 = 10.0$

and LCL = $4 - 6 = -2.0$.

Since number of defects cannot be negative, let us take the LCL at zero.

Value of C, control limits and number of defects per casting are plotted on the graph paper, as shown in Figure 9.15. It is concluded that since all the values of C lie within the control limits, the process is under control.

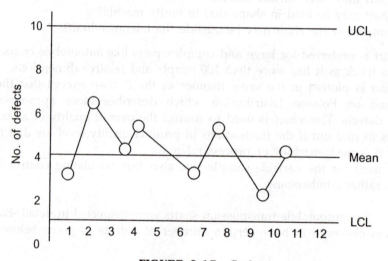

FIGURE 9.15   C chart.

9.9   STATISTICAL PROCESS CONTROL

Statistical Process Control (SPC) is a management technique and a 'reliability engineering tool' to control the reliability of a manufacturing process through regular sampling and statistical analysis.

Statistical process control focuses its attention in measuring the product output from a process on a regular interval and evaluates the process performance from this output. The entire process of statistical process control—right from sensing to the collection of data, analyzing the same and taking suitable corrective actions and putting the process back into its original desirable track—is achieved by the computer aided statistical process control system.

The computer aided gauging automation for the in-process control of the manufacturing system is integrated through the Program Logic Controller (PLC) of

Computer Integrated Manufacturing (CIM), which makes the process error-free and actually achieves an integrated manufacturing and quality control system known as 'autonomation', where it is impossible to produce a defective product. In this computer aided statistical process control system, the attainment of 'zero defect' becomes automatic.

If the output is within the control limits, the computer only keeps track of the data generated, and monitors them and gives simple statistical analysis like what is the population of components checked, how many are ok, How many are on the borderline of dimension, how many are outside the control limit, etc. The computer further analyzes the data and determines the mean, range, standard deviation and the control charts. In case there is some deviation developed in one of the dimensions, the gauging system as well as the computer senses the deviation through the sensor and activates a warning system like an electric hooter or a revolving red light on the top of the machine indicating that the process has started producing the defective parts and it warrants immediate attention. The system simultaneously stops the manufacturing process to prevent it from producing more defective parts. Now the supervisor/machine operator resets or adjusts the machine or corrects the defect by manual corrections and restarts the machines after ensuring that the deviation has been removed. This can be automatically done by the machine itself, provided it is integrated with the quality control system or with the automated gauging system.

The 'sensors' can be a mechanical device like a dial gauge or a pneumatic or air plug for internal diameter measurement or an air caliper or an air ring gauge for external diameter measurement. The sensor can be an electronic probe mounted on a suitably designed fixture for the measurement of the external or the internal diameters. Out of the three, the most accurate are the pneumatic sensors. The output from the sensor can be displayed on a mechanical gauge like a dial gauge, an air gauge unit or an electronic gauging unit. The mechanical and air gauge unit can only display the readings. The electronic display unit can directly read the mechanical and electronic sensors indirectly through a converter converting the pneumatic signal into the electronic signal. In case the electronic unit senses the signal in analogue units of micro current or voltages, the signal needs to be converted through an analogue signal to digital signal (A/D) converter into a digital signal. The electronic display unit displays the reading on a linear scale or in absolute digital unit. At the same time, the data output is connected to a computer to do a complete analysis of the data, its interpretation, and suitable process correction to ensure zero defect output from the system.

9.9.1 Principle of Statistical Process Control

The entire 'computer aided quality system' for 'reliability engineering' or 'statistical process control system' is explained schematically in Figure 9.16.

Figure 9.17 is an actual printout of such computer aided manufacturing system integrated with the quality known as 'autonomation' in the latest modern manufacturing technique developed inline with the 'TPS' or 'The Toyota Manufacturing System' followed by the Japanese industries.

The formulas used to calculate the summary statistics are in-built in the computer program. The system can also draw the control charts.

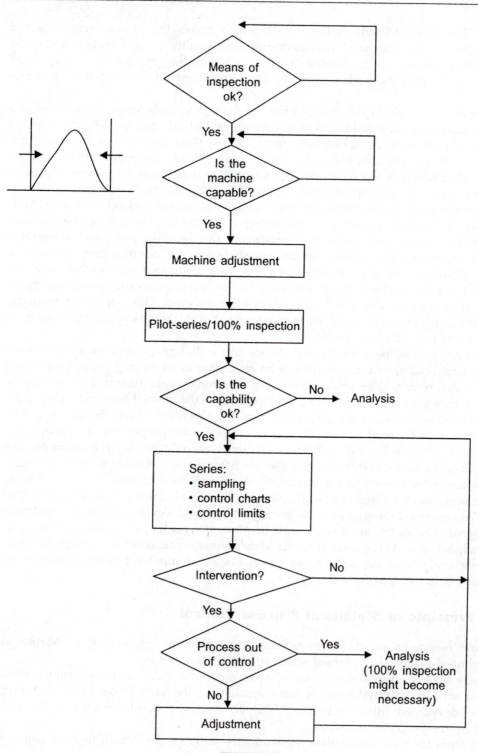

FIGURE 9.16

A1 HISTOGRAM STATISTICS

Histogram Summary Statistics

HISTOGRAM c01	ENT
n	418
min [177]	4.9877
max [333]	5.0111
Ave	4.99987
SD	.00352
−3s	4.98931
+3s	5.01043
CP .95	CPK .94

Rej	Wrj	Acp	Wrk	Rwk	
0%	8%	85%	7%	0	= 7

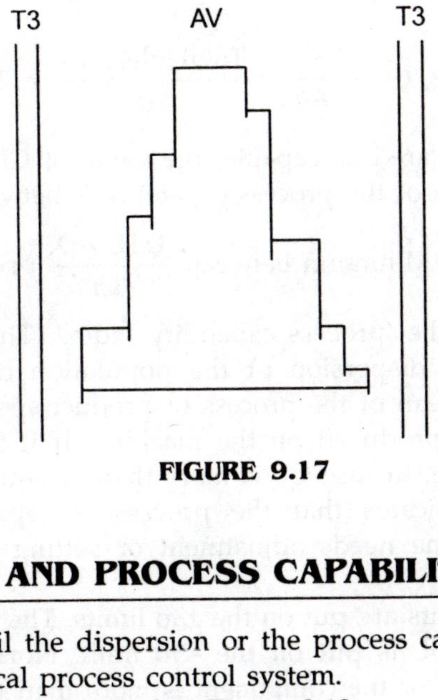

FIGURE 9.17

9.10 DISPERSION AND PROCESS CAPABILITY

Before discussing in detail the dispersion or the process capability, let us define certain basic terms of the statistical process control system.

The dispersion curve is depicted in Figure 9.18.

LTL = Lower Tolerance Limit
UTL = Upper Tolerance Limit
UCL = Upper Control Limit
LCL = Lower Control Limit
T_d = Total Tolerance
$\mu \approx X$ = mean value of the samples
R = Range. (It is the difference between the maximum and the minimum value. It shows the dispersion or the spread.)
σ = Estimated standard deviation.

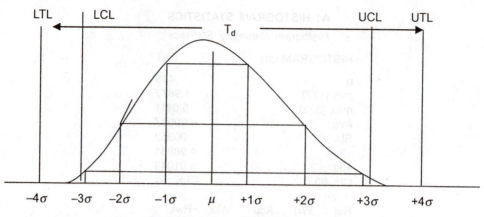

FIGURE 9.18 Dispersion curve.

$$\text{Process Capability Index, CP} = \frac{T_d}{6\sigma} = \frac{\text{Total tolerance}}{6\sigma} \geq 1.0$$

For a process to be declared as capable, the value of CP should be more than or equal to one. The ideal figure of the process capability is between 1.27 to 1.33.

$$\text{Centering index, CPK} = \text{Minimum between } \frac{\text{UTL} - \text{X}}{3\sigma} \text{ or } \frac{\text{X} - \text{LTL}}{3\sigma} \geq 1.0.$$

This is also known as the 'process capability index'. This is the measurement of the central tendency of the dispersion of the population or the components being measured. The central line mean of the process or product specification should coincide with the components being produced on the machine. If it is the same, the value of CP and CPK will be the same. In case CP is more than or equal to one and CPK is less than one, the situation indicates that the process is capable but the process of manufacturing or the machine needs adjustment or setting to put the process back around the mean.

Normally the control limits are put on the ±3σ limits. The upper control limit is put on the +3σ limit and the LCL is put on the −3σ limit. Normally the tolerance limit specified on the product, part or the component is more than this limit. Hence the UTL should be beyond +3σ limit and the LTL should be beyond the −3σ limit for the process to be capable.

As is already explained, the ±3σ limit gives a confidence level of 99.73%, i.e., there is a probability that 27 parts out of 10000 numbers produced will be outside the control limits. The latest trend in software and some other industry is to achieve a performance level of ±6σ, which gives a confidence level of 99.99997%, i.e., the probability of a component or the process going out of control is only 3 parts per million.

The statistical process control normal distribution curves with reference to the various process capability and process capability factor indexes are given in Figure 9.19 for a better understanding and analysis of the statistical process control system.

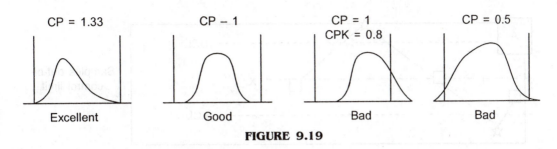

FIGURE 9.19

9.10.1 Abnormal Distributions

Abnormal distributions have been already explained in detail in the beginning of this chapter. More examples are given here with specific figures of skew and kurtosis. Refer to Figure 9.20.

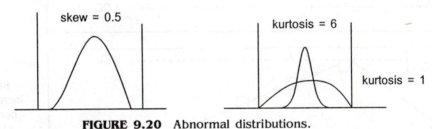

FIGURE 9.20 Abnormal distributions.

Ideal figure for the skewness is 0 ±0.4 and for the kurtosis is = 3 ±1.

The normality test depends in fact on the lot size and should be done whenever standard deviation is used.

We will now discuss some typical cases of analysis of the control charts and the recommended corrective actions to be taken. Some typical control charts and their analysis has been given below. All the probable forms of the control charts from the author's personal experience have been given along with the possible solution for handling the control charts in real-life situations.

9.11 ANALYSIS OF PROCESS OUT OF CONTROL

9.11.1 Actions for Corrective Actions

For any of the deviations and shift from the normal distribution curve, the three steps to be taken are given below. We will also simultaneously discuss the various situations depicted in Figure 9.21.

- **Identify the problem.** The statistical process control charts popularly used are the Mean chart or the $\bar{X}$ chart and the Range chart or the R chart. The chart is the most important and it indicates the process capability of the manufacturing system to meet the product specification requirement. The range chart basically

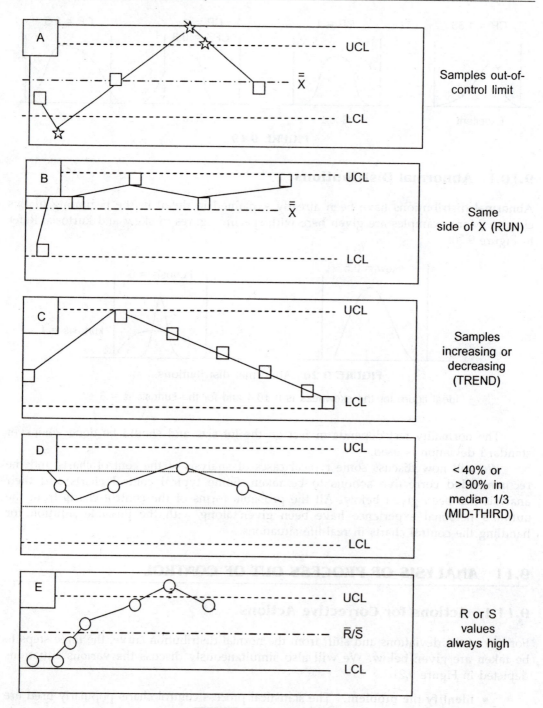

FIGURE 9.21 (Contd.)

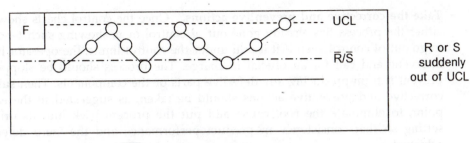

| G | CP or CPK < 1 | | H | Distribution on more normal |

FIGURE 9.21

monitors dispersion of the components produced on the machine and basically concerned with the machine capability and the process adjustments. Even if the control charts are within the limits, its tendency indicates how the process is performing and when it needs to be corrected or adjusted. This constant monitoring of the process control chart and its parameters is a vital aspect of the statistical process control system.

- **Evaluate the cause.** Once the problem has been identified with the components being produced outside the control limits or showing a tendency to go out of control limits shortly, the root cause of such occurrence has to be evaluated and suitable corrective actions must be taken to put the process back on proper track. In Figure 9.21A, the process capability for manufacturing the component is not there. A radical redesign of the component or the process is necessary. The immediate action is to revert back to 100% inspection.

In Figure 9.21B, the process capability for manufacturing the component is there. However it needs the process adjustment or resetting of the machine around the mean or shortly the parts produced may be outside the control limit. This tendency of process being one side of the Mean is known as 'RUN'.

In Figure 9.21C, the process capability and machine capability for manufacturing the component is there. This is a common type of 'trend' chart where the tool gets worn out as it machines the components. The amount by which the tool gets worn out, the component dimension changes slowly in one direction. For the external diameter of the component gradually increases for outer diameter machining as the tool get worn out. The tool needs to be re-sharpened and reset as the corrective action.

Figure 9.21D, shows that the process capability and machine capability for manufacturing the component is much above the laid out standard.

Figure 9.21E, is an advanced case of Figure 9.21B, where the parts produced have gone beyond the control limit. The corrective action is the same as stipulated in the case of Figure 9.21B.

Figure 9.21F, shows that the process suddenly goes out of control. This is due to the sudden tool breakage or machine failure.

The cases of Figure 9.21G and 9.21H show that both the process capability and the machine capability is not there and 100% inspection may be necessary.

- **Take the corrective and preventive actions.** Once the control charts show that either the process has already gone out of control or is showing such tendency to go out of control even if it is still under the control limits, the operator has to intervene and call for an official in charge. The process should be stopped to prevent it from producing any defective parts or the components. Then suitable corrective and preventive actions should be taken, as suggested in the earlier point, to eliminate the root cause and put the process back into its original setting so that consistency in product performance and the 'zero defect' is achieved.

9.12 CAUSES OF PROCESS VARIATION

- **Tool.** The process variation can occur due to the selection of wrong tool, excessive tool wear, lesser tool strength, etc.
- **Machine.** The process variation can occur due to the bearing wear or clearances between the moving parts, thereby producing erratic inconsistent dimensions. It can also happen due to worn-out machine parts.
- **Material.** The process variation can occur due to lack of homogeneity in the material, with sudden spots of dimensional or hardness variation leading to excessive load on the machine as well as cutting tools used for machining. Use of a material different from the specified one will need total change in the processing parameters or the desired results cannot be achieved.
- **Operator.** The process variation can occur due to variation in operators' skill, his training level, eyesight, physical health, habits like drinking, etc. and other human factors. Every processing needs certain amount of operator skill and this is an important process variable.
- **Process.** The process variation can occur due to the method of doing the job or variation in the process itself. A job can be machined in a lathe, shaping, milling or pantograph machines. Depending on the speed, feed, depth of cut and the type of machine used, the process of value addition will be different, which will be typical of a certain process and may not be acceptable under all circumstances.
- **Maintenance.** The process variation can occur due to inadequate or improper maintenance, leading to faulty machine operation. Lack of lubrication, regular checking and tightening of the V-belt tension, routine replacement of bearings will all lead to disturbance of the setting and process performance. This will produce faulty and defective products.
- **Environment.** The process variation can occur due to fluctuation in the environment factors like variation in the power supply leading to lower power output in the machine. This will lead to the overloading of the machine and burning of the electric motors, poor finish of the component, overloading of the tool and machine, leading to their failure. This may also lead to the vibrations in the components. The temperature variation may lead to dimensional deviation if the accuracy is measured in microns.

EXERCISES

1. Explain the probability theory and the fundamental logic behind the statistical measurement.

2. Explain the concepts of Normal Distribution Curve, Mean, Range, Standard Deviation and Variance. Give the relevant formulae.

3. Explain in detail all the statistical sampling techniques, i.e., single sampling, double sampling, multiple sampling and sequential sampling.

4. Explain the concept of control charts and explain in detail the P chart, C chart, X chart and R chart.

5. Define 'Statistical Process Control'. Explain the principle of working of the statistical process control system. Explain the concepts of process capability and the process capability factor.

6. Elaborate on the methodology of analyzing the SPC charts, i.e., the process of reliability analysis of the process or the process output and undertaking of the corrective and preventive actions.

7. Explain the computer aided quality management system and elucidate how it ensures 'zero defect' in the output products.

8. 25 components were manufactured on a machine and their diameters (in mm) as measured are given below:

   10.2, 10.3, 10.2, 10.3, 10.4, 10.2, 10.3, 10.2, 10.3, 10.4, 10.2, 10.5, 10.1, 10.3, 10.5, 10.2, 10.4, 10.3, 10.1, 10.3, 10.2, 10.5, 10.3, 10.4, 10.1

   Draw the frequency distribution table, the frequency distribution curve, bar chart and histogram.

9. The dimension for shafts being machined on a lathe machine are as follows: 6.2, 6.3, 6.3, 6.5, 6.5, 6.4, 6.0, 6.2, 6.3, 6.3, 6.4, 6.1, 6.0, 6.3, 6.2. Calculate the mean, range and the standard deviation.

10. A number of samples are selected and their average values and range are tabulated in the table below:

Sample lot No.	Mean (X)	Range (R)
A	8.0	2.5
B	8.5	2.0
C	8.0	3.0
D	9.0	2.5
E	10.0	3.5
F	7.0	2.0
G	8.0	3.0
H	8.5	3.0
I	9.0	2.5
J	8.0	3.0

Calculate the mean, range and standard deviation. Draw the $\overline{X}$ chart and the R chart. If the tolerance limit specified for the mean dimension is given as ± 2.0, calculate the process capability figure CP and the process capability factor CPK.

11. A manufacturing factory's inspection results for six consecutive days are given in the table below. The number of pieces inspected every day is 700 and the number of defective pieces found on each of these days are also given in the chart. Calculate the fraction defective and the percent defective and draw a P chart.

Date	Number of pieces inspected	Number of defective pieces found
June 5	700	12
June 6	700	15
June 7	700	18
June 8	700	20
June 9	700	16
June 10	700	13

Chapter 10

Six Sigma

CHAPTER OBJECTIVES

In this chapter, we will discuss the following:

- The concept of Six Sigma and its features
- The Six Sigma enablers and the goals of Six Sigma
- The Six Sigma problem solving approach
- DMAIC and the DMADV approach of Six Sigma

Six Sigma is a statistical control limit giving to the process of execution of a job or assignment, in part or in whole, a confidence level of 99.9997%. This means that the chance for the process or the product failure is only 3.4 part per million. The concept of statistical process control to the level of performance of $\pm 3\sigma$ (i.e., totaling Six Sigma) was practiced by industry for a long time for ascertaining the 'process capability'. CP and CPK, i.e., the process capability and the process capability factors were the important paradigms of process control. The control limits are fixed on $\pm 3\sigma$ and the tolerance limits have to be beyond that for the process to be capable. The computer aided quality management mechanism ensured to stop the process the moment it crossed the control limits. The products which are on the borderline or just crossed the control limit are still under the tolerance limit as the tolerance limit is fixed always beyond the control limit for the process to be capable. It ensured 'zero defect'. The Six Sigma is nothing but an extension of the control limits from the $\pm 3\sigma$ limit to the $\pm 6\sigma$ limit. The chance of a part going outside the control limit of $\pm 3\sigma$ is 27 parts in 10000 and that of $\pm 6\sigma$ is 3.4 parts per million. This means that the probability of the parts produced going outside the control limit is much higher in the $\pm 3\sigma$ limit system than in the $\pm 6\sigma$ limit system. This will lead need more process correction and may need stoppage of the machine in $\pm 3\sigma$ system than in $\pm 6\sigma$. However, whether you work under $\pm 3\sigma$ or $\pm 6\sigma$, the end result will not differ. It will be the same as your computer aided quality management mechanism will stop the process the moment it crosses the control limits.

However, in the manufacturing industry, the implementation of $\pm 6\sigma$ control limits will make the processing cost shoot up in terms of more accurate costlier machine tool, costlier cutting tool, etc. It may go up exponentially, thereby needing a cost-benefit analysis to justify such revision vis-à-vis the benefit realization. Hence the practical feasibility of implementing $\pm 6\sigma$ level of performance in manufacturing industry is still debatable. However, in the software industry, the shift in control limits from the $\pm 3\sigma$ limit to the $\pm 6\sigma$ limit basically needs a change in mindset more than any investment. Additionally, a software has to be foolproof and error-free. The hardware for control mechanism is missing like in manufacturing industry. The computerized system has to handle huge amount of data and the essence of its performance is 'zero defect'. A miniscule error even to the extent of $\pm 6\sigma$ will also lead to production of large number of errors. Hence the software industry is talking about six sigma performance level because that is probably the best that they can achieve today. But according to me, this is also not enough. It has to beyond this and attainment of 'zero defect' here is mandatory.

The 'Black Belt' and 'Green Belt', etc. are nomenclatures given to the people who have completed certain project involving the principle of the 'Six Sigma'. Black Belt is given to a more experienced person who has successfully completed two or more projects involving the Six Sigma principle and has mentored at least two Green Belt projects to successful completion. Till date there is no official international or local body which recognizes these nomenclatures officially. The norms that are followed today are set by either Mikel Harry of the Motorola Corporation or Jack Welch of 'General Electric (GE)'.

Jack Welch of GE, Azim Premji of Wipro, and Bob Galvin, and Mikel Harry of Motorola are some of the well-known names who strongly back up the Six Sigma concepts for implementation. They provided total commitment to ensure continued success of the Six Sigma. The Six Sigma was originally started at Motorola in 1979. The Six Sigma results at Motorola from 1987 to 1997 were reflected in five-fold growth in sales, with profits climbing 20% per year. Cumulative gains from the six sigma efforts were estimated at USD 14 billion. Motorola stock prices gained compounded to an annual rate of 21.3%.

Mikel Harry left Motorola in 1993 to join ABB. The Six Sigma effectiveness was proved in ABB by 68% reduction in defects and 30% in product costs.

Mikel Harry and Richard Schroeder started the Six Sigma Academy in 1994. Jack Welch, the CEO of General Electric popularized the Six Sigma drives across the globe by implementing it strongly in all its divisions as well as its vendors. Today, TCS, Wipro, Infosys, and Patni Computer Systems, all practice Six Sigma due to their tie-up with GE. Apart from these organizations, the other Indian organizations that have implemented Six Sigma are Tata Motors Ltd., Reliance Industries Ltd., Asian Brown Boveri Ltd., TVS Motors Ltd., ICICI Prudential, Larsen & Toubro Ltd., Tata Steel, Johnson & Johnson Ltd., Asian Paints Ltd. etc.

'Six Sigma' can be defined as 'a statistical measuring system to gauge and attain perfection of the product, process and services'.

There are many incidents where you cannot afford to fail even 3.4 parts in a million or at the Six Sigma performance level also. These are instance like landing system of aircrafts, your own heart beat, loss of important documents, failure in a surgery, testing of a nuclear plant and management of dangerous affluent.

However, under such circumstance the organization has to attempt to do the best that is possible and attempt to achieve at least a performance level of Six Sigma. However, the Six Sigma philosophy always attempts for an error-free performance.

Six Sigma follows the same main organizational objective as described earlier in the book as that of the maximization of customer satisfaction and maximization of the return on the investment. It incidentally has the same two business objectives. Six Sigma or Total Quality Management should be taken as a philosophy by the organization to transform the organization and change the people's mindset. Six Sigma as a strategy ensures rapid growth of the organization and it is also a tool to reduce costs, increase productivity, rejection, rework, etc.

10.1 FEATURES OF SIX SIGMA

Six Sigma has the following important features:

1. Six Sigma shifts the paradigm quality as the cause of good business performance and not the effect. Earlier all process and product improvement techniques were aimed at continuous improvement of quality. Six Sigma propagates that all-round quality performance (error-free performance excellence with continuous improvement) is bound to result in the attainment of the desired business excellence in terms of reduction in cost of production, maximization of customer satisfaction and return on investment.
2. The philosophy of Six Sigma is to make fewer mistakes in all the organizational activities and keep on reducing the mistakes.
3. The Six Sigma is a business strategy to reduce the cost by attaining good quality.
4. It is a statistical process control technique aimed at achieving total confidence in the company's products and service performances for the customers as well the management.
5. It is a philosophy of achieving the ultimate goal of 'Do it right the first time every time'.
6. It is a performance measure. The sigma and part per million (ppm) are correlated as indicated here.

Sigma	Defects per million
2	308537
3	66807
4	6210
5	233
6	3.4

Historically, the $\pm 3\sigma$ indicated a performance level of 99.73%. However, the Six Sigma has redefined the performance level at $\pm 3\sigma$ at 93.32%, $\pm 4\sigma$ performance level at 99.38% and $\pm 6\sigma$ performance level at 99.99966%.

This implies that as compared to the 3σ performance level, the $\pm 4\sigma$ is ten times improvement in performance and as compared to 4σ performance level, the 6σ is 1800 times improvement in performance.

7. Sigma in statistics is used to indicate the standard deviation. A sigma value indicates the ability of a process to perform defect-free work. The higher the sigma value, the better the process is performing and the lower the probability that a defect will occur.

8. Six Sigma reduces the defect and variations in the product be improving the process that produces and delivers the product.

9. The Six Sigma is not delegable. The involvement of the top management is a must.

10. The Six Sigma principles and philosophy are equally applicable to the manufacturing and the service industry.

11. The Six Sigma is not new. It makes use of the same problem-solving tools in a structured manner.

12. The Six Sigma's main objectives are reduction of variation, defects, costs and cycle time, aimed towards maximization of customer satisfaction.

13. The focus of Six Sigma is on the following areas:

   a. Independent variable to the process.
   b. Root cause of any problem and its elimination/prevention.
   c. Focus is on the inputs to the process and not on the output.
   d. Focus is on the problem and not on the symptom.
   e. Focus is in controlling the problem or the deviation and not on monitoring.

14. For a software or the information technology industry, CMM levels are important whereas for the manufacturing and other service industries, the ISO 9001:2000 certification is important. The ISO, CMM and Six Sigma have to be integrated in the system as the situation may be. The ISO 9001:2000 brings in a 'Quality Management System' with process-orientation and continual improvement of the process, product and system by taking corrective and preventive actions. CMM focuses on process improvement and Six Sigma looks for the tools and techniques for improvement to reach perfection. Six Sigma is a rigorous analytical process for problem-solving.

10.2 SIX SIGMA ENABLERS

Leadership commitment

The top management and senior leadership must give their total commitment in making the Six Sigma activity successful. Both Jack Welch and Bob Galvin provided total commitment to make Six Sigma successful in GE.

Change in culture

Six Sigma is directed towards specific, tangible, time-bound business objectives. The culture changed because of a shift in outlook towards delivering the above tangible results.

Change in mindset

The Six Sigma warrants an altogether change in the mindset of both the management and the people working in the organization. They have to convert themselves to a highly proactive, self-renovated, focused group on the end objective with the process of continual improvement through defect elimination.

Challenging standards

The Six Sigma approach sets aside the 'business as usual' attitude and sets challenging standards which are difficult but feasible and focused. The achievement of these new challenging standards can only catapult the organization to a new height of performance.

Customer focus

The Six Sigma process is aimed towards completely satisfying the customers' needs profitably. Six Sigma views processes and process measures completely from the customer's point of view. It is a statistical measure of a process's ability to meet the customer's requirements (CTQs).

Continual improvement

Six Sigma integrates the processes and daily work and executes in a manner that there is continual improvements in whatsoever is being done to attain the end objective of customer satisfaction.

10.3 GOALS OF SIX SIGMA

The principal six goals of Six Sigma are detailed below. However, depending on an organization and its circumstances, the gains can be in many other areas as well.

1. **To reduce variations.** The main objective of the Six Sigma practice is to ensure consistency in performance so that the users and customers can develop confidence in the quality and reliability in the products and services offered by the organization. The Six Sigma practice is oriented towards developing a manufacturing and/or service set-up which has zero variation in both the product and the process. The variations or the deviations are minimized in the Six Sigma practice.
2. **To reduce defects/rework.** The principal objective of the Six Sigma practice is to eliminate or reduce the defects and rejects to practically zero. Six Sigma is a process control technique. By ensuring that the process is under control, the product can never be defective. The Japanese mantra of 'Muda' ensures elimination of all wastages. Any rejection or rework saved gets straightway added to the bottom line in terms of the profit of the organization.
3. **To improve yield/productivity.** A single rejection saved is an additional piece produced. Any time saved in reworking is time utilized for effective production of the products and services, which again adds to the productivity. One of the main objective of the Six Sigma practice is to improve the yield or the

productivity by optimum utilization of the men, machine and material along with the elimination of the seven wastages. Higher productivity leads to more production, lower cost of production and better quality and competitiveness in the marketplace.

4. **To enhance customer satisfaction.** The concept of customer satisfaction will be dealt in detail later on in the same chapter. Customer satisfaction is achieved by providing the products and service of right quality, in right quantity at the right time, right place and right cost, fulfilling the customers' stated and implied needs. One of the main objectives of the Six Sigma practice is to achieve the highest level of customer' satisfaction, which is the prime objective of an organization, for sustenance and survival of the organization. By providing defect-free products and services of consistent performance and quality, the Six Sigma practice definitely enhances the customer satisfaction.

5. **To improve the bottom line.** The most important other objective of the Six Sigma practice is to improve the profitability and return on investment by reduction in the cost of production and processing by continuous process improvement. The other way to improve the profitability and return on investment is by reduction and elimination of wastages, rework and excess consumption of material, men or machine hours. The Six Sigma activity improves substantially the bottom line, without any investment, just by training and changing the employees' mindset and garnering their greater involvement in their work and the organization.

6. **To improve the top line.** The other immediate objective of the Six Sigma practice is improvement of the organizational reputation in the market and society at large by providing products and service of good quality without any deviation in terms of performance or user-friendliness and reliability. This creates a strong brand image in the market, leading to an increase in the sales and attainment of the market leadership position. The Six Sigma practice also leads to the development of better work culture, better relationships with customers and employees and improves the top line substantially.

10.4   ORGANIZATION FOR SIX SIGMA

The organization for Six Sigma should ensure the involvement and participation of all the employees as well as the top management. The Six Sigma process can only be successful with a focus on the end objective and a systematic structure for problem-solving and continuous process improvement. The detailed structure is given in Figure 10.1.

The Quality Council or the Apex Council is the apex body formed by the Heads of the functions with its chairman as the Chief Executive Officer or the Managing Director. This Apex Council controls and periodically reviews the entire Six Sigma activity, including project identification, performance of the project teams and the effectiveness of the solutions and their implementation.

The sponsor sponsors the project, reviews and monitors its progress on a day-to-day basis and ensures the implementation of the improvement suggestions.

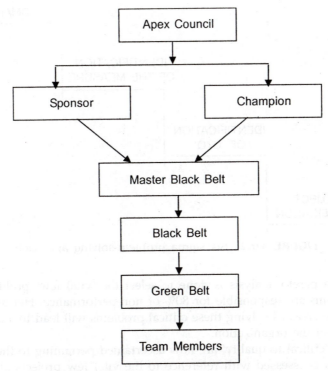

FIGURE 10.1 Six Sigma Organization.

The champion provides the 'vision' and 'business decisions'. He provides the leadership for the Six Sigma activities, projects and reviews their progress. He is not a part of any specific project. He is available for the expert help, as needed.

The 'Master Black Belt' has completed the Black Belt certification and has mentored at least 15 or so projects to completion. The parameter may vary from organization to organization. The Master Black Belt leads the initiative, trains and coaches the team and mentors the project. He also monitors and reviews the progress and takes suitable actions accordingly.

The 'Black Belts' should have completed the Black Belt certification and mentored four projects to successful completion. The 'Green Belt' should have completed the Green Belt certification and completed one process improvement project successfully. The 'Team Member' is a fresher initiated to the Six Sigma project after initial training only. The team as stated above undertakes the process improvements and implements them successfully. They run specific time-bound projects with defined objectives. The Black Belts provide the leadership to the team. The team together mobilizes the commitment for change and prepares and implements the action plan for process improvements.

10.5 SIX SIGMA PROBLEM-SOLVING APPROACH

The Six Sigma problem-solving approach is depicted in Figure 10.2. It starts with project identification. All the problems which are detrimental for the organization's prosperity

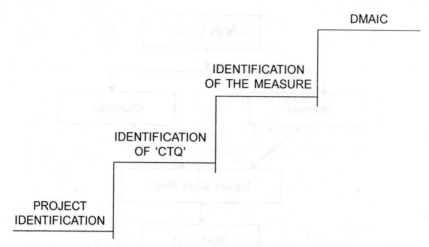

FIGURE 10.2   Six sigma problem-solving approach.

are listed. Now a pareto analysis is done to select the 'vital few' problems. These vital few (20%) problems are responsible for 80% of non-performance. Hence the projects are identified in these areas as solving these critical problems will lead to a quantum jump in the performance of the organization.

The factors 'critical to quality' are now ascertained pertaining to the quality and are listed down. This is assessed with reference to the vital few projects already identified. These factors are taken up for suitable corrective and preventive actions to eliminate them.

The next step is to identify and put into the practice the unit of performance measurement. Benchmark against the best technically sound organization and the relevant problem or process or the product that the organization has to ultimately outperform to stay in business.

The final stage of the problem solving involving the Six Sigma approach is either 'DMAIC' or the 'DMADV', which will be discussed in the following section.

10.6 'DMAIC' OR 'DMADV'

The Six Sigma follows either 'DMAIC' or the 'DMADV' approach step by step.

The steps in the **DMAIC** approach are as follows:

- **DEFINE:** Determine the project to be undertaken, its objective, scope, etc.
- **MEASURE:** Determine the 'Voice of the Customer (VOC)'. Convert it into 'Critical To Quality (CTQ)', obtain data to quantify, determine process performances.
- **ANALYZE:** Analyze data to find out root causes of defects.
- **IMPROVE:** Intervene in the process to improve performance.
- **CONTROL:** Implement a control system to maintain performance over a period of time.

The DMADV approach is described step by step as follows:

- **DEFINE:** Determine the project to be undertaken, its objective, scope, etc.
- **MEASURE:** Determine the 'Voice of the Customer (VOC)'. Convert it into 'Critical To Quality (CTQ)', obtain data to quantify, determine process performances.
- **ANALYZE:** Analyze data to develop design concepts and produce a high level design.
- **DESIGN:** Develop detail design, validate and implement the new design, integrate with the existing system.
- **VERIFY:** Check the completed design and ensure its transition to the customer.

We will now explain in detail the various steps of DMAIC.

Define

The success of the Six Sigma project depends substantially on the correct and proper definition of the project. The general statistics is that over 50% of the projects fail or get delayed due to inadequate 'scope' definition. Proper project definition facilitates the project execution and sets the common goals for the team and the chairperson. The definition should create customer-orientation and integrate the customer view and the supplier's process.

In the Six Sigma project, the 'customer' is defined as both the internal or external agencies impacted by the output of the product or the services produced by the project in question. 'Quality' is defined as the fitness for use as per the performance standard expected by the customer.

The requirements of the output of the process are called the 'Critical To Quality' (CTQ). The 'CTQ' can be derived from the customers' requirements, government regulations, economics and scale of operation and the business risks. However, the critical factor of the 'CTQ' are the customers' prospective requirements in quantified terms in a given time span.

The definition should capture the 'Voice Of Customer' (VOC)—internal as well as external—and convert it into a process. For this, the team selects the customers and collect information about their expectations and requirements. The process of converting the VOC to CTQ consists of collecting VOC, identifying real customer needs, identifying CTQ elements and validating with the customers. The CTQ should be measurable and quantified and segregated in terms of the process-related or the product-related. Also, they have to be identified in terms of what is critical to the business and what is critical to the customer. The CTQs should be defined in terms of both their efficiency and effectiveness.

The 'Quality Function Deployment' (QFD) is another method to convert the 'VOC' into the CTQ. The QFD has already been explained in detail in Chapter 3.

The Six Sigma project ideas come from the following areas:

- Brainstorming
- Process mapping
- Customers' complaints

- Customers' suggestions
- Bottleneck areas
- Under performance below the decided level in product, process or system
- Quality function deployment
- Statistical process control parameters and control charts
- Competitors' performance matrices
- Benchmarking data and gap analysis

The definition phase needs to define the following clearly without any ambiguity:

- **Project goal statement.** It may be in terms of targeted improvements, area impacted, directions, deadlines, progress measures, etc.
- **Project scope.** The project scope is to be defined in terms of the focus areas in terms of customers, markets, products, locations and processes.
- **Project schedule.**
- **Roles, responsibilities.**
- **Resource requirements.**
- **Problem statement.** It must be in terms of what, where, when and extent of deviation from the standard and its impact.
- **Likely business impact of the project.** It has to be estimated in terms of benefits.
- **Project description.** This needs to be in terms of the process charts, control points, etc.
- **Alignment with the organizational business objective.**
- **Process mapping of the project.**

Measure

After defining a problem, the team has to measure in quantitative terms 'how much' is the problem and what is the opportunity for the improvement. The measurement system should determine what to measure and validate the measurement system. The current performance has to be quantified and the improvement target needs to be estimated. The project objectives are to be enumerated quantitatively. It must be ensured that the current situation is understood by the process owners from different perspectives.

'Y' is the dependent variable, i.e., the output. 'X' is the independent variable, i.e., the input in terms of material, men, machine, method and environment. The aim to get the control of 'X' or the input variables to the level of Six Sigma so as to get the 'Y' right in terms of the product or the services that affect customer satisfaction. Determine what to measure in 'Y', establish the units of measurement and the process of measurement. After completion of all these activities, validate the measurement system.

The measurement deploys statistical process control techniques and sampling as described in detail in Chapter 9. Measure the mean, range, standard deviation, dispersion, central tendency, control charts, control limits, dispersion and ultimately the reliability and the confidence level of the process to produce the right product and services. Also measure the process capability measure of CP and the process capability factor CPK.

The measurement should be accurate, repeatable, reproducible and stable. The total observed variation always has a component of measurement error. The job is to ensure minimal variation due to measurement process. An understanding has to be developed as to how the measurement error impacts the customer.

All the processes, products and services cannot be exactly the same. The difference for the same parameter can be called as 'variation'. The variation is inherent in all activities producing an output which is repetitive in nature. However, this variation beyond the acceptable limit induces inconsistency in the product and service performance, leading to customer dissatisfaction.

The random causes of variation are inherent, predictable and have small impact on the product and services or the 'Y'. They are also known as the 'common causes' of variation. These variations cannot be controlled and should be left as it is. The 'assignable causes' of variation are special causes of variation. These causes of variation are sudden, not always present, unexpected, unpredictable and have substantial impact on the 'Y'. The main sources of variation in the process are from the independent variable 'X', i.e., the machines, materials, methods, men, measurements and the mother nature. According to me these are the 'SIX 'M' OF VARIATION'.

The assignable causes of variation have to be identified in terms of their current contribution to the cause of the variations or inconsistency in performance as well as the current trend of shift of the process which is likely to go outside the expectable limits of performance in the near future. Both situations needs to be corrected and prevented at the earliest. For this the seven tools of total quality control described in Chapter 2 along with the 'Quality Circle' have to be employed. The common tools are the histogram, run charts and the control charts to identify and ascertain the causes of variation.

The 'process capability' is the most important tool to ascertain the assignable causes of variation. The process capability graphs are drawn with continuous data. The central tendency of mean, mode and median as well as the dispersion in terms of range, standard deviation, variation (the 'Z' value) and span are determined. The process capability CP and the process capability factor CPK are determined. A process following the normal distribution curve has only the common causes of variation. Tools like histogram and run charts can be used to understand the process visually. The standard deviations and variance or the Z-value helps us to compare processes with varying complexities.

The process capability figures clearly indicate the flaws and opportunities of the process under study. The rolled throughput yield illustrates the complexity of a multi-process system affecting quality. The rational sub-grouping helps to separate out the common and special causes in the process. The sum of squares indicates the different types of variations.

A subgroup that contains only the common causes of variation indicates the short-term capability of the process. The long-term process capability represents the state of subgroups of the process having both the common causes and assignable causes of variations. The main objective of Six Sigma is to increase the process capability.

Analyze

The input to the process of 'analysis' is the data collected during the measure phase. The problems must be identified. Graphical analysis of data determines both the stability of the process and the process variation. Process capability is already established. Now the potential root causes need to be found and validated using the data collected in the measure phase. Avoid decisions based on intuition and preconceived notions. Derive specification limit for the vital process input 'X'. Revise the project scope, if necessary, and determine the potential benefit of the project.

The main function of the 'analyze' phase is to use the clues from the data to establish the hypothesis. The organization should determine the key drivers for the process variations. This phase makes use of suitable simple or the advance statistical tools to test the hypothesis. The organization shifts the focus from the 'Y' to 'X' during the analysis phase where 'Y' is the output measure or the symptom and 'X' is the process variable or the root cause. The variations in the output depend on the process as well as the process input variables. The organization should identify the 'vital few' of such process variable mainly responsible for the deviation of the output or the root cause to the problem.

The organization should use the 'data door' to identify the potential causes.

Segmentation is a process used to divide a large group into smaller, logical categories for the analysis. The organization collects the 'Y' data with the possible segment information. This segment information for data analysis identifies the possible causes. The organization should use appropriate display tool for the information analysis. The organization uses the histogram, run chart, etc. as a tool for the segmentation analysis. The segment which is generating the maximum number of deviations needs to be stratified and corrective actions taken.

Along with the data door, the organization uses the process door of lean manufacturing or the lean process as an effective analytical tool. A lean process uses only the absolute minimum of resources to add value to the output. In a lean process, every person is involved in the value addition process and the lead time is minimal. The lean concepts are useful in identifying the non value added activities. They also help in locating the wastes inherent in the business process. The lean concepts show that most of the process activities do not add value top to the end product or the services. The various concepts of the lean manufacturing system have already been explained in the previous chapters. However, the concepts of the lean manufacturing system are as follows:

- Customer pulled demand management system of manufacturing eliminating the excess inventory and reducing the chances of product obsolescence.
- Continuous flow type of manufacturing as explained in the Just-In-Time (JIT) manufacturing and purchasing system.
- Quick change-over and elimination of set-up time as explained in the Computer Integrated Manufacturing (CIM) system and Single Minute Exchange of Dies (SMED).
- Takt time is the minimum time between the units of production output integrated to the customer demand. The takt time calculations establish the drumbeat of a process and links it to the customer and aims at reducing the variations in the drumbeats.
- The visual management employing the principle of good housekeeping of '5S' as explained in Section 6.

- Establishment of a three-tier organization structure focused on the attainment of the organization's vision and mission.
- Deployment of '3M' practices of the Muri, Mura and Muda as explained in Section 2.12.

The process analysis is carried out in detail to ascertain the root cause of the problem as well as to eliminate the wastages and improve the process performance or 'X' elements to result in the improvement of the product and service performances or the 'Y' element. For this purpose, the process analysis and the sub-process mapping is necessary. The sub-process mapping consists of the following steps. The organization first forms a team who is fully aware of the current status of the process and its working. The organization should define the boundaries of the process by using the high level process map from the 'define' phase. The organization should now write down the list of all the activities that are to be carried out to complete the process in a sequential manner. Sequence the steps and draw a flow process chart. Maintain focus on the current process. Now verify that the flow is complete.

Process mapping is normally done by the process flow chart. This can be supplemented by the deployment or the responsibility chart or a top down flow chart. During the process map analysis, three factors are to be taken into consideration and suitable steps taken to make the process more efficient and effective. These factors are the moments of truth, value addition and the flow of the work itself. Let us understand these points in brief.

Moments of truth. Every process delivers certain products and services for the customers. The process invariably culminates into a point of interaction between the supplier and the customer. During these touch points, positive or negative impressions can be formed. These are the moments of truth. The feedback to the organization regarding these moments of truth is extremely important.

Value addition. This important topic has been discussed in detail in Chapter 3. The product or the service features, i.e., component 'Y', that add value to the customer have to be separated from the parts of the product and services which do not add any value. The parts, components of the product and services which do not add any value have to be eliminated from the system, thereby saving the cost of conversion as well as saving the time. The criteria for the value addition are the retaining and improving of the parts and processes that add value to the product and services and for which the customer is ready to pay. These processes transform or change the product and service features which add value and do it right the first time. The value addition process can be retaining the same value but reducing the cost by either elimination of non value adding parts or activities or retaining the cost but enhancing the value by modification, alteration or combination of such parts and processes, increasing the value of the end product from the customer's point of view.

The types of non value added work are the internal failures inside the factory and the related corrective steps, external failure at the customer's end having a tremendous damaging effect on the market reputation of the organization and high cost of correction, control or inspection, delays due to set-up time, changeovers or waiting for the mating part and the non value adding movements of the men or material.

Flow of work. The flow of work is depicted in the most effective and efficient manner in the 'flow process chart'. The flow process charts are drawn using five symbols of operation, inspection, delay, storage and transport. It is easily understood that out of these five activities, only 'operation' is adding value to the product or the process. The balances four are the non value adding activities. The flow of work involves calculating the amount of time that each sub-process step takes. The cycle time is normally the sum of the value added or non value added time. The objective of drawing the flow process chart is to identify all these non value added time and activities, i.e., activities of inspection, delay, transport or movement of men or material and storage of material or products. Once these non value added activities are identified, they are eliminated from the system or their effect nullified by an activity known as 'SCAMPER', which is explained below.

- **SUBSTITUTE:** Input raw material, components and men which are not adding value.
- **COMBINE:** Mix, integrate or combine with other value adding assemblies or services.
- **ADAPT:** Alter, change or use part of another element which is adding value.
- **MODIFY:** Modify process or product attribute, change shape or form, increase or reduce in scale to arrive at attributes which are adding value.
- **PUT:** Put to another use at another place where it is adding value.
- **ELIMINATE:** This is the most desirable action and the first option. Eliminate parts, components and processes that do not add value to the end product and services.
- **REVERSE:** Reverse or turn upside down or inside out and find out how it can add value.

We have used the 'data door' and the 'process door' to identify the possible causes affecting the product or the service performance output 'Y'. Now we have to prioritize the potential causes by using the pareto principle and identify their root cause for the deviation in performance. The root cause identification is done by the brainstorming (Chapter 3) and cause and effect or the Ishikawa diagram (Chapter 2).

Identify the possible causes. There can be only six sources of variation known as 'Six 'M''. They are the men, machine, material, method, measurement and the mother nature. The cause and effect diagram singles out the variation sources. It is a graphical tool to identify and organize all the possible causes that affect the outcome, as shown in Figure 10.3.

The next step of the 'analyze' phase is 'Hypothesis testing'. In order to improve the process, it is necessary to identify the factors that have a significant impact on the central tendency and dispersion of the output metric. Simultaneously, objectivity of the decision is important. Hypothesis testing starts with an assumption likely to be the most significant factor known as the 'null hypothesis'. The other possibilities are the alternative hypothesis. This assumption or the null hypothesis may be then mathematically proved to be true or false. Consequently, we either reject or accept the hypothesis. The hypothesis which meets all the 'musts' associated with the products and the services (Y) and maximum umber of 'wants' with the least consumption of the resources in terms of men, machine and materials is the ideal decision or the best way to

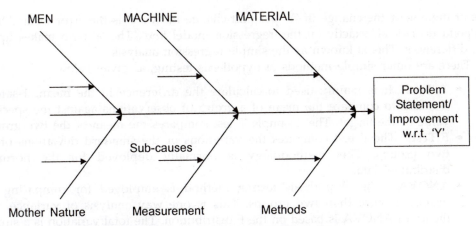

MEN   MACHINE   MATERIAL

Problem
Statement/
Improvement
w.r.t. 'Y'

Sub-causes

Mother Nature   Measurement   Methods

FIGURE 10.3 Cause and Effect diagram.

do the job. The ideal solution gives a perfect correlation between the independent (X) and the dependent (Y) variable.

A regression analysis and the establishment of the correlation proves the hypothesis. Coefficient of correlation 'r' value gives the nature of the relationship regression coefficient (R^2) which defines the strength of relationship. A line of the best fit can be plotted for the scatter diagram, as shown in Figure 10.4. The equation for this line is:

$$Y = mX + C + e$$

This equation can be used to predict the value for the 'Y' for a given value of 'X' where 'C' is the intercept or the predicted value of 'Y' when the 'X' is zero. 'm' is the

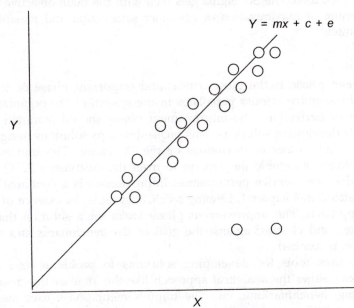

$Y = mx + c + e$

Y

X

FIGURE 10.4 Scatter diagram.

slope of the line or the change in 'Y' per unit change in 'X'. 'e' is the error term. All the data point do not fall exactly on the 'regression model line'. The 'e' term makes up for these differences. This is known as the simple regression analysis.

There are other simple methods of hypothesis testing, as given below.

- **T Test.** It is mainly used to calculate the difference in the mean. 1-sample T test is to compare the mean of a group of observations against the specified value or the target. The 2-sample T test compares the mean of the two groups.
- **F Test.** The F test compares the variations or the standard deviations of the two groups. This methodology is normally deployed for the normally distributed data.
- **ANOVA.** This hypothesis testing method is employed for comparing the means of more than two groups. This is one way analysis of variance. The theory of ANOVA is based on the F distribution. The total variation is a sum of the variations within plus the variations within the subgroups.
- **Chi-square Test.** This methodology is employed for comparing the frequencies or the proportions of multiple groups. The chi-square test is used to identify the difference in proportions. This test verifies the frequency of the actual occurrence against the frequency of the expected occurrences to help decide whether significant change has occurred.

In the 'DMAIC' model, the 'analyze' phase is the most important phase upon which the entire success of the Six Sigma program depends. Correct analysis of the data and its interpretation and synthesis itself gives solution to the problem or the improvement of the performance. The Six Sigma level of performance is the ultimate aim of any organization. It is perfection and its attainment needs a lot of focus and commitment, employee involvement, strategic direction and a sound base of quality management system like ISO 9000:2000. The Six Sigma gels well with the main objective of world-class management system of maximization of customer satisfaction and maximization of the return on investment.

Improve

The 'improvement' phase is the most critical and important phase of Six Sigma. The actual benefit of the entire activity percolates in the system of the organization taking it to a new height of perfection. The improvement phase should maintain the customer perspective while developing solutions. This phase develops solutions designed to reduce or eliminate the root causes of deviations or the 'X' factor. The improvement phase optimizes the solution to enable the process to meet the customer's 'CTQ' or the factor 'Y', i.e., the product and service performance. Improvement is a continual process done in stages. As is stated in Chapter 1, Deming's PDCA cycle is the essence of the continual improvement approach. The improvement phase looks for a solution that is planned, prioritized, piloted and checked against the goal or the benchmarks and refined till an optimum solution is reached.

This phase uses tools for developing solutions to problems or for the system improvement using either the analytical approach like the 'doe' or the creative approach like brainstorming, benchmarking, etc. The improvement phase uses methodology as described in Figure 10.5 to improve the performance to the Six Sigma level.

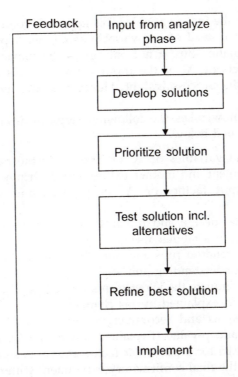

FIGURE 10.5 Methodology of the 'Implement' phase.

The improvement phase utilizes the input from the analyze phase and develops solutions for optimizing 'Key Input and Process Variable (KPIV)' or the vital input process variable 'X'. It then prioritizes and test alternative solutions and selects the most suitable one. The improvement phase confirms the improvements and then refines the solutions and implements the best one under controlled condition. Lastly, it gives the feedback on the improvements and its benefits or its failure, as the case may be, for further improvement and perfection next time.

Analytical approach. The analytical approach uses the 'Design Of Experiments (DOE)' approach.

The DOE approach determines which 'Xs', factor or the input variable have the most impact on the product or the services output or 'Y'. It determines where to set the 'X' values so as to optimize 'Y' or the output to meet the customers' requirements in terms of the stated and implied needs and its satisfaction. It also determines where to set 'X' values so as to reduce the effects of uncontrollable variables 'Z'. The DOE approach selects the input variables of 'Six M' or the men, machine, material, method, measurement and mother nature and determines their status and conditions as they are the factors or the causes that effects the performance of the 'Y' or the output. It uses the cause and effect diagram to measure the effect of these 'X' factors on the 'Y' or the performance of the product and the services.

The benefits of the DOE approach are that it is a quick and efficient way to identify the most significant 'X' or the input variable. This approach conducts simultaneous trials with multiple 'X' or input instead of one variable at a time. It provides a mathematical treatment, i.e., $Y = f(X)$ relationship. It not only gives the impact of 'X' on 'Y' but also gives the interaction effects of 'X' or the input variables. This approach requires less number of trials to get the process insight. Hence it is the most economical way of experimentation.

The DOE approach now takes the following steps to design an experiment. The sequence of steps is explained below.

- Identify the input variables of 'X' of 'Six M' or the men, machine, material, method, measurement and mother nature and determine their status.
- Identify the output factors or 'Y' of product and service output to the customers.
- Select experimental design and full factorial experiment and trials and design the data collection in a tabular form.
- Now conduct the random runs and note the results and responses in a tabular form for ease of understanding and analysis.
- Now this phase conducts the experiments and collect the data.
- Analyze the data as explained in this chapter.
- Draw the conclusions and recommendations based on the experiment data, graphical output and p-value (Explained in Chapter 9). If the p-value is more than or equal to 0.05 for a particular factor, then it is significant.
- Now we conduct the final confirmatory experiment with optimized value of the input factors 'X' and note down the output results and conclude that the new application is better in terms of quantifiable output.

Hence we can conclude that DOE is an experimentation beyond normal working range. It conducts experimentation with multiple factors at a time to gain process insight through interaction effects and simultaneously establishes the cause and effect relationship between the output 'Y' and the input 'X' and the vital 'X's. It is used for both the incremental and exponential process improvements. It can also predict accurately the future process performance.

Creative approach. While the DOE approach is a routine approach for improvements and gives reasonable improvement in performance, the creative approach may give breakthrough improvements.

The creative approach starts with the brainstorming process to develop the solution. The process of brainstorming, creative thinking, nominal group technique and whole brain thinking has been explained in detail in Chapter 3. The next phase of the creative improvement approach is 'benchmarking'. It is a management technique of learning from the best. The process of the benchmarking has been explained in detail in Chapter 3. Benchmark the best process, product and system for conversion and value addition and adopt the superior process for the desired improvement in the shortest possible time. The organization should keep in mind the 'value analysis' principals for value addition to the products and service, as explained in detail in Chapter 3.

While developing the solution, keep in mind the lean manufacturing system and the principles of the TQM. Also employ the principles of 'Poka Yoke' and 'FEMA', as explained in Chapter 12, for eliminating the mistakes, errors and failures. Every mistake corrected, every error rectified and every failure eliminated means one improvement.

The organization should employ the 'TRIZ' or 'The Theory of Inventive Problem Solving'. The organization and its employees should overcome the psychological inertia (PI) to accelerate the creative thinking for inventive problem-solving. The psychological inertia (PI) is a combined factor of the individual's personal opinion and biases, previous experience, technological knowledge and his nature and comfort zone. PI limits the scope of the solution space. The out-of-the-box creative thinking eliminates the mental blocks and enables the individuals to work out creative, unconventional solutions.

The ideal solution at the Six Sigma performance level should be maximizing the value addition to the output products and the services. The ideal solution at the Six Sigma performance level should be opting for the lean manufacturing system, minimizing the cost of production or the value addition as well as making the end products and services error-free. The quality of the solution developed will depend on the complexity of the problem, availability of the data and the problem-solving experience and competence of the team.

The solution can be refined by pilot testing and statistical analysis of test and the pilot phase data with respect to the baseline, which gives ample opportunity for the refinement of the solution. In the refinement stage, the improvement techniques and methodology are repeated using the various tools and techniques like FEMA (Failure Mode and Effect Analysis), DOE (Design Of Experiments), Benchmarking, Triz (Theory Of Inventive Problem Solving), Poka Yoke (mistake or error proofing), value analysis, etc.

The next phase of the improvement phase is the solution prioritization using rating on desirable attribute basis and working out a matrix diagram. The cost-benefit analysis of implementation of each solution has to be carried out before implementing the solution. The payback period for a Six Sigma project should normally be less than a year.

The next phase of the improvement phase is confirming the improvement. The selected optimum solutions are implemented in stages. The improvements are confirmed by using the same statistical tools and techniques with the identified baseline in the measure phase. Based on the feedback and confirmation of the improvements, further refinement is done. The solutions are tested to gain confidence and to ensure that the product and the service have improved, the root causes are eliminated and the improvement is sustainable. The solution then is implemented in the limited area under close supervision. The pilot testing exposes the opportunity for the improvements and refinement. The pilot testing gives confidence for full scale implementation and ensures smooth final implementation. It also validates the success of the solution.

The next phase of the improvement phase is validation and implementation of the solution. Confirm the improvements by measuring and using various statistical tools like histograms, control charts, and assessment of performance figure like the 'process capability index' and the 'process capability factors' along with the sigma values and variance. Now the organization confirms the solution and the improvement and identifies opportunity for the further refinement of the solutions. The next phase of the improvement phase is to identify other similar areas for improvement and undertake spin off projects.

Control

Control is an important element of the entire Six Sigma process. The perfect control mechanism is required to effectively and efficiently implement the improvements and hold the gains obtained out of the improvements. It does not allow the performance to slip back from the improved level. It ensures that a step taken forward is never retracted under any circumstances. The control parameters are focused in the control of the process, product and service performance and the quality management system performance.

The control mechanism insists for a 'quality plan', which is a documented plan whose purpose is to ensure that all product characteristics or process requirements stay in conformance. The quality plan must contain the process documentation and standards as well as the process controls. The most powerful and accepted control mechanism is the statistical process control as detailed in Chapter 9 and the ISO 9000:2000 Quality Management System, as detailed in Chapter 6. The control mechanism includes a well laid out quality plan including the statistical process control techniques and tools like the control charts and process performance figures like the process capability index CP and the process capability factor CPK, standard deviation and variance, management review meetings, internal quality audit reports, quality improvement teams like 'Quality Circle', 'Kaizen Gemba', 'JQI', 'Quality Improvement Projects', the root cause analysis for the process and product failure as per ISO 9000:2000 clauses and taking the corrective and preventive actions. These are all the manifestations of the control mechanism. The same tools and techniques are followed in the Six Sigma process, also for the 'control' phase of the Six Sigma.

The objective of the control mechanism is to design and put measurement point at the key process and product performance characters. Compare the actual performance against the quality plan and its directives. In case there is no deviation, continue with the periodic defined measurement system. The statistical figures of process capability, process capability factors, standard deviations, etc. are evidence of the product and process performance under control. But in case of deviation, the control mechanism should identify and release warning signals sensitizing the planned triggers for taking the suitable corrective measures to put the process back into the original track. However, every such deviation must be investigated to identify the root cause for it and preventive steps must be taken so that such type of deviation never ever occurs in future.

EXERCISES

1. Define 'Six Sigma'. Explain the concepts and features of Six Sigma.
2. Elaborate on the goals and focus of 'Six Sigma'. Explain the Six Sigma enablers in detail.
3. Design an organization structure for Six Sigma.
4. Explain the Six Sigma problem-solving approach.
5. Compare the two methodologies of the Six Sigma implementation—DMAIC and DMADV.

6. In the 'DMAIC' methodology of Six Sigma implementation, explain in detail the process-orientation and the project definition phase.

7. In the 'DMAIC' methodology of Six Sigma implementation, explain the measurement phase.

8. In the 'DMAIC' methodology of Six Sigma implementation, elaborate on the analysis phase.

9. In the 'DMAIC' methodology of Six Sigma implementation, explain in detail the improvement phase.

10. In the 'DMAIC' methodology of Six Sigma implementation, explain the control phase.

11. Implement the 'Six Sigma' in the following sectors:

  (a) A software development industry.
  (b) A mobile phone manufacturing company.
  (c) An automobile manufacturing unit.
  (d) An electric goods manufacturing company.

Chapter 11

Various TQM Related Tools and Concepts

CHAPTER OBJECTIVES

In this chapter, we will discuss the following:

- Poka Yoke
- Failure Mode and Effect Analysis (FMEA)
- Taguchi's Quality Engineering

This chapter deals with the TQM tools which have not been discussed so far. These are some typical TQM tools used in a sporadic manner for typical application. However, they have their own usefulness for the recommended application. These are some tools that are applicable for failure or mistake proofing, product design, etc. The principle of their functioning may be on a similar line that is already explained with reference to some other topic or subject. However, the understanding of these subjects in brief is required from the point of view of understanding the subject of Total Quality Management.

11.1 POKA YOKE

'Poka Yoke' is a Japanese word meaning 'mistake proofing' or 'error proofing'. The errors mainly result due to the assignable causes or the random causes. The random errors are predictable, within the control limits, miniscule and tolerable. The causes of the random errors are inherent in the process, its design, machines, etc. and normally they are left unattended as they have got negligible effect on the product and the process. The assignable errors are sudden, unpredictable, quite substantial and have quantum effect on the performance of the product and the process.

The process defects and variations are directly proportional to the amount of human factors of either interventions or involvement in the process. Inspection is not a solution to avoid errors and defects. To reduce the chance of error, we need to devise the system or processes in such a manner that the human element is removed from the vital input 'X' variable, which are critical for the performance of the product or the service output.

Under the principle of 'Poka Yoke', the methods of preventing errors in the processes and making them human independent as far as possible are to begin with the systemization of the way of doing the work. For this a 'Standard Operation Procedure' or the 'SOP' is written so that the errors are minimal and there is consistency in the performance. The process runs as per the written down method of working, that is the 'SOP'. The process performances are measured by periodic audits with or without a checklist. The process can also be measured by the control charts. These are the methods which measure and record whether the process or the product is as per the specification and within the norms or outside it. In case the product, service or the process is not as per norm and outside the control limits, suitable warning mechanism as well as the corrective measures have to be taken to first stop the process and then correct it and restart it and ensure that the process output in terms of the product and the services is as per the desired performance level. This identification of occurrence of the errors or the mistakes, issuing warning signals, stopping the machine or the process and taking corrective action and restoring the process back to the desired performance level can be done manually or by suitable automation. The permanency of control mechanism increases manifold as we move from manual to automation. The objective of 'Poka Yoke' is to prevent errors in the processes and make them human independent as far as possible.

In the improvement phase of the 'DMAIC' of Six Sigma process, as explained in Section 10.6, for the vital 'X' or the input variables, the organization needs to devise solutions by which the organization can minimize and avoid human intervention. We are giving below a few examples of the human independent process controls.

Computer Integrated Manufacturing (CIM) system as explained in Chapter 9. The moment the process starts producing products outside the control limits, the sensor in the automatic in-process gauging system senses the error and stops the machine and simultaneously starts a warning mechanism in the form of a hooter or a warning red light. The process correction can be done manually by the operator or automatically by the program logic controller and the auto tool re-sharpening mechanism and readjusting the machine to the original setting as programmed in the memory of the machine. This is a perfect case of 'Poka Yoke'.

- Auto e-mail generation for meeting deadlines.
- Automatic regression testing.
- Drop down menu.
- Pop up menu for wrong entry.
- Auto validation check for incorrect field.

The 'Poka Yoke' or error proofing either minimizes or eliminates the opportunity for error. For reducing the opportunity of error, the 'Poka Yoke' lays down some implicit rules of procedural guidelines or the explicit rules of back-up resources in case of non-availability of the process owner. The 'Poka Yoke' also minimizes the opportunity for error by incorporating low level of physical intervention of pop up reminders periodically with a checklist or in case something goes wrong in the system. The common example given can be the Windows XP/2000 operating system. The 'Poka Yoke' also looks for eliminating the opportunity for errors by high level physical intervention or automation. There are innumerable examples of data bank which enables correct response depending on the nature of query.

In short, the 'Poka Yoke' systematically and scientifically tries to identify probable errors much before they occur and take pre-emptive steps of eliminating these errors as and when they occur by way of suitable corrective and preventive measure with the end objective of a 'zero defect' performance of the product or the process. The 'Poka Yoke' is a system of error proofing to eliminate the need for inspection. The focus is to eliminate the errors in the design stage or the process stage itself.

11.2 FAILURE MODE AND EFFECT ANALYSIS

Let us first understand the meaning and the interpretation of the Failure Mode and Effect Analysis (FMEA). The 'failure mode' can be defined as the manner in which a product, service or a process can fail to meet the specification. The failure mode is basically associated with a non-conformance or a defective product or a deficient service to meet the customer expectations. The 'effect' is the impact on the customer if the failure mode is not prevented or corrected. The customer could be an internal customer or an external customer. The 'cause' is a deficiency that results in a failure mode. The causes are the sources of variability associated with the 'X' or the input variables. The failure mode is an in-process defect or deficiency in the input variables 'X' and the effect is the impact of such deficiency or defect in the process on the output product and the services.

FMEA is a structured approach to identify ways the product, service or the process can fail to meet critical customer requirements and to work out a plan to prevent these failures. FMEA involves estimating the risk of specific defined causes with regard to these failures and evaluating the current control plan for preventing these failures from occurring. It prioritizes the actions that help to improve the process.

FMEA identifies the potential failure modes and rates the criticality of their effect. It evaluates objectively the occurrences of the causes and the ability to detect the causes when they occur. The potential products and processes are ranked with reference to their severity. FMEA focuses on eliminating product and process concerns and helps prevent problems from occurring.

FMEA is carried out when the new products, processes and systems are being designed or when the existing process or the designs are being changed. It is also carried out when the carryover designs and processes are used in the new application or the new environment. It is also implemented after a problem-solving study to prevent the recurrence of the problem.

FMEA is measured by the numerical number 'RPN' or the 'Risk Priority Number'. This decides the risk of a particular failure mode.

$$RPN = SEV \times OCC \times DET$$

The scale fixed is 1 to 10, where 1 is for the best or the minimum severity or effect of the failure and 10 is for the worst or the most severe effect of the failure.

'SEV' stands for severity or how significant is the impact on the product and services and ultimately on the customer who could both be internal or external.

'OCC' represents the occurrence. How likely is the cause of the failure mode to occur?

'DET' stands for detection. How likely is the current system to detect the cause of failure mode if it occurs?

11.2.1 Benefits of FMEA

The main benefit of FMEA is to make the output 'Y', i.e., the products and services of the organization error-free. The general benefits of FMEA are elaborated below.

- FMEA ensures better quality and reliability of the output products and services.
- It ensures customer satisfaction.
- It reduces the product and/or services development timing and cost.
- It maintains the documents and tracks the actions taken to reduce the risk.
- It increases the safety of the product and/or service usage.
- In the 'improvement phase' of 'DMAIC' of Six Sigma, the organization needs to identify the risks for vital 'X' or Input using 'FMEA' to optimize the input resources or the 'X'.

11.2.2 FMEA Process

FMEA is a well structured process of error' or mistake proofing wherein certain steps are to be followed, as detailed below.

- FMEA is a breakthrough exercise.
- First construct a 'FMEA sheet' with complete details. Every 'FMEA sheet' is typical to the organization and should be designed as per the organization's specific requirement.
- FMEA takes into account the organization's current process and the product and the 'FMEA form' must be filled in after assessing the current situation. The rules for this exercise are detailed hereafter. List the process steps for the product components. List the mode of operation for each process component. List the effect of each failure mode. Now rate the severity of the effect of each failure to the customer on a scale of 1 to 10. The next step is to list the causes for each failure mode along with the linkage of the causes with a process input out of specification. The FMEA team assessing the situation must rate how often the particular cause or the failure mode occurs, on a scale of 1 to 10; 1 for not often and 10 for very often. The FMEA team documents how the cause is currently being controlled in the process. The FMEA team should also rate how well the cause or the failure mode can be detected. On a scale of 1 to 10, this translates to 1 for defect every time and 10 for defect not happening. Now finally the 'RPN number' or the risk priority number is worked out.
- After developing a FMEA on the current process and product, the next important step in FMEA is to work out an improvement plan. An improvement plan is required when the RPN number is more than 120. FMEA identifies a particular project or the process and prepares separate improvement sheets for each such project of product or process improvement. FMEA first conducts a

pareto analysis to identify the 'vital few' products or the processes where the RPN number is the highest. These highly potential failure areas are taken up as a project using FMEA. After assessing the current status and finding out the root causes of them, it takes the suitable preventive actions and documents recommended actions. The FMEA improvement plan now delegates the responsibility of taking the action and completing the project as per the plan to a particular team. After the action is taken and the improvements are carried out, the RPN number is reassessed to ensure that the improvement steps are effective and the project or the process is under control and the chance of failure is remote.

- To conclude effectively the 'improvement phase', FMEA is built on the new solution or the process to find the possible risks inherent in the solution. The steps are devised to eliminate the risks. The FMEA team should devise the mitigation plans for the high RPN items.
- FMEA now carries out the proactive and preventive steps to reduce the likelihood of failure. It also works out the damage control steps and recovery plan in case of the failure. Normally 'error proofing' and 'robust design' are the most likely preventive steps taken in 'FMEA".

FMEA success stories and cases are used to assist the identification of similar potential failure areas and for taking suitable pre-emptive steps to rectify and prevent their occurrence. FMEA focuses on the critical areas or the project steps, high cost areas and the product features that impact maximum customer satisfaction. It also looks at the high probability problem areas. FMEA use brainstorming and data analysis methods including cause and effect diagram or the Ishikawa diagram to identify and find out the key failure modes.

11.3   TAGUCHI'S QUALITY ENGINEERING

Prof. Genichi Taguchi, Director of the Japanese academy of quality and recipient of the prestigious Deming's prize did pioneering work in the field of experimental design and off-line quality control. Taguchi's method of experimental design is basically a statistical experimentation tool concerned with the application of pre-production quality control techniques at the pre-production stage to asses the viability and effectiveness of the input process design and output product design. This product and process engineering is independent of the production experimentation and analysis. This is a method which eliminates the need for mass inspection by building quality into the product, process and service at the design stage itself. Taguchi's method of experimental design incorporates the quality considerations at an early stage of product designing–prototype and final and the process designing—designing and installation of a manufacturing process onwards. The potential weaknesses of the product and the process is identified at an early stage and eliminated even before the same is installed or produced.

11.3.1   Quality and the Loss Function

If any product or service does not perform as per the targeted performance level fulfilling the customer's needs and expectations, the products or services create loss to the society which is given by the Taguchi's equation as

$$L(Y) = \frac{M}{D^2}(Y - t)^2$$

The above equation is a measure of the loss to the society due to faulty supply of the product or services. The cost includes the tangible cost of warranty and servicing cost as well as the loss of the product cost, including the manufacturing, shipping and the government taxes levied on the product. The cost also includes the intangible cost of customer dissatisfaction, loss of future sales, loss of market reputation and increased marketing effort to overcome this damaging effect of product non-performance. Taguchi's focus is more on controlling the variation in product performance. According to him, a product does not cause a loss when it is just outside the limits or a slight deviation from the target. Taguchi's loss function approach establishes a value base for the development of the quality products. According to him, the main objective of the quality improvement program should be to minimize the product performance about its target value. The smaller the performance variation, the better the quality. The larger the deviation from the standard, the greater the loss to the society, i.e., greater the loss of the consumer and the producer together. Taguchi's loss function approach unites the financial loss with the function specification through a quadratic relationship. This loss is proportional to the square of the deviation from the target. Figure 11.1 gives a graphical representation of the loss function $L(Y)$ when the performance Y of a product deviates from the desired target t. M is the producer's loss in monetary terms when the product tolerance D is exceeded.

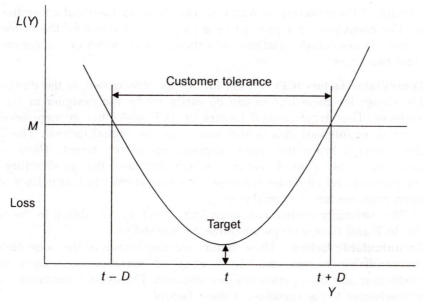

FIGURE 11.1 Taguchi's loss function.

11.3.2   Philosophy of Taguchi's Experimental Design

Taguchi's main objective is to identify the factors which are responsible for the product and the process variation and control their settings to optimal level. The main objective is to minimize the variations in product performance while keeping the mean response on the target. Taguchi's parameter design stage removes the bad effect of the cause rather than the undesirable effect of the cause, thereby achieving a more robust, stable and higher quality products and services. Since the method is applied in a systematic and scientific way at a pre-production stage offline prior to the setting of the manufacturing process, it can eliminate a number of time-consuming and costly tests to determine the cost-effective process conditions, thus saving the cost and preventing wastage of products.

The main point of the Taguchi's philosophy is to apply the quality control technique to offline from online. The objective is to build the quality into the product and the process so that there is no need to inspect the output products and services. The philosophy is that the root cause of variance is not one factor but a combination of multiple factors working together. Hence the experimental design procedures should conduct multi-variant statistical experimental design techniques.

The other important consideration of Taguchi's philosophy was his definition of quality and the objective of experimentation as 'achieve the target and minimize the variability' rather than 'achieving conformance to specifications'. Taguchi postulated the theory of changing the attitude for dealing with the uncontrollable factors, that is to remove the effect and not the cause by appropriately tuning the controllable factors.

11.3.3   The Principle of Factorization

Taguchi introduced the principle of factorization based on the product or the process parameters. The behaviour of a product or a process is defined by the factors or the parameters and the associated variations with them. These factors or the parameters are separated into two types.

- **Controllable factors (CF).**   These factors are also known as the design factors. The values for these factors can be easily set by the designer or the process engineer. The target control factors or TCF affect the average level of the response of interest. This is also known as the 'signal factors'. The TCF and their settings bring the mean response on to the target. There could be additional 'cost control factors' which increase the profitability of the organization and eliminate wastages. The cost control factors neither affect the mean response nor the variability.

    The variability control factors or VCF affect the variability in the response. The VCF and their settings minimize the variability.

- **Uncontrollable factors.**   These factors are also known as the noise factors. The uncontrollable factors are the sources of variation associated with the production and the operational environment. The overall performance should be insensitive to the variation of these factors.

    Noise are normally the input variables and factors causing variations which are impossible or extremely difficult to control. The noise factor or 'NF' can again be divided into two types—the outer noise and the inner noise. The 'outer noise' consists of the operating conditions and the environment and the 'inner noise' consists of the deterioration in the process and product control factors and the manufacturing imperfections. The objective of this segregation is to make the product and process robust against noise factors.

The basic difference between the Taguchi method and the statistical process control methodology is that Taguchi's method concentrates on variability and takes preventive steps during the design stage rather than at the production or the post-production stage. The main objective of Taguchi's method is to reduce the variability by changing and controlling the variability control factors and maintaining the required performance through adjustments of the process to the target control factors.

11.3.4 Parameter Design and Performance Measures

Taguchi's method identifies those settings of controllable factors that eliminate the performance variation caused by the noise factors. At the same time, the response of interest is kept on the target. The attempt is to reduce the effect of the noise factor. In this regard the fractional orthogonal inner array row are formed. In this design, every level of setting of a factor happens with other factors in the other level equal number of times. Refer to Figure 11.2. A fractional orthogonal array can be formed to understand the level combination of the noise factors in the outer array. The setting which minimizes the variability can be obtained by simulating the variability effect of the noise factors on each controllable noise setting.

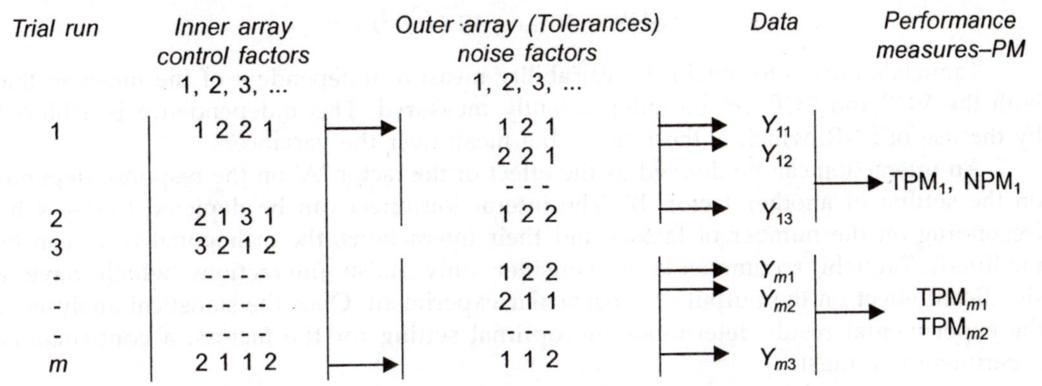

Trial run	Inner array control factors 1, 2, 3, ...	Outer array (Tolerances) noise factors 1, 2, 3, ...	Data	Performance measures–PM
1	1 2 2 1	1 2 1 / 2 2 1 / - - - / 1 2 2	Y_{11} / Y_{12} / Y_{13}	TPM_1, NPM_1
2	2 1 3 1			
3	3 2 1 2	1 2 2 / 2 1 1 / - - - / 1 1 2	Y_{m1} / Y_{m2} / Y_{m3}	TPM_{m1} / TPM_{m2}
.	- - - -			
.	- - - -			
.	- - - -			
m	2 1 1 2			

FIGURE 11.2

For each of the rows in the inner array, the n rows of the outer array will provide the equal number of n observations on the response. These observations will be computed to give certain performance measures for the members of the inner rows. The outer array is the carefully selected subset of the noise space.

If N_i is the noise factor chosen with a linear effect and known distribution, then N_i is tested between two levels ($m_i - s_i$) and ($m_i + s_i$) where m stands for the mean and s stands for the standard deviation. If N_i is assumed to have a curvilinear effect, then it is tested at three level, i.e., at $(m_i - s_i 1.225)$, m_i and $(m_i + s_i 1.225)$. However, the noise factor is assumed to be having a symmetrical distribution.

A response model can be developed through the computer simulation trials or the physical trials, if feasible. The whole exercise could work out to be extremely costly or may not be practically feasible. Hence the fractional experimental designs studying factors at the most at two or the three levels is carried out. This 'response model' should relate the product, process and service performance characteristics to the controllable noise factors, both internal and external.

Two performance measures are calculated, viz.

1. **The Noise Performance Measure.** The Noise Performance Measure (NPM) reflects the variation in the response at each setting. The analysis of the NPM identifies the variability control factors and the optimum combined setting of these factors to minimize the variability can be determined.
2. **The Target Performance Measure.** The Target Performance Measure (TPM) measures the process average performance at each setting. The analysis of the TPM will determine the controllable factors other than the variability control factors. These factors have a substantial effect on the mean response. This target control factors can be manipulated to bring the mean response to the required target level.

Taguchi devised the Signal to Noise Ratio (SNR) to decide on the target value for the response. The SNR measures the ratio μ/σ where the μ is the process mean and σ is the standard deviation. n is the number of observations in each trial. For each experimental trial, the SNR is computed as:

$$SNR = 10 \log 10 \, (\hat{y}^2/s^2)$$

Taguchi's idea is to obtain the variability measure independent of the mean so that both the VCF and TCF can be independently measured. This independence is achieved by the use of SNR, which is the ratio of the mean over the variance.

An interaction can be defined as the effect of the factor 'A' on the response depends on the setting of another factor 'B'. The interaction effect can be depicted by $(A \times B)$. Depending on the number of factors and their interactions, the orthogonal rows can be modified. Taguchi recommends to consider only those interactions which have a significant effect on the output of a particular experiment. Once the statistical analysis of the experimental result determines the optimal setting for the factors, a confirmatory experiment is a must.

If the output of the 'parameter design' does not give the desired result of removing the noise factors, Taguchi recommends 'allowance design' which brings in additional probable factors not considered earlier. If one wants the expected results to reach a still higher level of performance, Taguchi recommends to consider the tolerance of the products and its components and redesigning of the tolerances. This means retaining the mean as it is; the tolerance of certain crucial factors or components are reduced in an optimal and cost-effective manner to reduce the overall variability in response to an acceptable level. At this stage the decision is taken to remove the noise factors after having failed to remove their effect. Therefore, 'tolerance redesign' is resorted to as a last resort.

11.3.5 Implementation of Taguchi's Experimental Design and Off-line Quality Control

Taguchi suggested steps to carry out the experimental design and offline quality control are detailed below in nine defined steps.

1. **Define the problem.** Provide a clear statement of the problem to be solved. The features of the problem and its likely effect on the product, process and service parameters must be stated clearly. The boundary of the problem and its symptoms should be defined clearly.

2. **Determine the objective.** Determine the desired output characteristics or the response to be studied, optimized and the target performance which should be quantified and measurable. Work out the method of measurement and the measurement reliability. There could be a single or multiple objectives clearly defined against which performance can be measured.

3. **Factorization.** Conduct a brainstorming session involving the managers and operators closely involved with the production process or the product under consideration. The output of the brainstorming session is to decide on the controllable and the uncontrollable factors and to define the appropriate factor level. The team should also define the experimental range. The objective of the brainstorming session should be to consider as many factors as economically viable. The interactions should be as minimum as possible.

4. **Experiment design.** The team should select the appropriate experimental designs. The controllable factors and their interactions should be depicted and analyzed at the columns of the inner array. The outer column represents the noise factors in the outer arrays (see Figure 11.2).

5. **Conduct the experiment.** The team should select the experiments to be carried out. The team then performs the experimental trials and collects the experimental data. It should ensure that the experiment is conducted in a controlled condition on the defined parameters and the results are obtained with minimum measurement errors.

6. **Analyze the data.** Now both the target performance measures and the noise performance measures are evaluated for each trial run of the inner array. The data is then analyzed, synthesized and interpreted using appropriate statistical analysis technique.

7. **Interpret the result.** Identify the Variability Control Factor (VCF) and the Target Control Factors (TCF) and select their optimum levels. For the VCF the optimal levels of the process inputs are those which reduce the variability. For the TCF the optimal levels of the process inputs are those which bring the mean response to the target value. Now the team should be able to predict the process performance under optimal conditions.

8. **Conduct a confirmatory experiment.** It is important to confirm by some follow-up experimental trials that the new parameter settings have improved the performance as compared to their value at the initial settings. The team should run a confirmatory experiment to verify the predicted results. A successful confirmation experiment will remove the fears of wrong choice of

factors or the experimental design and increase the confidence level of its successful implementation.

9. **Validate the experiment.** A successful confirmatory experiment will validate the end result of foolproof solution to the problem. However, if the predicted results are not confirmed or the results are unsatisfactory, additional experiment may be required to validate the end solution to the satisfactory process and product performance.

Taguchi's experimental design for quality control is a unique concept which tries to foolproof the manufacturing system at the design stage itself so that everything is just the right product, process and service moving towards a 'zero defect' or 'zero failure' performance. This is an offline quality control system, thereby propagating a principle of 'do it right the first time'. Taguchi's experimental design is a straight-forwarded, well-integrated system of implementing the statistical experimental design with computer simulation.

Deming pushed the world from product-orientation to process-orientation, thereby eliminating the need for inspection since if the process is under the control limits, it can never get rejected. Taguchi moved further backwards to integrate the quality at the design stage itself.

EXERCISES

1. Define 'Poka Yoke'—the mistake proofing technique. Explain its concepts and features. Explain the process of 'Poka Yoke'.

2. Define 'FMEA'—Explain the concept and benefit of FMEA. Also explain the process of 'FEMA'.

3. Explain the concepts, objective and planning of Taguchi's quality engineering.

4. Explain the principle of factorization, quality and the loss function.

5. Explain Taguchi's concept of the parameter design and tolerance design. What are the performance measures, i.e., TPM and NPM and SNR?

6. Explain the procedure by which an organization will implement Taguchi's experimental design and offline quality control?

Case Studies

This section of the book deals solely with case studies which elaborate the practical implementation of the TQM principles. However, these case studies may not necessarily reflect the implementation of the Theory of Holistic Management for World-class Performance. The case studies show how the implementations of the TQM principles have benefited the various organizations partially or completely depending on the objective of the organization and their strategic quality planning as well as the extent of soundness of their foundation and infrastructure. Most of the cases are real-life situations. The information pertaining to the cases has been collected during the author's visit to these organizations, holding training sessions there, interacting with and interviewing the relevant officials as well as going through the literature available on the subject. The names are not published to retain the confidentiality of the organization. The cases have been explained in brief, elaborating only the key points without any jargon to make them easy-to-understand.

SECTION I

This section lists the major cases of the application of the TQM principles and practices leading to the implementation of the Theory of Holistic Management for World-class Performance.

The theory of Holistic Management for World-class Performance has been developed by the author himself and it focuses on the application of the TQM principles in a manner that the benefits accrue to the organization as a whole and not just to a specific operational area.

CASE 1: Implementation of the Theory of Holistic Management for World-class Performance in the Manufacturing Sector

The case pertains to the implementation of the 'Theory of Holistic Management for World-class Performance' including TQM in a manufacturing sector and how it helped the organization to achieve the world-class performance level. The case talks about a leading tractor manufacturer in India which started its TQM initiatives to attain its objectives of being a market leader. The company was faced with the daunting challenge of implementing TQM across more than 4000 employees, about couple of dozen area offices, around 500 dealers and more than 300 suppliers.

Prior to 1990, in the pre-liberalization era, the license raj existed in India, preventing competition. Like the other industries, the organization was in sellers' market and hence the focus was more on quantity production to optimize the plant capacity. There was no emphasis on the development of new models and to give improved features excepting the introduction of direct injection engine. However, this development of the direct injection model demonstrated that the organization had a sound base or foundation oriented towards continuous improvement.

The manufacturing activity was more inspection-oriented detection rather than the prevention of defects. The interaction with suppliers was purely need-based and the sales and service activity lacked standardization and varied from dealer to dealer. The rework and rejection percentages were high and the employee involvement in improvement activities was limited.

In the late eighties, the tractor market saw a slump in the demand partially due the government's change in policy of subsidy and the nationalized banks' credit policy pertaining to the change in rules and regulation for giving soft loans for procurement of tractors in the rural sector. Liberalization and globalization were on the horizon. The competitors were introducing new contemporary models of their collaborators with wide range of models at competitive prices, and were also increasing their capacities. As has been already explained, this organization had a sound foundation and was always proactive in its business decisions rather than being reactive. The organization decided to implement the TQM at the beginning of 1990 with the objective of achieving 'market leadership by performance excellence'.

The implementation of TQM was done in stages which are detailed hereafter.

As was the case with most organizations, TQM was started in a sporadic manner in the area of quality improvement or solving of day-to-day problem in working area. The implementation started with 'quality circles'. Each quality circle had six to eight people working in the same area and was led by the first line officer from the same area. At the peak of the activity, almost one-third of the workforce was involved in the initiative. These circles solved many operational problems, resulting in improvement in quality, safety and housekeeping and reducing costs. But improvement in the mindset of the employees and people development were relatively the more important benefits. This activity ensured 'Total Employee Involvement'. This success encouraged the company to pursue the path of TQM to attain and retain the market leadership position and grow further.

The TQM journey was in three phases, viz., the Introduction phase, the Promotion phase and the Development phase. The first two phases were of three years duration and the development phase is an ongoing activity.

The first phase objectives were focused more on the continuous improvement activities, process control bringing in a customer focus at all levels in the organization and working out the strategic quality plan for the long-term as well as the short-term implementation. This laid a solid 'Foundation' for the organization.

The step taken in this direction was the working out of a strategic quality plan for the next ten years to attain the market leadership position with a well-defined 'Mission' and 'Vision' statement. The customers' requirements were ascertained and accordingly the quality was improved through process control by implementing statistical process control (SPC). The quality of bought-out components was improved by initiating the supplier support activity. The organizational profitability and the return on investment were increased by increasing the productivity and reducing the cost of poor quality (COPQ). The introduction of initiatives like Juran's process of quality improvement (JQI) helped the organization to solve the chronic cross-functional quality problems. Other TQM activities like Business Process Re-engineering (BPR) were also carried out simultaneously in the manufacturing area. All these TQM activities created a solid foundation for the organization to go forward towards its aim of market leadership.

In the second phase, the focus was towards creating a sound infrastructure by introducing the various 'Quality Management Systems'. TQM in the second phase included the standardization of all operations as per the international guidelines and further improvement upon them. Accordingly, certification for the world-class management system as specified in the ISO 9000 was obtained. Subsequently, the industry-specific standard QS 9000 for the automobile industry was obtained. Policy deployment/daily work management technique and certification to environment management system standard ISO 14001 were introduced at the same time. The continuous improvement activity was also stepped up considerably. The employee involvement was almost 100 per cent during this period.

The benefits derived over the years by the implementation of the TQM activity can be summed up as substantial reduction in rework, rejections, reduction in rejection at suppliers' end as well at receipt stage at the manufacturing plant, improvement in field quality indicated by reduction in the number of consumer complaints during the first 250/500/1000/2000 hours of tractor operation, increased productivity, customer satisfaction, employee involvement in continuous improvement, and introduction of new models—15 models in three years. The main objective of attaining market leadership in India was achieved around the year 2000 and the position is retained even till date. The organization has been expanding its market globally in last few years with outstanding success stories. This can be an example of implementation of TQM and above all holistic management for world-class performance.

Questions

1. Explain the high points of the case.
2. Discuss whether the case followed the 'Theory of Holistic Management for World-class Performance'?
3. Explain the factors that helped the organization to defend and retain its market leadership.
4. Enumerate the critical success factor (CSF) of the organization.
5. What have you learned from this case study?

CASE 2: Implementation of TQM in a Manufacturing Organization

The case talks about the implementation of TQM initiatives at an automotive spare parts manufacturing company in the late 1990s. The actual process of the implementation of the TQM was started in the year 2000–01.

The implementation of the TQM in the organization is explained in detail in this case along with the relevant benefits realized by the organization. As the group comprises multiple companies with multiple plants, a three-tiered promotion structure was formed.

At the tier 1, group level TQM Apex Council was formed comprising of the group chairman, vice chairman, presidents and the total quality (TQ) coordinators of group companies and group TQM coordinator. Tier 2, which is at the company level, is called TQM Promotion Committee. This consisted of the president, senior management group of the company and plant and head office TQM coordinators. Tier 3 is at the plant level and is known as TQM Promotion Team. This team consisted of plant and head office functional heads, plant functional heads, head office department heads and TQ coordinators for the plants and the head office.

The company had a TQ Coordinator to monitor implementation and provide necessary alerts to senior management. Each plant of the company had a plant TQ coordinator who was responsible for facilitating TQ practices in the plant. The company and plant TQ coordinators worked closely to ensure that the practices were spread uniformly across plants.

Challenges encountered were mainly to change the basic outlook and orientation of the employees and the top management for the successful implementation of various TQM activities and the basic TQM philosophy in the organization.

The major challenge was to change the mindset of the employees to help them appreciate the TQM philosophy. Training programs were organized for the employees to create awareness about the utility of TQM. This enhanced their motivation to embrace TQM. Initially, there was a feeling that TQM was only for the shopfloor and not for non-manufacturing functions. Slowly, the company realized that standard operating procedures (SOP) and Kaizen were as much applicable to processes in functions like finance, marketing, materials as they were for the manufacturing process. It realized the need for writing SOPs for these processes to insulate them from human error. The organization implemented company wide TQM activities embracing all the functions and every employee in the organization.

The benefits derived by the organization from the TQM activities were phenomenal. During the initiation period of the TQM activities in the year 2000–01 and post 'TQM' implemented era in 2004–05, the organization's sales figured jumped three times. There was a lot of focus on customer satisfaction. This led to the development of a number of customer-oriented products and services. Compared to the 5% contribution to total sales by the newly developed products in the year 2000–01, in 2004–05 the contribution of the new product sales were nearly 30% of the total sales. The customer line rejection dropped from the percentage (%) level to the ppm. The energy cost vis-à-vis the net sales came down from around 3% to 1.86. The intangible benefits include the company becoming more customer-focused with improvements in business processes, system-orientation and cross-functional working along with the total involvement of the employees.

Questions

1. Discuss the high points of the case.

2. What benefits did the organization derive from the implementation of total quality management?

3. Based on this case, discuss the critical points for the implementation TQM and its various aspects.

4. What have you learned from this case study?

CASE 3:   Total Quality Management Implementation at 'BHEL' for World-class Performance Excellence.
(Also validates the 'Theory of Holistic Management for World-class Performance'.)

BHEL is an acronym for Bharat Heavy Electricals Limited. The Government of India started this Public Sector Undertaking (PSU) in the field of heavy electrical industry in India with the establishment of the first plant of BHEL nearly four decades ago at Bhopal. BHEL is today the largest engineering enterprise of its kind in India, with an excellent track record of performance, making profits continuously since 1971.

BHEL's business operations cater to core sectors of the Indian economy like power, industry, transportation, transmission, defense, etc. and fulfill the vital infrastructural needs of the country.

Today, BHEL has about 13 manufacturing divisions, 9 service centres and 4 power sector regional centres, in addition to over 150 project sites spread all over India and abroad to provide prompt and effective service to customers.

BHEL was one of the first organizations in India to recognize the potential of total quality management in business excellence and world-class performance. BHEL was probably the first Indian organization to implement 'Quality Circle' in all its plants way back in the 1970s. Its commitment in this regard was so high that it published a book on the subject of quality circle and the seven tools of total quality control. This book incidentally was also my first exposure to the subject of TQM and Quality Circle way back in my college days. BHEL has acquired certifications to Quality Management Systems—ISO 9001, Environmental Management Systems—ISO 14001 and Occupational Health and Safety Management Systems—OHSAS 18001 and has also adopted the concepts of TQM.

The company has also entered the international market and has tied up with Siemens, Germany. It regularly bags export orders from various parts of the world. It has built up a huge base for itself in south Asia because of its superior technology and unique facilities. Within the country, BHEL has joint ventures with NTPC and has been assisting IOC and ONGC in various projects. BHEL's Haridwar unit has installed almost 200 power generating units in various categories of 200 MW, 250 MW and 500 MW.

The manufacturing units of BHEL are located at the following locations spread across the entire country.

1. Haridwar : 2
2. Bhopal : 1
3. Hyderabad : 1
4. Tiruchirapalli : 2
5. Bangalore : 2
6. Jhansi : 1
7. Jagdishpur : 1
8. Ranipet : 1
9. Goindwal : 1
10. Rudrapur : 1

The BHEL employees are from all caste, creed and religion and from various parts of the country, but they have one common language of world-class performance excellence that each employee of BHEL speaks.

BHEL's operations are organized around various business sectors to create a strong customer focus and market-orientation. These sectors are power, industry and international operations.

1. **Power Sector.** The Power sector business of BHEL comprises of thermal, nuclear, gas and hydroelectric power generation. BHEL supplies electric power generating sets, accounting for more than 60% of the country's total installed electrical power generating capacity in the country. Till the late 1960s, most of the power generating sets were imported before the installation of the capacity at BHEL.

   BHEL undertakes turnkey power projects from the concept to commissioning, and manufactures boilers, thermal turbine generator sets and auxiliaries up to 500 MW to 1000 MW rating. The capacity might have increased further recently. BHEL has the technology to supply gas turbine generator sets up to a unit of 150 MW. Co-generation, combined cycle plants and regeneration of waste heat have also been introduced to achieve higher plant efficiencies.

   To make efficient use of the high ash content coal available in India, BHEL supplies circulating fluidized boilers. BHEL manufactured 235 MW nuclear sets and has also commenced production of 500 MW nuclear sets. Custom-made huge hydroelectric power generating sets of Francis and Kaplan types for head-discharge combinations are also engineered and manufactured by BHEL.

   The power plant equipment manufactured by BHEL is of the highest level of international quality and at the same time cost-competitive. BHEL's service in this sector is also of international standard. BHEL also undertakes successfully the renovation, maintenance and life extension of the power plants.

2. **Industry Sector.** BHEL manufactures the components, equipments and systems for various industries like cement, fertilizers, refineries, petrochemicals, steel, paper, mining, defense and telecommunication. The range of systems and equipment supplied include captive power stations, high speed industrial drive turbines, industrial boilers and auxiliaries, waste heat recovery boilers, gas turbines, electrical machines, pumps, seamless steel tubes, heat exchangers, thyristor devices, simulators, process control equipments, etc. It has recently entered the aviation industry with the introduction of a light trainer aircraft.

It also manufactures various products and systems for high voltage power transmission and distribution, transformers, switchgears, capacitors, etc. High Voltage Direct Current (HVDC) technology is also available for economic transmission of bulk power over long distance. In the field of oil and gas, BHEL is supplying various types of offshore and onshore drilling rigs.

In transportation, BHEL's traction and traction control equipments have been used in the trains of the Indian Railways. BHEL supplied drives and controls are used in India's first underground metro of Kolkata. The company supplies 3900 hp broad gauge AC locomotives to the Indian Railways and diesel shunting locomotives to various industries. The first 4700 hp AC/DC locomotive developed and manufactured by BHEL was supplied to the Indian Railways. The first 5000 hp AC locomotive prototype is undergoing tests. Battery powered road vehicles and locomotives are also manufactured by the company.

For the development of remote and rural areas, the company has developed many non-conventional energy sources like wind generator, solar power based pumps, lighting and heating systems which have been installed at the Indian station, Dakshin Gangotri in Antarctica. For meeting demands of wind farms, the company has manufactured wind electric generators of 250 kW rating. BHEL has also commissioned a 3 MW wind farm at Ramagiri in Andhra Pradesh on Build-Own-Operate (BOT) basis. It has also commenced manufacture of large desalination plants to help augment the supply of drinking water to the people.

BHEL's products, services and projects have been exported to all over the world, including the advanced countries like USA, New Zealand, etc. For excellent performance in exports, BHEL won the Top Exporters Shield from EEPC for the year 1994–95 in the project exporter category and also the Capexil Shield. BHEL has upgraded its products and related technologies by acquisition of new technology from world-leading organizations, viz., Siemens, Combustion Engineering, General Electric, Nuovo Pignone, Asea Brown Boveri, Hitachi, etc.

The company is embarking upon an ambitious growth path through the implementation of the TQM principles. The organization's clear Vision, Mission and committed values to sustain and augment its image as a world-class enterprise is detailed below.

Vision of BHEL

A world-class, innovative, competitive and profitable engineering enterprise providing total business solutions.

Mission of BHEL

To be the leading Indian engineering enterprise providing quality products, systems and services in the fields of energy, transportation, infrastructure and other potential areas.

Values of BHEL

1. Meeting commitments made to external and internal customers.
2. Foster learning, creativity and speed of response.
3. Respect for dignity and potential of individuals.
4. Loyalty and pride in the company.
5. Team playing.
6. Zeal to excel.
7. Integrity and fairness in all matters.

Quality Policy

In its quest to be world-class, BHEL pursues continual improvement in the quality of its products, services and performance, leading to total customer satisfaction and business growth. Through dedication, commitment and team work of all employees, BHEL is following the 5S system of housekeeping for the improvement of work environment. (This has been explained in detail in Chapter 2.)

Towards meeting its quality policy, BHEL is utilizing the Quality Management System, i.e., the ISO 9001:2000 series of standards certified by the internationally acclaimed certifying agency BVQI.

Corporate quality and unit level quality structure enables requisite planning, control and implementation of company wide quality policy and objectives which are linked to the company's Vision statement. Corporate quality derives strength from direct reporting to the Chairman and Managing Director of the company.

Other than traditional quality functions, today the focus is basically on propagating the Quality Management Systems and Total Quality Management in the entire organization and formulating, implementing and monitoring 'improvement plans' with focus on internal and external customer satisfaction as well as the investigations and preventive actions on critical quality issues.

Calibration and testing laboratories of BHEL are accredited under the National Accreditation Board for Calibration and Testing Laboratories (NABL) scheme of laboratory accreditation, which has got mutual recognition with Asia Pacific Laboratory Accreditation Conference and International Laboratory Accreditation Conference.

As a result of its thrust on quality and technology, BHEL enjoys national and international recognition in the form of product certification by international bodies like ASME, API, etc. and plant approvals by agencies like Lloyds Register of Shipping, U.K., Chief Controller of Explosives India, TUV Germany, etc.

In its movement towards business excellence and with the objective of achieving international level of quality, BHEL has adopted European Foundation for Quality Management (EFQM) model for business excellence. Through this model and annual self-assessment exercise, BHEL is institutionalizing continuous improvement in all its operations. Apart from the organizational quality policy, BHEL has also defined the 'Occupational Health and Safety Policy' and the 'Environmental Policy' which are detailed.

BHEL has a strong commitment to the 'Occupational Health and Safety' norms. The organization ensures the compliance with applicable legislation and regulations. The organization has got the set objectives and targets to eliminate, minimize and control risks due to occupational and safety hazards. An appropriate structured training of employees on Occupational Health and Safety (OH&S) aspects is carried out followed by the formulation and maintenance of OH&S management program for continual improvement. There is periodic review of OH&S Management system to ensure its continuing suitability, adequacy and effectiveness. In pursuit of these policy requirements, BHEL will continuously strive to improve work practices in the light of advances made in technology and new understandings in occupational health, safety and environment science.

BHEL's 'Environmental Policy' is to strive to be an environment-friendly company in its activities, products and services through compliance with the applicable environment legislation and regulations, continual improvement in 'Environment Management System' to protect the natural environment and control of pollution. BHEL will ensure the promotion of the activities for conservation of resources by the environment management. It will also assist the industries and the government in the environment management activities offering the company's capabilities in this field.

The Total Quality Management and Quality Circle movement has created an atmosphere of continuous improvement and total employee involvement with a customer focus. Strategic quality planning gave the organization a well-defined business direction. All these created a solid business 'Foundation'. The total employee involvement along with implementation of sound Quality Management Systems like ISO 9000 and ISO 14000 created a strong 'infrastructure' on which the organization carried out its TQM activities. This is the reason why BHEL not only obtained the market leadership position in whatever it did, but also defended and retained the same for more than two to three decades in spite of the international competition and globalization. BHEL is a classic case of validation of the 'Theory of the Holistic Management for World-class Performance".

Over the years, BHEL has emerged as a world-class engineering and industrial giant, the best of its kind in entire South East Asia. Its business profile cuts across various sectors of engineering and power generation industry. The company today enjoys national and international presence featuring in the 'Fortune International 500' and is ranked among the top 12 companies in the world in the manufacturing of power generation equipments. Nowadays everybody is talking of privatization. Here is a Public Sector Undertaking (one of the 'Navaratnas') which is miles ahead in performance excellence in terms of business efficiency, technology and effectiveness than most of the organizations in the private sector.

Questions

1. Describe the high points of the case.
2. Analyze the case in detail.
3. "BHEL is an ideal case for the validation of the 'Theory of Holistic Management for World-class Performance'. Discuss.
4. How will you create a world-class organization like BHEL?
5. What have you learned from this case study?

CASE 4:   Total Organizational Involvement in Implementation of TQM for Market Leadership in Automobile Sector

This is a case of achieving market leadership by performance excellence through the deployment of Total Quality Management.

This case illustrates how a successful American auto manufacturer transformed the organization from an economic model to a TQM model of the firm and the resultant benefits accrued by it. The transformation has become necessary because a business enterprise organized around the TQM philosophy draws upon mainly the systems and the human capital to meet and overcome international competition. The competition in most industries, including the auto industry, forces costs to decrease due to elimination of the wastages or the non value added activities while the quality, productivity and rate of innovation must increase on a continuous basis.

The Total Organizational Involvement (TOI), i.e., the involvement of the suppliers of raw materials and components along with the employees of the organization and the customer in the business process of the organization, is a key factor for the success of a world-class organization. The alliance between the organization's one of the assembly plants and one of the vendors explains in great depth how the TQM paradigm can be applied to build up an excellent supplier-organization relationship.

The transition of the organization from the economic model to the TQM model began in the early 1980s with a 'Quality is Job 1' initiative. The transition continued in the 1990s with a 'Quality People, Quality Products' initiative. The success of this transition reflected in better quality products, stable employment of the firm's workforce and management and of course in the increased profitability and better customer satisfaction. The organization has been a leader in the partnership concept with its suppliers for several years. The relationship with supplier in this particular case brought this practice to a new level. This particular assembly plant of the organization produced automobiles which dominated the mid-size auto market. The plant began production of these brands in the mid-eighties and by the beginning of 1990s, the automobiles had earned several awards and had become the number one company selling vehicle in its class. Its popularity is a convincing external measure indicating the success of the organization's this particular assembly plant in meeting the competitive forces of the auto market.

In the partnership between the organization and the supplier, the supplier supplies the specified material and components taking up the total responsibility. The comprehensive nature of the program is analogous to outsourcing management. A responsible person from the supplier's end works as the in-house representative at the organization's plant. This supplier is classified by the organization as a Tier I supplier, which means that all specified raw materials and components under this program are supplied and managed directly by the supplier. If the supplier does not supply a particular component or the raw material itself, it contracts with a Tier II supplier to provide the plant with the required raw material or the component of the right quality at the right time.

This program covers a wide spectrum of responsibilities. The supplier's representative is responsible not only for the raw material/components and the related inventory, but more importantly also for the quality of the output from this process. This means he must control the equipment used in the process of manufacturing and understand the processes' proceedings and follow the application to provide a quality product to the organization.

The supplier must maintain the equipments and process under control and dispose of waste products as per the parent company's specifications, which meet or exceed federal, state and local requirements.

Joint organizational goals are the backbone of the organization and the supplier's partnering relationship. Establishing an active, continuous improvement environment with a quality focus in meeting the customer's needs and wants is the primary goal. The reason for this focus is simple: A quality product that meets customers' needs translates into financial success. When poor quality occurs because of incorrect process, profits are consumed. When the defect is discovered internally, the vehicle must go through additional processes which increase the cost of the production substantially. When a customer discovers a poor quality in the product, the costs and damages are beyond imagination to the organization.

Organizational goals for this supplier-organization collaborative program are listed in a handbook outlining each partner's responsibility to the relationship. The details of the handbook are proprietary, confidential and unique to each such organization. The advantage of the handbook is that both partners know and understand their range of duties. Its tone is cooperative and fosters a working partnership relationship. The essence of the handbook is that this program has to be proactive with a supplier-assembler working relationship to increase quality and productivity and decrease the cost of production. Quality serves as the central focus of the relationship.

The handbook takes on the dynamic perspective when specifying each party's responsibility. It stipulates quality, productivity and cost target specifications. Because the specifications are expected to change as process improvements emerge, the handbook includes a section outlining how changes to the original targets will be managed. It is essential that the financial impact of any change must benefit both the supplier and the assembler equally. This is a very important component of the handbook because the strength of a continuous improvement operating environment rests on cooperation, interaction, and trust that the organization will not force the supplier into a situation that is financially unacceptable when changes occur.

This program has in its purview the scope and environment for fostering the 'individual goals' of the employees also. The fulfillment of the individual goals integrated together leads to the fulfillment of the organizational goals for this partnership. Employees in a successful transformation need to understand why changes are needed, what new attitudes are required, and how to respond within their realm of responsibility. The organization should empower its workforce and the supplier's representative to contribute to the process. The handbook calls for the representative to train the organizational employees about the raw material/component/assemblies supplied by the supplier and how to use them in the auto assembly process. In turn, the parent organization's employees train the supplier representative in process control techniques as they are practiced at this assembly plant. Normally the organization's employees train the supplier's employees in statistical process control and continuous improvement techniques as they relate to the material supplied by the supplier. This empowerment reflects the organization's position regarding who is responsible for producing a quality product—both management and the workforce.

This exchange of knowledge creates individual goals for the supplier and the organizational employees to improve quality and productivity at a reduced cost. The entire process involves everybody, including the workers, the organizational managers and the supplier representative and everybody understands that achieving these goals is essential to maintain a competitive position in the auto industry. This is why performing at something other than 'the best you can do' is socially unacceptable to both the organization and its suppliers alike.

Financial rewards encourage continuous improvements. The organization annually rewards its employees and managers with profit-sharing. In addition, an active suggestion program encourages participation by sharing any savings resulting from an idea with the individual who presented the idea. The supplier is also motivated to follow the same rewarding system.

Organizational and individual goals drive the next three elements of the TQM program. Statistical process control (SPC) is the primary measuring and control device for these elements. The supplier's representative and the organization's employees jointly establish the required flow charts, control charts and sampling techniques necessary for measuring the respective processes to ensure quality. These tools are used by both the supplier and organizational employees to keep the processes under control and reveal possible improvements. Information is openly shared.

The process of conversion with the raw material/components supplied by the supplier may sometimes not produce the right result. It is signaled that the process is out of control. The first concern and responsibility of the supplier's representative is to fix the problem according to a predetermined 'reaction plan' to ensure quality. The supplier's representative also has the authority and knowledge to reconfigure the process to increase quality, decrease cost, or both. The impact of this change is measured by the SPC. Each attempt at continuous improvement is studied and evaluated before it is implemented. Quality improvement is considered as the most important factor in the decision-making process.

Significant to this partnership is the fact that the supplier representative is free to run continuous improvements without the burden of red tape. He is entrusted with the management of a key sub-assembly process. Continuous improvement is achieved by empowering both supplier's representative and the organization's employees to take action as necessary and when opportunities surface. This arrangement represents aligning process information with accountability.

An innovative financial system supports this partnership. The supplier is paid on a per automobile basis. The supplier guarantees an increase in the productivity over the contract period. This is a sharp departure from the traditional in-house partnership in which the supplier is paid simply on a material quantity order basis with little incentive to improve the process. The immediate benefits to the organization are that it has got control over the cost of production and its reduction as an ongoing process. The operating system promotes continuous improvement because management and operating decisions are made on the basis of process quality.

Using a simple spreadsheet, the supplier tracks the cost of material flowing through supplier as a Tier I supplier. He knows immediately the cost of materials used in each process and using quality as a benchmark, maintains and continuously improves the process. Describing the process for setting the original per car compensation rate demonstrates how the financial aspects of this partnership were transformed from an adversarial to a cooperative relationship. Negotiations over the original compensation rate began, with each party analyzing its cost records. The organization tracked the inventory purchase, inventory holding, and freight costs paid for the relevant materials over the previous two years. These costs were standardized on a per unit basis. Then, using these data, the organization set a pay rate per automobile. The supplier worked out a rate it was willing to accept based on its cost records plus cost estimates from Tier II suppliers. The process of negotiation was held between them and an acceptable rate was eventually agreed upon. However, the rates are subject to revision depending on the change in process, technology, market situation, raw material price, etc. on a mutual consent basis so that the relationship is on a win-win situation for both the organization and the supplier.

The principles of work design and company boundaries were well-demarcated and defined between the organization and the supplier.

The supplier's representative, being situated in-house, has access to information before and after each process including how the product performs in the marketplace. He is expected to use this information to introduce new products and processes that offer significant productivity advantages, cost savings and quality improvement. The organization and the supplier jointly study all proposals, with quality improvement as the fundamental guide to all final decisions. Diffusing the boundaries between the organization and the supplier enables the organization to achieve quality at a lower cost as well as increased productivity. Beyond the supplier's own product line, improved quality and savings are also captured by better management of Tier II suppliers. The supplier's representative is responsible for the process and application of Tier II supplies and their continuous improvements. The in-house representative with a vested interest in quality and cost will outperform a supplier who 'checks in once a week.'

The organization and the supplier partnership focuses on organizational and individual goals on quality. The responsibility of process coordination, control and information has been turned over to those best suited for decision-making—the supplier's representative and the manufacturer's workforce. The continuous improvement process inculcates the effort to increase productivity and quality as well as innovation. Each product or process improvement contributes to the organization's competitive position in the global automobile marketplace.

All of these opportunities can be created by transforming supplier-buyer relations into a collaborative and cooperative environment under a TQM framework. This globally renowned automobile manufacturer's success story demonstrates that most businesses can strengthen worldwide competitiveness by using basic TQM techniques in their supplier-organization relationships as well as in other areas.

Questions

1. Explain the high point of the case.
2. Explain in detail the process of supplier-organization symbiotic relationship for business performance excellence.
3. Elaborate on the areas where the TQM philosophy and techniques has been deployed.
4. Describe how TQM has helped the organization to gain the market leadership position?

CASE 5: Implementation of TQM in the Service Sector

ITES and BPO are the buzzwords since 2000 onwards till date and the sector is contributing a substantial amount to India's GDP as well as creating lot of employment opportunities for the educated Indian youth. With lots of offshore business coming to India, ITES companies are on an expansion spree. New facilities with high deployment capacities are opening and new Indian players are coming into the picture. The organization is a major player in the ITES-BPO sector as well as part of one of the largest group in India in the software industry. The parent organization as well as the entire business group has successfully implemented TQM and various TQM techniques like Six Sigma, CMM, etc. and is recognized worldwide as a world-class organization because of its performance excellence. The organization under discussion has recently scaled up its operations and therefore needed more employees for its operation. The main challenge is to train and retain the competent employees who are vital to the organization's performance excellence.

Along with the increased hiring, training the recruited workforce is a major challenge and upgrading their skill to the international level of performance is a prerequisites for meeting the quality concerns demanded by the clientele. The performance of the BPO industry rests on the rapidness to scale up operations and at the same time ensuring that the processes are efficient, cost effective and of world-class quality. The performance of the organization has to be proved as per the global standards of performance excellence. The organization has to use resources efficiently and maintain productivity levels. The organization introduced iBaan's smart route planning system for obtaining the desired results.

The challenge and the crucial task is to keep the employees motivated and keep them in their best of physical and mental state. Most of the issues are handled by the organization very well and the systems and processes are kept in place by employing the TQM philosophy and practices. However, the organization faced a peculiar but critical issue to develop an effective and economical pick-up mechanism. Most of the 'call centres' provide their employees with a pick-up facility since the employees are expected to work at odd hours when the public transport system is either not available or not safe particularly for the female employees. The organization had to constantly alter its transport system to meet the needs of its employees who were located in diverse locations across the city. And with the hiring of each additional employee, this problem increased. The biggest problem that the organization faced was constant change in the to-and-fro movement of vehicles along diverse routes. The manual planning of the routes and the to-and-fro movement of the vehicles to accommodate each and every new employee resulted in an increased operational cost for the organization. The transportation cost per employee increased at a rapid rate.

The whole pick-up system was needed to be planned immaculately with an employee-friendly automated structured system to provide feasibility, sustainability, flexibility, cost-effectiveness, operational efficiency and timeliness in the process. The organization designed a geographical information systems based program that would enable them to quickly adjust to changes in the route taken by the vehicles.

Baan's iBaan RoutePro was the system chosen to be implemented since the solution had a capability to cater to the organizational priorities. The solution promised to enable a bird's eye view of the entire area where the vehicles would ply, right up to the doorstep of the employee safely and securely. The software was first implemented in one of their facilities and subsequently it was implemented in all their centres. The software was compatible with the existing hardware and the cost was marginal to the organization.

Benefits became apparent soon after the deployment of the system. Earlier there were cases reported that the employees were not picked up or dropped at the right destination and at the right time. This reduced the quality of the process in place and had major effects on the functioning of the organization as each employee is a mode of revenue generation on per call basis. The new system reduced the frequent changes in routes. The routes designed for each vehicle became more or less streamlined, thereby leading to better utilization of the vehicles. The vehicles now travel to predefined areas, eliminating the need to cover huge geographical areas. The software works out the optimal route mix enabling the vehicles to pick up and drop the maximum number of employee in time, every time at the least cost.

With the help of this solution, the organization has divided the entire city into various geographical pockets covered by one route. All the employees falling under a particular pocket are picked up in a single round by the same vehicle. The package provides a digitized map of the entire city with details of house and street names. This enables the drivers to easily find their way and saves lot of time and provides the facility of rescheduling the route in the event of emergencies. On-time arrival has increased the number of call engagements than before, which has ultimately led to an increase in revenues. The organization has been able to see a return on investment within a short span of three months after the implementation.

Questions

1. Explain the high point of the case.
2. Explain the areas where the TQM philosophy and techniques have been employed.

CASE 6:   Validation of Theory of Holistic Management in the Cutting Tool Industry

The organization is the manufacturer of abrasives and ceramics grinding wheels and polish papers used by the engineering industry for grinding, finishing and the super finishing of parts and components like gear shafts, crank shafts, bearings, etc. used in the automobile, steel and other industries. The organization is one of the first manufacturing companies of the 1.2 billion USD group from southern part of India. The organization is the market leader in India in its field of operation. In the 50 years, the company has established itself as a major Indian player competing in the global abrasives and ceramics market.

The organization has successfully defended its market leadership in India in spite of the entry of major global players in India in the post-liberalization period. After defending its market share and gaining more confidence of its product performance against the internationally leading product in the same category, the organization has successfully entered the global market in a big way. The organization has a vast dealer network all over the country with more than 200000 counters selling its products. The organization has an expansion plan to double its sales in the next 3 years. The organization has recognized Total Quality Management as the strongest tool for achieving this success and achievement of its business objective. The organization has always been having a strong customer focus and sound strategic quality planning exercise which is largely responsible for market leadership in the domestic market. This has been the organization's main foundation along with its continuous endeavour to improve its product, process and system performance.

The organization has developed the infrastructure through total employee involvement providing an experimental and innovative atmosphere, a sound quality management system under ISO 9000:2000 and an efficient logistics and supply chain management, to ensure the availability of right product, at the right place, at the right price and at the right time. The organization has also got ISO 14000 certification for its environmental commitment, conservation of natural resources and power generation.

The company has implemented TQM along with total productive maintenance. The organization has a perfect prevention based and growth-oriented quality plan with well-defined 'Mission', 'Vision', 'quality goals' and 'quality policy'. The organization has implemented Statistical Process Control (SPC) for all its manufacturing operations. It has a number of quality improvement teams working in tandem for all-round improvement in product, process and system performance.

The organization has received a number of business excellence and commendation awards. With the above said techniques of holistic management for world-class performance, the company has achieved tremendous results on all fronts with increase in its sales and exports exponentially. It has achieved both total customer satisfaction and maximization of the profit and the return on investment on a consistence basis. The case is a perfect validation of the Theory of Holistic Management for World-class Performance.

Questions

1. Discuss the learning points of the case.
2. 'The case is a perfect validation of the Theory of Holistic Management for World-class Performance' Please explain.
3. What are the high points of the case?
4. Describe how TQM has helped the organization to gain the market leadership position?

CASE 7: Implementation of Total Quality Management in an Indian Two-wheeler Manufacturing Unit

This case pertains to a two-wheeler manufacturing unit which is part of a major industrial house in the southern part of India. This group has a history of pioneering achievements in the field of the Total Quality Management. One of the group companies was the first in India to have the ISO 9000 certification for a world-class quality management system implementation. Another group company was the first to receive the prestigious Deming Award from Japan for the implementation of the TQM system in India.

The two-wheeler manufacturing unit of the group manufactures the full range of two-wheelers consisting of the mopeds, mini scooters, scooters and motorcycles. The company has been in existence for more than two decades. The organization was the first to introduce 100 cc current generation motorcycle of contemporary design in the country. In line with the group philosophy, the company is always in the forefront of implementation of TQM and the related activities. The organization has a strong Quality Management System of ISO 9000:2000. The organization has a strong foundation of strategic quality planning of long-term of 'Vision', 'Mission', 'quality policy' and 'quality objectives and a sound plan for the business development on short-term as well as long-term basis. They have number of quality improvement teams working simultaneously on various quality improvement projects. The organization has implemented statistical process control on its shopfloor in the entire manufacturing and the assembly line. It has gone for sophisticated computer aided gauging automation in the quality control of the processes resulting in producing components with zero defects. The company continuously collects the market feedback and develops customer-oriented vehicles which are normally big hits in the market. The organization's commitment on TQM has enabled it to win the prestigious Deming's Quality Award from Japan a highly rated award in the field of TQM and world-class performance excellence.

The organization made achievement of this rare distinction possible with the company wide effort towards continuous quality improvement of all processes, products and services with total employee involvement. All these efforts and achievements resulted in increasing customer satisfaction, loyalty and improved the business results. The organization is the undisputed market leader in the two-wheeler segment in southern India and enjoys a strong market position in other parts of India as well. The export market of the organization has shown a significant increase over the past three years. The organization's overall sales figure has shown an increase of almost 50% for the past three consecutive years, enabling the organization to cross the Rs. 3000 crore mark.

Apart from the increase in the sales figure, the organization's focus on TQM and continuous improvements in the product, process and system has led to the reduction of wastages at the various levels of operation. This has led to an increase in the operational efficiency of the organization, thereby resulting in increase of the overall organizational profits. The employees are empowered to carry out their tasks efficiently and effectively. The organization has a high level of customer loyalty as its vehicles always provide a high level of customer satisfaction. The overall all-round performance excellence of the organization has made it a world-class organization.

Questions

1. Explain the high point of the case.

2. Elaborate on the areas where the TQM philosophy and techniques has been deployed.

3. Describe how TQM has helped the organization to gain the market leadership position?

CASE 8: Implementation of TQM in a Glass Bottle Manufacturing Company

The organization is a glass bottle manufacturing company and is a part of a leading industrial house in the country. The industrial group has one of the top three pharmaceutical organizations under its ownership. The glass bottles manufactured by the company are basically for the use by the pharmaceutical industry. The organization therefore has a large number of captive customers within the group itself. The entire group has played a pioneering role in the implementation of the philosophy and the practices of Total Quality Management. It has been extremely successful through a strategy of being focused on the needs and expectations of the customer. The organization is also a leading manufacturer of glass packaging for cosmetic products.

The organization has focused on becoming the leading provider of 'flaconnage' type of glass containers for the quality conscious pharmaceutical and cosmetics industries. With a compounded consistent annual sales growth of over 35% every successive year, the organization enjoys a leadership position in the niche pharmaceutical packaging segment. Its market share has almost doubled in last few years. The organization is the only company in India and one of the few in the world who manufacture and market the entire pharmaceutical range of glass bottles and vials in amber and flint colours in both soda lime and borosilicate material.

The TQM principles and practices were implemented successfully in its various business processes. The organization has imbibed all the elements of a systematic approach to excellence in results. The organization was the first in the glass industry to receive ISO 9002 certification from the internationally recognized Bureau Veritas Quality International (BVQI). The organization has established world-class quality management system by getting itself further certified under the ISO 9001:2000. It is also one of the first organizations in the glass industry to attain the ISO 14001 certification. The organization has been focused extensively on Total Quality Management. It has invested extensively in people development and information technology. The ERP system in use is MFG-PRO and aims to bring in increased efficiencies in the various business processes. A major B2B initiative has been the enabling of transactions between the organization and its customers through the website. All this is aimed towards enabling the organization to provide speedy, prompt and better service.

The organization has been the proud recipient of the Best Vendor Award in packaging from the Organization of Pharmaceutical Products of India (OPPI) for two years in succession, leading it closer to becoming the most admired packaging company in India. OPPI rules prevented two-year-consecutive award winners from being rated for two subsequent years. After a forced gap of two years, the organization has, once again, been rated the Best Vendor in packaging for the year 2000.

The internally conducted periodic customer satisfaction studies rate the organization as superior to others in the industry. Even the study conducted by an external agency has rated the organization as a company with an admirable customer satisfaction index. Ratings for the organization on various parameters were quite high from the hundreds of studies conducted by the reputed external agency. The organization's strong relationship with the customers has lead to a high level of customer satisfaction. This is an example of strong sustainability of market leadership through customer-orientation.

The organization has been continuously raising the standards of its performance on the quality front. Working together with its customers from various pharmaceutical companies has helped the organization in the Total Organizational Involvement (TOI). The task forces formed jointly by customers and the organization have led to significantly better performance where objectives were set. The organization has introduced the just-in-time (JIT) concept to ensure that customers do not have to hold huge inventories. Warehousing facilities at their plants and elsewhere are ample evidence of their desire to lower customers' inventory carrying cost.

Questions

1. What are the learning points of the case?

2. Explain how the organization attained all-round performance excellence by following the TQM principles and practices.

3. Explain whether the organization has a solid foundation and infrastructure for implementing the TQM principles and practices.

CASE 9: Implementation of Juran's Quality Improvement Technique in the Textile Industry and Need for 'Holistic Approach for Performance Excellence'

This case is of one of the better known companies in the textile industry. The organization is a part of a leading industrial house in the country. The industrial group has a turnover of more than Rs. 3000 crores. This textile unit was once the organization's flagship company. This is a typical case of the implementation of Juran's Quality Improvement (JQI) projects in a particular area of manufacturing. The project involves increasing the productivity of the new pneumatic jet looms.

The problem faced by the company was related to the efficiencies of new pneumatic jet looms. The company assigned a team of 6 members who were cross-functional and formed the JQI team. The JQI team conducted around 30 meetings and collected the previous and current data regarding performance of these pneumatic jet looms. During the pareto analysis it was found that the vital aspect of the performance of the air jet looms is the functioning of the pneumatic jet tools. This followed the identification of the root cause through brainstorming, pareto analysis and Ishikawa diagrams as part of the 'diagnostic journey'. Some 24 theories were put forward, out of which 5 were finally selected to be tested and implemented during the 'remedial journey'. The result of the program was that the efficiency and productivity of the pneumatic jet looms increased from around 60% to more than 85% after the implementation. To hold the gain of the program, periodic audits on implemented remedies were carried out. The targeted level for the measured performance was finalized.

For this JQI project, there is neither a clear-cut mission statement nor any clear-cut objectives (in quantified terms). Though the company has tried to follow the JQI program but still some inherent weaknesses can be seen such as no process capabilities are measured regularly. The other relevant concerned parties like suppliers are not invited in the program. Thus in the end it can be concluded that, though the results are good at present, keeping this healthy rate for a long time would be difficult to manage without proper infrastructure and quality management processes.

The organization is not following the other aspects of the TQM principles and practices. Following only sporadic, localized, isolated quality improvement projects does benefit the organization in some areas of performance. But the same is not enough to make the organization have world-class performance excellence or sustain the pressures of globalization and international competition. In spite of doing more than 50 'JQI' projects, the organization's performance slipped below average due to the lack of a holistic approach. The sporadic benefits were loosely structured and therefore it did not have additive effect in the organizational performance. The customer focus or the market-orientation was missing. The organization had only dealer-orientation and therefore lack of actual contact, and hence understanding the customers' needs and developing products and service as per that was missing. This made the organization lose its market leadership position over a period of time. There was no brand loyalty among the customers. Whatever old reputation was there due to the organization's existence in the market was lost to more aggressive and dynamic competition. There was lot of old organizational politics and favouritism in the handling of employees, leading to the lack of involvement from the bulk of employees. Even if the organization did have an ISO 9001 certification, the quality management system was in existence only during the external audit of the 'QMS'.

The result was evident. The organization lost the market to its competition and the sales plummeted. The manufacturing cost increased due to not having control over wastages and various other factors. The share prices fell in five years from around Rs. 250 to Rs. 270 to less than Rs. 15. The organization had multiple successful units operating all over the country. The units started closing down one by one. There was all-round fall in the performance. Hence implementing a few tools of TQM in a sporadic manner like only the 'Kaizen', 'Quality Circle', the 'JQI', 'Six Sigma' or the 'ISO 9000' definitely gives some benefit to the organization, but not enough for world-class performance and market leadership and sustainability in the current business environment of globalization and liberalization. The average performance is not enough. Therefore the 'Theory of the Holistic Management for World-class Performance' integrating the entire business operation under a structured manner with solid foundation and a well-organized TQM program can only lead to the world-class performance and market leadership, as explained in Chapters 4–7.

Questions

1. Explain the lessons learned from this case?
2. Discuss why sporadic implementation of quality improvement activity is not enough for the survival and performance excellence of an organization?
3. Elaborate on the JQI project methodology.

CASE 10: Validation of Theory of the Holistic Management and Implementation of TQM by a World-Renowned Car Manufacturer

The organization is located in northern India and is the current market leader in the field of car manufacture. The organization's collaboration and joint venture project with the world's leading small car manufacturer from Japan represents the sowing of the seeds for a world-class organization. The agreement with the Japanese car manufacturer allowed the transfer of technology for manufacture of a range of four wheelers, including a small car, a van and a multi-utility vehicle.

The organization was searching for a partner among various international automobile manufactures. The organization chose the Japanese car manufacturer for two reasons. First, it wanted to concentrate on the small car segment easily affordable by the Indian customers and the second reason was heightened by Japan's resounding success in the world car market. The Japanese car manufacturers were successful in selling high quality, cost-effective automobiles in all international markets, including the US and Europe. The success of Japanese automobile manufacturers in the international market was attributed to their TQM-oriented manufacturing technology leading to high productivity, high quality and cost-effective products and services. The collaborator was the world's largest manufacturer of small cars (under 1000 cc engine size). The collaborator had a broad based understanding with the organization for cooperation in all areas of operation extending beyond simple transfer of technical documents and implementation.

The joint venture in its fifth year of operation itself achieved the project implementation in terms of establishment of production facilities for the manufacture of one hundred thousand vehicles a year as per its strategic quality planning. The step-by-step approach in project implementation proved to be very cost-effective and productive. The organization implemented the JIT manufacturing system following Taichii's Ohno's 'TPS' or the popular Japanese Toyota Production System. The production shops were established in tandem with the user downstream activity with full functional approach resulting in minimizing the idle capacity at any time as well as minimizing the inventory in the system. The organization had the total support and co-operation from its collaborator. The project implementation was so much efficient in terms of the time and cost-effectiveness that it was the benchmark for not only the other domestic industries but also the collaborators themselves. Hence from the very beginning the organization believed in world-class performance and continuous improvement by implementing the TQM principles and practices. The initial market survey and developing the cars as per the market need developed a culture of strong customer focus from the very first day. Even today the organization consistently gets the rating of highest customer satisfaction year after year. The organization therefore created a solid 'foundation' consisting of customer focus, continuous improvement and effective strategic quality planning, based on which organization proceeded further in its journey for the implementation of TQM principles and practices.

The organization created an environment of 'Total Organizational Involvement' by getting regular feedback from the customers. The suppliers were treated like their own employees and were taken into confidence during the entire process of technology transfer and component development. The organization's quality engineers visited the suppliers' shopfloor regularly and helped in the development of the process and technology. The statistical process control and process capabilities were strictly employed both at the suppliers' end as well at the organization's own shopfloor. The organization even participated in the equity of the suppliers' organization and sometimes even helped them to identify the right collaborator to solve their technical problems. The interesting part of the technology transfer process of handing over the knowledge is through personal training and example-setting rather than through technical documents alone. From the beginning, the collaborator's engineers, technicians and supervisors had been present in the various production shops, assisting the organization in the supervision of the erection and commissioning of the equipment as well as training the organization's own technicians and suggesting ways and means of achieving highest productivity through the same equipment and manpower. This was made possible by the process of developing the components, locally and developing Indian suppliers for the components. The outsourced components constituted over 75% of the requirements of the automobile components, which otherwise would have been a demanding task. Because of the low level of technology and low volumes at which the Indian automobile and auto component industry had been operating before the entry of this organization, it has not been easy for the suppliers to upgrade their technology and expand their facilities to meet the organization's stringent quality and delivery norms. In this effort the organization has received unstinted support form its collaborator. Being a Japanese collaboration, all these efforts resulted in the development of TQM principles and practices leading to a sound Quality Management System. The organization also implemented JIT and logistic and supply chain management. All the three factors combined together created a sound 'infrastructure' which has enabled the organization to quickly adapt to the changing market situation and defend its market share and retain the market leadership even under intense international competition.

The organization's collaboration efforts with the Japanese collaborator have not been limited to the transfer of technology alone. It has sought to learn and understand from its collaborator TQM principles and practices and how it can be adapted in the Indian context. Once again the Japanese personnel working at the organization and at its vendor's end have assisted in establishing various TQM principles and practices. These include the popularization of voluntary quality improvement activities, such as quality circles, among shopfloor workers. The organization has also implemented successfully the quality control activities like Statistical Process Control. The workers from groups meet periodically. They discuss and find solutions to their common problems. These solutions result in savings to the company and improve the product and process performance efficiency and effectiveness. These quality improvement activities also improve the morale and motivation of the workers. The employees are suitably rewarded financially also based on the benefits derived from their suggestions. An individual suggestion scheme is also in operation in the company. The organization receives on an average more than 1000 suggestions every month. Catchy slogans regarding quality, safety and cleanliness are suggested by the workers themselves and put up in different shops in the form of posters to reinforce among all people the company's emphasis on these issues.

The organization's emphasis on implementation of the '5S' in terms of quality, cleanliness and orderliness in the factory has succeeded in creating good housekeeping and making the employees understand its significance. The different shop employees in the factory take pride in keeping their workplace clean and well-organized. This creates a clean and exciting work environment. The employee productivity in terms of the number of vehicles manufactured per employee per year is already exceeding the norm of the originally set Asia target. Attendance at the plant is around 95%, which is higher than what most plants in India have ever achieved. The productive working time at the plant is more than seven and half hours out of a working shift of eight hours, which is again much higher than an average productive time of around four to four and half hours achieved by most manufacturing plants in India.

In the post-liberalization period, the organization faced stiff international competition due to the launch of contemporary international models and its market share in India was threatened. The organization had a tough time in the beginning of the current millennium. However, the organization overcame this challenge by following the 'Demand Technology Cycle'. It upgraded all its existing vehicles with Euro-II compliance, superior 'MPFI' fuel injection system, superior coil spring suspension and better upholstery and looks and recycled the product which was reaching the decline stage of the product life cycle. This made the existing models contemporary and the sales surged ahead of the competition again due to the organization's superior service network. Simultaneously, the organization launched a number of contemporary, stylish, superior models in each product range to achieve the market leadership and defend it.

This is a classic case of implementation of the TQM principles and practices and validation of the 'Theory of Holistic management for the World-class Performance.

Questions

1. Explain the learning points of the case.
2. Explain the 'Theory of Holistic Management for World-class Performance' in relation to the case.
3. Explain the critical success factor of the organization.
4. Elaborate the various instances of the implementation of the TQM principles and practices.

CASE 11: Two Global Leaders Compete through TQM

The organization 'ABC' is one of the world's largest producers of earth-moving equipments and machineries. The organization had sales running in billion US dollars, with more than 50% of the same being international sales.

The organization's powerful global rival throughout the 1980s and the beginning of 1990s had been a Japanese organization whose global earth-moving equipments and machineries' sales were also in billion US dollars and approximately half of the organization's sales by mid-nineties. The Japanese organization's objective was to catch up with this organization and overtake it on the global marketplace. It had the advantage of lower cost of labour and strong foundation of customer focus, strategic quality planning and total employee involvement.

In the mid-1980s, the Japanese organization's US market share was close to 15%. By the end 1980s, it started a joint venture in the US for the manufacturing and distribution of earth-moving equipments and machineries. The combined US market share of the Japanese organization jumped to more than 20% while the US market share of organization 'ABC' was 35%. It appeared that the Japanese organization might overtake 'ABC'.

The organization 'ABC' fought back to sustain its leadership position by making substantial investment in the upgradation of its plant facilities with a strong commitment to quality. The organization implemented the TQM principles and practices. It developed a business excellence model of its own, following the TQM principles and practices. The idea included Total Quality Control (TQC), Computer Integrated Manufacturing (CIM) and JIT production and purchasing systems. This business excellence model was a purely customer-driven manufacturing philosophy. The organization created its own 'quality institute' where the organization educated its employees as well as its suppliers in the quality improvement methods and various TQM principles and practices.

The organization kept its cost down so that the competitors did not achieve a substantial competitive cost advantage. The organization also kept its suppliers' costs low by educating its suppliers to use quality control techniques to reduce wastages and eliminate rework as a way to reduce the cost of manufacturing. The organization strengthened its dealer network further to provide prompt services to its customers. By mid-nineties, the organization's dealers' sales rose five time that of its Japanese competitors in the US and Canadian market. The organization recognized the importance of suppliers and dealers as part of its quality management system leading to the implementation of 'Total Organization Involvement' system to provide value to the customer which was the organization's main competitive strategy.

The organization's commitment to quality, its cost controls and its networks of motivated suppliers and dealers paid off by mid-nineties. The organization gained market share at its Japanese competitor's expense in the US. The organization's market share grew steadily and the profits were growing equally strongly in its entire product range. The organization formed quality improvement teams to reduce the percentage of defective items. Initially conflicts arose between the inspectors of the Quality Assurance Program and the workers. Some of the older employees felt that they were being insulted whenever a quality problem was traced to their work. This resentment was cleared by imparting proper training to the workers and explaining them the methodologies to improve their performance. This brought in greater involvement of the employees and the organization reached a new high in terms of elimination of wastages and rework, thereby reducing the cost of production substantially as well as making a better quality product giving consistent reliable performance to the customers. The organization's market share boosted and it has sustained its global leadership position.

Questions

1. State and discuss the learning points of the case.

2. Explain how the TQM principles and practices help an organization to sustain its market leadership position?

3. With the help of this case explain how will you implement 'TOI' in an organization?

4. 'Training is must for the successful implementation of the TQM principles and practices'. Discuss.

CASE 12: Implementation of the TQM in Hotel Industry

The organization is a reputed name in the hospitality industry, having a range of hotels spread across the continent. The hotel chain is reputed for its high commitment to quality and offers world-class service at all its hotels. It has got its own manual for imparting world-class services to its clientele with a quantified and defined service level. The organization is the first hotel company to win the prestigious Malcolm Baldrige National Quality Award. The name of the hotel alone evokes images of luxury and quality. The organization treats quality as the heartbeat of the company. This means a daily commitment to meeting customer expectations and making sure that each hotel is free of any deficiency. This is a benchmark case of implementation of the TQM principles and practices in the service industry.

In the hotel industry, guests buy an experience when they stay at the hotel. It is purely a service-oriented industry where the quality is difficult to quantify. Therefore, creating the right combination of the service elements in terms of the food, service and the ambience to make the experience stand out is the challenge and goal of every employee, from the maintenance department to the management.

Long before applying for the Malcolm Baldrige Quality Award, the company management undertook a rigorous self-examination of its operations in an attempt to measure and quantify quality. A process-oriented approach was developed with well-defined inputs, outputs and value addition requirement by each process. Nineteen processes were studied, including room-service delivery, guest reservation and registration, message delivery and cycle times for all these areas ranging from room service delivery times and reservations to valet parking and housekeeping efficiency were determined for the maximization of the customer satisfaction. The results were used to develop performance benchmarks against each activity/process against which the future activity performances could be measured. With specific, quantifiable targets in place, the hotel chain managers and employees now focus on continuous improvement. The goal is 100% customer satisfaction. If a guest experience does not meet his expectations and needs, the hotel risks losing that guest to competition.

The company has put more commitments behind its quality efforts by organizing its employees into self-directed work teams. The employees' work teams determine work scheduling, what work is needed to be done and what to do about quality problems in their own areas. Employees are also given the opportunity to take additional training in hotel operations so that they can understand the relationship of their specific area to the overall goals as well as improve their performance. Total quality management principles and practices are implemented. The hotel management believes that a better trained and informed employee is in a better position to take decision in the best interest of the organization.

Questions

1. Identify and discuss the high points of the case.
2. State the role of employees in the successful implementation of Total Quality Management.

CASE 13: The Implementation of the TQM Principles and Practices in a Japanese Organization

This Japanese firm is a major conglomerate with key interest in the manufacturing of aerospace and motor vehicles' parts and components. The company's 80% of the sales come from the automotive business which is the prime source of growth for the company. Japan as a country and Japanese industries in particular depend mostly on exports for their growth and prosperity. The high value of the Yen compared to the US Dollar had hit the exports hard for most of the Japanese industries in 1990s. The organization's bottom line was hit hard by this situation and the company's survival was at stake. The organization had responded to this crisis by systematic deployment of TQM principles and practices. The organization first focused on substantial improvement on its existing products, processes and systems. The organization improved the existing products and simultaneously went for the development of new and market-savvy contemporary products. The organization opted for the process improvement techniques while maintaining the existing productivity levels. The organization also went for the reconstruction of the company from within.

The long-term program included simultaneous strategic action plan on the quality improvement with cost reduction, employee motivation and increased education and training and the specific, defined, time-bound targets. The focus of the organization was on the achievement of zero defect in its products and services, zero accident on the shopfloor and zero downtime of the entire operations. This alone led to 20% increase in the labour productivity.

These objectives were achieved by the implementation of Kaizen Gemba and formation of Kaizen teams in each individual department and section, leading to the overall improvement in all organizational operations along with the individual improvement activities. The customer focus, long-term strategic planning along with short-term intensive activities on the continuous improvement created a sound foundation for the organization.

Based on this solid 'foundation', an equally strong infrastructure was built by the organization by developing Quality Management Systems like ISO 9001 certification, Total Preventive Maintenance (TPM), Single Minute Exchange of Dies (SMED) and proper development management. This was further supplemented by the Total Organization Involvement (TOI) by imparting education and training to the employees, suppliers and closer interaction with the customers regarding the proper use of the organization's products and services.

The organization set up separate task forces to deal with each area, and developed a formal structure aimed at promoting the TQM principles and practices. In particular, the organization emphasized Total Productive Maintenance (TPM) which targeted quality improvement around machine reliability and availability.

The organization worked out a three-year mid-term plan for focusing and refocusing attention on continuous improvement. It adopted a three-pronged approach for the TQM principles and practices. First, TQM tools and techniques were aimed at increasing productivity and quality. The second major step was to adopt the 'TPS', i.e., Toyota Production System, aimed at waste reduction and a customer-oriented approach implementing the JIT manufacturing system. The third step was to implement 'TPM' simultaneously aimed at obtaining high machine efficiency and availability and at increasing production rates through more reliable plant and machinery.

There was continuous effort for the upgrading of the equipments and operators. There were display boards throughout the factory, including a master giant chart tracking the progress to date and plans for the near future. Each work group met daily in its own department and tried to solve the problems as a group and find out ways and means for improvement. This team daily reviewed the performances and the improvement cycle. Small and regular inputs of training and one point lesson system were introduced. The organization regularly held motivational events. Individual Kaizen team activities as well as quality circles were formed to inculcate continuous improvement. The organization introduced the 5-S activities of housekeeping to ensure workplace analysis. All activities were carried out as per a well-structured strategic action plan as per a step-by-step approach with voluntary participation and high commitment from all the employees as well as the top management.

Policy deployment is the link between the organization's broad objectives and the specific improvement activities at shopfloor level. For each of 'Quality Improvement Projects (QIP)', there are specific targets which can be decomposed into improvement projects. For example, do the routine machine maintenance by yourself, increase efficiency of the machines, reduce material wastage in a particular operation, reduce start-up times of process, savings in power, fuel or expenses in any particular area or operation, improve the saleability of a particular product, increase the market share in a particular market segment, etc. These vague signposts are quantified and analyzed in terms of how they can be achieved and the problems which would have to be solved to make that happen using simple tools such as '5 Ws' and one 'H' or the Ishikawa diagram and brainstorming session. Diagnosis is top-down in terms of setting the actual numerical targets or the extent to which operators can maintain their own machines. A team of specialist engineers carried out this diagnostic journey. The company placed strong emphasis on mechanisms for embedding these behaviours in the culture of the organization so that they became the way things were done and taught to others. An important aspect of the current mid-term plan was to find mechanisms for doing this. These included training in TQM and in its other related aspects like 'TPM' and then 3 hours/month additional training on the job. They were also allocated 30 minutes per day to carry out their individual maintenance and to learn and improve this.

In addition to this, operator development and individual improvement, there were also continuous long-term improvement projects like JQI in a particular area on which groups worked as team. There were more than 30 quality improvement groups working in the organization. Group leaders spent half their time with the groups, facilitating, training, etc., and the reminder acting as a floating resource to cover sickness, holidays, etc.

The evolution of Kaizen had been through early team activities going back 20 or more years in Japan. The first organized seeds were sown by the 'Quality Circle' activities. Individual Kaizen team ideas did not come through at first. Hence a campaign was launched with the theme of what makes the operator's job easier? In the suggestion scheme, the focus was outside the individual operator's own job area. The evolution of suggestions scheme into the 'Kaizen' or the 'Quality Circle' made the improvement activities more structured, performance-oriented and measurable, thereby making them more effective. The organization started receiving around 15–20 suggestions per employee per month. The generation of some 30000 to 40000 suggestions per month created a problem as to how to process them. Hence the responsibility of studying these suggestions and implementing them was transferred to the group leader. Many of the ideas were minor changes to standard operating procedures and foremen/team leaders were authorized to make these.

The importance of recognizing and rewarding the low level simple ideas was implemented effectively motivating the workers and building a structure for continuous improvement. Strong top-level commitment multiplied the motivation at all levels of the organization.

The result was obvious. The organization's turnover multiplied to five times within a span of five years. The profitability grew exponentially in times. The return on investment grew substantially, leading to cash surplus situation and the organization set up additional plants in Europe and America to service their overseas customers more effectively and efficiently. There was no looking back for the organization and it became the global leader in its line of the products manufactured due to world-class performance excellence.

Questions

1. State the learning points of the case and discuss the same.
2. How did the organization turned round its performance to become a global leader?
3. Why did the organization adopt the TQM principles and practices?
4. Explain the various TQM activities carried out by the organization.
5. Total Quality Management is an integrated holistic approach and not a standalone program or activity'. Discuss.

SECTION II

The cases taken up in this section are relatively concise cases focused more on only one aspect of Total Quality Management rather than a holistic approach. Hence the success derived by the implementation of these cases gives some marginal benefit in a specific operational area and not on the overall organizational performance. Nevertheless, these cases are simple to understand and easy to implement and improve the performance of a product or process in selective manner. The learning points from these cases can be deployed in so many other areas in the same organization for getting useful results. The cases are discussed in a brief manner without much elaboration as they are simple to understand. These cases may turn out to be quite useful in case of initiation of Total Quality Management in an organization as well as the implementation of TQM improvement projects in a sporadic manner as standalone activity to solve some work-related problems.

CASE 1: Implementation of Juran's Quality Improvement Technique in the Engineering Industry

The organization is an engineering manufacturing company. The organization has a dominant position in the field of manufacturing the high speed cutting tools, including drills for creating holes in metal or any other surface. This case demonstrates a focused quality improvement project in the focused area of the prevention of drill breakage.

This problem faced by the company was costing it not just in terms of money but also in terms of lack of customer satisfaction. The quality council had formed a cross-functional team for solving the problems faced by the customers with the company's product. There was no historical data available in this organization in this respect. The team used the data on the customer complaint to do a pareto analysis. The vital root cause of the product failure was drill breakage during the process of drilling. This single cause was responsible for more than 80% of the product failure. The brainstorming session was done by the team involving some senior technical members of the company as special experts on the subject, including the metallurgist. After the cause-effect analysis, various theories were put forward as the likely solution to the problem, out of which three were tested. The results were good and satisfactory. The solution was focused on improving the process of manufacturing and the heat treatment process. After validating the solution by numerous tests and field trials, the process was standardized. There were substantial gains from the program both monetary, i.e., Cost of Poor Quality (COPQ) was reduced substantially, and non-monetary in the form of better morale and working conditions for the staff. The maximum benefit was derived from the marketplace due to superior product performance and better customer satisfaction. The company had also roped-in measures to hold the gain in the form of controlling the process, measuring chronic level of rejections and COPQ, analysis of customer complaints, etc. The company has followed Juran's Quality Improvement (JQI) program earnestly.

CASE 2: Implementation of TQM Technique in the Marketing Function

The organization is an engineering company and leader in India in the field of cutting tools. The power saw sales constituted 55% of the organization's sales. In the recent past, its nearest powerful competitor had intensified its effort both in terms of Marketing and product development, leading to a drop in the organization's market share. Some of the market feedback had reported a superior product performance by the competitor in selective market segment.

Hence the company faced the problem of decline in the market share of one of its main revenue generator. A cross-functional team was thus appointed for the purpose to help in boosting the market share of the company. After doing a pareto analysis, the team came to the conclusion that there should be special emphasis on improving the salebility of power saws. The team then formulated a clear-cut mission statement with quantifiable goals to be achieved in a time-bound manner. The diagnosis was done with the help of questionnaires keeping in mind the important parameters required by the customers. Also a lot of data analysis was done with respect to the process, the competitors vis-à-vis the company and an analysis of the non-user segment. After the analysis stage, four theories were put forward and tested and their results were put forward in the form of remedial action which was proposed to be taken. The remedial actions were taken and found to be effective in the existing product. Simultaneously, a new product was developed with different cutting angle and tooth geometry for the non-user segment of the industry requiring cutting the alloy steels and the relatively hard metals. The test results were validated and the remedial actions were taken by superior existing model along with the new model for the non-user segment as described above. The results were that the company scored gains in financial results in the form of conversion of non-customers to customers and non-financial gains such as better customer awareness about the company and its products. To hold the gains, company had laid down ISO 9000 norms and customers' interactions with the dealers were maintained regularly.

It can be seen that the company worked in the right direction by focusing on the customer and good quality planning has set its objectives and foundation strong. Also by a good interaction with its customers and ISO 9000 norms, the company placed the right infrastructure which, along with the quality management processes, resulted in not only superior financial gains but also enabled the company to have better and more satisfied customers. This case is the implementation of the 'Theory of Holistic Management for World-class Performance' for achieving world-class performance.

CASE 3: Implementation of TQM Technique in the Materials Management Function

The organization manufactured electric lamps. The company used more than 50% glass shells from the glass factory and the rest from the stores. The current case study referred to the procurement of the shells completely from the glass factory and its resultant benefits. The team comprised of senior members of various functional departments. The historical data was analyzed by the team with the process flow chart to identify the project and based on the above, a quantifiable mission statement was developed. The brainstorming session led to the formation of certain theories which were put forward. Also, during the testing, pareto analysis and scatter diagram were put to use to eliminate unnecessary ones. The best solution was chosen and tested to validate the best one. There was resistance from the staff due to closure of certain departments in the organization where the cost of production was higher than from procuring from the outside vendors. This problem was overcome by discussions and gainfully employing the employees from the closed sections to the other sections. This was possible as the organization's manufacturing cost of the final electric lamp dropped by 10% due to cheaper external source and elimination of certain processes. The market responded to a cheaper and better product from a reputed well-known manufacturer and the organization's market share increased substantially. This led to the expansion of capacity of the organization and resultant requirement of additional trained employees who were readily available from the sections of the closed uneconomical operation. It turned out to be a win-win situation. The project in the end led to substantial financial benefits. Apart from the financial benefits the intangible benefits, like reduced cycle time, better co-ordination, etc. resulted in increasing further operational efficiency. To hold the gains, regular data collection was done.

The project was manifestation of fulfilling a critical business necessity leading to the cutting down of the cost of manufacturing and improving the product performance to gain market leadership. The team utilized the right approach to solve the problem technically and emotionally. There was also full backing of the company in terms of the Quality Council. Also, care was taken that the gains were not squandered away. This is an ideal case of focusing on a specific area of business operation which is a critical success factor (CSF) for the organization and implementing the TQM principles and practice to attain the market leadership and all-round performance excellence.

CASE 4: Implementation of TQM Technique in the Manufacturing Function in a FMCG Industry

The case study concentrates on a limited area of reduction in loss of a product in liquid form while filling in the bottle. The company is a known player in the FMCG sector and manufactures a popular brand. The organization is an acclaimed leader in the market for the product manufactured by them. The organization is well-known for its modern management systems. It is practicing the various TQM principles and practices in various parts of the organization. It has successfully carried out number of Juran Quality Improvement Projects in its various operational areas. The organization faced a lot of problems in terms of loss of the liquid product during its manufacturing stage. The company appointed a team from across various functional departments who were at high positions in their respective departments. The team analyzed the historical data on such losses by pareto analysis and fixed an objective mission statement. The main cause for the loss was identified as the loss of the liquid product during filling the bottles. With brainstorming, the team short listed six theories which were tested with the help of Ishikawa diagrams. The result of the program was that loss reduced by 50% from the existing level in a span of a month or so. The benefits ran into lakhs of rupees as the scale of operation of the organization was quite high. To hold the gains, proper training and retraining at regular intervals to workers was given priority apart from measuring process capabilities. This is a classic case of implementation of simple quality improvement projects in a selected focused area of operation.

CASE 5: Implementation of TQM Technique in Improved Housekeeping

This is again a classic case of implementation of simple quality improvement projects in a selected focused area of operation. The company is known for its consumer durables, especially air-conditioners and refrigerators. The data on the Cost of Poor Quality (COPQ) showed losses of certain valuable metal used in the condensers worth a few lakh of rupees. Thus the quality council nominated a cross-functional team to look into the case. As no relevant data was available on the problem, fresh data was collected and after the pareto analysis, the mission statement was stated and was approved by the council. Diagnostic journey through brainstorming and Ishikawa diagram led to the formulation of four theories which were put to test. On the basis of these theories, various recommendations were put forward, which led to the net saving of a few lakhs from improving the shopfloor conditions and housekeeping. The product was also better and control over its manufacturing increased, leading to better confidence for the customer in terms of timely delivery in better conditions. To hold gains, constant recording of rejections were applied. The team was given a project, which was the need of the company. Also, the implementation was rather sporadic and principles of quality management process were not applied in the right earnest. As after application, no process capability studies were put into practice to look for new avenues of improvements in the process.

CASE 6: Implementation of TQM Technique for Saving Electric Power in an Automobile Manufacturing Industry

The organization is a leading automobile manufacturer in India and it is renowned for its product quality and orientation towards the implementation of quality improvement projects. However, the organization was implementing the same as a standalone activity in isolated areas. This is an example of one such quality improvement project of reducing the electricity consumption by 25 to 30%. The electricity cost was quite high for the organization compared to its competitors as percentage of the cost of production for various commercial equipment vehicles. It was seen by the quality improvement team that the plant was consuming a lot of electricity. Thus, a pareto analysis was conducted and various major sources of electricity consumption were identified. The team also utilized the help of line staff for the project and with the help of them the cause and effect diagram was drawn. This was followed by the brainstorming session and various theories were put forward. Based on these theories, recommendations were made. The recommendations were implemented, which resulted in saving of electricity cost by about 28% per year. Also, to hold the gains, checkpoints were established and monitoring of power factor was done.

As can be seen, the company saved a lot of money but this project is sporadic in nature rather than a continuous improvement one. There is no mission statement, no data available for the program. The project seems to measure the gains only on the data of electricity consumption.

CASE 7: Implementation of TQM Technique to Reduce Wastages

This case pertains to reducing the engineering downtime in one of the process areas. The company is a well-known manufacturer of components for the automotive industry. It was well-known that there is a large amount of time required for processing of the components which adds to the cost. Thus the mission statement for the team was designed to solve the same problem. Also, the company calculated the opportunity cost could be almost ten millions of rupees for the project. A cross-functional team was formed following the JQI project methodology. The team conducted a pareto analysis based on the data available and broke the project into sub projects which were supposed to be handled independently. After further brainstorming and drawing the cause and effect diagram of each sub project various theories were put forward and remedial actions were taken. Also, the team designed individual actions holding on the gains from sub-projects. The company made some improvements in elimination of the wastages and saved at least fifty percent of the targeted amount.

As can be seen, the company could not reach its goal itself as this kind of project required support from the higher level and coordination throughout the organization. Also, after doing the project, no process capability studies were initiated and thus continuous improvement is not visible in future also. There is some saving in the organization by this quality improvement project. But considering the scale of operation, this saving is a miniscule percentage. The original level could be worse, but the revised level may still be very bad even if the project has reported some improvement. Hence there is a need for a holistic approach for all-round performance improvement for the sustainability of an organization.

CASE 8: Implementation of TQM Technique to Reduce Field Failure and Improved after Sales Service

The company is a known manufacturer of air-conditioners and this case study refers to the problem faced by the company in the industrial installations during the warranty period. The objective of the project was the elimination of the compressor error during the commissioning and the warranty period. The compressor is a critical part without the proper functioning of which, the unit will not be working.

The company appointed a high-level cross-functional team to look into the problem. After an analysis of the customer complaint data through pareto analysis, the team short-listed the problems to be tackled under this program. The team formulated the mission statement for the program. It further analyzed the data through brainstorming, Ishikawa diagram and process flow charts. The data analysis led to the formation of about five theories which were put forward to test. The remedial actions based on these theories led to good results as per the company standards. Apart from the main result, there were other benefits such as improved inspection, better delivery and improved and reliable data of field failures.

As has been seen, the problem taken by the team was the one which required to be tackled urgently as the customers were suffering. Also, both in the mission statement and the results, no quantifiable data and numbers were provided. Although as part of the ISO 9000 standard implementation, the data had been collected, neither the process capability study nor audit of records have been incorporated to hold the gains for the future. Thus, it can be stated that the project was more of a single time effort than a part of continuous improvements or part of a structured effort.

CASE 9: Implementation of TQM Technique to Improve Safety in the Factory

The organization is a leading manufacturer of elevators and lifts and a well-known engineering industry known for its quality products and timely services of the products and projects installed by the organization. This case is an isolated standalone case of quality improvement project for the reduction of hazards in the factory.

The organization is a known company in the same business and faced a lot of problems due to accidents resulting in loss of time and cost associated with it. Thus the company formed a team of employees, mostly from manufacturing department, to look into the problem. The team from the historical data of accidents in the factory did a pareto analysis and looked into the major areas of concerns. Further, with the help of brainstorming and Ishikawa diagram, it suggested the remedial action, which after implementation resulted in the decrease of loss up to 70% in the concerned area. To hold the gains, the workers were provided regular training and the data of accidents were analyzed regularly.

The company has missed the essence of the JQI program. It blindly followed the problem without first quantifying the reduction in the problem though a mission statement. The workers were the ones who were most affected and no team member from them was chosen. Also, it seems that problem was taken on a basis of urgency rather than paving the way for implementation of continuous improvement projects under the JQI program.

CASE 10: Implementation of TQM for Business Process Improvement

The organization is a leading automobile manufacturer in the country and reputed for its commitment for the implementation of the TQM principles and practices. The organization undertook a focused project on improving the internal mailing system in a specific business operation.

This project was selected out of a few projects and the JQI methodology was used. It came under the head of administrative expenses. A cross-functional team was set up involving people from various departments. The team met on a regular basis and upon brainstorming, the problems were identified. The need for an efficient mailing system was felt by one and all and the company too faced its problem. For taking decisions on the basis of data, check sheets were distributed to the departments to assess their needs and requirements of mail. Direct delivery of mail was a major component and the mail never reached its destination in one day. So after consensus, the target of one day for mail delivery was set. Further brainstorming was initiated to gather information on the manpower requirement, location of mail department types, size, numbers and location of mailboxes, time schedule to deliver, etc. On the basis of preliminary data, the new service was communicated to all department heads well in advance. A system was started for constant feedback and suggestions for improvement were welcomed. Also, for proper delivery of mails, the legible and correct address was to be written by the sender. As everyone was involved in the process, there were few surprises and a wholehearted support was obtained. As a result, the mail delivery was more than 90% in one day as against 25% earlier.

As the changes are reversible in nature, a proper audit system was put in to oversee and suggest improvements.

CASE 11: Implementation of TQM Technique to Reduce Accidents

The organization is a mini steel plant and well-known for its commitment to the implementation of the TQM principles and practices. The organization has been able to sustain its profits and performance in the face of intense competition in the global and the Indian steel industry. The objective was to take up a focused project using continuous quality improvement methodology for reduction in burn injuries due to splashes in the steel casting section of the organization.

The project was selected by the quality council to learn the root cause of the accidents and take preventive actions to eliminate the same. The team appointed by the council was from across all functions in the company which did the detailed study of all the past data and after pareto analysis reached the consensus that the main problem of accident was burn injuries on account of the splashes in the steel casting section. To solve the problem, the team put forward various theories through Ishikawa diagrams and also interviewed those involved in the accident. Apart from this, various related equipments were standardized which were directly used by the concerned people and the dos and don'ts were mentioned in Hindi and Marathi wherever this work was conducted. To follow up the project, audit of the process at regular intervals was institutionalized.

TQM principles, practices and methodology were successfully tried in areas of safety of the internal customers of the company. By the follow-up through audits, the team has in effect reduced accident rates to a large extent and also reduced the number of man-days of production lost due to the accidents.

CASE 12: Implementation of TQM Technique for the Improvement in the Yield

Over the years, the company has built up its reputation as the producer of one of the finest steel products in India for the railways, locomotive, engineering, bearing and other industries. The problem faced by the company is related to losses during the pouring of molten steel. After a pareto analysis taking data from more than 150 incidences, the base, base joints and area around it and the fire clay bricks were identified as the main problem area accounting for more than 70% of the loss. Fresh data was taken and after brainstorming and Ishikawa diagrams, various theories were put forward. The most likely theory for solving the problem was selected and implemented, leading to reduction in the losses.

Though the company was able to reduce the losses, still this gain was short-term in nature as although a cross-functional team was utilized and commitment of shopfloor workers was there, no higher level authority was directly involved in the project to make such an affair a continuous one. Apart from this, the goals which were attempted had no quantification in terms of numbers or any measurable parameters like the cost, quality, time, etc. Another flaw seen here is that no process capability was measured, neither there was any feedback loop in terms of control charts to monitor the output on regular basis. Neither any flow diagrams of the process have been studied to further quantify the theories proposed.

Thus in the end, I would like to conclude that though the company is able to reduce the waste but there are defects not only in its process management but also the way they had gone about the program by semi-implementing it as no measure was undertaken to look for the above in a continuous fashion.

CASE 13: Implementation of TQM Technique for Improvement in the Product Performance

This is again a classic case of implementation of simple quality improvement projects in a selected focused area of operation of improvement of the product performance. The company is known for its consumer durables, especially air-conditioners, refrigerators and material handling equipments. It is part of a famous group which is famous for its business excellence model. The project is for the improvement of product performance by reducing the failure rate of certain key parts of the product. The material handling business division of the organization manufactures a wide range of industrial trucks. There was an average failure rate of around 10% for the past few years due to the failure of a certain component. As per the JQI methodology, the quality council formed a cross-functional team of people from various departments. After analysis of the data, it was observed that one particular model only accounted for the 90% of the failure. A pareto analysis was done for the performance pattern of the components and it was found that the failures of the seals were involved in 80% of the causes for failures. The brainstorming was done and about 28 theories were proposed; 15 were shortlisted and then only three were nominated for active implementation. The material and the design of the seal were changed to a contemporary design for prevention of failure. This reduced the rate of failure substantially and the product performance improved, leading to better customer satisfaction and improved market share.

CASE 14: Implementation of TQM Technique in the Improvement of the Business Process

The organization is a pioneer and market leader in the field of white goods, particularly in the consumer durable industry. This is ideal case for the implementation of the TQM technique in the improvement of the business process. The business process under discussion is the reduction of the dispatch time by 25%. Due to delay in dispatch, the company was losing lots of repeat orders, affecting the image of the company. This also led to the loss of money due to the late receipt of materials. The JQI methodology was adopted, wherein the quality council selected the project and the team was formed of officers from the various departments. Detailed data was collected from all the divisions of the organization. A pareto analysis was done from the data collected and the 'vital few' causes for the delay in delivery were ascertained. Brainstorming was used in conjunction with the cause and effect diagram to propose more than fifty theories. Among the theories, three were chosen as the most likely cause for the delay in dispatches. The team found out and recommended the solutions which were tested and remedial action was taken in these three valid ones. They were then analyzed over two months. As all the actions were reversible in nature, a proper audit system was designed and implemented. In terms of tangible benefits, the absence of system would have resulted in a loss of interest of around Rs. 25 lakh. There was also high customer satisfaction leading to repeat orders and thereby increase in the market share. The organization was facing tough domestic and international competition. The improvement in the business process definitely helped the organization increase its business. However, this was not a 'vital few' or the critical success factor (CSF) of the product's salability criteria. This also resulted in high employee motivation. After the implementation of the new system, 95% of all dispatches were made within 3 days instead of earlier time period of 10 days.

CONCLUSION OF THE CASE STUDY ANALYSIS

After analyzing the various case studies, it is evident that the Indian companies are opening up to the world demand for the production of quality products. The quality improvement programs like the JQI programs and Kaizen improvement initiatives are conducted across the board from automobile industries to the engineering industries and from textile to the service industry. Also, the companies have realized that quality products reduce the cost of production and are looking at data for the Cost of Poor Quality (COPQ) to reduce the cost to become more competitive in the marketplace. Outside Japan, Indian industries have won the highest number Deming's Quality Award to prove to the rest of the world that the Indian products are truly good quality products. Almost all the leading Indian manufacturing and service sector industries have adopted the ISO 9001:2000 certification to create a strong infrastructure of the Quality Management System or the QMS. Even to be a supplier to the automobile industries like Tata Motors Ltd., or any organization of the Tata group, the Bajaj Auto Ltd., the Mahindra Group, the 'RDSO' approval for supplying to the Indian Railways or for the Defense sector approval as a supplier and most of the reputed Indian and international organization, the ISO 9001:2000 certification has become mandatory. There are lots of improvements that have taken place over the years in terms of quality consciousness among the Indian industries. However, from the analysis of other relevant factors, it is observed that many of the companies which have followed such quality improvement programs have not done well in terms of all-round performance excellence. These companies had followed the program in an abrupt manner or, to be more precise, to solve the problems which were very serious or imminent with the help of a particular program. Apart from this, all the companies, big or small, had not done proper data recording initially or after the programs were concluded, thus defeating the cause for which such programs were held. Almost all the companies followed a similar pattern of using pareto analysis and brainstorming with fishbone diagram to solve problems through the QIP program. Apart from this, the bigger and well-known organizations had some quality councils which directed the quality team and had proper mission and vision statements. Almost all of them hold the gains by the ISO 9001:2000 system, internal audit systems and training of employees. Most of them had not conducted any process capabilities studies throughout the program, which could have given vital clues and shown patterns.

What is important about these case studies has been that despite that the chosen areas of the program range from employee protection to reduction in cost to marketing related problems, still these follow a pattern in following the TQM program.

The organization had empowered top-ranking officials as a part of a cross-functional team who had independent authority on the program. They had all the necessary historical data available with them to be used to look into the area of concern. Also, with each stage of analysis of data, the mission statements were made precise to focus just on a particular area. The brainstorming and Ishikawa analysis were supplemented by process flow diagrams which help in revealing a lot of data about the area of concern. Also, in the remedial action, the suppliers (internal/external) were involved and in the final outcome, the gains were held through proper control on the process with the help of control charts, data and audit under the arms of a high-ranking official.

Looking at these cases, from the point of view of the hypothesis, many similarities can be seen; such as they had a strong foundation at the base in terms of customer focus (in the first case, the internal customer—the employee), executive leadership in the form of high-ranking individuals being members of the team and strategic quality planning in terms of picking the mission of the program and the manner to go about it. As far as the required infrastructure was concerned, the team made the concerned employees to have proper training, proper measurements and data collection were done and finally total organizational involvement was also seen. The management processes of QI, QP and QC was implemented. These teams tried to follow them in the right earnest, wherever possible, in their respective cases. All this finally resulted in reduced quality costs, increased revenues, empowered employees and enlightened customer.

Finally, the point I would like to add is that it is not that others have not done these procedures. They have done them partially and have gained substantially in both monetary and non-monetary terms out of these improvement exercises. But those organizations who have not completely followed Total Quality Management in the right spirit, their gains have been or are likely to be for the shorter term and of sporadic/intermittent in nature rather than on continuous basis and sustainable for a long period.

The Total Quality Management Implementation in India and the World

The stress and strain of globalization and liberalization has created the business pressures hitherto unseen and inexperienced by the most of the industries across the world. This situation is not unique to India, it is global in nature. The floodgates of intense international competition have swept the industries off their feet. The rapid technological advancement, emergence of cheaper and better substitute products, information technology explosion, leaner and flatter organization, and flexible manufacturing system have made at least one thing clear to all enterprises—only good performances in isolated sporadic areas are not enough for the survival of an organization; the organization should have an all-round performance excellence to be the best among the betters for survival. Almost all the organizations across the globe practice the TQM principles and practices for their survival. However, what makes the difference between the 'leader' in the field and the 'also runs' is that the leader practices the TQM principles and practices in a holistic manner with proper strategic quality plan, foundation, infrastructure and total quality management consisting of quality planning, quality control and quality improvement, whereas the 'also runs' practice the TQM principles and practices in bits and pieces, following only one aspect of Total Quality

Management, like either JQI or Kaizen or ISO 9000 or TPM etc., thereby giving marginal result. These 'also run' organizations may be satisfied with the marginal gains considering the fact that they have got some benefit from their effort as most of them implement the TQM principles and practices as a fad rather than with a proper understanding of the system and specific direction for attaining world-class performance excellence.

The implementation of the TQM principles and practices comes naturally to a Japanese organization. It is the practice on these TQM principles and practices that have made the Japanese organizations the world leaders in their respective fields of operation. From nowhere compared to the west in 1950, when Japan was totally struggling to revive from the ruins of the second world war, to mid-seventies, when the Japanese industries had only one focus in their working—the implementation of the TQM principles and practices with a vision to be the global leader in their respective fields by 1970. What actually happened is history. One by one the Japanese industries in their respective fields became the world leaders not exactly by 1970 but between 1975 and 1978. The most important factor in their progress was that the Japanese organizations not only became the world leaders in their respective fields, but they have sustained the leadership for more than three decades till date. Even today in entertainment electronics, i.e., CTV, etc. sony is the world leader; in the watch industry, Citizen, Ricoh, etc., in the electrical industry, the Matshusita Heavy Electrical Industries; in earth moving equipment and heavy automobiles (HCVs), the Mitsubishi industries and the Komatsu; in the automobile segment of cars and 'SUVs', the Toyota, Honda and Mitsubishi industries; in small car segment, Suzuki Motor Corporation; in the two-wheeler segment of motorcycle and scooters, Honda, Yahama and Suzuki; in the photocopying industry, Canon and in the Camera and Photography, Minolta, Yashica, etc.; in cutting tool industry, Kyocera Corporation; and Casio in the electronic goods are the instances of such cases of rising to the global leadership from an obscure position and sustaining the leadership for substantial period of time till date. Practices which gave them this global leadership is nothing other than the implementation of the TQM principles and practices in a holistic manner. That is the reason why the entire world started talking about and practicing the TQM principles and practices. However, most of the TQM principles and practices come natural to the Japanese business practices. All Japanese believe that they have to behave in an improved manner and implement the same in their individual work today as compared to yesterday and tomorrow as compared to today. The reason is that they become older by a day and must learn something during the day that adds to their experience and therefore results in better knowledge and experience to do things at the workplace or at home. These practices are an integral part of the Japanese lifestyle. This is only the practice of Kaizen or continuous improvement. The rest of the world has to work hard to practice Kaizen whereas it is natural life practice for the Japanese society. The entire Japanese industry is customer-oriented and has a customer focus. All the Japanese products are user-friendly. They have a customer focus in-built in their lifestyle. The Japanese practice long-term strategic planning not only for every business organization but also every individual at personal level as well as at the family level. Hence the important three aspects of 'foundation', viz., 'strategic quality planning', 'customer focus' and 'continuous improvement' are part and parcel of the Japanese lifestyle. They have practiced for long the 'Company Wide Quality Control' or the

'CWQC' from which the TQM system evolved. This is nothing but the ISO 9000:2000 Quality Management System. The Japanese industries developed and practiced closely-held integrated performance with their suppliers as well as their customers leading to the Total Organizational Involvement. These factors led to the development of a solid 'infrastructure'. The Japanese organizations derived the maximum benefit out of the implementation of the TQM principles and practices due their holistic approach to the implementation of the TQM comprising of quality planning, quality control and quality improvement activities and not only sporadic implementation of quality improvement projects in selective areas and calling it as the implementation of TQM principles and practices. From the above analysis, it becomes apparent why the Japanese industries got the maximum benefit out of the implementation of the TQM principles and practices which was singularly responsible for their acquiring the position of global leadership and sustaining the same for more than three decades. They have not run after anything that is either a new management theory or a fad or mindless computerization or sporadic working in an isolated management theory without making the same a part of the whole existing system. This is the main difference between them and the rest of the world where the TQM principles and practices are implemented as a fad or more as a ritual without the involvement of the top management and the employees, thereby giving temporary marginal benefits. In particular, the top management and the employees are excellent 'cheer leaders' and thus probably not even the surface of the TQM principles and practices have been scratched there. Nevertheless, the JUSE and the Japanese government gave prime importance to the implementation of the TQM principles and practices and named the award in this regard as the Deming's Quality Award for performance excellence in the field of TQM principles and practices implementated in an organization. The Korean industries worked closely emulating the Japanese working system as they have an almost similar culture and way of life. Like the Japanese industries, all the Korean Industries practice the implementation of TQM principles and practices like the Samsung group, the Daewoo group or the industries belonging to the Hundai group. These organizations also in their own way have attained global leadership following the implementation of the TQM principles and practices.

While the Japanese industries were implementing the TQM principles and practices and bridging the gap between them and the western world leader in a particular industry, the western industries were continuing with their 'product-oriented model', 'Ford's mass production model', 'machine-oriented model' and 'manufacturing facility optimization inward looking organization'. The industry leader from Europe or America was comfortable with stagnation due their complacency of global leadership. When they started losing their leadership position one by one to the Japanese industries, they were startled and could not believe the situation. However, as they realized and accepted the facts, they started adopting the implementation of the TQM principles and practices, which was a big shift in their mindset. To implement the TQM principles and practices, they had to shift the focus from product-orientation to process-orientation, from the Ford's MPS to Toyota's TPS or Toyota Production System or the Just-in-Time production system, from the 'automation' to 'autonomation', from 'machine-oriented model' to the 'people or the employee-oriented model' and from the 'manufacturing facility optimization inward looking organization' to the 'customer-oriented outward looking model'. In Europe and America, the 'TQM' principles and practices were accepted as the key management practice for the performance of a business organization. Based on the 'Deming Quality Award', America developed its own performance excellence business model based on the TQM principles and practices and recognition of its implementation was the 'Malcolm Baldridge Quality Award' and Europe declared the same as 'European Quality Award'. Most of the leading European and American organizations now practices the TQM principles and practices. The International Standard Organization (ISO) formed a formal Quality Management System in 1987 based on the organization wide quality assurance model with representatives from more than 70 countries across the world and this is probably the formal worldwide recognition of the TQM principles and practices. The systems standard was revised marginally in the year 1994 and substantially modified in the year 2000 to the TQM principles and practices with the acceptance of more than 118 countries across the globe. The automobile industries formed their own manual based on the TQM principles and practices known as the QS 9000 which adopted the ISO 9000 standard along with the best business practices adoption of organizations like the Ford Motor Company, Chrysler Corporation, General Motors Corporation, Mack Trucks Inc., Navistar International Transportation Corp., PACCAR Inc., Volvo Truck North America, Mitsubishi Motors–Australia and Toyota–Australia. All these organizations worldwide were committed to the implementation of the TQM principles and practices as the key factor for their performance excellence. General Electric and Motorola pioneered the implementation of the 'Six Sigma' across the globe as a powerful TQM tool. The 'Six Sigma' approach is adopted by all the Indian software and information technology firms like Tata Computer System Ltd., Patni Computer System Ltd., Wipro Technologies Ltd, Infosys Ltd., Satyam Computers Ltd., etc. apart from the attainment of the CMM level. The Tata Group, including Tata Motors Ltd., Tata Iron Steel Ltd., Tata Chemicals Ltd., Tata International Ltd., and other Tata group companies follow a 'business excellence model' in line with the Malcolm Baldridge model of quality award criteria. The ISO 9000 Quality Management System implementation as well as the implementation of Juran's Quality Improvement (JQI) projects in various functional areas is practiced in all the Tata Group companies. The TQM principles and practices have become the mainstay of the automobile industries. Tata Motors, Mahindra & Mahindra automotive division and tractors division, Maruti Suzuki Ltd., Hero Group, Bajaj Auto Ltd., the RDSO of the Indian Railways as well the Indian Defense organization all insists on the implementation of the TQM principles and practices to its suppliers. They have made the ISO 9001:2000 certification compulsory for all its suppliers and ancillaries. The Government of India gives an immediate reimbursement for the ISO 9000:2000 certification cost up to Rs. 75000 to the business units registered under the Small Scale Industry (SSI Sector).

The TVS group is famous for the implementation of the TQM principles and practices. Sundaram Fastners Ltd. was the first organization in India to get the prestigious ISO 9001 certification. Sundaram Clayton Ltd. from the same group was the first Indian organization to be awarded the prestigious Deming Quality Award followed by TVS Motors Ltd. of the same group. The other members of the group, like the Lucas TVS Ltd. or the Brakes India Ltd., also got similar recognition in the implementation of the TQM principles and practices.

Mahindra & Mahindra's automotive as well as tractor divisions are also well-known for the implementation of TQM principles and practices to defend the market leadership of the products manufactured by the organization. They have implemented various TQM principles and practices like JQI projects, ISO 9001 Quality Management System implementation, business process re-engineering, benchmarking, statistical process control, logistics and supply chain management, etc.

In the Ajay Piramal Group, the Nicholas Piramal Ltd. in the pharmaceutical industry and Gujarath Glass Ltd. in the packaging industry particularly for the pharmaceutical industry, have reached the market leadership position respectively in last decade and half from an inconsequential position, with the sheer implementation of the TQM principles and practices by way of ISO 9001 quality management system implementation, JQI projects implementation, implementation of logistics and supply chain management, employees training, etc.

Maruti Suzuki Motors, being an organization in collaboration with the world's largest small car manufacturer from Japan, has implemented all the TQM principles and practices, which is the key to its market leadership position and its success at defending the same for the years together in spite of intense market competition.

The TQM principles and practices can be employed in all sorts of industries in both the manufacturing and service sectors. The Ritz Carlton Hotel in the hospitality industry; Bombay Dyeing Ltd., Mafatlal Industries and Arvind Mills in the textile Industry, Tata Iron & Steel Industries Ltd. (TISCO), Steel Authorities India Ltd. (SAIL), Mukand Ltd., etc. in the steel industry; Voltas Ltd., Godrej group of industries and Videocon International Ltd. in the consumer durable manufacturing industry and Marico Industries Ltd., Asian Paints Ltd., etc. in the FMCG industry are the examples wherein TQM principles and practices have been adopted and the resultant world-class performance excellence and market leadership has been achieved and sustained.

In the engineering industry, Bharat Heavy Electriacals Ltd., Carburendum Universal manufacturing industries Ltd., Otis Elevators Ltd., Philips India Ltd., Hindusthan Motors Ltd., ISUZU Engine Plant at Prithampur, Bajaj Tempo Ltd., Crompton Greaves Ltd., Godrej group of Industries, Larsen & Toubro Group of Industries, Aditya Birla Group of Industries, Reliance Group of Industries, Modi Rubbers Ltd., Gujarath Heavy Chemicals Ltd., Amul, etc. are all the examples of companies attaining world-class performance excellence through the implementation of the TQM principles and practices.

Internationally, apart from the automobile industries where the principal focus for world-class performance and sustainability in the business is the implementation of the TQM principles and practices, there are other sectors like the Eastman Chemicals Ltd. including the Eastman Kodak, world leader in the photographic materials, Xerox Corporation Ltd. pioneer in photocopying business, Microsoft Industries Ltd., IBM International Ltd., Velcro Ltd., Florida Power Corporation, Boeing Airlift & Tankers(AT&T), Motorola, General Electric, Merril Lynch Credit Corporation, Solar Turbine Inc., USA, Florida Regional Medical Centre, USA, Holston Valley Hospital and Medical Centre, Dynamic Seals, USA, Printed Circuit Board, etc. are all examples of the implementation of the TQM principles and practices to attain world-class performance excellence in their field of operation.

These are obviously just few examples. There are many more organizations in India as well as in the world, who have achieved world-class performance excellence and market leadership through the implementation of the TQM principles and practices.

However, most of the organizations, barring a few, have implemented the TQM principles and practices in a sporadic manner in selective areas just as a problem-solving technique and tool, neglecting the principle objective of world-class performance through holistic approach of all-round performance excellence. The TQM principles and practices should be implemented following the theory of the 'Holistic Management for World-class Performance' for attaining sustainable growth with market leadership and maximization of customer satisfaction and return on investment.

The implementation of the TQM principles and practices has made a tremendous difference to the acceptance of the Indian products in the international market where the 'Made in India' brand had difficulty in selling itself as compared to the 'Made in Japan' or the 'Made in USA' or the 'Made in Germany' emblems. The Indian organizations securing the ISO 9001 certification from a world-renowned certification agency like BVQI, TUV, DNV or KPMG as per the standards of (ANSI) American or (Queen's Crown) United Kingdom or German standard gave them a positioning as a world-class organization and they could realize good value for the products manufactured by them unlike other Indian manufacturers who have to match the international quality but have to sell the products manufactured by them as commodity on weight basis without their brand name.

The ISO 9001 certification is supplemented by many organizations with the globally acclaimed Deming's Prize for TQM practices. Five Indian organizations have already bagged the prestigious Deming's Award for quality and eight more are in the process of acquiring it shortly as they are implementing the criteria for the Deming's Prize given by JUSE for performance excellence in the field of TQM. India has suddenly acquired the position of having the maximum number of Deming's Prize winners next to only Japan. This by itself has resulted in the 'Made in India' brand gaining recognition as a quality brand in the rest of the world.

The Japanese Institute of Plant Management has rewarded eighteen manufacturing plants in ten Indian companies for excelling in Total Plant Maintenance (TPM). This is another powerful tool for the implementation of the TQM principles and practices. Prof. Yasutoshi Washio, a world renowned TQM expert, has predicted that Indian manufacturing quality will overtake Japan by the year 2013.

India has already become one of the prominent global players in the field of the Information Technology. We are now in for a grand success story in the field of manufacturing, riding on the back of the implementation of the TQM principles and practices. India is a warehouse of competent qualified engineers of more than two million working in the manufacturing sector, making it as one of the soundest, technically experienced and competent industry with many of the companies progressing at a revolutionary rate of more than forty percent per annum. Indian industry is on a journey towards total quality. But it has to refine the approach by adopting a holistic approach to be an international leader in the respective fields of operation. The interest shown by the global manufacturing companies in sourcing parts and components from India is on the rise as the recognition to the Indian industries' commitment to quality. Today the American, European and Japanese firms are seeking outsourcing deals with the Indian manufacturing firms. Toyota is sourcing transmission parts from India. Ford is sourcing the entire car engine from India. The Suzuki Motors corporation has leveraged on Maruti's capability to make it the sole manufacturing facility of manufacturing many of the Suzuki's models for the international market in India as well as sourcing parts and components from many Indian organizations. Yahama and Mitsubishi have announced to make India a global sourcing hub for automobile components and parts in the two-wheeler segment. Tata Motors is selling Indica cars to Rover for the United Kingdom market. Mahindra & Mahindra is selling its Scorpio model of SUV all over the world, including Asian and European countries successfully. Bajaj Auto Ltd. has been selling its scooters in the world market for many years. The United States market leader in retailing and a global leader, Wal-mart, intends to increase outsourcing from India from the current level of USD 1 billion to USD 10 billion in the next couple of years.

All these success stories and information build up the resolution for the companies who are not implementing the TQM principles and practices to immediately go for the same. This is the reason why most of the management & engineering institutes have introduced 'Total Quality Management' as a compulsory subject in their syllabus. The only way the organization can survive and excel in the current global environment of intense international and local competition is by the implementation of the TQM principles and practices. The most interesting part of the entire exercise for the industries is that it is a 'Zero Investment Activity' which maximizes the productive use of the plant and machineries as well as all other resources. The implementation of the TQM principles and practices simultaneously gives customer satisfaction as well as the market leadership position and maximization of return on investment, which are the vital factors for attaining global leadership and world-class performance excellence.

Bibliography

Adam, Everette E. Jr. and Ronald J. Ebert, *Productions and Operations Management*, 5th ed., Prentice-Hall of India, New Delhi.

Benbow, W. Donald and T.M. Kubiak (2005), *The Certified Six Sigma Black Belt Handbook*, Pearson Education.

Besterfield, Dale H., Carol Besterfield, Glen H. Besterfield, and Mary Besterfield (2004), *Total Quality Management*, Pearson Education.

Bowersox, Donald J. and David J. Cross (2000), *Logistic Management—The Integrated Supply Chain Process*, International Edition, Tata McGraw-Hill, New Delhi.

Caroselli, Marlene (1996), *Quality Games for Trainers*, McGraw-Hill, New York.

Celente, Gerald (1997), *Trends 2000*, Warner Books Inc.

Christopher, Martin (1998), *Logistic and Supply Chain Management—Strategies for Reducing Cost and Improving Service*, 2nd ed., Times/Pitman Publishing.

Cole, W.E. and J.W. Mogab (2000), *TQM*, Blackwell Publisher, UK/Infinity Books.

Covey, R.S. (1992), *Principle Centered Leadership*, Simon & Schuster, Great Britian.

Creech, Bill (1994), *The Five Pillars of TQM*, Truman Talley Books, Dutton, New York.

Crosby, B. Philip (1980), *Quality is Free*, Mentor Publisher, New York.

_____ (1995), *Quality without Tears*, McGraw-Hill, New York.

_____ (1988), *The Eternally Successful Organization*, McGraw-Hill, New York.

David, Drennam and Steuart Pennington (1999), *12 Ladders to World Class Performance*, Kogan Page, London.

David, Goestch L. and Stanley B. Davis (2001), *Total Quality Handbook*, Prentice-Hall Inc., New Jersey.

Eliyahu, Goldratt M. and Robert E. Fox, *The Race*, North River Press.

Eliyahu, Goldratt M., *Theory of Constraints*, North River Press, Great Barrlington, Massachusetts.

Endres, A.L. (1997), *Improving R&D Performance—The Juran Way*, John Wiley & Sons Inc., New York.

411

Eugene, Grant. L. and Richard S. Leavenworth, *Statistical Quality Control*, 6th ed. (International Edition), Tata McGraw-Hill, New Delhi.

Ford Motor Company (1990), Ford Quality System Standard Q 101–1990, Ford Motor Company.

Ford Motor Company (1990), Q Preferred Quality Award – 1990, Ford Motor Company.

Ford Motor Company (1993), *Production Approval Process*, Ford Motor Company.

Hammer, Michael and Steven A. Santon (1995), *The Reengineering Revolution*, Harper Business.

Heizer, Jay H. and Nathan Jay (2004), *Cases in Total Qualitry Management*, Thomson South Western.

Imai, Masaaki (1997), Gemba Kaizen—A Commonsense, Low-cost approach to Management, McGraw-Hill, New York.

Imai, Masaaki, *Kaizen—The Key to Japan's Competitive Success*, McGraw-Hill Inc., New York.

ISO 9000:2000 Quality Management Systems Standard, International Organization for Standardization.

ISO 9001:2000 Quality Management Systems Standard, International Organization for Standardization.

ISO 9004:2000 Quality Management Systems Standard, International Organization for Standardization.

ISO 14000:1996 Environmental Management Systems Standard, International Organization for Standardization.

Joseph, Martinich S., *Productions and Operations Management*, John Wiley & Sons Inc.

Juran, Butman John (1997), *A Lifetime of Influence*, John Wiley & Sons Inc., New York.

Juran, J.M. and Frank M. Gryna, *Juran's Quality Control Handbook*, 4th ed., McGraw-Hill Inc., New York.

Juran, J.M. and A. Blanton Gobfrey, *Juran's Quality Handbook*, 5th ed. (International Edition), McGraw–Hill Inc., New York.

Juran, J.M. and Frank M. Gryna, *Quality Planning and Analysis*, 3rd ed., McGraw-Hill, New York.

Juran, J.M., *Juran on Planning for Quality*, The Free Press, New York.

Juran Institute (1992), Bench Marking for World-class Leadership, Juran Institute, Wilton.

Juran, J.M., *Managerial Breakthrough*, Revised ed., McGraw-Hill Inc., New York.

Juran, J.M. (1992), *Juran on Quality by Design*, The Free Press, New York.

Korgaonkar, M.G. (1992), *Just in Time Manufacturing*, Macmillan, Delhi.

Kotter, P. John (1997), *Matsushita Leadership*, The Free Press, New York.

Logothetis, N. (1992), *Managing for Total Quality*, Prentice-Hall of India, New Delhi.

Lulla, Suresh, Qimpro Consultants, ISO 9000 + CQI = PROFIT (Indian Experiences), D.L. Shah Trust, Mumbai.

Mody, Suresh M., *Bench Marking and Process Improvement—Book Four*, D.L. Shah Trust, Mumbai.

Oakland, S. John and Leslie J. Porter (1994), *Cases in Total Quality Management*, Butterworth Heinemann, Oxford.

Pande, S. Peter, Robert P. Neuman and Ronald R. Cavanagh (2000), The Six Sigma Way— How GE, Motorola and the top companies are Honing their Performance, McGraw-Hill, New York.

Peters, Tom, *The Circle of Innovation*, Coronet Books, Hodder & Stoghton.

QS 9000, *Quality System Requirements*, 3rd ed., March 1998, International Organization for Standardization, Ford Motor Co., Chrysler Corp., General Motors Corp.

Russell, S. Roberta and Bernard W. Taylor III, *Operations Management*, 2nd International edition, Prentice-Hall Inc., New Delhi.

Schonberger, J. Richard (1982), *Japanese Manufacturing Techniques*, Simon & Schuster, Great Britian.

Seurat, Silvere (1979), *Technology Transfer—Arealistic Approach*, Gulf Publishing Company, Houstan.

Sharma, Sunil (1997), *TQM in Indian Engineering Industries*, Business Publications Inc., Mumbai.

Walton, Mary (1990), *Deming Management at Work*, A Perigee Book by Berkley Publishing House.

William C. Miller (1993), *Quantum Quality*, Quality Resources.

Index